NEW YORK'S WAR OF 1812

CAMPAIGNS & COMMANDERS

GREGORY J. W. URWIN, SERIES EDITOR

CAMPAIGNS AND COMMANDERS

New York's War of 1812

Politics, Society, and Combat

Richard V. Barbuto

University of Oklahoma Press : Norman

Library of Congress Cataloging-in-Publication Data

Names: Barbuto, Richard V., author.
Title: New York's war of 1812 : politics, society, and combat / Richard V. Barbuto.
Description: Norman, OK : University of Oklahoma Press, [2021] | Series: Campaigns and
    commanders ; volume 71 | Includes bibliographical references and index. | Summary:
    "Analyzes the intense and crucial participation of New York state's people and government
    during the War of 1812"—Provided by publisher.
Identifiers: LCCN 2020029679 | ISBN 978-0-8061-6833-3 (hardcover) ISBN 978-0-8061-9082-2
(paper)
Subjects: LCSH: New York (State)—History—War of 1812. | New York (State —History—
    War of 1812—Biography. | United States—History—War of 1812.
Classification: LCC E359.5.N6 .B37 2020 | DDC 974.7/03—dc23
LC record available at https://lccn.loc.gov/2020029679

New York's War of 1812: Politics, Society, and Combat is Volume 71 in the Campaigns and
Commanders series.

The paper in this book meets the guidelines for permanence and durability of the Committee on
Production Guidelines for Book Longevity of the Council on Library Resources, Inc. ∞

*This work is dedicated to
the memory of Sergeant James R. Wheeler,
Infantry, U.S. Army, Korean War.
My father-in-law's love for the history
of New York inspired my own.*

CONTENTS

Acknowledgments

This work could not have been brought forward without the assistance of a small army of scholars, friends, librarians, archivists, and local historians. I am honored to thank a few.

Independent scholar Gary Gibson attempted to fill this soldier's head with an inkling of nineteenth century naval ways. He shared his vast scholarship and reviewed various chapters pertaining to the war on Lake Ontario. This work is better for his contribution. Patrick Kavanagh, a local historian on the Niagara frontier, made available countless pages of letters, articles, and newspaper clippings that filled in much of the detail and added color to the narrative. Anthony Gero, whose work on militia uniforms is unsurpassed, drew my attention to primary sources dealing with the state's attempts to raise and maintain a wartime army. Kate Emerson, Niagara County Historian, brought to life Betsy Doyle, our own heroine. I am proud to bring Betsy's story to a larger audience.

Throughout the years, Paul Lear, site manager of the Fort Ontario Historic Site, and Connie Barone, director of Sackets Harbor Battlefield Historic Site, have supported my research efforts in many ways. They and their crews keep the memory of the state's military history alive.

Dave Bennett, who organizes and runs the War of 1812 in the West Symposium, provides a forum for historians and buffs to share the latest scholarship. Discussions with Dave and Hal Youmans, a frequent participant, never fail to reveal a clearer understanding of the relationships of persons and events.

My friends from the Old Fort Niagara Association, Executive Director Bob Emerson and board of directors' member Harry DeBan, have supported my scholarship in so many ways for many years.

I want to thank the many site historians and docents who provided unpublished correspondence as well as assistance in understanding the details of geography, infrastructure, and local politics of the war years, particularly: Arthur L. Simmons III, Executive Director of the Rome Historical Society,

Pat Talley of the East Bloomfield Historical Society, and Don Gray, who brought to life his ancestor, Nicholas Gray.

Since 1986, Fort Leavenworth's Ike Skelton Combined Arms Research Library has supported my research. On this particular project, librarians Nora Walker and Dan Barbuto helped me find dozens of sources. My deep appreciation to them and the entire CARL staff.

I am indebted to the deans of War of 1812 scholars, Don Graves and Don Hickey, for their scholarship and inspiration throughout my professional life as an historian. My work is better for their profound insights and thoughtful suggestions.

Adam Kane, Kent Calder, and Greg Urwin of the University of Oklahoma Press and its Campaigns and Commanders series have encouraged me and provided useful perspectives in ushering this project through to publication. My thanks to Erin Greb as well for turning my drawings into useful maps. My dear friend and scholar Jonathan House reviewed this manuscript early in its life and provided insights that shaped the final product.

Finally, and most importantly, my loving spouse, Ann, who edited the work multiple times and enabled me to achieve more clarity. Ann provided countless suggestions that have improved my efforts. She is a wonderful traveling companion in many visits to the sites at which the events in this narrative occurred. Her perceptive questions opened new avenues of investigation that have enriched the story. My history profession has been akin to a vow of poverty, and Ann's forbearance has been essential in bringing this project to completion.

INTRODUCTION

The War of 1812 was New York's war. While there was substantial military and naval activity elsewhere, New York state was at the center of decisive operations. President Madison's offensive strategy could not be accomplished without military operations based in and launched from New York. After initial military setbacks, it was in New York state that the war effort found its footing. The army and navy achieved tactical parity with their British and Canadian foes, and New York turned back the final invasion across the northern border. Lack of success in and around the state moved the British toward a peace settlement. The federal government could not conduct war without the ample human and material resources provided by the state governments. In this regard, New York rose to the challenge, led by the most competent and effective of war governors, Daniel D. Tompkins.[1] Tompkins's political skills maintained support for the war, thus sustaining the national effort. The people of New York paid a disproportionate cost of the war effort in military service as well as loss of life and livelihood. Our understanding of how and why the conflict unfolded as it did is incomplete without an appreciation of the political, social, and military aspects of the war in New York.

The War of 1812 was a direct result of the larger conflict between France and Britain. The intense efforts of each to ravage their opponent's economy resulted in the loss to American shippers and merchants of hundreds of vessels. Adding insult to injury, the Royal Navy impressed thousands of seamen from American merchant ships. Native Americans pushing back on white westward expansion carried weapons acquired from British traders, and the widespread assumption on the frontier was that British authorities condoned and even instigated warfare on America's frontiers. By 1812, most Americans had had enough with what they perceived as Britain's blatant disregard for American sovereignty, leading Congress to declare the nation's first foreign war on June 18, 1812.[2]

1

Madison's war aims were to gain Britain's recognition of America's version of neutral shipping rights and to cease impressment; additionally, British authorities in Canada would have to stop providing Indians within American territory with the means to conduct war.[3] Clearly, the American military was unequal to challenging Britain directly, but President Thomas Jefferson and his successor, James Madison, perceived that Canada was vulnerable. Seizing Canada, substantially accomplished by capturing Montreal and possibly Quebec, might force Britain to negotiate a settlement. American privateers would damage Britain's merchant fleet, applying additional pressure. If Britain refused negotiations, then the United States would retain Canada. With Britain fully occupied in an existential struggle with Napoleonic France, Madison seized the opportunity to strike decisively across the northern border. Thus, New York was geographically at the center of military operations.

At the time that Congress declared war, Britain's resources were focused on defeating France. The British goal in its new war with America was intentionally limited to maintaining the physical integrity of British North America. In 1813, the ministry, headed by Lord Liverpool, expanded its commitment by adding naval forces to blockade portions of the American coast, and British land and sea forces operated in Chesapeake Bay to tie down American forces that otherwise might be committed to fighting along the Canadian frontier. With Napoleon's abdication in April 1814, Britain was then able to substantially increase its military and naval commitment to North America. British strategy now included offensives to gain possession of American territory in Maine and New York in order to improve its negotiating position. However, the ministry decided that the strategic requirements in the postwar settlement in Europe being negotiated in Vienna were the highest priority. Therefore, it moved for peace in North America and dropped its demands for territorial cessions. As the federal government approached bankruptcy and the Madison administration had little hope of securing its war aims, the American negotiators came to agreement with their British counterparts. Britain retained its maritime rights as well as the territorial integrity of British North America. With the war in Europe over, America's overseas commerce was no longer subject to seizure, and its sailors were no longer impressed. American forces had effectively crushed Native American resistance along the frontier, and the flow of settlers to the American West grew to a torrent.[4]

Combat on land and sea is the central component of warfare and the ultimate test of policy and strategy. Evaluation of the wisdom and effectiveness of national and state leaders requires an examination of how their decisions ultimately played out on the battlefield. This study looks at battles and engagements for three reasons. First, the narrative would be incomplete without an investigation of the linkage between policy and battlefield success and failure. Second, a look at the number and scope of military and naval engagements demonstrates New York's centrality to the war effort and the size of its human and material contributions. Third, an exploration of battlefield activity points out the particular roles of New York's participants that are often missed in general accounts.

While the war saw much fighting in other regions and on the seas, the largest campaigns occurred within New York State or close to its borders. Among these were the invasions of Canada culminating in battles at Queenston Heights, Lacolle, Stoney Creek, Chateauguay, Crysler's Farm, and the four-month-long 1814 campaign on the Niagara River. The Battle of Lundy's Lane was the second-most expensive engagement of the war in terms of casualties, second only to the Battle of New Orleans. The Battle of Plattsburgh blunted Britain's major counteroffensive of 1814. The largest shipbuilding effort of the war occurred on Lake Ontario at Sackett's Harbor. The War Department focused its war-making efforts in and near the state. For example, in the summer of 1814, 62 percent of the effective strength of the regular army was either stationed in the two military districts comprising New York or under orders to march there.[5] The efforts to improve the defenses of New York City eclipsed comparable endeavors in other major American seaports. While plunder and destruction by the Royal Navy on Chesapeake Bay over two years was vast and ugly, the burning of virtually every house along the Niagara River and the killing of civilians in a period of twelve days in December 1813 was singularly ruinous. Thousands of refugees fled dozens of miles into the snowy forest seeking shelter, many never returning to the site of their former homes. New York also witnessed what was perhaps the most significant technological advancement that came out of the conflict—Robert Fulton's *Demologos*, the world's first steam-powered warship and the largest steamer in the world.[6]

At no time since the American Revolution was joint federal–state cooperation in war-making more evident than in the War of 1812. Essentially, the Madison administration could not conduct the war without the active collaboration of the governors of key states. The failure of state governments under Federalist control—particularly in New England—to resource offensive operations impaired the war effort. In striking contrast, Republican governor Daniel Tompkins wholeheartedly supported the war and, as commander in chief of the state militia, commanded an organization larger than the regular army. Starting as soon as he entered office in 1807, Tompkins began readying the state for the conflict he saw coming. He guided the legislature in acquiring weapons and placing them closer to the frontiers. He ensured that the militia was generally officered by fellow Republicans, who presumably would be more supportive of the national party's efforts to resolve the growing tensions with Britain. More than any other person in state government, Tompkins was fervently proactive in positioning the militia for the defense of state lands. The battlefield efforts of the militia were mixed at best; nevertheless, the militia had the means and the leadership to defend hearth and home. It is doubtful that any other politician could have accomplished as much. Had the governor been a Federalist or a Republican less determined than Tompkins, it is quite possible that the northern border of New York State would have been pushed some miles southward.[7]

Madison recognized the competence and energy of the governor and, in the crisis of 1814, he made Tompkins the commander of the Third Military District. In so doing, Madison entrusted Tompkins with the command of both federal and state troops, including those New Jersey militia units charged with the defense of America's largest port. At no time since 1815 has a state's role in the conduct of warfare so closely approached that of the federal government.

Upon the publication in 1898 of *Public Papers of Daniel D. Tompkins: Governor of New York, 1807–1817*, state historian Hugh Hastings wrote in the introduction, "The history of the second war with Great Britain has never been written, because no writer has yet undertaken to show the superb services which were rendered to the American cause by the State of New York, and by the great war Governor of that State, Daniel D. Tompkins."[8] The 1911 Albany fire damaged the state museum and destroyed countless militia records and much of the governor's official correspondence, thus crippling any comprehensive study of the state's forces. However, this work is an attempt to overcome that impediment and to address the gap in the historical record.

This book is not a conventional history of the war, with balanced coverage of all the participants—British, American, Canadian, and Native Peoples. That balanced approach is generally achieved in the current scholarship. Readers will quickly note the explicit and intentional focus on New Yorkers and the Native Americans residing within the state. This study seeks balance in its coverage of the tensions between civilian and military; various ethnic groups; Federalist and Republican; army, navy, and privateer; federal and state forces; federal and state governments; and urban and rural residents.

Such examination is important because it expands and shapes our understanding of an underappreciated war. This conflict was an early test of federal–state cooperation in war-making. President Madison did not wage this war alone; Governor Tompkins was at his side every step of the way, along with tens of thousands who supported Madison for better or worse. This study is also a remedy to past general histories that have minimized the state's contribution to the war effort in favor of that of the federal government, or have emphasized notable battles elsewhere. The burning of Washington, the sinking of HMS *Guerriere* by USS *Constitution,* and the Battle of New Orleans were dramatic events to be sure, but they were not essential to the outcome of the war.

Given the state's centrality to the fighting, the contributions and suffering of its people, and the immense role of the state government in support of operations, it is fair to say that New York's war was the War of 1812. It is past time for New Yorkers to take pride and ownership of these events of more than two centuries ago.[9]

CHAPTER 1

PRELUDE TO WAR

British attacks on American sovereignty had been ongoing for years, but in April 1806, the insults rose to the level of wanton violence. Three British warships appeared off Sandy Hook, New Jersey, intent on examining merchant vessels entering or leaving New York Harbor. Royal Navy gun crews fired shots across the bow of craft, forcing them to stop to be searched. On April 25, HMS *Leander* fired upon the sloop *Richard*, killing the helmsman, John Pierce, a New Yorker. The population of New York City was outraged. The citizenry conducted a public funeral. New Yorkers held rallies denouncing the British and calling on the federal government to defend the harbor and maintain the honor of the nation. Men rushed to join volunteer militia companies. However, the demonstrations were generally local and eventually the public's fury subsided.[1] The following year, HMS *Leopard* fired upon the U.S. Navy frigate *Chesapeake*; the outrage was now national and the march to war began.

In 1810, New York state had a population of 959,049 in forty-six counties. Ten percent of New Yorkers resided in New York City, including about 2,000 free persons of color and 1,700 slaves. New York City was the most populous city in the nation, having grown nearly 40 percent in the twelve years prior to the war. Washington Irving, then a local literary celebrity, coined the nickname "Gotham" for the city prior to the war. In 1812, New York City and New York County were synonymous with Manhattan Island and Governors, Ellis, and Bedloe's Islands in the harbor. The compact city occupied the southern tip of Manhattan, with small villages extending northward toward the Harlem River. Unlike today, the city did not include the five boroughs. Queens, Kings, and Richmond were separate counties. The Bronx was then part of Westchester County.

The population of the state capital, Albany, was 10,000 in 1810. The rest of the state population resided in smaller cities and villages located along rivers, the shorelines of lakes, and on Long Island. Yeoman farmers living close to villages and around larger cities comprised as much as 70 percent of the population.

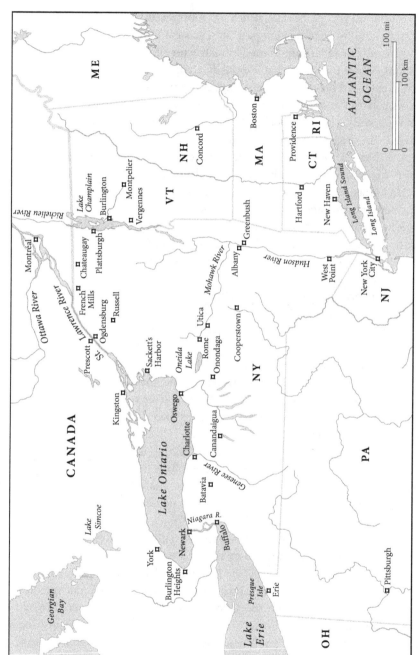

New York theater of war. Map by Erin Greb Cartography.

In the western part of the state, which was most recently opened to settlement, farming families were moving past subsistence and now producing surplus. However, the inland transportation infrastructure limited most selling to local markets. Water transportation, especially along the Hudson River and Long Island, extended the range for sale of agricultural produce.[2]

A small and marginalized part of the population were Native Americans. Approximately 4,500 Iroquois and other tribespeople lived on eleven reservations. The largest tribe of the Iroquois was the Seneca, who resided in the western part of the state. The War Department administered treaties and affairs between the reservation natives and the federal government through Indian agents. Erastus Granger was the agent to the New York Native Americans between 1803 and 1818. He and the sub-agent, Jasper Parrish, were well respected by the Iroquois. Indians had captured Parrish during the Revolution, and he had lived with them for several years. He also served as the agency's primary interpreter. The Indians would become key participants once Congress declared war in 1812.[3]

Two important lines of transportation connected New York City with the upstate population. The first was the Hudson River–Lake Champlain–Richelieu River corridor. Other than a short portage between the Hudson and Lake Champlain, water access existed between New York City and the St. Lawrence River. The second line started at Albany and traversed a sixteen-mile-long portage bypassing the Great Cohoes Falls and entering the Mohawk River at Schenectady. Vessels then proceeded up the Mohawk River portaging around Little Falls. At Rome, batteaux or Durham boats carried cargo through the short, narrow Rome Canal that connected with Wood Creek. This shallow waterway emptied into Oneida Lake. Vessels moved across the lake and down the Oneida and Oswego Rivers to Lake Ontario. Oswego Falls interrupted the flow, and teamsters portaged cargo around that obstacle. Both lines of transportation were also historic routes of invasion that had figured heavily in New York's colonial wars and the Revolution.[4]

State politics echoed the intensely partisan national condition. The Federalist Party, seemingly diminished by the election of Jefferson, experienced a resurgence in the run-up to war. The Republican Party, while generally supportive of Madison's press toward war, also included a substantial anti-war faction. The quest to establish the nation's sovereignty in the face of unremitting British and French incursion resulted in a fiercely divided citizenry and markedly limited the state's ability to sustain the national war effort largely unfolding on the state's periphery.[5]

The state constitution, in effect since 1777, prescribed that the governor serve for three years, senators for four, and assemblymen for a single year. Elections were conducted over a three-day period at the end of April. Winners took office on July 1. However, the legislative session did not begin until the last Tuesday in January and lasted as long as three months. The governor could prorogue (dismiss) a legislative session or call for a special session. The state had an unusual two-tiered suffrage requirement. Free males age twenty-one or older who had a "freehold estate" valued at $50 or who were tax-paying tenants met the qualifications to vote for state assemblymen and U.S. congressmen. However, a higher criterion was necessary to vote for governor and state senator—a freehold valued at $250. Roughly 60 percent of eligible voters could meet this higher threshold.[6]

State politics began with the Revolution. George Clinton had served as governor from 1777 to 1795 and again from 1801 to 1804. A Republican, he served as vice president under Jefferson and Madison from 1805 until his death in 1812. Clinton was fiercely opposed by New York Federalists John Jay, Stephen Van Rensselaer, Alexander Hamilton, and Philip Schuyler. Clinton did not seek reelection to the governorship in 1795, making way for John Jay. However, the treaty that Jay had negotiated with Britain in 1794 came to light after the gubernatorial election. Republicans considered Jay's Treaty a national travesty and humiliation because it gave too much to the British with little in return. The ensuing national debate over the treaty led to a coalescing of the Republican and Federalist movements into political parties. Republicans in New York City found a home in the Society of Tammany. This influential group was antimonarchist, anti-Jay, and tilted toward France and away from Britain. Aaron Burr was largely responsible for turning the Tammany Society from a social club into a political society.[7]

The Federalists in New York City also had a political organization, the Washington Benevolent Society, whose primary function was electioneering for Federalist candidates. In 1798, Jay was reelected, winning over Republican Robert R. Livingston by more than 2,000 votes. Criticism of the Jay Treaty was subsiding as the quarrel with France grew.[8] However, Federalism was on a decline in New York because of the backlash against the Alien and Sedition Acts. Many people believed that enforcement of these laws was haphazard and exceptionally partisan.

New York politics is unintelligible without reference to the Council of Appointment, a body unique to the state. The council controlled the appointment of about 7,000 state officials and the commissions of about 8,000 militia officers. The council was composed of the governor and four senators elected annually by the State Assembly, each of whom had a single vote. It was a clearinghouse for party patronage and could remove incumbents. Thus, when the Federalists controlled the Assembly, it was very likely that the council would have a majority of Federalist members who would replace Republican office-holders. A Republican governor would have difficulty placing his supporters into positions that had become vacant through resignation or death.[9]

In July 1801, George Clinton reassumed the governorship and served until he was elected to the vice presidency in Jefferson's second administration. By then, Republican leadership fell into three factions: followers of Clinton, followers of Livingston, and followers of Aaron Burr. The Clinton and Livingston factions used the Council of Appointment to reward their followers and to shut out those of Burr. With the turn of the century, political leadership was slowly moving to a new generation—those who had not participated in the Revolution.

A major player in the Republican Party was George Clinton's nephew, DeWitt Clinton. Born in 1769, DeWitt was valedictorian of Columbia College's class of 1786. He served as secretary to his uncle during the latter's governorship from 1789 to 1795. In 1803, DeWitt Clinton resigned from the U.S. Senate to become mayor of New York City. The executive power in the city was invested in the municipal corporation that was composed of the appointed mayor and ten elected aldermen. The mayor had authority to appoint a number of city officers, an authority each mayor used to thank his supporters. DeWitt Clinton was ambitious, ruthless, and intolerant of those with differing opinions. Yet, would-be politicians sought his patronage. Inimical Councils of Appointment removed Clinton from the mayor's position twice; however, he remained mayor during the war.

The Livingston and Clinton factions feuded. The Livingstons were members of New York's aristocracy. Morgan Lewis was among them, having married Livingston's sister, Gertrude. Lewis decisively defeated Aaron Burr in 1804 and served three years as governor. DeWitt Clinton's brother-in-law was Judge Ambrose Spencer. Clinton and Spencer wanted to defeat Lewis and promoted Daniel D. Tompkins's candidacy in the 1807 gubernatorial election. Martin Van Buren supported Tompkins, and the two became close political associates. The contrast between Tompkins, the son of a farmer, and landowner Morgan Lewis could not be more stark. Tompkins won by more than 4,000 votes. The Federalists had no candidate, most of their votes going to Lewis. Tompkins's biographer, Ray W. Irwin, noted, "Practically the only strikingly-new development in this election was the elevation to the governorship, for the first time in the state's history, of a person without personal wealth or important family connections."[10] The new governor was assisted in his election by the votes of many newly naturalized refugees from the failed United Irish Rebellion of 1798. Thomas Addis Emmet delivered the Irish vote. He had been arrested by the British just prior to the rebellion and imprisoned until 1802. He emigrated to New York the following year and became a prominent

Governor Daniel D. Tompkins, by John Wesley Jarvis. Courtesy New-York Historical Society.

lawyer. When Tompkins was reelected in 1812, he rewarded Emmet with the attorney generalship.

Daniel D. Tompkins was governor of New York throughout the war. Tompkins was born in 1774 in Westchester County. He would serve twice as vice president of the United States, but that was in the nation's future. During the Revolution, Westchester County was a combat zone between British forces occupying New York City and George Washington's Continentals, who loosely surrounded their foe to ensure that the British could not depart their sanctuary without being challenged. Tompkins's father, Jonathan Griffin Tompkins, was an unabashed patriot and a man of modest means. He was a tenant farmer who purchased a farm near Scarsdale just before Daniel's birth. In the confusion and danger sown in the early years of the conflict, Jonathan took his family, including two-year old Daniel, to relative safety in Dutchess County. They returned after the war to their farm.[11]

Tompkins entered Columbia College in 1792, graduating valedictorian three years later. During his collegiate years, he wrote essays challenging slavery, capital punishment, and the treatment of Native Americans.[12] In 1797, Tompkins opened a law office in New York City, and he married Hannah Minthorne. Hannah's father was a prominent Republican active in the Tammany Society. Becoming a Republican was easy for Tompkins given his upbringing in an impecunious household and the legacy of a Revolutionary father. Tompkins worked strenuously to gather support for Republican candidates in the 1800 election, coming to the attention of the Republican leadership. He was one of New York City's delegates to the 1801 constitutional convention and served in the State Assembly in 1803. He was elected to Congress in 1804 but resigned without serving so that he could accept an appointment as an associate justice on the state supreme court during the governorship of Morgan Lewis.[13]

On June 22, 1807, HMS *Leopard* attacked the American frigate *Chesapeake* off Norfolk, Virginia, killing three sailors and wounding eighteen others. News of the attack arrived in New York as Tompkins was sworn in as governor. Americans of all political bents were incensed. The threat of imminent war was palpable. Knowing the nation was unprepared for war, Jefferson would attempt to use the nation's economic power to achieve national goals via the Embargo Act.[14]

During the crisis at hand, various communities along the border with the province of Upper Canada (present-day Ontario) formed committees of safety and requested arms from the state. Tompkins ordered state arsenals to make some arms available, only to discover insufficient state weaponry to meet the immediate demands. Tompkins noted rather sternly that militia laws required citizens provide their own arms and accoutrements. He also commented that he, the governor, was personally responsible for issuing the weapons; therefore, he expected their return in good condition when the emergency subsided.[15] However, Tompkins anticipated the real possibility of a major conflict and began taking steps to prepare the state for its own defense.

On July 6, 1807, and in direct response to the *Chesapeake* Affair, Jefferson directed that state governors requisition a total of 100,000 militiamen and hold them in readiness to "march at a moment's warning." New York's share was 12,704, which represented about 13 percent of the state's common militia. These citizen-soldiers were selected from the common militia and assigned for temporary service to the detached militia until the emergency passed. The governor would appoint the officers of these new organizations. The state would pay wages earned while serving in detached units and requisition the federal government for reimbursement. In office for only fifteen days, Tompkins ordered his division commanders to identify militiamen who would serve. He was confident "that a considerable portion, if not the whole of the Quota required, will consist of companies voluntarily and cheerfully tendering their services." However, as late as December, several division commanders had not submitted the required rosters of detached militiamen. In January 1808, although some returns were still missing, Tompkins was pleased to report to the legislature that "all the artillery of the detachment, and most of the cavalry and infantry are volunteers. "[16]

The War Department was concerned about the Canadian population in the event of war. Thousands of settlers in Upper Canada had been born in the United States and had moved north for cheap land. To what degree would they support the British government? Erastus Granger's position as Indian agent gave him access to information not otherwise attainable by the national government. He and Jasper Parrish kept abreast of conditions in the Canadas through interviews with Indians who crossed the international border. Within weeks of the attack upon the *Chesapeake*, Secretary of War Henry Dearborn directed Granger to make an intelligence analysis of the military and social situation in the north. Granger's assessment was borne out by events.

> In speaking of the loyalty of the people, I think I am warranted in saying that a very large majority of the inhabitants, say 7–10th, would greatly rejoice at a union with us. Still, however, if war takes place, it will be between the United States and Great Britain. We therefore ought not to calculate with any degree of certainty on a part of her subjects taking up arms in our favor to reduce the rest. The people at present feel no oppression from their Government. They have rather been fostered hitherto by his Majesty. We therefore can only calculate on their neutrality and good wishes for our success.[17]

In December 1807, Congress passed the Embargo Act, and news of this drastic response inflamed the state's commercial interests. Nonetheless, Tompkins gave wholehearted support to Jefferson. In his first address to the state legislature in January 1808, Tompkins cited the "unprovoked and unprecedented attack" upon the *Chesapeake*, impressment, and the unlawful seizure of ships and cargoes. He stated that Jefferson's embargo reflected a "sincere desire" to avoid war with Britain, and the citizenry should accept "temporary privations and inconveniences" rather than resort prematurely to armed conflict. He noted the ongoing partnership with the federal government in fortifying the city of New York but warned the lawmakers not to "be unmindful of the exposed situation of our brethren upon the northern and western frontiers of our state." Tompkins implored the legislators to correct deficiencies in the militia laws to achieve greater efficiency in mobilization. He completed his list of concerns by asking the legislature to approve funding for a powder magazine to be built near New York City. Both houses of the legislature responded positively to the governor's defensive measures. The Assembly noted that the "defence-less state of our principal sea-ports and our Western and northern frontiers" would "not fail to receive our earliest attention." The Republican-dominated state senate agreed. A senate committee responding to the governor's speech wrote, "We cannot admit the absurd and degrading idea, that the rulers of a free and enlightened people, with ample means to defend themselves, can possibly be capable of pursuing measures subservient to the views of any nation."[18] Tompkins had wasted no time in taking major steps in readying the state for a possible, even likely war.[19]

Congress renewed a requisition of militia in March 1808. This time, the War Department set New York's quota at 14,389. Tompkins once again issued a general order establishing quotas for the divisions and separate brigades. In April 1809, Jefferson issued the order to stand down the requisitioned militia; the immediate crisis had passed. The two statewide requisitions served to exercise militia officers at all levels to call up and select their citizen-soldiers for detached service.[20]

Understandably, the Embargo Act prompted an increase in the ranks of the Federalist Party. Farmers saw prices of their produce plummet as foreign markets dried up, and they voted Federalist. The Federalists gained control of the State Assembly in 1809 and would not approve any of the governor's requests to improve the state's defenses. In January 1810, the Federalist-dominated Council of Appointment began a wholesale replacement of Republicans. "Republicans holding office as judges, sheriffs, surrogates, county clerks, district attorneys, and justices of the peace were made to realize the power of this colossal engine and were ruthlessly removed, merit, fidelity, ability counting as naught." Fortunately for the Republicans, they recaptured the Assembly and replaced hundreds of Federalist officials with members of their own party beginning in January 1811.[21]

The embargo also caused ruptures among New York's Republicans. DeWitt Clinton condemned the Embargo Act, noting that American commercial interests should assume the risk and protect themselves rather than give up trade altogether. Their opposing views caused the beginning of a rift between Tompkins and DeWitt Clinton. Madison, upon taking office in 1809, was loathe to reward appointments to known followers of DeWitt Clinton. For his part, Clinton reconciled himself to the Embargo Act rather than further split his own party in the face of a resurgent Federalist Party. Yet, as the nation began a five-year drift toward war (from the attack on the *Chesapeake* in 1807), DeWitt Clinton emerged as leader of the anti-war Republicans.[22]

Unsurprisingly, the Embargo Act engendered a thriving culture of smuggling, particularly along the northern border. Canadians paid inflated prices for potash, salted pork, salt, flour, and lumber. One customs collector reported, "Sleighs pass at Sackets Harbor ten miles from shore, and all the force I can raise is not sufficient to stop them. They appear determined to evade the laws at the risk of their lives." Customs officials and local sheriffs received little help from the local populace in enforcing the law, and Governor Tompkins reluctantly called out the militia. Militia officers posted a small detachment on the Oswegatchie River in Jefferson County. The customs collector at Sackett's Harbor reported that "the people in the vicinity of their station are hostile, and refuse to accommodate them with anything, even to admit them into their houses. They are in a suffering condition, and the snow is three feet deep."[23]

A serious incident occurred in Oswego in the summer of 1808. Sixty armed men arrived at that port proclaiming they would seize a shipment of Canadian flour that the customs officer had captured. They were driven off by militia dragoons, and Tompkins maintained a militia presence in Oswego until a newly recruited company of regulars replaced them. However, Tompkins was much more comfortable using civilian law enforcement than militia. He wrote to Jefferson, "I am persuaded a few prosecutions and convictions would have a greater tendency to make the laws respected than the appearance of a military force." He advised the officers of the regulars that "by a discreet exercise of moderation, circumspection, prudence and firmness resorting to force only where persuasion and caution prove unavailing, you will meet with little mortification or difficulty."[24]

Sometimes smugglers resorted to violence to intimidate revenue officials. Peter Sailly was a staunch Republican who had served in the state legislature and in Congress. Since 1809, he was the collector of customs in the District of Champlain and responsible for seizing many goods intended for illegal entry into Lower Canada. In January 1812, a group of men entered his home in Plattsburgh at night brandishing pistols. Sailly met them and fired his own weapons, wounding two. The intruders fled. From 1813 onward, Sailly served as keeper of stores in Plattsburgh as well as a customs official, and he worked tirelessly to ensure that soldiers received the best food available—a considerable challenge.[25]

Tompkins worked closely with Secretary of the Treasury Albert Gallatin to identify and replace ineffective customs officials.[26] In February 1809, Tompkins appointed Gen. Benjamin Mooers of Plattsburgh to command the detached militia on Lake Champlain and charged him with assisting the customs officials in enforcing the Embargo Act.[27] Mooers was a veteran of the Revolution, having served in the Second Canadian Regiment commanded by his uncle Moses Hazen. In the last days of the Jefferson administration, Jefferson signed into law the Non-Intercourse Act, which lifted the embargo on all ports except those under French or British control. His action removed the major point of contention between parties, although the Federalists remained competitive if only as an active opposition party. With his stalwart support of Jefferson's trade policies, Tompkins strengthened the political bonds between the New York and Virginian wings of the Republican Party. Tompkins handily won reelection in 1810, and Republicans took the legislature.[28]

From the *Chesapeake* Affair onward, Tompkins was increasingly preparing the state for war. Along its western and northern frontiers, New York shared more than four hundred miles of land and water boundaries with Lower and Upper Canada. The traditional Richelieu River—Lake Champlain—Hudson River invasion corridor led from Montreal along a mostly water route past Albany and directly to New York City. Long Island and New York City were open to direct assault by troops landed by the Royal Navy. In the event of war, New York presented numerous targets for British attack. While the United States Constitution gave the federal government the sole responsibility to declare war and the primary responsibility to protect the states from invasion, it was well understood that warfare was a shared task between the states and the federal government. Governor Tompkins directed the state's efforts generally along two lines: upgrading the militia to better defend communities and territory, and improving fortifications to protect likely targets.

The Constitution gave the Congress power "to provide for calling forth the Militia to execute the Laws of the Union, suppress Insurrections and repel Invasions." Congress gave structure to the militia through the Militia Acts of 1792 and 1795, but each state enacted its own laws in conformance to federal law. In April 1809, the legislature updated the state Militia Act. In general, all free able-bodied white male citizens between the ages of eighteen and forty-five were enrolled in the common militia. State law exempted some professions such as clergy, teachers, college students, firemen, sailors, and some state officials such as judges. In peacetime, the few full-time paid militia positions in the state included the adjutant general, the commissary of military stores and his deputy, and the superintendents and guards at the two state arsenals. Armorers were contracted as necessary to repair weapons.

The expectation was that the common militia would defend the local community and support the sheriff in enforcing the law and quelling domestic violence if called upon to do so. The militia also served a social function, especially in sparsely settled areas. The semi-annual days of muster and training were opportunities to meet fellow citizens and perhaps discuss local and national issues. Thus, muster days were tinged with varying degrees of partisan political expression.

In 1807, the state militia was an impressive organization on paper.[29] The size of a local company varied; none normally exceeded a hundred militiamen.

The state organized eight or nine companies into a regiment; a battalion was a collection of companies smaller than a regiment. The state further paired regiments into brigades commanded by a brigadier general. A varying number of brigades were organized as a division, commanded by a major general. Men with a martial inclination and motivation to greater social or political standing organized themselves into volunteer companies, acquiring their own uniforms and weapons and choosing their own officers. Rather than organize as generic infantry, the volunteer companies typically armed and equipped themselves into something more exotic such as rifle, dragoon, or artillery companies. The state recognized the volunteer companies and exempted them from enrollment in the local militia and mandatory training. However, the state assigned volunteer companies to militia regiments.

At least one unit of volunteers had an ethnic origin. Thousands of Irishmen emigrated to the United States after the failed 1798 Rebellion. Many saw service in militia units as a way to both express loyalty to their new home and demonstrate their deep-seated animosity toward the British. Francis McClure of New York City raised a volunteer rifle company composed of Irish immigrants and later expanded this unit to battalion size. The men volunteered to serve in the requisition of March 1808. Tompkins sent his personal thanks to the commanders of companies that had volunteered. Tompkins wrote to McClure, "The Gallant Sons of Erin have experienced the bitter fruits of persecution and Arbitrary power in their native soil; many of those who have sought an asylum in the United States justly value the privileges and happiness of a free Government. This is honorably and satisfactorily evinced by the unanimity, spirit and enthusiasm with which the Battalion of Riflemen under your command have enrolled themselves in support of the Government and laws of their adopted Country."[30]

This battalion eventually took the formal name Battalion of Republican Greens, an unsubtle reference to the political leanings of its members. However, the citizenry referred to McClure's volunteers more commonly as the Irish Greens. Tompkins held McClure in high regard, having written to a mutual friend that "the major is a disciplinarian and a patriot, who will not desert his country's standard upon any emergency." Upon the declaration of war, an anonymous writer in the New York newspaper *The War* noted that "their attachment to their new country and the abhorrence of the men who drove them from the land of their fathers, contributes to make them the most formidable enemies the British will have to contend with in the new world."[31]

The state also recognized another form of volunteers. Citizens not required to join the militia because of service during the Revolution, age, or other qualification, could self-organize into companies referred to as exempts. As war drew closer, several communities formed exempt companies and sought state sanction. As part of their state recognition, the men of a company of exempts agreed in an emergency to serve anywhere in the state.[32]

State law spelled out who was required to serve in the militia but was less clear on who would serve as officers. The appointment of officers was a joint function between the Council of Appointment and the governor. The council could grant commissions, but the governor assigned the officers to positions. In 1810, the Federalists controlled the Assembly and dominated the Council of Appointment. The majority of new militia commissions and promotions went to Federalists, yet Tompkins managed to evade putting some Federalists into high command by granting brevet promotions to Republicans. Brevet rank was a temporary rank that could be bestowed as a reward for meritorious service or for political support. During the war, Governor Tompkins brevetted officers in order to fill various command positions. For example, he could confer the rank of brevet lieutenant colonel on a major and assign that officer to command a regiment. The council could validate the promotion but could not remove the brevet or the officer from his position. The governor could also deny a command indefinitely, as he did to Maj. Gen. DeWitt Clinton during the war.[33]

A militiaman accepting a commission was expected to purchase an officer's uniform, equipment, and a weapon, not an inconsiderable expense. Militia officers met more frequently than their men, serving on court-martials and participating in officer training. Thus, commissions fell to those who were financially able to accept their role and who could control their time. Few yeomen farmers, especially on the state's frontiers, could meet these requirements. The overlap between a militia commission and upward social and political mobility was undeniable. Both parties exercised patronage in granting commissions, and many officers concurrently held civil office.[34]

In the run-up to war, the New York militia consisted of approximately 98,000 men organized in 164 infantry regiments, twelve cavalry regiments, and a varying number of artillery regiments and separate artillery companies.[35] The whole was organized into forty-two brigades and these were gathered into eight divisions. The governor was commander in chief of the state militia. Under the federal Constitution, the president was commander in chief of all federal military forces and also state militias in those few instances outlined in the Constitution.

The Militia Act of 1795 stipulated that each militiaman would provide his own musket, bayonet, flints, cartridge box, and knapsack. However, repeated musters demonstrated to inspectors that such was not the case nor would it be. Weapons and accoutrements to outfit a militiaman cost as much as $15, which was beyond the financial reach of most citizens, particularly settlers on the state's frontiers. Both the federal government and state governments provided weapons, so at least some portion of the men sent to war would do so with musket in hand. However, President Jefferson informed Tompkins that federal arsenals were so deficient in weapons that the state needed to meet the needs on the frontiers with Canada.[36] He noted that federal law allowed U.S. weapons only for militiamen mustered into federal service. Prior to war, and before the president called out the militia, New York would have to acquire weapons and stage them at population centers closer to the anticipated scene of action. Tompkins repeatedly offered to store federal weapons with state weapons in the various outlying arsenals; the federal government declined to accept.[37]

Responding to a request for weapons from a committee of safety in Ontario County, Tompkins noted that no state law allowed the issue of weapons when the militia was not formally called into service. Nevertheless, he wrote, "The importance and expediency of placing arms and ammunition within the reach of that portion of our fellow citizens who would be first and most exposed in case of an invasion by our Canadian neighbours, determined me upon adopting the measure and trusting to the good sense and justice of the Legislature to sanction it." In October 1807, without the approval of the legislature, Tompkins released 220 stands of arms (musket, bayonet and scabbard, cartridge box, and belt) for Niagara County. With no funds budgeted to transport the weapons from the Albany arsenal to the Niagara frontier, Tompkins required the committee of safety there to pay for transport.[38]

Prominent citizens from Jefferson County petitioned President Jefferson for arms and requested the federal government build and maintain a fortification within the county. Jefferson County bordered Lake Ontario and the St. Lawrence River and was thus exposed to attack. The land was settled very recently, and fewer than four hundred privately owned muskets existed among a population of 3,000 men. The sparse settlement and proximity to Upper Canada prompted the petitioners to note that "a sudden attack without previous measures of defence on our part might be attended with the most dreadful calamities."[39] On April 18, 1808, Jefferson forwarded this petition to Tompkins, reminding him that no federal law permitted issuing arms without a requisition of militia into federal service. Jefferson was making it abundantly clear that defense of New York's frontiers would be primarily the responsibility of the state.

In February 1808, the state legislature passed "An Act to Provide for the Defense of the Northern and Western Frontiers." This act directed the governor to store a total of 4,000 stands of arms in Onondaga, Genesee, Oneida, Jefferson, Clinton, and Essex Counties. Tompkins issued orders to the commissary of military stores, John McLean, to transport weapons, accoutrements, and ammunition and deliver them to state officials, often the local judges, who would oversee the security of the items until the state could construct proper storage facilities. Tompkins was thus expanding the system of arsenals that had been previously limited to Albany, Rome, and Plattsburgh. Construction began on arsenals at New York City, Batavia, Canandaigua, Russell, Onondaga, and Watertown. The state enlarged existing arsenals and also built fifty small gun houses between 1808 and 1812. This action brought some weaponry directly into the villages, where militia would assemble to deal with local emergencies or to support a general mobilization. This effort took time, yet it gave confidence to settlers that they had the means to secure their communities.[40]

The City of New York operated its own arsenal, so the new state arsenal expanded the capacity to store weapons and ammunition. The state also began construction of a separate powder magazine in New York City in order to isolate this potentially dangerous commodity. When ordered to muster, militiamen would draw weapons, returning them when their tour of duty was completed.[41] The state also made land in New York City available to the federal government for arsenals and magazines. By the time war was declared, the federal government operated two arsenals, a magazine, a laboratory, and a powder house in the city. A "laboratory" in the military parlance of the day was a facility where workers assembled cartridges and rounds of artillery ammunition such as grapeshot.

In 1808, the state contracted with weapons manufacturer Eli Whitney of New Haven, Connecticut, for 2,000 stands of arms for $26,000. The following year, the state contracted for 1,000 muskets from a new gun manufacturer, Lemuel Pomeroy of Pittsfield, Massachusetts. In 1811, the state contracted with Whitney for an additional 2,000 stands of arms, of which five hundred were delivered by the end of the year. However, Whitney was unable to complete delivery of the remaining 1,500 on time, which drew a rebuke from Tompkins. Eventually Whitney completed the order.[42]

In addition to muskets, the state owned a considerable number of artillery pieces. About two hundred pieces of field artillery, most of them brass, were issued out to the militia artillery companies or stored in the various arsenals. The field artillery ranged in size from three- to twelve-pounders, with three- and four-pounders by far the most numerous. A typical militia artillery company had two small guns for training. However, with caissons and teams in short supply, each company would have to use whatever means available to move guns in an emergency. The state also possessed about eighty heavy iron guns, mostly twenty-four and thirty-two pounders, positioned in the defenses of New York City.[43]

By March 1811, Tompkins reported to the legislature that the project of providing arms at strategic locations throughout the state had been largely completed. He reported that "the state is now supplied with an adequate part of artillery, fit for service; and . . . when the small arms now manufacturing are received, the supply of muskets and ammunition will be amply sufficient to equip as large a detachment of the militia of this state as will probably ever be called into service at one time." Tompkins also bragged that the requirement for gunpowder had encouraged entrepreneurs in Columbia County to establish a powder factory, the first in the state.[44]

Despite the best state efforts to arm the common militia, units were generally incapable of maneuver on the battlefield due to deficiencies in training. Untrained militia officers could not train their men. As one author has put it, "The local militia consisted of those whose military experience and discipline, had been acquired in no better school than the semi-annual backwoods muster; an enrolment, an answering to names; an imperfect 'inspection and review,' and, generally, an easy compliance with requirements, far from being either stringent or effective."[45] An incident occurring one year before the declaration of war is illustrative of the many deficiencies of the militia. Nineteen-year-old Henry Leavitt Ellsworth, a Yale graduate, was travelling through Goshen in Orange County and recorded his observations of a company on training day. He noted no one was in uniform, their muskets were exceptionally rusty, and few could properly perform even the simplest of commands. One constant of military service remained intact: When the men started idle chattering, "the orderly sergeant grew wroth and was denouncing his most bitter anathemas upon them for their disorderly behavior." However vivid a sergeant's invectives, they are not enough to turn civilians into soldiers.[46]

Tompkins took his duties as commander in chief seriously. As he could, he attended annual militia reviews and sent congratulatory messages addressing the appearance and drill of specific units. State law required the governor to review court-martial verdicts, and Tompkins disapproved judgments when proceedings were in any way irregular.[47] He considered requests to form new uniformed companies, and these applications multiplied as the probability of war increased. The governor also approved the frequent reorganizations of the militia in response to population growth. Finally, he oversaw the appointments and promotions of officers as the numbers of companies, regiments, and brigades increased.

Tompkins was concerned that when militia and regular formations came together on the battlefield, they would not share the same tactical doctrine. Trainers of the time used the term "discipline" to denote soldier's individual actions (such as handling a musket) as well as the movement of units (such as forming a line from a marching column). These movements allowed a large unit to maneuver on the battlefield in order to gain a positional advantage on the enemy. While militia officers trained their soldiers using Von Steuben's *Blue Book*, the regulars may have been trained using a more modern doctrine, a doctrine with different formations and commands. The *Blue Book* was entirely appropriate for use during the American Revolution; however, the French had developed newer modes of fighting that combined the strength of assault columns, the firepower of lines, and the close coordination of skirmishers. American officials attributed French successes in the wars of the French Revolution to these new tactics, as well as the enthusiasm of citizen-soldiers. In a letter to General William Paulding, Tompkins wrote, "It is certainly desirable that a national system of discipline and tactics for the militia and Regulars should be devised and sanctioned by Congress. Until something of that kind be done, we may expect to have a great many ignorant officers in both corps, and of course some very indifferent troops." Congress did not act on Tompkins's worthy suggestion, and the lack of a common tactical doctrine hindered efficiency.[48]

The lack of a common tactical doctrine frustrated the militia and regulars in working together efficiently, as did another factor. Regular units trained together, worked together, and lived together for months or years. This closeness bred an understanding of the strengths and weaknesses of each officer and soldier. In units that had seen combat, the men dealt with their initial fears and would perform better in subsequent fights. Each man knew that he could depend on his comrades to stand firm. The militiaman had no such advantage, thus making militia units brittle just as newly recruited regulars were unsteady. New troops, whether regular or militia, were much more liable to panic in their first encounter with the enemy.

While preparing an immense militia organization was important to the defense of the state, perhaps more important to the governor was the defense of New York City. The British occupation during the Revolution had indelibly stamped the minds of the citizenry of New York City with the hardships they would face if any hostile power were to gain control over their metropolis. The fires of 1776 and 1778 had destroyed about one-quarter of the city. The economy was degraded, and poverty soared. In September 1811, Tompkins wrote, "I feel no doubt, however, that as between Canada and ourselves there is no danger of their commencing hostilities. The sea coast, will, I think, experience the first injury."[49] The city was crucial to the war effort. Customs revenues provided about 90 percent of all income to the federal treasury, and New York City provided about one-third of all import duties. The loss of the city would lead to catastrophic losses to the federal treasury. Secretary of War William Eustis agreed with Tompkins in his report to Congress in December 1811 on the status of defense of the maritime frontier. "New York, from its exposed situation, and relative importance to the Union, together with the harbor of Newport, Rhode Island, claim particular attention and require additional means of defence."[50]

There were three ways to raid or seize New York City. The first and most threatening was a naval attack that passed the Sandy Hook peninsula and adjacent shoals and entered the Upper Bay through the Narrows. Warships could then fire directly into the city and land troops at the southern end of Manhattan Island. These invaders could easily seize vessels and start fires. The second avenue into the city was to land a force on Long Island and seize the area around Brooklyn. Once in Brooklyn, the enemy might conduct an amphibious assault across the East River. The British took this route in 1776. The third approach was to land in Flushing Bay. An amphibious force based there could take a number of routes onto Manhattan Island. This avenue of approach would necessitate crossing the Harlem River and passing across Harlem Heights. Tompkins and state and city officials gave their highest priority to blocking the entrance to the Upper Bay.

State and city officials were justifiably concerned with fortifying the water approaches to New York City. As early as March 1807, the legislature designated a state Board of Fortification headed by DeWitt Clinton. Tompkins and the Board of Fortification formed a partnership with Col. Jonathan Williams, chief of the regular army's Corps of Engineers. That year, Williams, along with Vice President George Clinton and Secretary of War Henry Dearborn, conducted a detailed survey of New York Harbor. The product was a document entitled "Outline of a Plan of Defence for the City and Harbor of New York."[51] Understandably, Col. Williams took the lead in the survey and the resulting defensive plan. Williams intended the fortifications to challenge warships passing the Narrows and then destroy them in the harbor. Warships of the time had distinct advantages, albeit weather-dependent. A ship of the line could bring forty or fifty heavy guns to bear on a target from an extended range and from any position in which the depth of water was adequate. However, accuracy was degraded by the roll of the ship. Also, wooden ships were vulnerable to hot shot—balls heated cherry-red in a furnace. Guns firing from masonry land fortifications had no such vulnerabilities.

Military engineers typically designed fortifications based upon the designs of Sébastien Le Prestre de Vauban, the foremost military engineer of the seventeenth century. Engineers laid out a polygonal trace of bastions that allowed defenders to bring fire upon assaults from any direction. While Williams used the basics of bastions, he also employed round masonry casemate designs, not unlike the popular Martello towers making their appearance in Europe. A casemate is a vaulted interior chamber that housed an artillery piece. Williams designed thick masonry structures of one to three tiers, each consisting of multiple casemates. The round design deflected some shot striking at an angle. Additionally, curved and thick masonry walls would be difficult to breach by a land attack. An added advantage, in Williams's calculations, was that curved walls required much less masonry and were therefore cheaper and easier to construct than bastioned fortifications. A multi-tiered casemate structure occupied a smaller footprint than a more traditional polygonal fort and required fewer soldiers to defend it. Nonetheless, state officials would also station militia to challenge land-based assaults. Williams also saw a role to be played by U.S. Navy gunboats roaming the harbor and bringing enemy vessels under fire as opportunities presented themselves.[52]

While Colonel Williams oversaw the entire enterprise, the state Board of Fortification appointed commissioners to manage the work and to authorize spending of state funds. Commissioners hired and paid carpenters, stonemasons, and common laborers between $1 and $1.65 per day. By comparison, private soldiers at this time received only $8 per month. Many of the city's working poor sought jobs on various defense projects. The commissioners authorized purchases of timber, stone, and brick, as well as wine and brandy for themselves. The vast undertaking was a joint effort between federal, state, and city officials.[53]

To pass from the Lower Bay to the Upper Bay and Manhattan Island, enemy warships would have to transit the Narrows, the mile-wide waterway between Staten Island and Long Island. Colonel Williams developed a comprehensive plan to fortify the Narrows, even though the federal government would only own the sites on the shores of Long Island—Hendrick's Reef and Red Hook. The state decided to build and retain ownership of the fortifications on Staten Island. Therefore, the state bought or leased land and began construction of Fort Tompkins and Fort Richmond. Fort Richmond was a semicircular structure at the water's edge, while Fort Tompkins stood atop a cliff overlooking and protecting Fort Richmond from land attack. Fort Tompkins was a pentagonal structure. Williams eventually chose an innovative design featuring circular rather than triangular bastions and built for all-around defense. Eventually, the state constructed two smaller batteries, Fort Hudson and Fort Morton, to supplement the fire from the two larger forts into the Narrows. Fort Richmond was capable of mounting twenty-five heavy guns. The supporting batteries, Forts Hudson and Morton, could accommodate ninety-two guns. However, by June 1812, only sixty guns had been mounted on Staten Island and none across the Narrows at Hendrick's Reef.[54]

Should enemy warships enter the Upper Bay, they could fire directly upon New York City. However, the enemy would have to pass three strategic islands, and the Board of Fortifications took advantage of this key terrain. The first order of business was to acquire land. Between 1807 and the declaration of war, the governor, the Board of Fortification, and Colonel Williams sought state or federal title to land on these islands. As early as 1800, the state legislature ceded legal jurisdiction of Governors, Ellis, and Bedloe's Islands to the federal government in anticipation of acquisition of land and an official transfer of ownership.[55] In 1808, Tompkins charged a group of persons skilled in evaluating property to assess a fair price for Ellis Island. The annual income that the occupants derived from harvesting oysters and netting shad, over $500 annually, amplified the assessment to $10,000. He sent this information to Secretary of War Dearborn to justify the unexpected high sale value. By the end of the year, the federal government had secured the title to Ellis Island.[56]

Governors Island was the largest of the three harbor islands and the site of Fort Jay. Williams reconstructed and expanded Fort Jay, a traditional four-bastioned polygonal structure, incorporating more stone and brick masonry into walls and buildings. In 1807, authorities renamed it Fort Columbus partly due to the unpopularity of Jay's Treaty with Britain. By the start of the war, Fort Columbus could mount as many as ninety-six guns. Workers also began work on Castle Williams and South Battery on Governors Island. Castle Williams, a modern casemate structure, was the crown jewel of the Upper Harbor defenses. When completed, it would consist of three tiers of casemates, each holding twenty-six guns. The structure stood forty feet tall. Its walls were eight feet thick, virtually impervious to anything the Royal Navy could bring to bear. Rounding out the fortifications on Governors Island was South Battery, whose ten guns faced Brooklyn. Williams also designed and oversaw batteries on Bedloe's and Ellis Islands.

As the masonry went up, the governor and Williams secured artillery guns to place inside the fortifications. By the time Congress declared war, much had been accomplished to put the Upper Bay fortifications into readiness. On Governors Island, Fort Columbus mounted sixty heavy cannon, and Castle Williams mounted fifty-two with room for further expansion. The batteries on Bedloe's Island mounted twenty-four guns, and Ellis Island had fourteen.[57]

If enemy warships could pass the three harbor islands and draw closer to Manhattan Island, they would have to contend with a new casemate fort. In 1806, the City of New York acquired subsurface land off the Battery at the southern tip of Manhattan Island. Slowly workers deposited stone to create the island upon which eventually stood the Southwest Battery, renamed Castle Clinton after the war. This circular single-story structure housed twenty-eight guns. The Southwest Battery served as the headquarters of the federal commander of the city and environs.[58]

Farther up the Hudson River stood the North Battery, commonly known as the Red Fort for its red sandstone masonry. This semicircular stone fortification housing sixteen heavy guns was built atop a small island about two hundred yards offshore and connected to the shore by a causeway. Farther still up the Hudson and at the water's edge stood another masonry structure, Fort Gansevoort. Gen. Peter Gansevoort, a revolutionary hero, commanded Fort Stanwix, at the portage between the Mohawk River and Wood Creek, during its three-week siege in 1777. The city whitewashed the sandstone masonry of Fort Gansevoort and gave it the common name, the White Fort. These three sites—the Southwest Battery, North Battery, and Fort Gansevoort—would make passage from the Upper Bay up the Hudson River exceptionally difficult.

The state's priority was clearly to defend the direct approach through the Narrows into the Upper Bay. However, the Board of Fortification also laid out defenses on Brooklyn Heights, the East River, and Harlem Heights. A series of earthen and masonry forts and gun batteries eventually arose as the fear of war grew stronger. Work on improving the defenses of the city continued unabated throughout the war. In 1814, when Britain had the means to attack the city, it briefly considered but quickly rejected that course of action, selecting Washington and Baltimore as targets instead. The advanced state of defenses of New York City contributed to that choice.[59]

As 1811 came to a close, the storm clouds gathered. Perhaps no New Yorker was more influential in bringing about the war than congressman and War Hawk Peter B. Porter. Porter was a graduate of Yale and moved to New York at the age of twenty. He settled at Black Rock on the Niagara River in 1810 and represented the westernmost congressional district of the state. On November 29, 1811, as chairman of the House Committee on Foreign Relations, he delivered a powerful speech condemning Britain for its violations of America's neutral shipping rights and the impressment of its sailors. Britain's actions were "so daring in character, and so disgraceful in their execution" that Americans must take action. He connected the citizenry to its Revolutionary legacy. "The patriotic fire of the Revolution still burns in the American breast with a holy and unextinguishable flame, and will conduct this nation to those high destinies which are not less the reward of dignified moderation than of exalted valor." Porter introduced a series of resolutions that increased the size of the army, authorized the president to call up the militia and to enlist volunteers, and required the navy to fit out its vessels and put them into commission. After a vigorous debate, the House passed these resolutions on December 16. The War Hawks were not ready to declare war until the nation was better prepared to conduct it successfully.[60]

Governor Tompkins wrote to Congressman Thomas B. Cook that he did not expect the Twelfth Congress to declare war despite Britain's manifest affronts to national sovereignty. He closed his letter, "I hope, however, that my prophecy may prove to be incorrect and that you will evince by your measures that we will forthwith gird on the sword rather than couch to insult any longer."[61] As

Peter B. Porter, by Lars Sellstedt. Courtesy Buffalo History Museum.

if to press home the point to his officers that war might well be imminent, the governor invited all the generals and field-grade officers in and around Albany to attend church with him on New Year's Day mounted and in uniform. There was a flurry of activity with the local tailors as the invitees made up shortages in uniforms. Tompkins remarked that "there has been as much commotion amongst them as if they had been attacked unawares by the Indians." On the appointed day, Albany was subject to an ice storm such that "scarcely a man or horse could keep upon legs."[62] Nonetheless, the governor and his officers attended services. Perhaps the storm portended the upcoming conflict. Within six months, the nation would be at war with one of the most powerful adversaries on the planet. The state's officials and its citizens would soon learn whether their extensive preparations since 1807 were sufficient to the tempest.

1812

CHAPTER 2

PREPARATION FOR WAR

As 1811 rolled into 1812, a majority of Republicans, including President James Madison, came to believe that war was the only path remaining that would lead to the end of Britain's infringement of American rights as a sovereign neutral nation. Clearly, economic pressure had failed to move Britain and had proven to be a double-edged sword, hurting many Americans involved in foreign trade—farmers, merchants, bankers, and shippers. Republican discourse revealed the numerous benefits of war, benefits that would outweigh the risks involved. A successful war would persuade Britain to respect America's neutral trading rights, end impressment, and withdraw support to Native Americans who were challenging white settlement on the frontiers. A less tangible benefit would be to establish the world's only democratic republic as an equal among nations. Furthermore, war would unify the Republican Party and diminish the Federalists, perhaps once and for all.[1]

The first five months of 1812 saw the federal government scrambling to put the nation onto a wartime footing in anticipation of a declaration of war. High on the list of priorities was expanding the regular army and mobilizing the deep reserves of militia. These endeavors required close cooperation with state governments. The national government had to prepare naval forces for immediate action and to protect the merchant fleet from destruction by the Royal Navy once the war began. Wars cost money, and the federal government needed to entice subscribers for a sizeable loan. Anticipating resistance from the Federalists, Republicans began efforts to create widespread support among the general citizenry. Madison, his cabinet officers, and congressional Republicans put the engines of federal power into motion. But first, Madison had to settle upon a national strategy that would convert human and material resources into accomplishment of the war goals.

How could the United States challenge Great Britain, a major power? The foremost American goals pertained to maritime issues, yet the U.S. Navy could

not possibly engage the Royal Navy with any hope of decisive victory. Therefore, the administration resisted calls to expand the navy; instead, it spent
money to mobilize the army. Yet, the high seas presented an opportunity to
support the national strategy. America could unleash hundreds of privateers
to prey upon British shipping. While commerce raiding would not by itself be
decisive, Madison reasoned that a successful invasion of British North America
could bring Britain to the negotiating table. American diplomats would offer
Canada back to Britain in exchange for maritime concessions. It was not lost on
Republicans that Britain was fully engaged in existential conflict with Napoleonic France. Perhaps Britain would make a deal quickly with the U.S. in order
to direct all of its resources against its most dangerous enemy. If Britain refused
Madison's offer, America would retain Canada. This action would break the
British–Native American alliance and secure the fur trade for Americans.

British North America was immense, yet it was also vulnerable to American
attack. The vast majority of the white population of Upper and Lower Canada
lived along the St. Lawrence River or near the shores of Lake Ontario. Quebec,
Montreal, and Kingston were the largest cities. The supply line for British forces
extended from Britain, across the North Atlantic, and up the St. Lawrence River
and into the Great Lakes. Cutting the supply line would eventually starve military and naval forces posted up the line. Naval forces were particularly vulnerable, as virtually every item needed to build a warship except timber originated
in Britain—guns, anchors, heavy cables, ropes, and sails. An American strategy
to seize Canada would have to include cutting the supply line. Thus, attacks to
seize Montreal and Quebec would yield strategic results. Attacks to the westward
of this slender supply line, such as across the Niagara or Detroit Rivers, would
yield only local consequences. Quebec was key. The St. Lawrence was navigable
by ocean-going vessels as far as that fortress city. No defense of Canada was
possible if Quebec fell. British attempts to retake Canada would have to start
with securing that city. For the Americans, the best path to Quebec ran through
Montreal, and the best path to Montreal originated in New York State.[2]

In February, Congressman Peter B. Porter offered a plan to accomplish
America's war aims. He noted that the effort to raise 25,000 regular troops was
proceeding too slowly to support a successful invasion of Canada in 1812. Yet,
delaying an invasion until 1813, when the regulars would presumably be available, allowed Britain too much time to bolster the defenses of British North
America. Porter argued that the invasion should proceed in 1812, as soon as the
government could raise 15,000 to 20,000 short-term volunteers. The invaders
would "over-run Canada, with the exception of Quebec, in a few weeks." After
cutting across the St. Lawrence River, these forces would conduct additional
training. They would then march "at their leisure, to the siege and reduction

of Quebec." Finally, an army of regulars and volunteers would depart New England and attack Halifax, thus completing the invasion. Like Porter, Madison believed that an attack made quickly that seized Montreal with available troops was preferable to waiting until a large regular army could be recruited. The president assumed that a large number of volunteers "would be readily furnished by the enthusiasm of the frontiers of New York and Vermont." Porter eventually became a brave and successful brigade commander. However, events would disclaim his and the president's overly confident optimism and simplistic strategic sense.[3]

Clearly, New Yorkers were divided on the wisdom of seeking war. Federalists bemoaned the anticipated economic disruption, both the trade out of New York City and the thriving commerce along the northern border with Canada. Back in Albany, Governor Tompkins supported the national Republican movement to war. On January 28, 1812, Tompkins addressed the opening session of the legislature. He noted Britain's continued affronts to national sovereignty and neutral rights. Tompkins observed that the militia had demonstrated improvements and that the state "may repose unlimited confidence in the patriotism, gallantry and efficacy of the militia, whenever the honor and safety of the country shall require their services." Was Tompkins justifying the years of investment in the militia? Did he believe his own words? The militia would expose its numerous defects once the state's commander in chief ordered it to the frontiers.[4]

The governor appealed for unity in the impending crisis, asking for an end to political differences and "that whatever may be our local and domestic differences, we shall be an united and formidable people, upon all questions which involve our national existence and privileges, or which affect the vital principles of independence." This call was generally disregarded. The Federalists had lost a major point of contention when Jefferson lifted the embargo in 1809. However, now they could take up the anti-war position to motivate the citizenry. The mixed sentiment concerning the drift toward war was reflected in the statewide April elections, in which the Federalists won a small majority in the Assembly, playing no small amount of mischief with the governor's programs.[5]

A component of the national strategy was the use of privateers to damage British commerce and cause social unrest. Thomas Jefferson stated the case vividly and optimistically: "Their fleet will annihilate our public force on the water, but our privateers will eat out the vitals of their commerce. Perhaps they may burn New York or Boston. If they do, we must burn the city of London, not by expensive fleets or Congreve rockets, but by employing an hundred or two Jack the painters whom nakedness, famine, desperation & hardened vice will abundantly furnish from among themselves."[6]

Madison and Jefferson understood that the U.S. Navy could not challenge the Royal Navy on the seas, while a large and active privateering effort could damage British trade and be just enough of an irritant to induce Britain to accede to American war aims. On June 26, Congress passed "An Act concerning Letters of Marque, Prizes, and Prize Goods." This law codified how the nation would conduct this aspect of naval operations. New York City would eventually be home port to about forty-four privateers. Only Baltimore, with fifty-two privateers, supported more of these commercial "warships." [7]

However, the seizure of Canada would be effected, if at all, by troops, not by privateers. On November 5, 1811, Madison asked Congress to add 20,000 men to the regular army. At the time, there were fewer than 8,000 soldiers serving in federal units. After a delay of two months, Congress authorized ten new infantry regiments, one additional regiment of light dragoons, and two new artillery regiments. Congress initially retained the five-year term of service. The recruits received a $16 bonus and, upon completion of their term of service, 160 acres of land and three months' pay. The long term of enlistment was widely perceived as a hindrance to recruiting, and Congress authorized the War Department to offer terms of eighteen months. These recruits, however, would not receive the land bounty. Once Congress authorized the regiments, the War Department began the monumental process of selecting more than eight hundred new officers. [8]

Secretary of War William Eustis brought in two officers to assist in the many tasks of expanding the army. The first was Col. Alexander Smyth. Smyth was born in Ireland and brought to America at the age of ten. He was an ardent Jeffersonian and a Virginian politician who had commanded the elite Rifle Regiment since 1808. Smyth was also the acting inspector general to Eustis. The second, Lt. Col. Alexander Macomb, was born in Detroit. His father, also named Alexander, was a land speculator who had purchased 3.6 million acres of land in northern New York. The senior Macomb moved to New York City when young Alexander was three. The Macombs enjoyed the friendship of Alexander Hamilton, who assisted young Alexander in securing an officer's commission in 1799. Macomb served as an engineer and received rapid promotions as a result of his competence and ability to get along with his colleagues, two uncommon characteristics in the prewar army. Eustis appointed Macomb acting adjutant general. As adjutant general, Macomb wrote and tracked responses to thousands of orders emanating from the War Department.

Once Congress authorized the new regiments, hundreds of men applied for commissions. Governor Tompkins received many requests for letters of recommendation and sent such for persons known to him or recommended by friends and associates. Political considerations were important. To a would-be

*Major General
Alexander Macomb,*
by Thomas Sully.
Courtesy of the
West Point Museum
Collection, United
States Military
Academy.

sponsor, Tompkins wrote, "The intelligence, moral & political character and standing in society of the candidates, are the points upon which I wish to be informed before I unite in a recommendation."[9] However, Tompkins did recommend qualified Federalists for commissions from time to time, although these were in a decided minority. Presumably, military experience would be a bonus. Madison and Eustis pored over these applications and the many letters of recommendation that accompanied them to select nominations to send to the Senate for confirmation. The Senate formed subcommittees composed of the two senators from each state to consider applications from their own citizens. This selection was an opportunity for patronage. The Senate started announcing confirmations in April 1812, and Smyth and Macomb sent letters of notification to the selectees.[10]

Among many others, four notable New Yorkers received commissions in the winter and spring of 1812. John Chrystie of New York City was of special note. Fourteen prominent New Yorkers, including Congressman Peter B. Porter and Senator Obadiah German, sent Madison a letter nominating Chrystie to be a lieutenant colonel. Chrystie had served three years as a captain in the Sixth U.S. Infantry until he resigned in 1811. The War Department in turn commissioned

Chrystie as an officer in the newly formed Thirteenth U.S. Infantry. The colonel encouraged his officers and men to sport mustaches, contrary to the style of the day. This gave the regiment its nickname, the Jolly Snorters.

Henry Leavenworth, of Delhi in Delaware County, was a protégé of Gen. Erastus Root, a prominent Republican politician. The War Department commissioned Leavenworth a captain in the Twenty-Fifth U.S. Infantry, a regiment largely recruited in Connecticut. Officers in the regular army served in whichever regiment had a vacancy. Thus, it often occurred that officers were from different states than the men they commanded. The Senate also confirmed the appointment of Mordecai Myers, a Jewish New York City merchant, as captain in the Thirteenth U.S. Infantry. Myers had extensive service in the militia and was an avid student of tactics. He was also a friend of Daniel Tompkins and a member of the Tammany Society. Finally, John Ellis Wool, a practicing lawyer from Troy, received a captain's commission in the Thirteenth U.S. Infantry. These officers resigned their commissions in the militia and went on to serve competently in the upcoming campaigns.[11]

Officer selection was critical to the recruiting effort. Once selectees accepted their commissions, the War Department assigned them to recruiting duty. Eustis established eight recruiting departments, each further subdivided into a number of recruiting districts. He assigned generals or colonels to command the departments and field-grade officers or captains to superintend the districts. District commanders contacted the new officers living in their districts and sent them out to begin recruiting. The recruiting officers distributed handbills, submitted announcements to newspapers, and hired musicians to gain attention in public areas. They accepted recruits who met standards and paid them a portion of their signing bonus to discharge their debts. As the district identified one hundred recruits, the commander swore them in and sent them to a rendezvous prescribed by the department commander. With few exceptions, the new officers were as ignorant of their duties as their recruits. Mordecai Myers, who had studied military matters, recalled that "great ignorance of military tactics prevailed in the new army, and the old one was not far beyond us in field duty. However, things soon took a better aspect, for we had some educated and scientific officers, and all soon improved who were capable of improvement."[12]

The War Department divided New York into two recruiting departments north and south of the 42nd degree of latitude, a line north of Kingston on the Hudson River. Col. Peter Schuyler commanded the southern recruiting department headquartered in New York City, while General Peter Gansevoort commanded the northern department from Albany. Smyth assigned New York a quota of twenty-eight companies, or 2,800 new soldiers, a goal that was not achieved in 1812. The army recruited three infantry regiments in the state—the Sixth, Thirteenth, and Twenty-Third—as well as companies for the Third U.S. Artillery, the Second U.S. Light Dragoons, and the Rifle Regiment.[13]

On March 27, 1812, the Senate confirmed the commissioning of New Jersey governor Joseph Bloomfield to the rank of brigadier general. He had served in the Revolution at Fort Ticonderoga and in the Mohawk Valley, and he had been seriously wounded at the Battle of Brandywine. He had also commanded state and federal troops during the Whiskey Rebellion. Bloomfield resigned the governorship in order to assume his commission. The War Department ordered the fifty-eight-year-old Bloomfield to command the defenses of New York City, taking over from Col. Henry Burbeck. Bloomfield commanded the regular army troops in and around New York City and would command militia units once they were brought into federal service. However, his immediate duties were to establish his headquarters and assemble a staff. When Peter Schuyler departed to command the Thirteenth U.S. Infantry, Bloomfield took over the recruiting department in the southern part of the state.[14]

The impact of the creation of new regiments for the regular army was that hundreds of men in New York were no longer eligible for service in the militia. Moreover, these new regulars had all volunteered for service as war approached, thus depleting the pool of potential volunteers from the militia.

The War Department was scrambling, even before Congress declared war, to build the offensive punch being readied in New York. Eventually, these forces came together to form the Northern Army under Maj. Gen. Henry Dearborn. Dearborn had served competently, even heroically, in the Revolution. He had also been President Jefferson's secretary of war. Madison called him to active duty as the army's senior officer in January 1812. The War Department rushed units northward. With few assets readily available, Smyth ordered Maj. Abram Eustis to bring three companies of the Regiment of Light Artillery to Albany from various stations in New England. He ordered Capt. George Armistead to move his company of artillerists from Fort McHenry in Baltimore to Bedloe's Island.[15] While the War Department directed the new regiments assigned to the Northern Army to Greenbush, near Albany, for training, it ordered some recruits directly to the front lines. In March, Smyth directed General Gansevoort to send some recruits at Albany to Fort Niagara to bring Capt. Nathan Leonard's artillery company up to strength.[16] Recruiting proceeded slowly, so slowly in fact that the War Department could not wait until a regiment was brought up to full strength before issuing marching orders. From Virginia northward, nearly as soon as regimental officers could assemble a full company, the War Department ordered the unit to start the long march from the recruiting rendezvous to Greenbush or the Niagara frontier.[17]

Greenbush (now East Greenbush) was across the Hudson and about ten miles southeast of Albany. The army camp, about a mile outside of the village, grew into the major rendezvous and training grounds for the army stationed in the north. Dearborn purchased the land in May 1812 from Stephen Van Rensselaer. Initially the men camped in tents, but eventually, the encampment consisted of eight two-story barracks, officers' quarters, and warehouses. The general's headquarters stood near the hospital. Hospital Surgeon James Mann served on the general staff and oversaw medical operations from Buffalo to Lake Champlain. The army had no doctrine to organize or manage hospital operations, so Mann and the regimental surgeons improvised. Mann kept detailed notes, not only on medical activities, but also on the diagnosis and treatment of the many illnesses that sent hundreds of soldiers to an early grave. Since units remained in Greenbush only as long as it took to prepare to march to the front, the population varied between 1,500 and 3,000 soldiers in 1812. The general hospital housed between one hundred and two hundred soldiers at any time.[18]

The federal government and New York underwent parallel mobilizations. In March, Secretary of War Eustis authorized Governor Tompkins to muster 1,600 militiamen for immediate deployment to the Niagara frontier, Oswego, and the vicinity of Sackett's Harbor. However, the secretary's letter did not specify the purpose of the requisition nor did it address issues such as command or equipping and feeding the militiamen. After Tompkins asked the relevant questions, Eustis agreed that the federal government would provide rations but not weapons or camp equipment because the new regular regiments were the priority. The two also agreed that this militia contingent would have a militia officer as commander until a regular army general took command. Madison biographer Irving Brant noted that the general condition of American militia was "not cheering. The single exception was Governor Tompkins's prompt dispatch of 1,600 New York militiamen to guard the Northern frontier."[19]

The federal government was unprepared to wage war with major shortcomings in manpower, money, warships, weaponry, skilled leadership, training, equipment, and transportation. Operations in New York in 1812 demonstrated all of these aspects. An additional deficiency was administration. No policies or procedures addressed the crucial interface between state and federal authorities and resources, especially as militia units transferred to federal service. Throughout 1812, the crush of sending thousands of state and regular troops to the frontiers revealed unnecessary friction in every aspect of mobilization. Tompkins identified numerous issues of nonexisting or ambiguous policy and procedure to an unresponsive War Department, itself floundering in the enormous enterprise of waging its first foreign war.

Unlike the disorganized and inefficient conduct of the war exhibited by the Madison administration, the British government had been waging war for twenty years.[20] The British ministry was clearly more efficiently organized and had administrative policies and practices that were well understood throughout the army, navy, and foreign services. Britain's global strategy was directed by three persons: Prime Minister Lord Liverpool, Secretary of State for War and the Colonies Earl Bathurst, and Foreign Secretary Viscount Castlereagh. This tight group ensured effective resourcing and integration of military, naval, and diplomatic efforts.[21]

Tompkins received Eustis's requisition on March 31, and two days later, he issued a general order setting this mobilization into effect. He ordered two of his eight division commanders to select and hold in readiness to march eight hundred detached militiamen to the vicinity of Sackett's Harbor and 250 to Oswego. Tompkins stated his preference that the militiamen selected would be volunteers. He requested the division commanders to nominate officers to command the two detachments, reserving the final selection to himself. He also ordered Maj. Gen. Amos Hall to send six hundred detached militiamen to the Niagara frontier under the command of Lt. Col. Philetus Swift, a veteran of the Revolution. Hall had been a fifer in his father's regiment during the Revolution. Hall and Swift served in the State Assembly and the Senate, Hall a Federalist and Swift a Republican. As senators, Hall and Swift had served respectively in the 1810 and 1811 Council of Appointment. Swift undid much of the Federalist mischief Hall had perpetrated in 1810.[22]

Brig. Gen. Jacob Brown wrote to his commander, Maj. Gen. George Widrig, on April 24, 1812, from Brownstown revealing a lack of progress in the mobilization. Widrig commanded the Fifth Division of common militia headquartered at Herkimer, while Brown commanded one of the brigades assigned to the Fifth. Widrig had ordered Brown to raise six hundred men from the Fifth Division. His orders stated that volunteers were preferred. Brown reported,

> But as volunteers are preferred and I am directed first to obtain if possible volunteers I am in obedience to the orders exerting myself to procure the volunteers but I cannot count with any degree of certainty upon raising my quota in this way. About 30 have volunteered since the reception of my orders which is now five days and I shall go on with the volunteer system a few days longer. Perhaps I may get a company in this way. You may rely upon my men being ready to march by the early part of May.[23]

The act of Congress authorizing the Voluntary Military Corps, passed on February 6, 1812, complicated the mobilization. This law authorized the president to accept into federal service up to 50,000 volunteers for one year. These volunteers would receive benefits beyond those of the detached militia and would serve under officers selected by the state. The benefits ranged from a clothing allowance to purchase uniforms of the unit's choice, pensions for wounded officers, and a death benefit of 160 acres of land for next of kin. Additionally, a soldier released from service after as little as one month could take his issued weapons with him. Tompkins received many offers from company commanders who volunteered their units for detached service. The governor followed up and offered these commanders the opportunity to extend the service of their men to twelve months under the act of February 6. Another important distinction, but one perhaps not entirely understood at the time, was that companies and battalions volunteering for the twelve-month option would be under direct federal control and therefore subject to serve outside the country while detached militia could not be ordered to do so.[24]

On April 10, Congress directed the states to call up a total of 100,000 militiamen. New York's share in this second mobilization was 13,500 detached militiamen. This quota dwarfed the levy for 1,600 men in March. New York had approximately 115,000 men eligible for military service, and this call-up affected 12 percent of the manpower pool. Hundreds had already joined the regular army and volunteer units, thus decreasing the pool further. Clearly, 100,000 militiamen was more than what was needed to enforce the embargo; Congress was evidently preparing for war. With little guidance from the War Department on the strategic plan, if any existed, Tompkins struggled with apportioning forces to best defend the state. The state effort to select soldiers and officers and to arm, equip, feed, and shelter them while moving them to the frontiers or to the defenses of New York City was immense. It required mobilizing and coordinating the human and material resources of the entire state. The governor and the various departments rose to the occasion.[25]

On April 21, Tompkins issued a general order for various commanders to select the men necessary to complete their assigned quota. Once selected, men awaited orders to muster into federal service. When these orders arrived, the men drew weapons and equipment from an arsenal or gun house and marched to the frontier. The governor gave senior commanders authority to appoint field-grade officers to command these units of detached militia.[26] Militia commanders throughout the northern and western counties assembled their men and asked for volunteers. If the number of volunteers failed to meet the quota, then the commander drafted the shortfall, typically by an arbitrary drawing. A drafted man could hire a substitute, a policy favoring the well-to-do. The substitute collected money from the man he was replacing as well as his military pay. State law required that every militiaman in a company must serve once, or hire a substitute, before he was required to serve a second time. Volunteers or substitutes could serve as many call-ups as they wanted.

Tompkins expected that partisan politics would interfere with a smooth mobilization. He wrote of his fears to Eustis that "these criminal machinations may possibly have the effect of introducing into the ranks of the detached Militia an extensive and dangerous spirit of insubordination to the command of their superiors." There is little evidence that such was the case during mobilization. However, party politics would come into play as summer turned to autumn.[27]

Once the preselected militiamen received notification to enter federal service, they had to put their personal affairs into order, gather up weapons, blankets, and equipment they might possess, and move to the designated rendezvous. For many, this meant leaving to their families the hardship of planting and harvesting. At the rendezvous, the commander of the detached company enrolled his men in the company book. This act started their pay and their tour of duty of about ninety days. The federal paymasters had insufficient funds to pay the men on time, and some men would not be paid until they

New York State Militia Officer, by H. C. McBarron. Courtesy Parks Canada.

were mustered out of service or well after. Upon mustering, the company or regimental commander read the articles of war to the men. This was official notice of what constituted a crime and the accompanying penalty. Military crimes included drunk on duty, sleeping on guard, absent without authorization, desertion, striking an officer, mutiny, and other activities that would negatively affect the capability of the unit.

The detached militia companies and regiments were composed largely of officers and men who did not know one another, having been culled from several units of common militia. Thus, whatever level of cohesion that existed in the common militia was lost. Unit cohesion is the glue that holds soldiers together in dangerous situations. It derives from shared experience and earned trust. The men would develop cohesion to some degree on the long march to the front and during training. However, cohesion in a militia unit would never approach that of a regular British formation, in which the soldiers had been together with the same officers, sergeants, and corporals for several years.

It happened fairly often in 1812 that many or all of the men of a volunteer company agreed to muster as a company. This was what these men had prepared for. These soldiers wore their distinctive uniforms and carried their own weapons and equipment. It was very probable that a volunteer company demonstrated greater cohesion than that found in a detached company.

The federal government was entirely unable to provide for the thousands of detached militia brought into service. It could not arm and equip militia units or pay the men at the conclusion of their tour of duty. Eventually the army maintained a staff presence in Albany, including a number of officers performing quartermaster and pay functions. While the federal government had an arsenal in New York City, it did not maintain an arsenal in Albany, closer to the expected fighting fronts. The War Department did not address the absence of a federal arsenal in the major theater of war until the summer of 1813, when the army built an arsenal near Albany. This facility initially made musket cartridges, an important if limited function.[28]

Tompkins, the state government, and the legislature had done a creditable job in acquiring muskets and positioning them along routes leading to the frontiers. Nearly 11,000 muskets and rifles were positioned at the twelve arsenals north and west of Albany. However, fewer than two hundred tents and seven hundred camp kettles were available at these sites. Since squads of six to eight soldiers shared a tent and a camp kettle, there were not enough of these critical items to support mobilization. Also lacking were axes, saws, and shovels, all necessary to build camps and field fortifications.

On April 18, 1812, Tompkins brought Peter B. Porter, the state's quartermaster general, onto active duty. He had an immense task to ensure the feeding,

arming, and supplying of the militia as it mobilized and marched to the frontiers. At the time, no regular army quartermasters or paymasters were present
in the state north of West Point; the militia had responsibility to maintain all
accounts and seek repayment from the federal government later. The federal
contractor charged with providing rations was Elbert Anderson, Jr. However,
if Anderson was unable to provide rations, Porter was authorized to purchase
and transport food. Tompkins appointed Major Darby Noon to assist Porter.[29]
In the absence of a senior quartermaster officer of the regular army, Porter
focused his efforts on the huge task of providing barracks and general logistical
support for both militia and regular forces deploying to the state's frontiers
between Buffalo and St. Regis, a Mohawk community near the St. Regis River
in northern New York, about one hundred miles northeast of Kingston.

Governor Tompkins complained that "the duty of dispensing the public
funds for defraying the expenses of the Militia . . . was imposed upon me by
the General Government without my suggestion or solicitation." Throughout
the war, the federal government provided funds directly to Tompkins, who,
in turn, transferred these to state officials to spend. In May, Secretary of War
William Eustis forwarded $50,000 to meet immediate demands.[30] During the
course of the war, Tompkins was personally involved in settling pay disputes
arising from the absence of clear procedures governing the interaction between
army and militia paymasters. In these events, militia officers went directly
to Tompkins for resolution and Tompkins corresponded with Robert Brent,
paymaster general of the army. In one case, the bank in Utica sued Brig. Gen.
Richard Dodge for a draft that army paymasters refused to clear. The draft
was entirely proper, yet no army paymaster would take responsibility. Tompkins complained to Brent that he was involved in duties that should have been
handled smoothly by a brigade quartermaster, a major's position.[31]

Tompkins understood that there remained serious shortfalls in equipping
the militia. In February, he wrote to Assemblyman Abraham Van Vechten, enu-
merating the shortages so that the assemblyman could introduce bills to address
the deficiencies. The state experienced difficulties constructing gun carriages for
artillery gun tubes without carriages or to replace numerous unserviceable carriages. The artificers used unseasoned timber, resulting in cracks that effectively
destroyed the usefulness of the carriage. Tompkins requested funds to procure
well-seasoned timber to be maintained in the armories. He requested that the
Assembly authorize funds to purchase 1,000 muskets annually for five years.
Tompkins recognized the serious shortage of tents, knapsacks, and camp equipment, and he asked Van Vechten to seek enough to equip 4,000 men. Tompkins
also requested that the Assembly consider mobilizing 4,000 militiamen for
one month to be spent in cantonments for the purpose of intense training. He

pointed out the requirement for 5,000 artillery gunners to provide crews for all guns then gathered in the fortifications around New York City. Understanding that militiamen assigned to artillery companies were poorly trained at best, he suggested that the Assembly mobilize these men for training as well. The governor had put his finger on the urgent requirements to complete preparations for war. In March, the legislative committees recommended bills that addressed most of the governor's concerns. Unfortunately for the soon-to-be mobilized citizens and the state in general, no time remained to achieve these goals.[32]

The federal requisition from March did not include troops for the Lake Champlain region. Tompkins placed detached militia from the second mobilization under the command of Maj. Gen. Benjamin Mooers. The governor noted that the citizens around Lake Champlain were "imminently exposed both to invasion by the enemy and to the depredations of savages."[33] Eventually, Eustis validated this order and took these troops into federal service.

In June, Tompkins organized the 13,500 militiamen from both mobilizations into twenty regiments and a separate corps of light infantry and riflemen. He grouped the regiments into eight brigades and organized the brigades into two divisions. He allocated five brigades to the First Division. These troops would defend the shores of Lake Ontario and part of the St. Lawrence River. Troops from the First Division would also conduct the anticipated invasion across the Niagara River. Tompkins assigned three brigades and a regiment of artillery to the Second Division to defend the eastern portion of the state from New York City to the Lake Champlain region.[34]

The governor's choice for command of the Second Division was easy. Maj. Gen. Mooers already commanded the Third Division of the common militia. Tompkins gave him command of the Second Division of detached militia as well. Because he was now dual-hatted, Mooers could more efficiently coordinate mobilization issues as citizen-soldiers left their local units and joined units of detached militia. Mooers lived in the vicinity of Plattsburgh for twenty-eight years and knew his subordinate officers well.[35]

The choice of a commander for the First Division was momentous. Tompkins assumed that a regular army general would lead the major offensive aimed at Montreal from the Lake Champlain region. Although the War Department had not been forthcoming in discussing strategy, Tompkins rightly assumed that a supporting advance across the Niagara River was in the offing. Here, militiamen would outnumber regulars, and it was very likely that a militia general would command both regular and militia units.

Tompkins considered two choices for this most important command. The Council of Appointment elevated DeWitt Clinton to the rank of major general just before the declaration of war. Clinton desired a field command. However,

Maj. Gen. Stephen Van Rensselaer was senior in rank. Neither had any significant military experience. Whoever commanded a successful invasion of Canada would reap considerable fame that could be parlayed into political capital. Clinton and Tompkins both had aspirations to the presidency. Madison gained the nomination of the Republican Party in his bid for reelection in 1812. Despite this nomination, the New York Republican caucus nominated Clinton in May to run for the presidency against Madison. Clinton, though a Republican, gained strong Federalist support for his anti-war stance. Tompkins remained a staunch supporter of James Madison; he would defer his presidential aspirations for a later time. Clinton's candidacy broke his relationship with Tompkins. One of the governor's biographers wrote, "The breach was so far widened that it could never again be healed."[36]

Tompkins expected to gain his party's nomination for reelection to the governorship in early 1813. He anticipated that he would run against Van Rensselaer, the Federalist candidate. Van Rensselaer was immensely wealthy and had hundreds of renters on his vast land holdings around Albany. Rather than give the potentially rewarding campaign to an anti-war Republican, Tompkins selected Van Rensselaer to command the First Division and presumably to lead the invasion across the Niagara River. Tompkins's choice for this important position appeared non-partisan; it gave the Federalists an opportunity to embrace the reality of a declared war. Perhaps Tompkins hoped that Van Rensselaer would refuse the command, thus appearing unpatriotic to most voters. Van Rensselaer agreed to command, although he stipulated that his cousin, Solomon Van Rensselaer, would serve as his aide.[37]

Solomon Van Rensselaer had been seriously wounded in the Fallen Timbers campaign in 1794. He served eight years in the regular army, rising to the rank of major. He had also served, on and off, as the state adjutant general between January 1801 and 1811. Solomon Van Rensselaer was a virulent Federalist. The governor had vigorously opposed a regular commission for Solomon in February, citing his "political intolerance."[38] In 1807, on State Street in Albany, Solomon attacked a Republican who had insulted Stephen Van Rensselaer. Others joined the fray, in which Solomon received serious wounds and became the darling of the Albany Federalists. Tompkins honored Stephen Van Rensselaer's request and reluctantly appointed Solomon to duty on the general's staff as a lieutenant colonel. Even though Stephen Van Rensselaer's potential battlefield success would make him a very popular candidate for the governorship, Tompkins supported him and the campaign on the Niagara unreservedly.[39]

Unlike Mooers, Stephen Van Rensselaer was not particularly well acquainted with the officers chosen to command the detached militia of his division, nor was he associated with the commanders of infantry units making up the common militia along the extensive border for which he was held responsible—475 miles from the Pennsylvania border to St. Regis. Van Rensselaer had been an officer of the common militia for many years. By 1812, he commanded the state's only cavalry division.

Nonetheless, Van Rensselaer had some excellent subordinates. Brig. Gen. Richard Dodge commanded the Fourth Brigade of Detached Militia, made up of four regiments. Dodge lived in Johnstown in Montgomery County. Brig. Gen. Jacob Brown commanded the Fifth Brigade of Detached Militia, consisting of two regiments. He hailed from Brownville in Jefferson County. Brown's responsibilities ran from Sackett's Harbor to St. Regis. Tompkins mobilized Brown's regiments first. As their ninety-day tour of duty expired, the governor mobilized Dodge's brigade.[40] Van Rensselaer deployed Brig. Gen. Daniel Miller's Sixth Brigade of Detached Militia and Brig. Gen. William Wadsworth's Seventh Brigade of Detached Militia to the Niagara frontier for the impending invasion. Both Miller and Wadsworth also commanded brigades of the common militia. Finally, Van Rensselaer also commanded the Eighth Brigade of Detached Militia. This brigade consisted of cavalry, light infantry, and riflemen raised from the state at large.

While the governor was willing to support Madison's strategy of invasion, his first priority was the defense of the state. The shores of Lake Ontario marked nearly two hundred miles of the state's frontier. Both sides became increasingly aware of the decisive nature of the lake's waters to the outcome of a conflict. Control of the lake offered a grand highway of invasion, raids, and supply for either opponent. Two important harbors lay on the Canadian side, Kingston and York (modern Toronto).

About thirty-seven miles across the lake from Sackett's Harbor lay the port of Kingston, Upper Canada. About 1,000 people lived in and around the settlement at Kingston. Harbor facilities were well-developed. The military presence was a small but growing army garrison, and the Provincial Marine, a water transportation service for the British army. No Royal Navy warships were present on Lake Ontario in 1812. York, with about six hundred residents, was the capital of Upper Canada. Its harbor was shallower and harder to enter than that of Kingston. A small garrison guarded a rudimentary shipbuilding facility at York. Kingston and York were the two major stops along Britain's extensive supply line connecting Quebec to the Upper Great Lakes.

On the American shore were a few settlements and anchorages. Vessels could enjoy some protection at Four Mile Creek, east of Fort Niagara. Farther east lay the small villages of Charlotte, at the mouth of the Genesee River, and Sodus Point on Sodus Bay. Fort Niagara, Oswego, and Sackett's Harbor were the most important military locations on the American side.

The supply line between New York City and Oswego was difficult, requiring a number of transshipments between water vessels and wagons. Oswego was the final transshipment point along the supply line between New York City and Sackett's Harbor and Fort Niagara. Crews of laborers moved cargo from river craft to lake vessels. When ice appeared on rivers and lakes, shipments halted. Crews left cargoes at various locations along the route until the interior waterways opened in the spring.

Sackett's Harbor grew into the largest American shipbuilding enterprise of the war. The small harbor was well protected from the worst of lake storms. However, two vulnerabilities challenged its effectiveness. First, it could be easily blockaded. It would be exceptionally risky to sail a squadron out of port in the face of even a small enemy presence. Second, British vessels could readily interdict the vital supply line between Sackett's Harbor and Oswego.

The U.S. Navy had a slender presence on Lake Ontario in 1812; the Madison administration did not comprehend the importance of controlling the lake until well after the commencement of hostilities. Lt. Melancthon Woolsey was the only officer posted there. Woolsey was born in Plattsburgh, son of an officer of the Revolution. Sackett's Harbor was home port to the U.S. Brig *Oneida*, Woolsey's only warship. The *Oneida* carried eighteen carronades, making it the largest warship on the Great Lakes. Its crew was inexperienced. The Provincial Marine's five vessels outgunned the fledgling American squadron in June 1812. Both sides conducted ambitious shipbuilding programs and numerous forays in order to gain control of Lake Ontario, a goal that remained elusive. However, that naval campaign was in the future.

Lt. Col. George Fleming of Aurelius commanded the detachment sent to Oswego in the first mobilization. Fleming served as an artillery officer during the Revolution. Maj. John Lovett, secretary to Gen. Van Rensselaer, declared, "The whole service is to him, as familiar as housekeeping."[41] In May, Tompkins appointed Lt. Col. Christopher P. Bellinger of Herkimer to command the detachment assigned to the Black River region. Tompkins explicitly directed, "The troops of whom you have the command are neither intended to enforce the Embargo Act nor to pursue any offensive operations, but are merely an advanced corps to defend & protect the Frontiers from invasion." Bellinger's men drew weapons from the state arsenal at Watertown. This facility was built in 1809 as part of the preparedness program. State Deputy Quartermaster General Darby Noon made arrangements to build barracks at Sackett's Harbor, Gravelly Point, and Ogdensburg to shelter Bellinger's troops.[42]

While the shores of Lake Ontario were open to raids, the Niagara frontier was more vulnerable. The Niagara River formed the western edge of Niagara County. Erie County was not formed until 1821. Maj. Gen. Amos Hall commanded the

Seventh Division of common militia. This division encompassed militia units from Cayuga County westward. Hall assisted in the mobilization of the detached militia moving to the Niagara frontier. Lt. Col. Philetus Swift of Phelps, Ontario County, commanded a detachment from the first mobilization. On April 29, Tompkins ordered Swift and his men to march to the Niagara frontier. Tompkins told Swift to take command of all troops, militia and regulars, along the Niagara River since he outranked Captain Leonard of the regular artillery at Fort Niagara. Swift reported to Tompkins that the fort's walls were in "a miserable and decayed situation which can present but a feeble defense." Swift also brought to the governor's attention the fact that if Fort Niagara should fall, the damage to the supply line would be considerable.[43]

Tompkins wrestled with the integration of militia and regular forces for effective defense. He needed to secure an agreement with the War Department in the event that regular commanders would come under militia officers as the mobilization grew in scope. Disturbing signs of friction between regular and militia officers were becoming apparent even before Madison sent his war message to Congress. On April 30, Tompkins wrote to Eustis that Captain Leonard "will not feel himself justified in surrendering the command to an officer of superior rank of the Militia ordered into service at that Post without some notice or instructions to that effect from the War Department."[44] Eustis responded. Alexander Smyth wrote to General Gansevoort in Albany, "You will please instruct the officer commanding at Niagara to admit into the fort such detachments of militia as may be ordered there on duty."[45] The War Department also directed Leonard to place himself under the command of Lieutenant Colonel Swift, who commanded along the Niagara until Maj. Gen. Van Rensselaer arrived. Leonard's reasons for keeping the militiamen outside the walls are unknown; however, it is very likely that he wanted to maintain a physical and administrative boundary between the militia and the regular forces.

Tompkins told his three commanders—Fleming, Bellinger, and Swift—to open a direct correspondence among themselves to keep one another informed and to coordinate activities. Thus, information would travel faster unhindered by any requirement to pass through the state commander in chief's hands first.

Tompkins gave particular attention to the Niagara frontier. No state artillery pieces were on the Niagara River, so the governor ordered Porter to issue two guns and 15,000 musket cartridges from the arsenal at Canandaigua. Tompkins also directed Porter to build a barracks at Black Rock for three hundred men. The governor apparently anticipated the upcoming war to extend into a second year as he directed Porter, "Let the roofs be made of good and durable materials & the siding of the best stuff that can be got so that they may, hereafter, be converted into Winter barracks."[46]

Tompkins received complaints about the quality of the rations provided by the federal contractor, Elbert Anderson Jr. He fired off a complaint to Anderson questioning whether the subcontractors issued the inadequate rations "for political purposes." Tompkins was sensitive that Federalist-leaning subcontractors were purposely attempting to create dissatisfaction among the detachments at Oswego and Sackett's Harbor. He warned Anderson that he would launch an inquiry and would inform the War Department of noncompliance.[47]

Regarding Indians, most Iroquois had supported the British during the Revolution. Many of those removed themselves to reservations near Montreal and the Grand River. There remained approximately 2,500 New York Iroquois on reservations within seventy miles of the Niagara River. Of these, about eight hundred resided on Buffalo Creek and 250 in the Tuscarora village near Lewiston.[48] Madison sought to keep the tribes living on U.S. territory neutral. As early as 1808, while Indian agent Erastus Granger distributed the Iroquois annuity, he laid out the relationship Washington expected of the natives. In the event of war, the Iroquois would be wise to remain neutral. In a stark warning, Granger stated, "All of our enemies will feel the weight of our strong arm. Be not deceived. If we go to war with Great Britain, and you join them, [your] destruction will follow."[49] However, even if the chiefs declared tribal neutrality, nothing could keep individual warriors from crossing into Canada to serve as allies of the British.

As Tompkins arranged for the defense of the border with Canada, he well understood that New York City was not prepared to defend itself against a determined raid by the Royal Navy.

Of the three brigades of the First Division of detached militia, Tompkins assigned one, the First Brigade under Brig. Gen. Gerard Steddiford, to the defense of New York City. However, the 450 artillerists assigned to this brigade were tardy in responding to the call-up. These gunners were to man the fortifications at the Narrows, the city's first line of defense. Tompkins fired a strong reprimand to the commander charged with mobilizing these key defenders: "I shall expect no further delay in organizing that detachment. Indeed I am ashamed of the delay which has already happened, & have written to the Secretary [of War] that I had no doubt before Tuesday last, the New York Detachment of Artillery had been reported to the Commanding officer in the harbor."[50] Federalist voters outnumbered Republicans in New York City as recently as the statewide election in April, and partisanship was vigorous. General inertia, administrative incompetence, and partisan foot-dragging combined to thwart preparedness.

Once called up, the brigade of detached militia was on duty full-time. The defenses of New York City were supported as well by the common militia, which consisted of those men not already selected for duty in the First Brigade of detached militia. The militiamen of the First and Second Brigades of Militia (infantry) and the First Artillery Brigade would be called up in an emergency. Approximately 3,000 militiamen from New York City and surrounding counties were members of uniformed companies, and several of these units volunteered in their entirety for detached service.[51] Tompkins streamlined the chain of command between himself and the common militia. For example, he consolidated all of the individual rifle companies in the city and Brooklyn with the Battalion of Republican Greens under the command of Maj. Francis McClure. The new organization was formally named the First Rifle Regiment, but it continued to be known as the Irish Greens.[52]

In June, Tompkins took advantage of Peter B. Porter's connections in Washington to suggest to the president that he appoint John Armstrong to an independent command of all army forces in New York City and its harbor defenses. The governor and other Republican leaders were disenchanted with Joseph Bloomfield. Armstrong outranked Dearborn during the Revolution, thus an independent command would sit better with Armstrong. Madison took this suggestion and eventually replaced Bloomfield with Armstrong.[53]

New York City was assisted by one of its most famous citizens. Robert Fulton returned to America in 1806 after a twenty-year absence in Europe. While in Europe, he invented a working submarine and numerous naval weapons. In July 1807, the month following the *Chesapeake* Affair, Fulton met with then–Secretary of War Henry Dearborn, who was inspecting the defenses of the city's water approaches. Fulton proposed building underwater mines, then called torpedoes. Dearborn forwarded Fulton's proposals to Jefferson, but the crisis was abating when the president reviewed the offer.

In the years preceding the war, Fulton partnered with Robert Livingston to build a commercially successful steamboat on the Hudson. The official name was the *North River Steam Boat* but it is remembered as the *Clermont*, named after Livingston's estate. Fulton referred to his craft as the *Steam Boat*. Fulton developed and ran a steam ferry between Manhattan and Brooklyn. The route presaged the trace of the Brooklyn Bridge. In 1809, Fulton ran an experiment in which a boat carrying a torpedo attacked an anchored ship. Commodore John Rodgers, who opposed Fulton's innovations, conducted the experiment. Rodgers's sailors surrounded the target ship with nets and booms. Nonetheless, the attacking craft managed to cut a fourteen-inch cable beneath the surface. The committee evaluating the experiment judged that the country could not depend on Fulton's weapons. Of course, an attacking squadron would not always have time nor inclination to emplace defensive booms and netting.[54]

Meanwhile in Washington, Henry Clay led his fellow War Hawks in preparing for war. In April, Congress established a ninety-day embargo. While the War Hawks insisted that this step was preparatory to war, many congress-men voted for the bill as yet another warning to Britain of the seriousness of American demands. Although the congressional debate was conducted in secret, some members of Congress leaked word of the impending embargo. Frantic merchants in every port contracted shippers to move cargoes before official word arrived at the port. In New York City, as many as one hundred ships departed for foreign shores carrying grain. Merchants along the northern border were furious at the new embargo, as their livelihood depended upon the sale of salt, potash, and food to Canadians.[55]

While Tompkins directed the state's resources preparing for imminent war, Federalists and anti-war Republicans pushed back. The business of New York City was commerce. Federalists organized the citizenry in petitioning Congress to end the embargo and halt the apparent rush to war. Federalists and their supporters, especially those involved in foreign trade, were especially active in the growing anti-war movement. The Washington Benevolent Society, the electioneering arm of the party, went so far as to promote draft evasion as a civic duty. In April's state elections, Federalists gained control of the Assem-bly with a majority of eight. They maintained control for two years, hindering Tompkins's efforts to support the war. Since the Assembly selected the senators sitting on the Council of Appointment, Tompkins had to deal with a Federalist-dominated council. The 1812 council replaced many Republican state officials with Federalists.[56]

Tompkins maintained his strong support for the war effort. In this, he stood in stark contrast to his peers in New England. During the congressional vote on the ninety-day embargo, a key gubernatorial election took place in Massa-chusetts. Federalist Caleb Strong narrowly defeated the Republican governor. The Federalists captured both houses of the General Court as well. Strong took his election as a mandate to block the militia from joining Congress's April call for 100,000 men. Likewise, the Federalist governors of Connecticut and Rhode Island refused to place their militia under federal control. The Republican gov-ernors of Vermont and New Hampshire lost their positions to Federalists the following spring, making Federalist control of New England complete. Thus, large numbers of relatively well-equipped militiamen were unavailable to the Madison administration.[57]

Madison sent his war message to Congress on June 1. Senator Obadiah Ger-man, a New York Republican, articulated the anti-war position of many of his party during the Senate debate. German's voting record fully supported defen-sive measures for the nation. He readily acknowledged that both Britain and France had committed acts of war. However, to his mind, the country was woe-fully unprepared to conduct a war outside the nation's borders. No one should consider the small U.S. Navy "competent to hold in check any detachment that Great Britain is able to send upon our coast from her thousand ships." Federal finances were in a shambles. "It is well known to every member of the Senate that our treasury is empty." German noted that the states whose congressional delegations had been most vocal in calling for war were the states least forthcoming in subscribing to the $11 million loan to finance the enterprise. He criticized the Madison administration for its failure to raise the 25,000 soldiers authorized by the previous Congress. He lashed out at Secretary of War William Eustis as being incompetent to put the army on a war footing. German noted that if the army could not seize Montreal in six weeks, the "conflict must be lengthy, and, consequently, more bloody, if not doubtful." German continued with his prescient analysis. A lengthy war would all but destroy foreign commerce. A failure to seize Canada would likely push the war onto American territory, "and your militia will be called out from their usual business and avocations of life into the field, as soldiers for the protection of the frontier settlements, and you will have all the expense of a regular campaign without any of its benefits." However, German could not dissuade his colleagues.[58]

In the vote to declare war, Republican Senator John Smith voted in favor, while German voted against. Eleven Republicans and five Federalists represented New York in the House. Six Republican congressmen joined the five Federalists in voting against the declaration. Three Republicans voted for war, while two abstained. One of those abstaining was War Hawk Peter B. Porter, who had departed Washington to take his commission in the militia. William Paulding Jr. also abstained from the vote; he was then serving in Albany as the state's adjutant general. One seat was vacant: Robert L. Livingston had resigned to accept a commission in the army.[59]

As expected, the declaration of war incited a large and active anti-war movement. Federalists organized rallies, sent petitions, and communicated with Federalists in other states. Groups formed secret "benevolent societies," membership in which included an oath not to bear arms except in case of invasion. John Jay and other Federalist leaders met with DeWitt Clinton, then mayor of New York City, to explore a potential association of Federalists and anti-war Republicans. Clinton understood full well that he was treading on thin political ice if fellow Republicans saw him cozying up to their political enemies.[60]

Clinton attempted to walk a narrow line between the pro- and anti-war factions. In a speech, he warned the citizenry that the United States was now at war and that previous business or political acts favoring the British might now be considered treasonous. "As it is morally impossible for every man, in a moment, to cease his old habit without the agency of some cause that immediately touches him, it is not to be wondered that many still express great partiality and regard for the enemy, and commit treason in their hearts; so long have they been accustomed to look up to Great Britain as the source of their profit." Clinton then appealed to the pro-war faction to be patient: "In the interim, while we carefully watch against crimes let us bear with the weaknesses of our brethren, and unite them in a pure love of country, with gentleness." Clinton's apparent equivocation completed the break with Tompkins. Nevertheless, the two leading Republicans in the state continued to work civilly and effectively in fortifying the city.[61]

The declaration of war was a political boon to state Federalists. In a special election, Federalist Rufus King took the seat occupied by Republican Senator John Smith. Republican Obadiah German's six-year term would not come to an end until 1815. Because of a dramatic increase in the state's population, the number of New York congressmen increased from seventeen to twenty-seven. In the December election, the Federalists took twenty seats, the Republicans seven.[62]

News of the declaration of war reached New York City on June 20. When word arrived in Albany, Governor Tompkins hastened preparations. Within four hours of receiving the news, he sent urgent dispatches to his commanders on the frontiers. The detached militia was already in place or on the march. As commanders passed through Albany, Tompkins met to discuss their orders and to provide them with state funds. When state money ran out, Tompkins used his personal funds. He directed his commissary of military stores, John McLean, to transport weapons, ammunition, and small artillery pieces from New York City to Albany, making use of one of the three steamboats operating on the Hudson if possible. Tompkins directed McClean to acquire enough tents, camp kettles, and knapsacks for 2,000 men. He wanted to infuse McLean with a sense of urgency, warning him, "You will not slumber upon the execution of this order." Two days later, to emphasize his point, he again warned McLean. "You will please to understand once for all, that prompt execution of orders in such an emergency as now exists is indispensable."[63]

Tompkins hired three additional commissary officers to manage the transportation of weapons and equipment and forwarded money to expedite purchases. He decided to remain in Albany to oversee the movement of equipment to the frontiers. On June 26, the first wagonloads of supplies departed Albany heading for the frontiers. Unfortunately, there were no tents or camp kettles to send. Tompkins wrote to both Eustis and Dearborn of these unnecessary difficulties. He reminded Eustis in particular that he had warned the War Department that the state arsenals had insufficient camp equipment and tents to support the large body of detached militia stationed on the frontier. Dearborn was then in Boston, and the federal quartermasters in Albany would not issue anything from the federal stocks without his orders. To make matters worse, about six hundred regular army recruits had gathered at Canandaigua, Rome, and Plattsburgh; however, the federal weapons were in Albany. Tompkins reminded Eustis that he had refused the governor's offer to maintain federal weapons at state arsenals at those locations. He also reminded Dearborn that the unarmed federal recruits at Plattsburgh were only fifty miles away from Britain's allied native warriors on the St. Lawrence River.[64] Tompkins had a much clearer concept of preparing for war and a greater sense of urgency than federal authorities.

In addition to his concern for the frontiers, Tompkins did not neglect the defense of New York City and particularly the fortifications at the Narrows. He wrote to Mayor DeWitt Clinton vesting the governor's authority with the Commissioners of Fortification, of which Clinton was the chief.[65] He also notified Brig. Gen. Bloomfield, then still in command, that Bloomfield would have at his disposal the entire detached and common militia from Westchester County, New York City, and Long Island. The governor ended his letter with a declaration that he devoted his authority "to a vigilant and faithful support of the constituted authorities of our beloved Country, in the prosecution of the just & necessary War into which they have entered."[66]

As soon as he learned of the declaration of war, Tompkins ordered Benjamin Mooers into active service as a major general commanding the detached division in the eastern part of the state. He also appointed Brig. Gen. Micajah Pettit to command the detached brigade in the northernmost part of the state as part of Mooers's division. Tompkins ordered Pettit to protect "our frontier brethren, and their wives and children from massacre by savages, and from the depredations of the enemies of the United States." Tompkins ordered weapons sent to Plattsburgh to augment those at the state arsenal at Elizabethtown in Essex County.[67]

Tompkins ordered Brig. Gen. Jacob Brown to assume active command of his brigade of detached militia and gave him responsibility for the Black River region and the border along the St. Lawrence River to the settlement at St. Regis. Brown responded, "Your Excellency will bear in mind, that this is a very new country; that the population is light, and generally poor . . . and that, if any more men are called from their homes, the crops which now promise a very abundant harvest must perish on the ground." Nevertheless, Brown went on to say that he would not be deterred "for a moment, from calling out every man in the county, if its defence requires it."[68]

On June 23, Tompkins ordered Brig. Gen. William Wadsworth of Geneseo to active duty in command of the detached militia on the Niagara frontier. Wadsworth wrote to Tompkins to confess himself "ignorant of even the minor details of the duty you have assigned me." He further requested that Tompkins send someone who might assist in making up his shortfalls. Tompkins ordered Quartermaster General Peter B. Porter to forward camp kettles and other camp equipment to the Niagara frontier immediately. In his order to Porter, he noted that additional troops would be marching to the Niagara frontier and that "great exertions must be made to have them accommodated in every respect." Tompkins also told his generals "the troops are of course to act offensively whenever an opportunity presents."[69]

As reports from the frontier arrived at Albany, the governor became alarmed at the poor condition of naval forces. In July, he sent a strongly worded letter to John Bullis, the Department of the Navy representative to New York, complaining of the emerging British naval superiority on Lakes Erie, Ontario, and Champlain. He pleaded that Bullis immediately send Lt. Melancthon Woolsey sailors, marines, and ordnance to retain command of these waters. Failure to secure navigation and to take the offensive quickly would lead to defeat and, as a result, the Madison administration would "be condemned as inefficient or insincere with respect to the conquest of Canada."[70] Tompkins' words were prescient.

New York and Canada shared considerable commerce, and families and friends straddled the border. As might be expected, espionage was rampant from the very early days of the conflict, and it continued throughout. The border between New York and Lower and Upper Canada was porous and insufficiently guarded. American and British travelers crossing the border offered information to military commanders; these authorities soon recruited and managed their own agents. For example, Maj. Gen. Isaac Brock, who was then acting as lieutenant governor of Upper Canada, sent a spy through New York. Former army officer Augustus de Diemer crossed over to Black Rock late in June. Passing himself off as a French citizen, de Diemer collected a wealth of information from Americans, including officers and government officials. He traveled through the Niagara frontier, Utica, Ogdensburg, Albany, Whitehall, and Burlington. He was stopped twice and jailed once, escaping quickly. During the war, intelligence flowed in both directions and informed military and naval decisions.[71]

In the last months leading to the declaration of war, the national government displayed institutional inertia and administrative incompetence. The recruitment of regular army regiments and the selection of officers proceeded at a snail's pace. The federal government could hardly train, uniform, and equip the thousands who were mustered into service, and very few of these new soldiers were standing on the frontiers ready to invade Canada—Madison's strategic imperative. Ineffectual federal administration clearly hampered New York's efforts. In every instance, the state government was ahead of Washington in anticipating and solving problems. The federal government could not arm, equip, feed, or pay the deep reserves of militia needed to back up major invasions.

Fortunately, the state government, under Daniel Tompkins's leadership, had taken major steps in preparing New York for war. Armed and reasonably well-led detached militia guarded key posts. Thousands more of the state's citizen-soldiers were on the march. Most had weapons. Nevertheless, chronic shortages in tents and camp equipment discouraged these soldiers. The defenses of New York City were still largely on the planning boards. New York's leaders, particularly Stephen Van Rensselaer, Benjamin Mooers, and Peter B. Porter, were determined to succeed. Yet, the citizenry, whether in camp or in their homes, was deeply divided on the wisdom of war with one of the world's greatest powers. Britain was fully engaged in war with France and could not immediately send reinforcements to Canada. There remained a narrow window of opportunity in which America might succeed in its military and national goals.

CHAPTER 3

THE BATTLE OF
QUEENSTON HEIGHTS

Much of the death, injury, and destruction of the War of 1812 fell to the New Yorkers and Canadians living along the Niagara River as well as to thousands of soldiers and Indians sent there. In October 1812, Madison's strategy to quickly capture Canada fell apart at the Battle of Queenston Heights. This major clash, and the farcical events that followed, demonstrated the utter unpreparedness of both the regular army and the detached militia to conduct offensive warfare. Combatants showed heroism and timidity, competence and inefficiency. The campaign also revealed the fatal tensions between regulars and militia as well as fierce partisanship that contributed in no small way to American failure.

In 1797, a group of Dutch investors, organized as the Holland Land Company, bought 3,250,000 acres of land west of the Genesee River from the Seneca, represented by Cornplanter, Farmer's Brother, and Red Jacket at the treaty of Big Tree. The Seneca retained designated tribal reserves. Red Jacket was an orator and diplomat and therefore the public face of the Seneca. The British gave him a uniform coat for services as a runner during the colonial wars, and the white community gave him his English name. By 1812, roughly 25,000 settlers were clearing land and planting crops. The land agent Joseph Ellicott promoted the organization of the militia and had an outsized influence in selection of militia officers.[1]

The settlements of Buffalo, Black Rock, Manchester (now Niagara Falls), and Lewiston along the Niagara River were the largest of Niagara County. This county had a population of about 6,032 in 1810. Batavia, where Ellicott located his primary office, was in adjoining Genesee County. Approximately 12,600 people made Genesee County their home. Buffalo was a village of five hundred residents in 1812. Rough roads connected Buffalo and Lewiston to Batavia.

The main Seneca settlement of about eight hundred people was located immediately south of Buffalo along Buffalo Creek. A small Tuscarora community established its settlement on the escarpment southeast of Lewiston. A third Iroquois settlement lay along Cattaraugus Creek, which flowed into Lake Erie. Other land reserved for the Iroquois lay inland from the Niagara River.[2]

In April, Governor Tompkins ordered six hundred detached militia commanded by Lt. Col. Philetus Swift to march to the Niagara frontier. These citizen-soldiers reinforced the regulars in Fort Niagara as well as the local common militia. News of the declaration of war arrived on the American side of the Niagara River on June 26, roughly a half-day after officials on the Canadian side received word. The people of Buffalo became aware of hostilities when the British captured a salt boat heading into Lake Erie. While there would be minor military activity across the northern border in 1812, the focus of New York's efforts would play out on the Niagara frontier.

Tompkins well understood the importance of transferring weapons, ammunition, and camp equipment from Albany to arsenals that would equip the detached militia as they marched to the frontiers. He gave priority of issuing muskets to these communities before arming the militia defending New York City. As for arming the detached militiamen moving toward the Niagara frontier, he gave orders to stock the arsenals at Batavia and Canandaigua with 3,500 muskets as well as artillery ammunition. However, camp kettles and tents were still in short supply at Albany. A deeper problem for the defense of the state was the general lack of skill and experience among the state's militia officers. Brig. Gen. William Wadsworth had earlier professed his lack of competence in military matters. Tompkins turned to Maj. Gen. Amos Hall of Bloomfield in Ontario County to moderate the effect of Wadsworth's deficiency. Hall arrived on July 28. Tompkins paid Hall from state funds because the general was not covered by the federal mobilization. Nonetheless, Hall worked feverishly to facilitate mustering the detached militia heading toward the Niagara.[3]

Among the first militia units to arrive on the Niagara frontier were two companies of one-year volunteers from Seneca and Ontario Counties. These militiamen found themselves building a gun battery at Black Rock. The militia leadership strictly proscribed any firing across the river. Nonetheless, when Archer Galloway, in charge of the battery, saw a British work party starting construction of a battery on the opposite bank, he believed himself obligated to intercede. In his words, his men "were tired of lounging and doing nothing." Galloway had his crew aim their cannon so that the shot would land in front of the work party, to scare them rather than to kill. The shot landed where intended. "The British were so completely enveloped in smoke and dust that not one of them could be seen, but as soon as they could be we found them

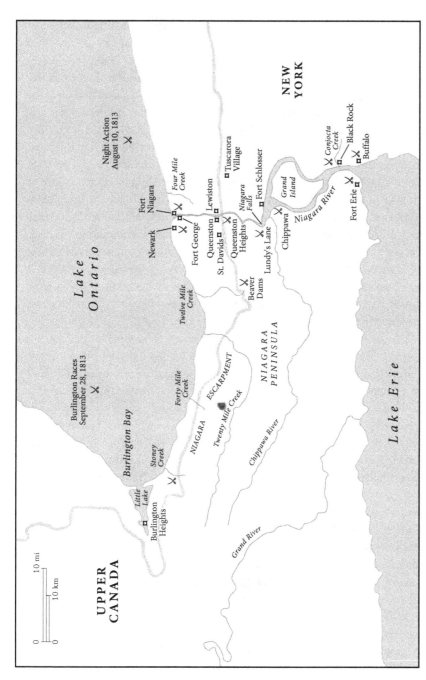

Niagara region. Map by Erin Greb Cartography.

running in every direction, some falling down, others over them." Galloway's superiors wanted to know who had disobeyed orders, but the crew pleaded ignorance. The officers "did not try very hard to find out." Galloway claimed that this was the first shot fired across the Niagara. However, the British had their revenge. The following day, they returned fire, inflicting heavy damage on American barracks. The New York militiamen got a taste of the excitement of war; the profound tragedy would follow soon enough.[4]

The war in western New York was also characterized by naval raiding parties along the lakes. On July 4, the HMS *Queen Charlotte* appeared off Canadaway Creek on Lake Erie in Chautauqua County. Her target was a salt boat that ducked into the creek. Salt was a valuable commodity for the British now that the war cut off supplies from New York. The boat was defended by its small crew and several local militiamen. Celea Cole, a widow and mother of eleven rode her plow horse four miles to the village of Canadaway (now Fredonia) to spread the alarm. Soon there were forty defenders of the boat and its cargo. A ship's boat carried thirteen crewmen toward its goal, but a ragged volley from shore drove them back to the *Queen Charlotte*. Raids like this plagued the citizens along the lakes' shores throughout the war.[5]

This incident impelled the people of Chautauqua County to petition the governor. "The British have a number of armed vessels lying off our shore, landing their spies to gain information of our strength, arms, means of defence and reconnoitering our shore, many of their people formerly accustomed to trade with us, are well acquainted with the landing places, which gives the Enemy great advantage to do us injury." The citizens requested that Tompkins send troops there, or to return the detached militia that was serving elsewhere. Claiming that it was almost impossible to furnish themselves with weapons, the petitioners requested five hundred stands of arms. Tompkins responded by sending 150 weapons from the arsenal at Canandaigua. The troops, however, were needed elsewhere.[6]

The Iroquois of western New York were well aware of the federal government's desire that the tribes remain neutral. Settlers in the Holland Land Purchase outnumbered Indians ten to one. For years, the Iroquois had voiced their numerous complaints to the federal government. Land payments and annuities arrived late. Settlers stole horses and cattle and cut timber from the reservations. The federal government had not compensated the Iroquois for these property losses. Open dispute remained over ownership of Grand Island on the Niagara River. The Seneca, New York state, and the federal government all claimed it. On two occasions and at the request of the federal government, Iroquois had met with western Indians to persuade them to maintain neutrality. Still, the War Department had not paid their travel expenses.[7] Despite these irritants, the bulk of New York Iroquois maintained neutrality in the coming campaign. However, Indian warriors on the Grand River in Upper Canada, fighting under their competent war chief John Norton, would have a major influence on the battle ahead.

In June, a delegation of New York Iroquois traveled to the Grand River settlement and met their fellow Iroquois in council. Little Billy, head of the deputation, made the case for tribal unity and neutrality. "God knows Great Britain has once cheated us, we will now try the United States. We are one people and you ought to unite with us for we are greater [more numerous?] than you." A Mohawk speaking for the Grand River Indians replied, "If you listen to the United States you will be destroyed and made slaves like the Negroes. The President wants you to lie still and hold down your heads. But I am a Mohawk. I will paint my face and be a man and fight Yankees as long as I live." The council ended with the understanding that Iroquois in New York would be neutral, while Grand River warriors would be free to ally themselves with the British if American forces invaded.[8]

In Albany on July 13, Stephen Van Rensselaer formally took command of the division of detached militia that was charged with the defense of New York from the Pennsylvania border to St. Regis on the St. Lawrence River. Tompkins informed Van Rensselaer that General Henry Dearborn had "a general superintending command" of all regulars and militia in the state.[9] It was more than that; Dearborn was Van Rensselaer's superior officer. However, it was not until August 7 that Dearborn himself understood that the Niagara frontier was part of his responsibility. The confusion resided in the War Department's correspondence with Dearborn, Tompkins, and Van Rensselaer. Tompkins had taken the initiative to order regiments of detached militia to move to the frontiers without waiting for permission from Washington. Dearborn, for his part, immediately ordered Maj. James Mullany to proceed with his recruits and report to Van Rensselaer. He also requested that Pennsylvania Governor Simon Snyder send 2,000 militiamen to the Niagara frontier. Unfortunately, the Pennsylvania troops experienced difficulties mobilizing and did not arrive until after the fateful battle on Queenston Heights.[10]

Tompkins officially appointed Amos Hall, a Federalist, to command on the Niagara frontier until Van Rensselaer arrived, at which time Hall would transfer command to Van Rensselaer. In his letter to Hall, the governor remarked that it would be a "feather in your cap" if Hall could capture Forts Erie and George before Van Rensselaer arrived. Thus, the victory would go to someone other than Tompkins's presumed Federalist opponent in the upcoming gubernatorial election. Tompkins was brimming with unfounded optimism, and he stated boldly that he was confident that as many as half of the Canadian

Major General Stephen Van Rensselaer, by Thomas Gimbrede. Reproduction courtesy of Institute Archives and Special Collections, Rensselaer Polytechnic Institute, Troy, New York.

militia would defect in the event of invasion and that the New York militia alone would take Canada.[11]

The governor sent another valuable asset to the Niagara frontier. Gen. Nicholas Gray was Tompkins's private secretary, a veteran of the Irish Rebellion of '98, and a military engineer and artillerist. Gray had been sentenced to death for his part in the rebellion but received a last-minute pardon. He was in generally poor health but willing to go on campaign. His honorific title of general came from his service in Ireland. Without a militia commission, Gray served as a civilian advisor to General Wadsworth to help him organize his staff functions. Tompkins told Gray to return to Albany "whenever the least inclination to dispense with his services is manifested." Tompkins valued Gray's service as secretary and complained to Peter B. Porter in September of the difficulty he experienced in writing orders himself. Putting his engineering skills to practice, Gray soon had three batteries erected, two at Black Rock and one atop Lewiston Heights, south of Lewiston. This latter position was known as Fort Gray [12]

General Van Rensselaer made his way westward, but upon hearing of alarms at Sackett's Harbor and Ogdensburg, he diverted his trip to visit those locations to do what he could to improve the defenses. At Ogdensburg, he cancelled a raid across the river to seize a Provincial Marine schooner when hundreds of volunteer militiamen backed out of the adventure when time came to load the boats. The general arrived in Buffalo on August 10. He soon met with Red Jacket and Cornplanter, who were working to keep their warriors neutral. The general inspected the defenses and wrote to Tompkins of his immediate need for artillerists and engineers. He discovered citizens but no army. Many of the militiamen had arrived shoeless from the long trek from the interior counties. While many had muskets, hundreds did not. Also insufficient were tents, camp kettles, tools, and all the items necessary to support an army. Now the general's aide, Lt. Col. Solomon Van Rensselaer, found full range for his organizational skills. Having served in the regular army, Solomon Van Rensselaer knew what to do. He laid out the major camp east of Lewiston. He organized a camp guard, established a regular distribution of food, and began a modest program of instruction. Soon, more troops were pouring into camp.[13]

In August, the federal government loaned 2,000 muskets to the state. Tompkins quickly issued these to deploying militiamen. The governor judged that it was time to put more detached militiamen on the road to the Niagara frontier. On August 13, Tompkins ordered Lt. Col. Henry Bloom's Nineteenth Regiment of Detached Militia to march to the Niagara frontier. Bloom was from Genoa in Cayuga County. Bloom's regiment was assigned to General Wadsworth's Seventh Brigade of Detached Militia. On August 27, the governor ordered Brig. Gen. Daniel Miller's Sixth Brigade of Detached Militia to muster into federal service on September 8. The Sixth Brigade was composed of Lt. Col. Farrand Stranahan's Sixteenth and Lt. Col. Thompson Mead's Seventeenth Regiments of Detached Militia. Stranahan was from Cooperstown and Mead from Chenango County. Their regiments would not arrive at the camp in Lewiston until the evening before the invasion. Stranahan was a Republican, and in May 1807, he had achieved notoriety for beating Judge William Cooper with a cane over an insult. The Federalist judge was the founder of Cooperstown and father of the future literary giant James Fennimore Cooper. Stranahan had been tried and fined $30 for the offense.[14]

As Tompkins had repeatedly warned the War Department, the state had insufficient tentage and camp equipment for the entire number of militiamen called into service. Tompkins had issued necessary orders in a timely manner to ensure that state assets, largely weapons and ammunition, be available at the various rendezvous sites. However, as mobilization unfolded, the governor learned that federal authorities, specifically General Dearborn and Quartermaster General Morgan Lewis, appeared unable to direct the movement of tents and camp equipment to appropriate locations along the route of march. The governor sent Lewis messages detailing the mobilization schedule, and he also directed state quartermasters to work hand-in-hand with their federal counterparts. Tompkins chided Dearborn for the failing. "Rely upon it, my dear Sir, that nothing is so much calculated to damp the spirits and ardour of Militia as a failure on the part of those public officers to whom it may appertain, to supply the accommodations promised to be ready at the times and places of Rendezvous and I, therefore, trust that proper measures will be taken to prevent the like deficiencies in future." The governor had worked diligently and successfully to ensure that the detached militia would be armed and ready to march promptly. He would not allow negligence on the part of the federal government to impair the defense of the state. However, two weeks later, he discovered that the tentage had not yet departed the federal storehouses in Albany. Tompkins personally intervened and got the equipment on the way westward. After the war, Tompkins remarked that in its opening weeks, there was not a camp kettle within four hundred miles of the Niagara, and his officers purchased what they could from the settlers they passed. Despite these efforts, the thousands of militiamen assembling on the Niagara frontier in the fall of 1812 would be short of necessary tents and equipment.[15]

Early in August, Lieutenant General Sir George Prevost, governor and commander in chief of British North America, proposed a general armistice to go into effect on August 9 and General Dearborn accepted. Prevost hoped that a pause would allow the Madison administration to consider Britain's repeal of the Orders in Council as a basis for negotiating an end to the war. The Orders in Council were British decrees to regulate neutral trade with European ports. Solomon Van Rensselaer and British Major General Roger Hale Sheaffe negotiated the details of the armistice, and the American won the concession to move cargoes on Lake Ontario. Boatloads of provisions and equipment moved from Oswego to the Niagara River to bolster the army on the Niagara frontier.[16]

Catastrophe hit on August 16 as Gen. William Hull surrendered Detroit to Major General Isaac Brock. The British captured more than 2,400 Americans, the bulk of whom were Ohio militiamen. Brock paroled the militiamen but marched the regulars eastward to prison in Quebec. Once paroled, the men could not fight until exchanged. Americans on the New York side of the river watched in horror as the bedraggled captives walked from Fort Erie to the village of Newark (now Niagara-on-the-Lake). General Morgan Lewis, writing from Albany, noted that "Many of the federalists cannot disguise their exultation, though they pretend to be much mortified." Solomon Van Rensselaer wrote to his spouse, "Had I been in the command of one thousand regular troops I would have risked every thing to have retaken them and in which I know I should not have been disappointed—the indignation expressed by all against the government and Genl. Hull were great indeed." Years after the event, an anonymous witness wrote, "Never did I see such an excitement of distrust on the part of our Troops, the idea spread through the camp that Hull had sold the Army, and it was soon ascertained that insinuations were made that Genl. Van Rensselaer would do the like." To the fear of death and injury was now added the possibility of a treasonous surrender and a slow death in a prison stockade somewhere in the bleakness of Canada.[17]

In late August, Tompkins moved his headquarters to New York City to oversee preparations there. About September 6, he was "thunderstruck" to learn that Hull had surrendered his army at Detroit. Tompkins realized the immediate danger posed to the state's western frontier and he returned promptly to Albany. Once there, he discovered that several regiments of detached militia had not yet moved to the Niagara frontier and to Sackett's Harbor, presumably for lack of tents and camp kettles. An irate governor wrote orders demanding these units to march immediately.

On September 9, Tompkins sent a long letter to Van Rensselaer. He informed his general that 2,000 Pennsylvania militia and 1,200 regulars were on the march to the Niagara frontier. He also affirmed that Van Rensselaer had full authority to call out the militia as necessary be they detached or common militia. Tompkins also mobilized about 1,000 militiamen from volunteer companies—artillery, rifles, and light infantry—and ordered them westward. He even ordered Lt. Col. Francis McClure's Irish Greens to move from New York City to Albany in preparation for deployment to Van Rensselaer's army on the Niagara. The governor assured Van Rensselaer of his full support and added, "I pray God, you may be able to maintain your post until reinforcements shall arrive." He added that "the government has at length been awakened to its duty with respect to the Command of the Lakes." Clearly, Tompkins was frustrated with the general incompetence of the federal government.[18]

Van Rensselaer kept his superiors, Tompkins and Dearborn, apprised of the dire situation along the Niagara. To Tompkins, he admitted his sense of personal deficiency. "To perform my duty, arduous as it is, is comparatively easy, but to determine what my duty is, in a wide field of action, where every thing is unshaped and uncertain, is often a task of no small difficulty." The general expected to be attacked and perhaps to be defeated. "A retrograde movement of this army upon the back of that disaster which has befallen the one at Detroit, would stamp a stigma upon the national character which time could never wipe away." The burden of command was weighty indeed.[19]

To Dearborn, Van Rensselaer reported his fear of being attacked before the army was prepared. He also provided a litany of shortcomings. Many of the men's weapons were broken, and the militiamen and regulars were insufficiently trained in the basics. It was impossible to acquire wagons and teams. They had little grain to feed the horses of the dragoons and artillery. He added an ominous note. "And to cheer up our hearts, we have picked up a Birch Bark, on which is written a Notice from the Soldiers to the Officers of this little army that unless they were paid, they would absolutely quit the field in 8 days from that time."[20] It was clear that many of Van Rensselaer's troubles were beyond his capability to resolve.

After the declaration of war, Tompkins assigned Porter to be the state's quartermaster general. Porter began buying or building barracks along the northern and western frontiers. On September 9, Tompkins focused Porter's tasks. Porter was to work in direct support of Van Rensselaer and was to have all the authority of the governor in the realm of logistics. The governor intended to "exert every nerve to put Genl. Van Rensselaer upon a respectable footing for force and equipments as soon as possible." The implication was clear—Porter was to carry out the governor's expectations, which meant unlimited support for the Federalist general. However, even Porter's skill and drive could not coax supplies from the now-empty arsenals of central New York.[21]

On September 13, Dearborn ordered Brig. Gen. Alexander Smyth to take command of the regular infantry brigade forming on the Niagara River and to report to Maj. Gen. Van Rensselaer upon his arrival. Smyth reached Buffalo on September 29. However, he failed to visit his superior, claiming to be too busy preparing his brigade. Smyth also failed to participate in planning the upcoming invasion. A staunch Republican, Smyth would avoid contributing to the success of a Federalist if he could. He also harbored an animus for militia officers promoted for political reasons. This was particularly ironic; Jefferson commissioned Smyth directly to the rank of colonel in 1808, largely for his political purity.[22]

About this same time, the intense partisan conflict between Porter and Solomon Van Rensselaer came to a head. Solomon had complained to his spouse of "the persecution of my Political enemies who even pursue me to this quarter of the Globe." Solomon uncharitably attributed the severe lack of supplies directly to Porter's neglect. He accused Porter of intentionally embarrassing the general's command for political reasons. Instead of "bringing the war to an honorable termination, . . . he [Porter] cared not how long it might last, provided he could make his fortune by it." Admitting later that his words were imprudent, he stated that Peter 'Belligerent' Porter was a "Damned Scoundrel." These fighting words proceeded quickly to the arrangement of a duel. Someone from Porter's camp informed Major General Van Rensselaer, who quickly stepped in to promise arrest if his two closest staff officers did not cancel their preparations.[23]

Two great divides contributed to the general dysfunction of the army gathered on the Niagara River. The first was the political partisanship that poisoned cooperation between Federalists and Republicans, even in a time of national emergency. Suspicions ran deep among some of the militiamen and their officers that the Federalist General Van Rensselaer was not earnest in his quest to invade Canada. Extremists whispered rumors that the general would surrender the army. The second great divide was between regulars and militia. Regular officers, many very new to their duties, disparaged their militia counterparts and resented service under a militia general. Smyth's treatment of his superior, General Van Rensselaer, was unconscionable. His actions created a command environment in which his officers felt free to openly discredit militiamen. The absurdity of this situation became evident at the end of the year, when the Porter-Smyth affair pitted the two Republicans in a duel. It was the consequences of these political and professional divides, as much as lack of supplies, that crippled operations and led to catastrophic defeat. Every leader in the army wanted victory. However, many could not overcome mutual suspicion and distrust. The army lacked cohesion, and Van Rensselaer's best efforts could not supply it.

The story of the faltering 1812 mobilization is told in the surviving records. Late in August, Tompkins called Lt. Col. Thompson Mead's Seventeenth Regiment of Detached Militia into active service and ordered it to march to join Van Rensselaer. The Seventeenth delayed its move while waiting for tents and camp equipment. Seven years after the war, Mead was still trying to collect repayment of his personal funds expended during the march westward. In his request to the New York legislature, he wrote, "no munitions of war, no arms, no tents, no provisions, and no hospital stores were provided, and that the Quarter-master's department was entirely destitute of every thing requisite for subsisting and quartering the troops." Mead had received $478.34 directly from the governor, and Mead ordered his regimental quartermaster to use it to buy food. When troops fell sick, Mead found civilians who would board and nurse the sick soldiers for a price. The governor told Mead to draw weapons at Batavia. However, when the regiment arrived, there were no weapons. They had been issued to units passing through earlier. The friction of war had defeated the governor's best efforts over several years to place trained, equipped, well-led soldiers on the state's frontiers.[24]

The regulars gathered at Buffalo were hardly better off than the militia. Capt. William King inspected the soldiers of Col. Thomas Parker's Twelfth Infantry and found them still in their linen recruit uniforms, entirely unprepared for the cold and stormy October weather. He reported that the junior officers were generally intelligent and were gentlemen, but "very ignorant of their duties." King judged the men to be "excellent recruits" but "very raw." There was insufficient ammunition and gun tools. Tents, canteens, and knapsacks were "very bad." King next turned his attention to Col. William Winder's Fourteenth Infantry and found weapons and ammunition in even worse condition. King believed that as many as 20 percent of the muskets should be condemned and "some of the cartridges are said to have been made up in 1794." Many of the men were without shoes and stockings. Their training was abysmal. "They are mere militia, and, if possible, even worse; and if taken into action in their present state, will prove more dangerous to themselves than to their enemy." King's pronouncement reflected his denigration of the militia but also indirectly pointed out the incompetence of the newly appointed regular officers.[25]

American morale soared with an unexpected naval victory on October 9. Lt. Jesse Elliott, commander of the Lake Erie squadron, assembled a hundred sailors, soldiers, and volunteer militiamen for a daring raid to capture two small Provincial Marine brigs anchored under the guns of Fort Erie. The senior militiaman was Capt. Cyrenius Chapin, a local doctor. Elliott and his raiders worked their way stealthily across the lake in two barges. Scrambling over the sides, the Americans quickly subdued the crews of the *Detroit* and the *Caledonia*. The real fighting began as Elliott brought the vessels downriver with little wind to assist. The makeshift crew brought the *Caledonia* to shore, but British guns severely damaged the *Detroit*. The *Detroit* grounded on the western side of Squaw Island. Unable to salvage the battered vessel, Elliott burned it. Elliott's raiders captured fifty-nine British sailors and soldiers and freed about forty Americans held aboard the two vessels. Congress awarded a sword to Elliott, and the army brevetted Capt. Nathan Towson to the rank of major for his part in the daring venture. Congress also awarded prize money of $12,000, to be shared among the raiders. One of the casualties of the engagement was militia Maj. William Cuyler of Palmyra. Although he had opposed the war, he volunteered for service to defend his country. He was riding along the shore when grapeshot fired from the Canadian side severed his spine. After the war, the body of the popular major was returned to Palmyra for burial.[26]

Navy Lt. Samuel Angus, who directed work at the Black Rock naval yard, sent carpenters to work on the *Caledonia* and three former private vessels.

However, following Elliott's raid, the British had "kept up such a constant fire with shot & shells upon the vessels and houses at Black Rock . . . that the Carpenters broke off and went to Batavia for safety and nothing could induce them to go back to their work." Nonetheless, the *Caledonia* sailed with Oliver Hazard Perry's squadron at the Battle of Lake Erie the following year.[27]

In the second week of October, General Van Rensselaer made the fateful decision to take his inadequately prepared army into Canada. The season was late and the weather was rainy. The men, inadequately sheltered, clamored to invade or to be released to their homes. Van Rensselaer received letters from friends in Albany warning that any delay would be taken by his political enemies as evidence of incompetence or treason. The editor of the *Buffalo Gazette* noted that the general had but two choices, "To risk a battle, or endure intolerable imputations upon his own character (for vipers began to hiss)." In a long letter to Dearborn, Van Rensselaer stated, "The blow must be struck soon or all the toil and expense of the campaign will go for nothing, and worse than nothing, for the whole will be tinged with dishonor."[28]

The two Van Rensselaers planned a two-pronged attack. The main attack would be a river crossing from a point south of Lewiston to the base of the escarpment. The troops would then seize Queenston Heights. Smyth would make a secondary attack. He would embark his brigade from Four Mile Creek on Lake Ontario and land near the village of Newark. This move would presumably tie up General Brock's troops around Fort George. Van Rensselaer set the invasion for October 11.[29]

The general's selection of a crossing site between Lewiston and Queenston was informed by a detailed reconnaissance made by Nicholas Gray. Porter ordered the construction of boats at Manchester, but only thirteen were gathered to support the assault.[30] The waters exiting the gorge were notorious for backflows and eddies, so Porter hired civilian pilots to steer the boats. A round trip took at least thirty minutes under good conditions. Because no more than about 350 men could be transported at one time, it would take hours to cross 4,000 men. While moving the boats in the dark from Lewiston to the embarkation point about a mile south of the village, militia Lieutenant Sims, who led the movement, mysteriously disappeared, along with oars and oarlocks. Due to these difficulties, Van Rensselaer postponed the invasion until October 13.

On October 10, Van Rensselaer ordered Smyth to march his troops "immediately" from Black Rock to the militia camp. Smyth started out the next day, but turned back because of the "badness of the weather and roads. . . ." Indeed, the rain fell in torrents. Smyth informed the commanding general that the troops needed to wash their clothing and would not move until the 13th. On the 12th, Maj. Gen. Amos Hall prodded the ungracious and transparent Smyth to meet Van Rensselaer face-to-face to coordinate the upcoming battle. Hall could not tolerate the regular general's obvious obstruction. Frustrated, Van Rensselaer was determined to continue without Smyth or his men. Yet the general was in despair that enough militiamen would volunteer to cross the river. When Lt. Col. Mead requested time to rest his troops and to draw ammunition, Van Rensselaer "replied, with some warmth, that the troops should cross that night if ever; that he did not know what would be done; that out of the two regiments stationed at Lewiston, viz. Cols. Allen's and Dobbin's, not more than 75 or 80 men would volunteer."[31]

On the evening of October 12, Lt. Col. and New Yorker John Chrystie brought five companies of raw recruits of the Thirteenth Infantry into camp and requested a command for the attack to take place the following morning. General Van Rensselaer agreed. Solomon Van Rensselaer adjusted his crossing schedule to accommodate the late arrivals. The first wave would consist of half of Chrystie's regulars and half of moderately well-trained militiamen. Regulars under Lieutenant Colonels John Fenwick and New Yorker James Mullany comprised the next two waves. Militia would follow as boats returned. However, when Solomon Van Rensselaer led his militiamen to the boats around 3 A.M., he found that Chrystie had filled all the boats with regulars. It is difficult to see this as anything other than evidence of regular-militia enmity. Van Rensselaer had no choice but to enter a boat with his staff and shove off. During the crossing, Chrystie's boat and two others returned to the New York shore, the pilots complaining about the adverse river currents.

Van Rensselaer and the regulars landed. Among the officers were Capt. John E. Wool and Lt. Stephen Watts Kearny. Wool was born in Newburgh and orphaned at an early age. He grew up in Troy. Kearny was born in New Jersey but entered the service from New York. He attended Columbia University for two years, served in the militia, and was related to the prominent Livingston and Watts families. Landing in the darkness, the group was fired on by British regulars. In the ensuing firefight, the Americans forced the British to withdraw but not before two officers were killed, and Van Rensselaer, Wool, and three other officers were badly wounded. The Americans did not know that Chrystie had failed to cross. Van Rensselaer received five or six musket wounds and could no longer retain command. Although wounded through both thighs, Wool volunteered to lead the soldiers in scaling the heights and assaulting the gun position part-way down from the summit. Wool's command succeeded in this daunting task. After sunrise, General Brock personally led an assault uphill to recapture the gun position. Shot in the wrist and chest, Brock collapsed, and the assault did as well. Brock died a hero's death.[32]

The boats that had been with Van Rensselaer returned to shore carrying him and the dead and wounded. The soldiers waiting to board were troubled by the bodies, and the blood welled up in the boats. Fenwick and Mullany crossed over in four boats. British from the high banks fired as the Americans approached, killing and wounding many. Faced with the desperate situation, Mullany filled a boat with wounded and unwounded and pushed off, eventually reaching the friendly shore. Fenwick, himself wounded, surrendered the rest of his men.

Except for sporadic fire from two guns across from Lewiston, British resistance ceased for a few hours. During this time, over 1,300 regulars, volunteers, and militiamen crossed the river and ascended the heights. Of the five regiments of detached militia, four of the battalion commanders crossed with some of their men. Only a few of the thirteen boats remained in service. Others had floated downriver or had been abandoned by their civilian pilots.[33]

Brig. Gen. Wadsworth was the senior officer on Queenston Heights, but he wisely yielded tactical command to Lt. Col. Winfield Scott. Wadsworth understood that Scott knew what he was doing and his commanding presence inspired some confidence in those brave enough to join the invasion. General Van Rensselaer crossed over during the lull in the battle to ascertain what might be needed. He rightfully understood that he could best influence the battle by directing resources from the New York shore. In his official report to Dearborn, he wrote, "By this time, I perceived my troops were embarking very slowly. I passed immediately over to accelerate their movements, but, to my utter astonishment, I found, that, at the very moment when complete victory was in our hands, the ardour of the unengaged troops had entirely subsided. I rode in all directions; urged the men by every consideration to pass over—but in vain. Lieutenant Colonel Bloom, who had been wounded in the action, returned, mounted his horse, and rode through the camp, as did also Judge Peck, who happened to be there exhorting the companies to proceed—but all in vain." The reality of death and injury had overcome patriotic intentions. No amount of encouragement from Van Rensselaer or their officers could persuade them otherwise.[34]

Meanwhile back at Fort George, Major General Sheaffe saw that there were no American boats poised offshore, thus he was free to move his regulars and militiamen to Queenston. The first to appear on the heights were Britain's Indian allies, about eighty Grand River warriors under the leadership of John Norton. Winfield Scott led an attack and Norton's men withdrew, keeping out of the range of American bayonets. However, Norton's Iroquois made a consequential contribution to the British victory. Their war cries were heard across the river and intimidated the wavering militia. Lieutenant Jared Willson wrote of his experiences.

The Battalion of Rifle-men, to which I belong were sent out after the first engagement, a mile or more from the main body to make discoveries. We had not been
gone long, when a party of Indian Devils—about two hundred, attacked us in
the woods. We were far inferior in numbers and of course compelled to retreat
precipitately. The savages, greedy for plunder, and thirsting for blood, pursued
us closely, firing and yelling, in a most frightful manner. They pursued us close
to the main body, but in their turn were compelled to fly to safety. By this time, I
thought hell had broken loose and let her dogs of war upon us. In short I expected
every moment to be made a 'cold Yanky' as the soldiers say.[35]

By 2 P.M., the Americans saw Sheaffe and hundreds of British regulars and
militia approaching. The Americans had the steep side of the gorge to their rear
and the crest of the escarpment to the north. Dozens fled the ranks, futilely seeking safety. There was no easy escape. Scott directed the insubstantial fire of those
stalwarts remaining with the colors. With his defense collapsing, Scott brought
the men down the slope to the river's bank—with no boats waiting. Earlier, militiaman Elihu Shepard had been wounded and returned to the American shore.
From there, he saw soldiers rushing toward the cliff to escape. "They had come
to a place so steep that they could not stop when they saw their danger, and were
killed instantly." Some Americans attempted to swim the wide river; none arrived
on the opposite shore. It was all over. Wadsworth surrendered his sword.[36]

Sheaffe's men took 436 regulars and 489 militiamen. Among the officers were
four of the five militia battalion commanders. Lieutenant Colonels Farrand
Stranahan and Henry Bloom, who had bravely returned to the battlefield, were
wounded. Sheaffe paroled the militia and sent most of the regulars to captivity in
Quebec. The British exchanged Scott and many of the other captives in November and they returned to the United States. Van Rensselaer reported sixty dead
and 170 wounded, more than twice the British and Indian casualties. Eventually,
more than a hundred of those wounded perished. He ended his report, "The
brave men who had gained the victory, exhausted of strength and ammunition,
and grieved at the unpardonable neglect of their fellow-soldiers, gave up the
conflict. I can only add, that the victory was really won, but lost for the want of a
small reinforcement; one-third part of the idle men might have saved all."[37]

Fourteen-year-old Eber Howe walked the battlefield the following day and
saw about twenty bodies of Americans, stripped and scalped. He watched as
they were buried in a shallow grave. "Three men would then take the body, two
with a stick under the neck, one hold of the feet, carry it to the hole and pitch it
in like a dead hog. . . . I then wended my way home, with many sad reflections
on the barbarities of war."[38]

General Van Rensselaer requested to retire from his command. Morgan
Lewis attributed his request to the extreme political partisanship in the camp

at Lewiston. The defeated general turned over command to Smyth on October 15 and returned to Albany to the praise of his many supporters. The common council of Albany arranged a public reception for the returning general. He remained a major general and commanded the cavalry division of the common militia but saw no more combat. Magnanimously, the general praised several of his subordinates, Republican and Federalist alike. Regardless of the fears and accusations of many in his army and in Albany, Stephen Van Rensselaer had successfully removed political partisanship from his dealings and his command relationships.[39]

Paroled militiamen returned to the American camp and were allowed to go home. They could not fight and were a drain on resources, particularly food. Many other militiamen drifted off without leave. A Federalist newspaper editor who departed with his company wrote of "the great desertion of militia by wholesale and retail, through starvation and disgust of the service and objection to serve under United States officers, few militia are left." None of the militia had as yet been paid for their service. Tompkins arrived at Buffalo about two weeks after the fight, and he set about addressing the new and painful situation. Years of preparation had not gained a victory. General Smyth consolidated the remaining militiamen into a battalion of fewer than five hundred men commanded by Hugh Dobbin of Junius. This was all that remained of the 2,200 detached militia who had marched to the Niagara frontier. Smyth segregated Dobbin's men at Fort Schlosser, so that there would be no regular soldier "within ten miles of them." He did not want defeatism to infect his regulars.[40]

Tompkins ordered Lt. Col. Francis McClure, then marching three companies of his volunteer regiment to the Niagara frontier, to place himself under Smyth's command. The governor also commissioned Nicholas Gray as a lieutenant colonel of militia to serve on Smyth's staff. Finally, citing the reduced number of militiamen present for duty and noting the arrival of a regular army deputy quartermaster, Tompkins discharged Porter.[41]

Tompkins made enquiries about the grievously wounded Solomon Van Rensselaer although he did not visit him even though they were billeted in the same hotel. For this slight, the governor received deserved criticism. Bad blood already existed between Lt. Col. Van Rensselaer, a stalwart Federalist, and the governor. In 1810, Governor Tompkins had sent a letter to Van Rensselaer, then serving as the state adjutant general, seeking his opinion on a matter of military law. Van Rensselaer had not responded to this official request. Tompkins could not have forgotten the snub, and in February 1812, he warned the state's congressional delegation not to commission Van Rensselaer in the regular army. On October 27, the governor returned to Albany to address the new legislature.[42]

While Tompkins had become brutally aware of many shortfalls in the state's military preparation, he posed a special problem to the legislature. He noted that the penalty for failing to muster when called up was only pecuniary and a "trifling" at that. Tompkins complained that "the affluent portion of the community do not participate in the danger and burthens of service at all . . . whilst the more indigent, perhaps with young families to support, are alone subjected to the sacrifices of supporting the government and defending the lives and the property of their fellow citizens, and receive a compensation, which, in comparison with their earnings at home, is but a mere pittance."[43] The poor were fighting the war, while the rich stayed safe at home. The legislature took no action.

Smyth immediately began planning his own offensive. He ordered Colonel Winder to start collecting boats; he needed enough to cross four thousand men, supporting artillery, and cavalry in one lift. Perhaps his ego got the better of him, for Smyth bypassed Dearborn, his superior officer, and complained directly to the secretary of war about the contractor supporting him on the Niagara. "He has no salt meat, and only damaged flour." Smyth warned Eustis to "Place no confidence in detached militia. They have disgraced the nation." He boasted, "Give me here a clear stage, and money, and I will retrieve your affairs or perish." As it turned out, he would do neither.[44]

Although Smyth had no use for militiamen, he nonetheless appealed to them to participate in his contemplated invasion. In a bombastic proclamation appealing to patriotism, Smyth asked, "Are you not related to the men who fought at Bennington and Saratoga? Has the race degenerated?" However, rather than encourage a strong flow of recruits toward Buffalo, the proclamation angered the many Federalists in the common militia. A few of them published their response to Smyth's call. Echoing their party's narrative, they wrote, "Why should our swords be drawn in redress of injuries which we have never felt, or which if they exist are beyond our reach? Why appeal to our valor for the destruction of our own happiness or that of others?" The defeats at Detroit and Queenston Heights, the appalling conditions in camp, and the risk of death from battle and disease discouraged the citizenry.[45]

Smyth received a long letter of guidance from Dearborn promising money and some reinforcements. "That you may be so fortunate as to succeed in retrieving and meliorating the state of our affairs is my most ardent wish." Dearborn also placed a requirement on Smyth, one that would necessitate a delay. He wrote that Smyth, "should, if possible, be prepared for crossing with three thousand men with artillery at once." Smyth needed scows to carry artillery. None were immediately available, and it would take at least twenty days to construct ten of them. Smyth was determined to cross if and when there were sufficient boats. He replied to Dearborn that he "would cross in three days if I had the means."[46]

The antipathy between regular army and militia increased after the poor showing of the militia in battle. Most militiamen had refused to cross, and of those who did, many withdrew from the battle lines in order to seek shelter from the deadly fighting. Col. Thomas Parker reflected the aversion of many regular officers. Consulted on the propriety of forming a brigade consisting of regulars, volunteers, and militia, Parker responded that he knew of only one militia company on the Niagara "that would not corrupt any regular troops that they might be associated with." As for Francis McClure's Irish Greens, who were daily expected in camp, Parker advised that it would be best "to keep the regular troops entirely distinct from them." Parker's attitude was deep-seated; he had served for seven years in Virginia Continental regiments during the Revolution and had ample opportunity to view militia.[47]

The myriad problems that had plagued Van Rensselaer continued to distress his successor. Smyth repeatedly complained to Dearborn that he had no money to build scows or to pay troops. In mid-November, he noted that two regiments of regulars mutinied while marching to Buffalo because they had not been paid. The army's district paymaster in Albany reported that he had no money to send but expected funds from Washington at any time. Colonel Winder, then in command at Fort Niagara, reported, "We are literally starving on this end of the line for bread, and unless the supply is more abundant, the contractor will be answerable for consequences more fatal to their country than treason." Smyth bypassed the contractor and ordered his quartermaster to purchase food with funds that would have been used elsewhere.[48]

On November 19, Smyth informed the British that the armistice would end the following evening. The commander of Fort Niagara, Lt. Col. George McFeely, ordered his artillerists to heat up iron shot in the furnaces. At 5 A.M. on the 21st, the British in Fort George opened fire on Fort Niagara, 1,000 yards away. The Americans responded immediately, and a heroine emerged that day. In his report of the eleven-hour cannonade, McFeely noted, "An instance of extraordinary bravery in a female (the wife of one Doyle, a private of the United States Artillery, made a prisoner at Queenston) I cannot pass over. During the most tremendous cannonading I have ever seen, she attended the six-pounder on the old mess house with red hot shot, and showed fortitude equal to the Maid of Orleans." Betsy Doyle was a hardy laundress in the First U.S. Artillery. She knew only that her husband, Andrew, was a prisoner. However, Winfield Scott warned the Secretary of War that a number of prisoners taken at Queenston Heights who had been born British subjects were sent to Britain in close confinement. Scott understood that these soldiers were to be punished because they had been "found in arms against the British King." The punishment for treason was a grisly death. Among the twenty-three taken was Andrew Doyle who had been born in Upper Canada. As for Betsy, she would have more opportunities to show her mettle.[49]

Smyth received reports that large numbers of his regulars were sick or dying. One officer looked in the hospital of the Thirteenth Infantry, where he saw five soldiers who had been dead for more than twenty-four hours but had not been buried for lack of coffins. The *Buffalo Gazette* reported that in the nineteen-day period between October 28 and November 15, twenty-four regular soldiers died in the hospital at Buffalo.[50] While the regulars were arguably more dependable than militiamen, Smyth would have too few to attack successfully. He had no choice but to include militiamen in his invasion plans.

With most of New York's detached militia now walking to their homes, citizen-soldiers arrived from another state. Governor Simon Snyder of Pennsylvania, an ardent supporter of Madison and the war effort, ordered a brigade of 2,000 detached militiamen to march to Buffalo. These militiamen had volunteered for service, and Snyder fully expected them to cross into Canada if ordered to do so. However, their mobilization was exceptionally difficult. Unlike Tompkins, Snyder had not taken steps before the war to prepare his militia, although he had been governor since 1808. There were few arms in the state arsenals. Snyder maintained that it was the responsibility of the federal government to arm, equip, supply, and pay state militia from the time they arrived at their points of rendezvous. The War Department could not provide weapons for 2,000 men, and would not feed, supply, or pay the troops until they departed Pennsylvania. Adding to the general discomfort of the Pennsylvanians, state law prohibited the governor from providing funds in advance to feed the troops. Snyder asked his commanders to feed their men from out of pocket and to provide receipts to him for reimbursement later.[51]

Snyder's notion that his Pennsylvanians would surely cross the border was fantasy. The brigade commander, Brig. Gen. Adamson Tannehill, ordered his four battalion commanders to query their troops to ascertain who would consent to cross into Canada. While the nominal strength of the brigade was 2,000, hundreds had already deserted. As it was, only 413 Pennsylvanians committed to fight across the Niagara.[52]

On November 22, Smyth addressed the Six Nations at a council in Buffalo. He politely refused the assistance proffered by various chiefs. "We understand that you are willing to help us if we ask it, yet we do not ask it. The quarrel is ours, and not yours; and we will fight our own battles." Smyth encouraged his own soldiers to kill those Indian warriors fighting as allies of the British. He offered "forty dollars to be paid for the arms and spoils of each savage warrior who shall be killed." The message was clear to his men—there was no need to take Indian prisoners.[53]

By November 27, Smyth had gathered more than 4,500 soldiers and volunteers at Black Rock. Among these were Colonel Philetus Swift's Volunteer Regiment and a few hundred men of the detached militia willing to cross. Before dawn on November 28, Smyth ordered preliminary attacks in preparation for the major invasion to follow. Two parties departed the American side of the Niagara River, one to disable some shore batteries near Fort Erie, the second to destroy the bridge at Frenchman's Creek. The raiders managed to spike a few guns, throw a caisson into the water, and burn a barracks, but they were unable to destroy the bridge.[54]

In these two hard-fought engagements, the Americans lost seventy casualties as well as thirty taken prisoner. The British suffered similarly, losing sixty casualties and twenty-four taken prisoner. These crossings presaged the potential bloodletting of Smyth's plan to cross directly into the strongest part of the British defenses. However, as the day dragged on, Smyth gave no order for a general crossing. The embarkation was slow, and the number of British arrayed directly across the river was growing. Certainly, the Americans were contemplating the slaughter inevitable in an amphibious assault directly into the guns of hundreds of British muskets. Late in the afternoon, Smyth convened some of his officers and asked them if they should cross at that time. The regular officers stated no. Only Philetus Swift argued for the crossing. Smyth then ordered the army to disembark. The soldiers had been shivering in the boats and were now quite disgusted. Smyth then issued a new order to cross on the following day. This news appeared to quiet the obvious unrest in the American camps.[55]

The next day came and passed. On December 1, only 1,500 men were willing or could be ordered to cross. This group included 276 of McClure's Volunteers and about one hundred of Hugh Dobbin's detached militia. Smyth convened a council of war of his regular officers; the militia and volunteers were not invited. Smyth reminded his officers that Dearborn had directed him to "cross with 3000 men at once." This group recommended that operations cease; there was little hope in persuading the demoralized militia to cross. Dismissing all but the regulars was all they could do.[56]

Many of the Americans were furious at the situation and rioted, firing their muskets at Smyth's tent. Others broke their muskets and headed for their homes. Porter was incensed and wrote a letter published in the *Buffalo Gazette* accusing Smyth of cowardice, a particularly daring move considering both men were prominent Republicans. Smyth challenged Porter to a duel, and after both fired and missed, Porter retracted the charge of cowardice and the two shook hands.[57]

Lt. Col. George Fleming wrote to Governor Tompkins on December 3 that he had reason to believe Smyth "has entirely lost the confidence of both the militia and the United States troops." Upon learning of Smyth's aborted invasions, Tompkins replied to Fleming, "I did not, indeed could not, anticipate such a scene of gasconading, and of subsequent imbecility and folly as Genl. Smith [sic] has exhibited. To compare the events of the recent campaign with those of the days of the revolution, is almost enough to convince one, that the race of brave men and able commanders, will before many years become extinct." Dearborn wrote discreetly to the president that Smyth "has not been as popular as would have been wished."[58]

Smyth's army was disintegrating quickly due to sickness and desertion. It seemed that the regulars were only a bit more resilient than the militia. One of Winder's officers wrote of Smyth that his men "will never fight under such a granny—our men are dying fast." Nearly one half of the regulars were sick at the beginning of December. Lt. Col. George McFeely, commanding at Fort Niagara, reported "that there has crept into this garrison a dreadful contagion, which upon an average carries off between three and five each day." As for the Pennsylvanians, there were only 267 men left at Buffalo; 1,147 officers and men had returned home without orders[59]

Smyth realized his general unpopularity and thus his entire loss of effectiveness. On December 17, he departed Buffalo on leave and headed back to his home in Virginia. Three months later, Madison ordered Smyth to be quietly dropped from the rolls of the army.[60]

Smyth spent the winter in Virginia, but the contingents of regulars, volunteers, militiamen, and sailors left in winter quarters suffered immensely. Capt. Mordecai Myers, whose troops were quartered in Williamsville, recalled that Col. Moses Porter frequently called soldiers to Buffalo in response to possible British attacks. No attack came. Yet in Myers's recollection, the soldiers at Williamsville trudged the eleven miles to Buffalo at least twenty times.. "And when there after a march, the tracks of which could be traced by the blood from the feet of the men (for they were nearly all bare footed) we were compelled to encamp in the streets being unable to procure quarters."[61]

In early January, Commodore Isaac Chauncey visited the naval contingent at Black Rock. He reported to Secretary of the Navy Paul Hamilton that the sailors were "living about in the woods in small huts, made of the leaves of trees, ever since they arrived on this station, and Lieuts. Elliott and Angus have not been able to procure quarters for them the consequence has been that we have lost many by sickness, and a number by desertion."[62]

The soldiers endured a comparable fate, as many as three hundred succumbing to disease. The doctors, both civilian and military, met on December 16 "to take into consideration the most approved method of arresting the progress of the present epidemical disease." The *Buffalo Gazette* reported on December 22, "The Fever which has made such a dreadful havoc among our soldiers and citizens continues to rage. The Physicians are taking unwearied pains to ascertain the character of the disease and to prescribe an effective remedy for it. Bloodletting is generally fatal in violent cases." The sickness was typhoid.[63]

Doctor Daniel Chapin and Indian Agent Erastus Granger coordinated the effort to deal with the hundreds of bodies. The ground was too frozen and rocky for proper burial, so work parties placed the dead in pine coffins and interred them as best they could. In the spring, the coffins were reinterred on land belonging to Chapin and Capt. Rowland Cotton. On July 4, 1896 Buffalonians dedicated a bronze marker on a granite boulder "To the memory of unnamed soldiers of the War of 1812 who died of camp disease and were buried here."[64]

The 1812 campaign on the Niagara River exposed the early failure of the experiment in federal-state cooperation in war making. Little agreement existed over the allocation of responsibilities or procedures to implement them. Federal officials failed repeatedly to deliver supplies and equipment or pay to militiamen, largely because they did not know how to do so. General Dearborn's ignorance over the extent of his command responsibility is evidence of the failure to establish the most fundamental requirement of military operations—unity of command. However, at the heart of the failure to cooperate for the public good was the culture of the federal officer corps. From John Chrystie's flagrant disregard of the order to load assault boats, to Alexander Smyth's unconscionable obstructionism at every opportunity, too many federal officers refused to accept militiamen as partners. Instead, they ridiculed militiamen as incompetent and unpatriotic and unworthy to fight alongside regulars. How could federal-state cooperation exist in this toxic environment?

Years of preparation under the leadership of Governor Tompkins enabled the state to place thousands of armed militiamen on the Niagara frontier, but it was not enough. Supply and equipment shortages and political partisanship sapped the army of its strength, as did tension between militia and regular troops. Leadership was insufficient to overcome the many critical defects or to motivate militiamen to risk their lives in a war that many considered unnecessary. The Battle of Queenston Heights, Smyth's abortive invasion, and a widespread epidemic resulted in many hundreds of deaths and injuries. Despite these sacrifices, the country was no closer to accomplishing its war goals. But New York's War was fought not only on the Niagara frontier, but also along the state's entire northern frontier.

CHAPTER 4

THE NORTH COUNTRY

While the major offensive efforts of 1812 were across the Detroit and Niagara Rivers and north along the Richelieu River, the governor of New York was worried about the defense of communities along the shores of Lake Ontario and the St. Lawrence River. Of particular importance were the ports of Oswego and Sackett's Harbor. The federal and state governments moved cargoes to Oswego for transportation to the Niagara frontier and the nascent shipyard at Sackett's Harbor. Therefore, the governor's initial efforts supplemented the federal government's meager defensives of the two communities. The geographic expression "North Country" was ambiguous during the war years, as it is today. However, military and naval operations were geographically unified from the Genesee River northwest to Ogdensburg on the St. Lawrence River.

Lt. Melancthon Woolsey was the only naval officer posted on Lake Ontario, and the brig *Oneida* was his only warship. The *Oneida* was armed with eighteen 24-pounder carronades—short-barreled weapons that could reach out to five hundred yards. However, these weapons were typically only accurate at ranges up to one hundred yards, leaving *Oneida* without a long-range punch.[1]

When Washington declared the ninety-day embargo in April 1812, Woolsey patrolled the lake and captured the *Lord Nelson*, a Canadian schooner. A second commercial schooner, the *Julia*, rounded out Woolsey's small command. Woolsey had too few seamen to adequately crew his three vessels. Once Congress declared war, Woolsey requested men and money to convert the two schooners into warships. The Navy Department neglected the war on the inland lakes and rivers during the opening months of the war, focusing instead on getting the frigates out to sea and fostering the privateering effort. Little of Woolsey's preparation was accomplished when the Provincial Marine appeared off Sackett's Harbor.[2]

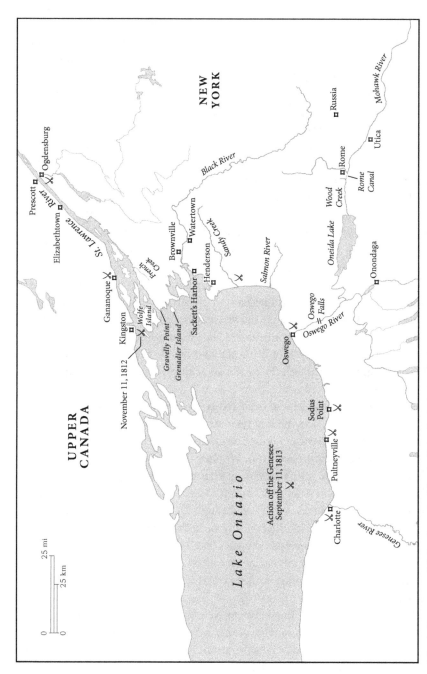

North Country and Lake Ontario. Map by Erin Greb Cartography.

With the declaration of war, the threat to American communities on Lake Ontario and the critical supply line came from the Provincial Marine. A component of the Quartermaster General Department, the mission of this small organization was the supply of army formations along the international border. Kingston, about thirty-seven miles across the lake from Sackett's Harbor, was home port to the small Lake Ontario squadron. By July, the squadron consisted of five warships. Three of the vessels were armed, and with their fifty-two cannon and carronades they easily outgunned *Oneida*. Isaac Brock replaced the elderly chief of the Provincial Marine; however, the officers and crews were inexperienced fighters not up to the demands of war.[3]

The British squadron arrived off Sackett's Harbor at dawn on Sunday, July 19, with the intention of destroying or capturing *Oneida* and thus gaining supremacy on the lake. Woolsey responded by anchoring *Oneida* close to shore and transferring nine carronades to a fortification above the shipyard. Already there was a 32-pounder with an effective range of one mile. However, there was no ammunition for this gun, and local legend has it that the crew wrapped 24-pound balls with carpet to achieve a snug fit. After exchanging several shots, the Provincial Marine broke off the attack and returned to Kingston. Sailing Master William Vaughan commanded the gun crew of the 32-pounder, and publicly claimed the honor of firing the first hostile cannon shot of the war. The garrison later improved the fortification above the navy yard and named it Fort Tompkins.[4]

The next naval engagement occurred two weeks later on the St. Lawrence River. The Provincial Marine sent two warships on a reconnaissance responding to reports of American civilian schooners at Ogdensburg, about seventy miles down the St. Lawrence River. Woolsey dispatched the schooner *Julia* to challenge the British. *Julia*'s armament consisted of the 32-pounder pivot gun that had been fired in defense of Sackett's Harbor and two long six-pounders. Acting Lieutenant Henry Wells caught up with the two British vessels near Elizabethtown (now Brockville) on July 31. In the three-hour cannonade, neither side could inflict serious damage. That evening, Wells brought *Julia* to Ogdensburg. The Provincial Marine arrived on August 1 but declined to attack. When news of the temporary armistice arrived, *Julia* and the civilian vessels returned to the lake.

The American supply line between New York City and Oswego was well inland and generally secure. However, the British supply line between Quebec and Kingston was vulnerable to attack along the one hundred miles of the Upper St. Lawrence River that served as the international boundary. The British war effort was dependent on supplies, naval stores, and reinforcements travelling this water route. Land transport was impractical because of abysmal roads and lack of wagons, teamsters, and animals. The British dedicated ever-increasing resources of men, bateaux, and gunboats to operate this vital supply line. By the end of the war, as many as 4,000 men drafted from Lower Canada were engaged in ferrying cargo along the St. Lawrence. Yet, American strategists did not add the mission of cutting the Upper St. Lawrence until 1814, and this task remained undone when peace was restored.[5]

In a report to the governor, Brig. Gen. Jacob Brown expressed concern that the militiamen at Sackett's Harbor and other posts expected discharge promptly three months after they mustered in, as well as $6.66 per month and a "reasonable amount of clothing." Brown warned that it would be a "knotty business" if the men were retained longer than their term of service. The governor disbanded the regiment on time on August 20, but there was no money to pay them. The lack of prompt pay discouraged volunteers for future recruiting efforts.[6]

While the navy focused on gaining control of Lake Ontario, Governor Tompkins worked with Maj. Gen. Henry Dearborn to allocate manpower to defend New York City and the North Country while reinforcing the two offensives across the Niagara River and toward Montreal. The governor released the militia raised in May at the end of their term of service. Dearborn requisitioned two brigades of detached militia to defend the frontier between Oswego and St. Regis. Tompkins ordered Brig. Gen. Richard Dodge's Fourth Brigade of Detached Militia to the defense of Sackett's Harbor. Jacob Brown's Fifth Brigade of Detached Militia was responsible for Ogdensburg and the length of the St. Lawrence River to St. Regis. The mobilization did not proceed smoothly. Federal authorities had failed to deliver the expected camp equipment and wagons at the rendezvous sites. On September 9, Tompkins wrote to Woolsey that he was "thunderstruck" that some parts of Dodge's Brigade had failed to march. Dodge arrived at Sackett's Harbor on September 23, at the head of about 1,800 militiamen.[7] Brown marched his men to Ogdensburg, arriving on October 1. Being senior to Brown, Dodge exercised overall command of both brigades. However, given the distance between Sackett's Harbor and St. Regis, 125 miles along poor roads, Brown effectively held an independent command.

Tompkins believed that the 13,500 detached militiamen authorized by the War Department were too few to defend the frontiers and New York City. Perhaps he harkened back to the Revolution, a time when native warriors allied to the British ran rampant throughout the Mohawk Valley. The dread of Tecumseh's warbands had been key to Hull's surrender of Detroit. Would Canadian tribes join that charismatic leader and bring the war farther east? Citing the "savage barbarity" expected of Britain's native allies, Tompkins ordered ten volunteer companies to active service, five each at Plattsburgh and Sackett's Harbor.[8]

A company of the First Rifle Regiment commanded by Capt. Benjamin Forsyth of North Carolina was part of the garrison at Sackett's Harbor. On September 21, Forsyth led about seventy riflemen by bateaux into the St. Lawrence River to raid the settlement at Gananoque. This village was a transloading point along the British convoy route. Arriving on the 24th, Forsyth's men easily drove off the sixty militiamen defending the village, destroyed some foodstuffs, and started their return voyage. When word of Forsyth's raid reached Kingston, the British sent out a force to intercept the Americans. They were too late; Forsyth's raiders had returned safely. The British party landed at Briton's Point and burned a block house before returning to Kingston.[9]

On October 1, the Provincial Marine's *Royal George* seized a sloop and a revenue cutter at the mouth of the Genesee River. The raiders left after harassing the villagers in Charlotte. Although outgunning the American squadron, the Provincial Marine was unable to control the lake. Its sailors had been unable to transition from transporters to warriors. Jacob Brown was aware of the number of schooners, both recently captured or still in civilian ownership, available on the lake. He wrote to Tompkins that bringing these vessels into American service with suitable crews "would at once command the lake and the St. Lawrence . . . and may I ask your Excellency, in the name of all that is holy, why this has not been done?"[10] It took presidential action to answer Brown's question.

Late in August, Madison was digesting the sour news of Hull's catastrophic surrender at Detroit. The war effort was faltering, and Madison resolved to put it back into motion. The president concluded that control of the Great Lakes was necessary to support operations. To that end, Madison gave the commandant of the New York Naval Yard, Capt. Isaac Chauncey, the daunting task of building up the naval forces on Lakes Ontario, Erie, and Champlain and destroying British naval power. The president gave Chauncey wide-ranging authority as well as the title "commodore."[11]

Chauncey's five years' experience overseeing ship repair and supply operations provided the right skill set to build a fleet at a frontier navy yard. He sent the talented shipbuilder Henry Eckford, along with 140 shipwrights, to Sackett's Harbor. Soon to follow were about six hundred officers and crewmen and one hundred marines. Among the officers was Lt. Jesse Elliott, who famously captured the *Detroit* and the *Caledonia*. Initially, Chauncey would have no staff at Sackett's Harbor, so he worked with John Bullus, the naval agent at New York City, to purchase and transport cannon, ammunition, cable, sails, anchors, tools, and a myriad of other necessary items. Three weeks after receipt of his orders, Chauncey finally headed north. He coordinated his operations with Dearborn and Tompkins in Albany, and then he and the governor continued on to Sackett's Harbor, arriving on October 6. He approved Woolsey's work and began the expansion of the facilities and the squadron. Chauncey wrote to Secretary of the Navy Paul Hamilton that he hoped to "proceed on service by the first of November."[12]

While at Sackett's Harbor, the governor was sorely impressed by the numerous shortfalls in preparedness. In a letter to Dearborn, Tompkins insisted that the defense of the naval base was "indispensable." The weather was growing increasingly bitter. Tompkins requested that Dearborn send blankets, overcoats, ammunition, picks, and axes immediately. He also requested a regiment of regulars to replace the uniformed militia who would be returning home in December. Finally, he opined that the garrison would still be "no more than barely competent" to protect the warships and shipyard. Dearborn responded that he had ordered ammunition for Sackett's Harbor, "but that by some mistake or fatality it had taken the route to Niagara." As the weather grew worse, Tompkins gave General Dodge funds to build huts so that the militiamen could move out of tents as soon as possible.[13]

Chauncey and Tompkins sailed to Oswego on October 18, where Chauncey bought more schooners to create a squadron of ten warships. He needed the vessels to transport guns to Sackett's Harbor. The commercial schooners were a stopgap measure while awaiting purpose-built warships. Adding guns to the deck raised the center of gravity, putting the vessels at greater risk in a storm. Also, a commercial schooner had detachable handrails rather than a warship's bulwarks. Bulwarks protected gun crews from enemy fire. However, the lack of bulwarks would be an advantage for schooners armed with pivot guns, allowing the gun's crew to lower the gun nearly to deck level. Chauncey returned to Sackett's Harbor while Tompkins proceeded to Buffalo, meeting with his militia commanders along the way. At each stop, he gauged the preparedness of units and commissioned or brevetted officers to fill vacancies in the companies and regiments.

The commodore prepared the merchant schooners for their new role as warships and, on November 8, brought *Oneida* and six schooners out of Sackett's Harbor in search of British prey. The Americans found the *Royal George* the next day and gave chase. *Royal George* gained the safety of Kingston harbor despite receiving some damage to sails and rigging. The Americans prowled around the eastern end of the lake until high winds and snow gales closed navigation. Chauncey had won temporary command of Lake Ontario. He bragged to Secretary Hamilton, "I think myself now so completely Master of this lake." His short voyage demonstrated the inability of the Provincial Marine to protect shipping; the Americans captured or burned three commercial vessels. Chauncey's shipbuilding efforts were rewarded with the launching of the corvette *Madison* on November 26.[14]

Dearborn finally responded to Tompkins's plea for regulars to protect Sackett's Harbor. Understandably, Dearborn had sent most of his troops to the Niagara frontier and Lake Champlain to support the planned invasions. He clearly could not depend upon militiamen to cross an international border, but regulars did not have this option. However, he agreed with Tompkins's assessment of the crucial importance of Sackett's Harbor, and he allocated a small number of regulars to join the permanent garrison. On November 8, Col. Alexander Macomb and about four hundred soldiers of the Third U.S. Artillery Regiment departed Greenbush on a 210-mile march.

Six days later, the artillerists passed through the town of Russia in Herkimer County. Perhaps the citizenry were anti-war Federalists or perhaps the soldiers had used fence rails for firewood or raided barns looking for food. In any event, a crowd confronted the soldiers as they were leaving town. In the ensuing brawl, three officers drove off four attackers, leaving one with a broken jaw. The fight drew a larger crowd. The adjutant recorded the following in the regimental order book: "After which the citizens of the said village Russia collected as posse comitatus in the road thereby impeding the progress of the rear guard. Lt. Biddle however aware of the efficiency of the bayonet charged upon this multitudinous assembly with the most undaunted bravery. This assembly being unable to withstand the resistless fury & impetuosity of the Guard, who threw this posse into a panic by the violence of their onset, fled the field in the utmost horror & distraction."[15]

On November 21, the Third Artillery arrived at Sackett's Harbor. The adjutant noted that it was "a miserable cold place on the shores of Lake Ontario." Chauncey was thankful for the regulars' arrival. Macomb's artillerymen were versatile, able to fight as infantry as well as crewing heavy guns. They quickly built log quarters, improved fortifications, and established a laboratory to assemble artillery ammunition. Macomb, the senior regular army officer, quickly established a cordial working relationship with Generals Dodge and Brown as well as with Chauncey.[16]

Captain Forsyth's September raid on Gananoque touched off a series of fights along the St. Lawrence River. Ogdensburg in New York and Prescott in Upper Canada were key transshipment sites along the river. Here, cargo brought downriver on deep-draft schooners was transferred to shallow-draft vessels to navigate the rapids en route to Montreal. Before the war, merchants of the two cities had carried on a vigorous trade—American potash, flour, and meat for European goods. By October, artillery batteries on both shores impeded trade important to both communities. Dearborn and Governor General Prevost both refused to condone raids across the border for fear of igniting a sequence of retaliatory actions that would bring suffering to civilians without commensurate military advantage. Sanctioned or not, local commanders saw advantages in further fighting.

Governor Tompkins recognized the importance of defending Ogdensburg. In a letter to David Parish, an extraordinarily successful landowner and merchant of that city, Tompkins noted that Ogdensburg was an important military station. Parish was also a major subscriber to the Treasury Department's loans that were needed to prosecute the war. Tompkins lamented that British control of the waterways and the "almost impassable state of the roads" precluded getting "a force proportioned to its importance" to Ogdensburg before spring. As the governor wrote, he was unaware that the first engagement at that place had already occurred.[17]

On October 4, Col. Robert Lethbridge led about 725 British fencibles and militia in an amphibious crossing to destroy American gun positions and open the British supply line, at least until the arrival of winter's ice. General Brown and 1,200 men, mostly militia, turned back the assault. As soon as the governor learned of the attempt to capture Ogdensburg, he asked General Dodge at Sackett's Harbor to send riflemen and two artillery pieces and crews, about 120 soldiers, to travel by land to reinforce Brown's forces.[18]

The British made a stronger assault across the ice on February 22, 1813. Major George Macdonell, known locally as "Red George," led his regiment, the Glengarry Light Infantry Fencibles, other regulars, and three hundred militiamen in a determined attack that surprised the American defenders. Newly promoted Maj. Benjamin Forsyth and his company of regular riflemen offered obstinate resistance and accurate fire. However, the militiamen largely left the fighting to the riflemen. Outnumbered, Forsyth withdrew before being encircled. The British destroyed the batteries, barracks, and gunboats. When word of the attack reached Albany, Tompkins ordered Jacob Brown to take seven hundred militiamen from his brigade to drive off the invaders. However, the British had returned to Prescott. Forsyth pleaded, "If you can send me three hundred men all shall be retaken, and Prescott too, or I will lose my life in the attempt."[19] Forsyth's superiors (Dearborn and Macomb) decided not to retake the village. For the rest of the war, British supply convoys passed the demilitarized American settlement, and civilian trade continued. Ogdensburg was also home to some Americans who actively passed information to both sides.[20]

Late in 1812, two small engagements disturbed the tranquility along the land border between New York and Upper Canada. On October 23, Maj. Guilford Dudley Young led about two hundred New York militiamen to raid the small British post at Akwesasne. Young forwarded the captured flag to Albany, and Tompkins displayed it in the state capitol. He noted that the gallantry of Young's men bore "ample testimony of the valor and patriotism of the militia of the State of New York."[21] Young's minor victory paled in comparison to the catastrophic loss at Queenston Heights just ten days earlier. The British retaliated one month later by raiding the militia post at French Mills on the Salmon River eight miles east of St. Regis. The raiders surprised the garrison and destroyed weapons, ammunition, and bateaux.

Over the winter, operations at Sackett's Harbor continued unabated. The first order of business was construction of additional barracks to replace the tents that were inadequate for the notoriously frigid weather. Work parties also improved Fort Volunteer to the east of the naval yard. Chauncey and Macomb contemplated attacking Kingston across the ice; however, they expended more mental energy in developing tactics to guard against British attack. They were wary of spies within the naval base passing information to the British in Kingston.[22] Navy and marine contingents kept ships' decks cleared of snow and maintained firearms and cutlasses in easy access. Crews broke the ice around the ships to deter storming parties and to open holes from which water could be drawn to douse fires. This practice also relieved the hull of the pressure produced by the ice. The crews remained on ship each evening. While sailors and marines defended the ships, soldiers and militiamen manned the several forts, blockhouses, and gun batteries on the periphery of the base. If the British hazarded a winter assault, they would not win for lack of American preparation or determination.

Nevertheless, Chauncey was dissatisfied with the militia. From the 1,000 militiamen assigned, Chauncey estimated that no more than six hundred were fit for duty. He complained to Navy Secretary Paul Hamilton, "even this number is every day diminished by desertion, discharges, and furloughs." The term of service expired at the end of December, leaving the base even more vulnerable to attack. He wrote desperately to Dearborn, "I am really alarmed Sir for the safety of our little Fleet collected here & trust you will deem their preservation of so much importance to our future operations against Canada, as to induce you to order to this post as soon as convenient 1000 additional regular Troops: the militia will not do." Dearborn, of course, had no soldiers to spare.[23]

Chauncey took a few weeks to oversee two of his other responsibilities—the naval activities at Black Rock and Presque Isle, Pennsylvania. Operations at the naval yard on Conjocta Creek were a grave disappointment. Lt. Samuel Angus commanded there, and apart from maintaining a few acquired commercial schooners, Chauncey believed the officer had done virtually nothing to prepare for the coming season. Angus insisted he had done everything he could, and Chauncey lost his temper. Chauncey arrested Angus for insubordination and put Lt. John Pettigrew in command. Both the commodore and Angus wrote irate letters to Hamilton. The Navy Department eventually reassigned Angus, a solution mutually acceptable to both officers.[24]

Chauncey was better pleased at Presque Isle, near the small community of Erie, Pennsylvania. He gave the go-ahead to Sailing Master Daniel Dobbins to construct gunboats and a brig for the nascent Lake Erie squadron. Once back at Sackett's Harbor, Chauncey accepted Master Commandant Oliver Hazard Perry's offer to join the commodore's command. A major challenge for Chauncey in 1813 would be to balance the resources provided to his Ontario and Erie squadrons commensurate with their strategic importance.

On November 11, Governor Tompkins reported to the Legislature that approximately 2,400 militiamen—volunteers, detached militia, and ninety-day common militia—were in service from Sackett's Harbor to St. Regis.[25] Tompkins paid off and discharged the detached militiamen from Dodge's and Brown's brigades. The governor replaced the militia with smaller units of volunteers who had enlisted for one year of service.[26]

The year had been eventful in the North Country, although the Americans had fallen short of their military goals. Raids on the St. Lawrence River accomplished nothing except to encourage the British attack in the following February. The failure of federal officials to provide transport and equipment to mobilizing militiamen contributed to the one-month gap in militia coverage at Oswego and Sackett's Harbor. Yet without a major battle in the region on the scale of Queenston Heights, the lack of federal-state cooperation was not evident. Chauncey had wrested temporary control of the lake, but Kingston remained out of reach. The arrival of the Royal Navy in 1813 would heavily challenge the commodore. Governor Tompkins, for his part, worked hard to overcome institutional inertia in maintaining a credible militia presence on the frontiers. The final act of the war in 1812 occurred to the east with Dearborn's invasion.

CHAPTER 5

LAKE CHAMPLAIN

The War Department's plan for 1812 was to conduct three simultaneous invasions. Brig. Gen. William Hull would attack across the Detroit River and Maj. Gen. Stephen Van Rensselaer across the Niagara River. Maj. Gen. Henry Dearborn intended the main attack to seize Montreal to cut the British supply line. Hull surrendered Detroit in August, and Van Rensselaer's invasion collapsed in October. The Battle of Queenston Heights presaged the failures of preparation that would appear in Dearborn's invasion. The general unwillingness of detached militia to cross the international border robbed Dearborn of manpower. Additionally, administrative incompetence and vast distances combined to yield an irresistible friction to Dearborn's plans. The federal government's inability to recruit, equip, move, and train sufficient regular troops in a timely manner condemned his operation to failure.

The regular army assembled at Greenbush for organizing, equipping, and training. From there, Dearborn sent regiments to the Niagara frontier and Lake Champlain. In August, Gen. Morgan Lewis provided President Madison with a summary of the status of the Northern Army.

> We have as yet but the shadow of a regular force—inferior even in numbers, to half of what the enemy has already in the field—ill supplied with clothing, camp equipage, ammunition and ordnance. Not more than a fourth of the artillery of the park is mounted—and of that most of the carriages fail from being constructed of unseasoned timber. The staff departments are defective in organization, and the war is decreasing in popularity from the intrigues of designing and pretended republicans, and the severe duties necessarily imposed on the militia; a body at all times inadequate to offensive operations.[1]

Activities at Greenbush through the fall demonstrated little evidence of improvement. Regular troops passed through that site, with about half heading toward the Lake Champlain region for the operation against Montreal.

Lake Champlain was part of the near-continuous waterway connecting New York City, Albany, and Montreal. New Yorkers and the people of Vermont could hardly forget the battles of Bennington and Saratoga that turned back a major invasion in 1777. Henry Dearborn creditably led a battalion of light infantry in that campaign. Now, Dearborn reversed the direction of invasion. However, in June 1812, Governor Daniel Tompkins focused on the state's defense. New York and Vermont shared Lake Champlain; thus, there were three persons with defense responsibilities—Dearborn, Tompkins, and Governor Jonas Galusha of Vermont. Galusha was a veteran of the Revolution and a Republican. He supported Dearborn's calls for militia, and he led the legislature in forbidding trade with Canada, an unpopular law to be sure. New York and Vermont smugglers exploited the growing British demand for food. Tompkins corresponded with Dearborn and Galusha to share information and coordinate defensive measures. Tompkins directed Gen. Benjamin Mooers to correspond directly with Col. Isaac Clark, commander of the Eleventh U.S. Infantry stationed at Burlington, "so that mutual assistance may be given." In a letter to Clark, Tompkins pledged "that everything in my power shall be performed to render the Canadian frontier on each side of the Lake secure from the Incursions of the enemy."[2]

Governor Tompkins exercised his authority to shore up the defenses in the Champlain Valley. He wrote to Robert R. Livingston, owner of the only steamboat operating on Lake Champlain and Robert Fulton's partner, requesting priority use of the vessel in moving troops and supplies from Whitehall to Plattsburgh. He made no secret that failure to approve use would result in state troops commandeering the steamboat. "The State of the Champlain Frontier and the necessity of reinforcing would justify me in putting the Steamboat in requisition or pressing her into the above service without the volition of the owners, but I prefer your acquiescence in the use which I propose to make of her." Livingston agreed and in closing added, "Permit me to offer your Excellency my acknowledgment for your polite attention to our rights."[3]

One of the first regular army officers to arrive at Plattsburgh was Capt. Mordecai Myers of the Thirteenth U.S. Infantry. His orders were to recruit and to guard federal stores and bateaux in the village. The citizens complained that a recruiting officer had paraded his recruits through the streets with drums and fifes "at unreasonable hours of the night." Myers halted the practice. However, the regular army Capt. Myers soon came into conflict with militia Gen. Mooers. Passing militiamen failed to give proper countersigns when challenged by Myers's guards, although Myers provided the parole and countersign to militia officers each day. The guards threw the offending militiamen, including an aide to Mooers, into the guardhouse. Myers released the offenders promptly.

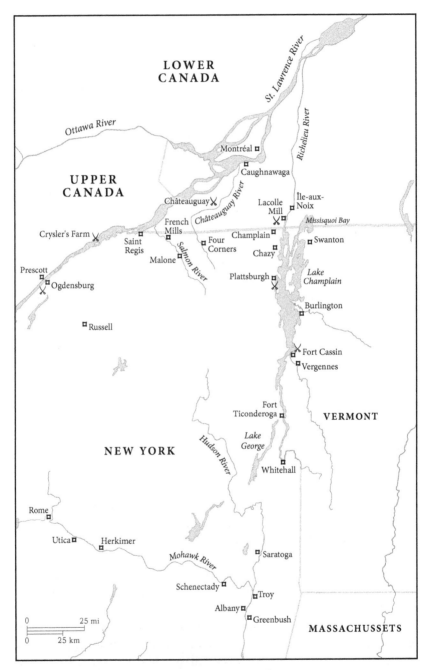

LOWER
CANADA

Ottawa River

St. Lawrence River

UPPER
CANADA

Montréal □

Caughnawaga □

Richelieu River

Châteauguay ✕

Châteauguay River

Lacolle
Mill ✕□

Île-aux-
Noix

Crysler's Farm ✕□

French
Mills □

Saint
Regis

Champlain □

Four
Corners □

Missisquoi Bay

Swanton □

Prescott □

Malone □

Salmon River

Chazy □

Plattsburgh □ ✕

*Lake
Champlain*

Ogdensburg ✕

Russell □

Burlington
□

Fort Cassin ✕
□
Vergennes □

Fort
Ticonderoga □

*Lake
George*

VERMONT

NEW YORK

Hudson River

Whitehall □

Rome □

Utica □ Herkimer □

Mohawk River

Saratoga □

Schenectady □

Troy □

Albany □
□ Greenbush

MASSACHUSSETS

0 ___ 25 mi
0 ___ 25 km

Lake Champlain region. Map by Erin Greb Cartography.

The next day, Mooers ordered the regulars out of the village. Myers protested, persuading Mooers to allow the regular-army contingent to resume guarding federal property. Negotiation diffused regular militia tension. It could not have hurt that both Mooers and Myers were Republicans and active in state politics.[4]

Of course, the militia was not free from internal tensions. Mordecai Myers recollected a dueling incident between two militia officers. They chose to stand in the lake's waters to circumvent the state law disenfranchising duelers. Their seconds had secretly loaded the pistols with blood instead of ball, perhaps to preclude actual bloodshed or as a prank. The antagonists fired and one of them fell into the water. His second pulled him up to find him covered in blood. Myers recalled that, "It was some time before he could be convinced that he was not mortally wounded."[5]

Regular reinforcements joined Myers, and by the end of September, three regular infantry regiments were at Plattsburgh. Col. Jonas Simonds commanded the Sixth Infantry, and Col. Zebulon Montgomery Pike commanded the Fifteenth Infantry. These formations were joined at the end of the month by Col. Simon Learned and the Ninth Infantry as well as Capt. Alexander S. Brooks's company of the Third Artillery Regiment.

The arrival of these regulars moved the governor to modify his command arrangements. Tompkins felt compelled to remove Mooers from command at Plattsburgh. As the governor explained to Mooers, Brig. Gen. Joseph Bloomfield had departed New York City to command the brigade of regulars at Plattsburgh. Since the regulars outnumbered the militia, a command arrangement with a state officer in overall command was unseemly. Furthermore, the number of soldiers—militia or regulars—did not justify a major general's command. Eventually Brig. Gen. Micajah Pettit of Washington County commanded the detached militia in federal service in and around Plattsburgh. The governor's actions supported healthy federal–state relations.[6]

On September 15, Tompkins ordered Lt. Col. Peter Vosburgh to bring his regiment of detached militia to Plattsburgh. The governor apprised Bloomfield of the move of Vosburgh's men and requested that Bloomfield train them "industriously." In particular, he noted the field officers were ignorant of their duties. However, the soldiers of the volunteer companies also marching to Plattsburgh were "tolerably well" trained. He added that "some of the privates of those Companies are amongst the most respectable young men of the towns to which they belong."[7]

Throughout September, Dearborn struggled to resource and coordinate two offenses: his and Van Rensselaer's on the Niagara River. He feared that Brock might attack Van Rensselaer before troops on the march could arrive. Dearborn was heartened that Madison finally understood the importance of control on Lakes Ontario and Champlain; nevertheless, it would take a while for that understanding to translate into warships. Dearborn's analysis troubled him. He wrote to Madison that he "was compelled to relinquish all ideas of offensive operations against Montreal or its dependencies this year & to confine my movements in that quarter to a feint—which would operate as a diversion in favor of our operations on the great Lakes." Dearborn gave his appraisal of the militia, the centerpiece of Republican military policy. "The expenses of the Militia are enormous, & they are of little comparative use except at the commencement of war, and for special emergencies. The sooner we can dispense with their services, the better—on every consideration." This could not have been pleasant reading for Madison.[8]

Control of Lake Champlain was essential to both offensive and defensive operations, but the establishment of a naval force on Lake Champlain was off to a rocky start. In the absence of a naval officer, the War Department purchased six sloops. When Lt. Thomas Macdonough arrived at Whitehall on October 13, he assessed the situation. Three of the sloops were able to accept naval guns. Macdonough used the others as transports. The "largest and best vessel on the Lake," the *President*, carried eight guns. Macdonough attempted to bring all six sloops under his command, but Dearborn refused to release the *President*. Dearborn had given command of *President* to a civilian who Macdonough grumbled was not even subject to martial law. Macdonough complained to Secretary of the Navy Paul Hamilton, "I am strangely deprived of more than half the force in having this vessel in the hands of those, that know not, what to do with her. Such a strange arrangement as this, having a Citizen to command the principal vessel on an expedition cannot but, be attended with fatal consequences." Macdonough had other serious problems. As late as October, no sailors or officers had arrived to crew the sloops, and Macdonough was unaware when they might appear. He was reluctant to ask for soldiers, considering them "miserable creatures on shipboard."[9]

In mid-November, American and British negotiators at Whitehall hammered out a treaty to release prisoners. Each side would immediately offer parole to their prisoners. Those accepting the offer agreed not to enter combat or perform any military service until officially exchanged. British officials agreed to transport American parolees to Boston while the Americans would move British prisoners to Saint John, New Brunswick, or to British stations on the border with New York. The treaty established procedures for exchanges and went far to relieve the unfortunate captives of the suffering sure to follow the onset of winter.[10]

During 1812, the federal and state governments attempted to persuade Native American tribes to maintain neutrality. This effort failed on the western frontier, but in New York, the tribes were inclined to stay out of the fight. However, Indian men wishing to create their reputations as warriors offered their services to the British, seeing the United States as the more threatening of white governments. Governor Tompkins met with the Indian community at St. Regis. He offered encouragement: "Brothers, I am informed that some of your young men have imprudently taken up the tomahawk and have gone to Montreal or some other place and joined the British. For this we do not blame you as a nation, but are satisfied that it was contrary to the opinion and advice of a great majority of the Sachems and Chiefs, and I hope that those young Warriors will see the impropriety of their conduct and return to their homes."[11]

Tompkins understood the deleterious effects of even a few Indian warriors to civilian morale. His efforts and those of federal agents appeared to achieve some success. British forces operating between Montreal and Plattsburgh were supported by some Indian adjuncts, but these were in small numbers and largely behaved within the standards of western warfare.

By the end of October, Dearborn regained his optimism about invading Canada. He wrote to General Smyth at Buffalo, "I expect that General Bloomfield will move immediately towards Montreal, and I calculate on his being able to beat up the several posts between his camp and the river St. Lawrence." He shared with Secretary of War William Eustis that Montreal might be taken "with but little risk." Despite an attack of rheumatism, Dearborn moved from Greenbush to Plattsburgh, arriving on November 15. Bloomfield moved his brigade northward the following day. However, Bloomfield fell ill. Dearborn took personal command of the offensive, and by November 18, the Americans were at Champlain, two miles from the border. Scouts reported that the British numbered as many as 3,500 regulars, militiamen, and Indian warriors. At that time, Dearborn had about 2,000 militiamen from New York and Vermont and as many as 2,800 regulars.[12]

Unfortunately for Dearborn, his militia officers reported that many of their men, perhaps as many as one-half, would refuse to cross the border. Dearborn called a council of war to examine his options. Understanding that their diminished force would probably not be able to fight its way to Montreal, and that wintering in Upper Canada would be extremely risky, the senior officers recommended that the army enter Canada, remain a short time as a demonstration, and then return to the U.S. to establish winter quarters. Dearborn agreed.[13]

On November 20, Col. Zebulon Pike led 650 soldiers of the Fifteenth U.S. Infantry across the border. About three hundred New York militiamen marched on a parallel route. Pike's troops drove off the small garrison at Lacolle, about five miles north of the border. As Pike's men were returning to the border, they came upon the militiamen. Mistaking the regulars for British troops, the militiamen opened fire. The regulars returned the fusillade with volleys of musketry. The mistake was soon discovered, but the fratricide had inflicted nineteen casualties. Dearborn marched his men back to Plattsburgh. What was supposed to be the major offensive of the campaign year had come to naught.[14]

Entries in the orderly book of a company of detached militia captured the ruinous nature of the campaign.

> November 18   Had a General Review & the Militia are called upon to know who would go into Canada in case they were wanted for a present expedition—but few volunteered.

> November 19 & 20   Col. Pike's Regt with a part of the Militia Volunteers went about six miles into Canada to the River La Cole. Kill'd two of their own men, wounded five others, drove back about 12 Indians, burnt an old log house, & returned inglorious.[15]

Dearborn's offensive failed for a number of reasons. Foremost among them was the general failure of the recruiting efforts of the regular army. Transportation of people and necessities to Plattsburgh was slow. New officers hardly knew how to train or discipline their men. The refusal of so many militiamen to cross the border put the burden on the regulars. The net result was that Dearborn's army started the campaign too late and with too few soldiers to capture Montreal.

As for the experiment in federal-state cooperation, the campaign showed mixed results. The friction resulting from regulars jailing militiamen for failure to use the countersign was resolved by compromise. Likewise, Tompkins's removal of Major General Mooers from overall command was correct and enacted before it became an issue. However, Dearborn's negative attitude toward the value of militiamen in general was certain to pervade the regulars. This negative mindset was certainly reinforced when only fifteen percent of the available militiamen volunteered to set foot on British territory.

After the aborted invasion, Dearborn dismissed the militia. He sent Bloomfield's Brigade of three regiments of regulars into winter quarters at Plattsburgh and Gen. John Chandler's Brigade, also of three regiments, to Burlington, Vermont. Bloomfield requested and was granted leave to return to his home. Madison reassigned the former governor of New Jersey to command the Fourth Military District and specifically the defense of Philadelphia.[16]

The winter encampment was particularly brutal for the troops. Bloomfield had done little to prepare shelters for his men. Surgeon's Mate William Beaumont, who later achieved fame for his observations of the working of the human stomach, was the regimental surgeon for the Sixth Infantry wintering at Plattsburgh. The men slept in tents with only a fire at the entrance to warm them. By late December, the soldiers moved into huts they had built at Camp Saranac, about four miles from the village.[17]

Sickness was rampant during the fall, with as much as one-third of Dearborn's army contracting measles. While not deadly in itself, the illness weakened the men. Doctors used mercury and opium as treatments, along with various herbal medicines. During winter quarters, dysentery, pneumonia, and typhus were killers. Typhus, carried by body lice and fleas, was magnified by overcrowding in tents and crude shelters. Beaumont recalled that the treatment for pleurisy and pneumonia was "copious bleeding." During December and January, as many as four hundred soldiers died of disease at Plattsburgh and Burlington.[18]

In December, the ladies of Hudson and Newburgh knitted hundreds of pairs of socks and mittens for the militiamen serving in the North Country. Tompkins sent his personal appreciation to the "amiable and benevolent ladies" for their "female tenderness and generosity."[19] The men also required wool blankets and overcoats to maintain their health. Neither the state nor federal governments had the foresight to acquire these items. As 1812 closed on the frontiers of the nation, Madison's war effort had all but collapsed.

CHAPTER 6

NEW YORK CITY

In addition to supporting two invasions of Canada and the general defense of its immense frontier, New York state officials were frantically assembling a creditable defense of the nation's largest city and major port. Although the federal government could spare few regular forces, it harnessed some of the city's energy and resources to launch privateers upon the ocean and to build the lake squadrons. New York came alive to adapting to wartime life and engaging in the presidential campaign of 1812.

News that Congress had declared war on June 18, 1812, reached New York City on June 20 and Albany three days later. Tompkins, with his adjutant general, Lt. Col. William Paulding Jr., moved to New York City. As commander in chief of state forces, Tompkins put troops into motion for the defense of New York City. He ordered the First Brigade of Detached Militia into service, along with artillery and cavalry units selected for service in detached units. Brig. Gen. Gerard Steddiford, who led state troops during the Revolution, commanded the First Brigade. Tompkins directed his militia commanders to coordinate movement routes directly with Brig. Gen. Joseph Bloomfield of the regular army, under whose command the militia would now fall. New Jersey's quota of the 100,000 detached militiamen was 5,000. Several New Jersey units fell under General Bloomfield's command and were prepared to serve in the city's defenses if called upon.[1]

Lt. Col. Jonas Mapes led one of Steddiford's regiments. His regiment was raised in New York City and Staten Island. The rolls prepared for Mapes's unit at the time of muster reveal a bit about the process. Capt. Robert Hyslop's company was typical. One man was discharged for being underage, another because he was already in the regular army, and a third because he was an alien. Three men were released from service because they were a fireman, a college student, and a schoolmaster. Another never saw service because he was in prison, and four "absconded," apparently not showing up for muster.

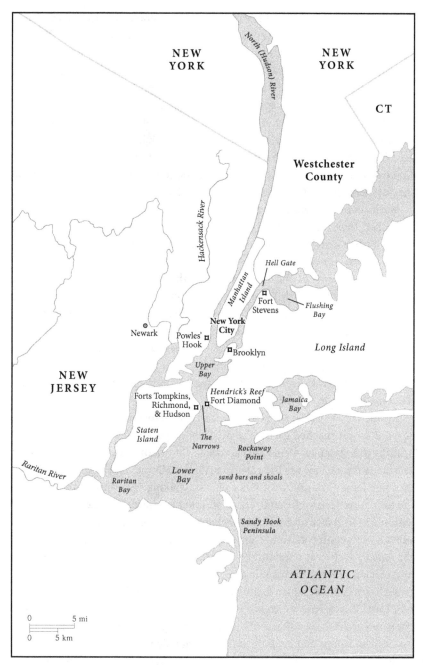

New York City and vicinity. Map by Erin Greb Cartography.

Other companies discharged persons for being overage, for already serving in state artillery units, for being a Quaker, or for being "unfit for duty." This last category carried no further explanation. Service in the detached militia offered shelter, meals, and continual employment for many of the city's working poor.[2]

The Madison administration had initially resisted calls to expand the navy. The war would be won by capturing key Canadian cities, supported by the success of privateers. However, it became clear that mobilization of the army was proceeding slowly, thus delaying the administration's land war. Secretary of the Navy Paul Hamilton issued the necessary orders to his captains to sail. American merchant vessels needed protection returning to port, and the Treasury desperately needed to collect import duties.[3]

Naval commanders in the city reacted to the news of war as soon as it reached them. On June 21, Commodore John Rodgers sailed out of New York's harbor with the frigates *President*, *United States*, and *Congress*, and the sloops-of-war *Hornet* and *Argus*. Rodgers chased off the blockading vessels. Capt. David Porter of the *Essex* departed the bay on July 3, but not before he dispatched an English-born sailor to the city, tarred and feathered by his crewmates.[4] Porter became the first navy officer to capture a British warship when he defeated the *Alert* in August. Shortly after Porter's departure, the Royal Navy returned to the lower bay and began capturing stray merchant vessels. However, during the temporary absence of blockading warships, dozens of merchant ships slipped into the harbor. Their import duties were a welcome benefit to the federal treasury.[5]

Royal Navy vessels captured American merchants on the high seas as soon as word of war reached them. The *Minerva* departed New York City in April, heading to Ireland. HMS *Acteon* captured *Minerva* in July as the merchantman was on its return voyage. The captain of *Acteon*, David Smith, impressed crewmember James Tompkins of Ulster County, along with three others. When the four Americans refused to serve on his ship, Smith had the men whipped with over 180 lashes over a three-week period. Smith ordered the men to fight when *Acteon* confronted and captured a French vessel, but they refused. When the *Acteon* docked at London, the Americans gained their liberty through the intercession of the American Consul.[6]

As Royal Navy warships tightened their hold on New York City, the economy trembled. Prices rose as goods became scarce. Within months, the British government acted to preserve the shipments of grain from American ports to feed British troops and civilians on the Iberian Peninsula. Many of these shipments left from New York City. British authorities sold licenses to American grain shippers that would protect vessels and cargoes from capture. U.S. Navy warships and privateers, however, sought to capture these merchantmen because they were violating the Embargo Act of April 4, 1812. The British licenses were so valuable that at least one New Yorker printed and sold counterfeit licenses.[7]

Many politicians, Thomas Jefferson and Henry Clay among them, supported the trade with the British, as it brought much needed specie into the country. However, Congress eventually supported President Madison and in July 1813 passed the Foreign License Bill, which specifically condemned the grain trade. The issue was rendered moot that year as Napoleon's Continental System was effectively eviscerated and European flour fed British troops.

Locals clandestinely rowed out to British ships guarding the Lower Bay to sell food for the crews. Local authorities questioned whether spies passed information such as cargo ship departures to Royal Navy captains. The federal government enacted a measure to identify British citizens on American soil, requiring enemy aliens to register with U.S. marshals. By 1813, about 2,300 British citizens were in or had passed through Manhattan. The federal government's lenient policy toward enemy aliens was in stark contrast to that of Governor Sir George Prevost in Quebec, who had ordered all Americans to leave British North America unless they took an oath of allegiance and agreed to bear arms if called upon.[8]

The U.S. Navy maintained facilities and operational units at New York. Capt. Isaac Chauncey was commandant of the navy yard at Brooklyn. Chauncey served during the Quasi War with France and the First Barbary War. Secretary of the Navy Hamilton needed Chauncey's skills for bigger things and, in September, ordered Chauncey to command naval forces on the Great Lakes. On September 23, Chauncey, now elevated to the title of commodore, departed for Sackett's Harbor. Once the warships departed New York, Chauncey's operational forces consisted of twenty gunboats, each armed with a twenty-four-pounder long gun or similar weapon. Sailors rowed the gunboats; thus, they could still move when a lack of wind rendered sailing vessels immobile.

Several civilian shipyards dotted the East River, the most prominent of these being those owned by shipbuilders Adam and Noah Brown. Christian Bergh, who operated his own yard, had superintended the construction of the frigate *President*. Bergh had built *Oneida* on Lake Ontario at Oswego. Near Bergh's facility on the East River was that of Henry Eckford. Isaac Chauncey hired Eckford to head up the shipbuilding effort at Sackett's Harbor, while Noah Brown oversaw construction of the Lake Erie squadron. Meanwhile, Bergh and Adam Brown recruited ships' carpenters and other skilled workers and sent them to the navy yards on the Great Lakes. Eckford built some of the vessels in Oliver Hazard Perry's Lake Erie squadron at the Black Rock shipyard, as did Noah Brown at Erie, Pennsylvania. On Lake Champlain, the Browns built several privateers as well as warships. Much of the success of the U.S. Navy

Manhattan and upper bay. Map by Erin Greb Cartography.

on the Great Lakes was due to the management skills of these New York City shipbuilders and hundreds of their carpenters and workers.

A sizeable increase in the number of exempt militia companies during the first six months of the war reflected a general burst of patriotism. Tompkins recognized these volunteers and appointed their officers. No one expected that the exempts would deploy; their contribution to the war effort was entirely local. These men could provide security and general service to the community while other citizens served their tour of duty with the detached militia. The presence of the exempt company meant that there was a body with purpose and direction to resolve local issues in the best interest of the community. While a number of exempt companies were in existence prior to the declaration of war, beginning in June, the governor recognized twenty-eight additional companies. The new organizations chose names such as the Silver Greys, the Franklin Volunteer Exempts, and the Madrid Veterans. The expansion of the number of exempt companies reflected not only an expression of patriotism, but also a spirit that the defensive effort was everyone's duty. Thus, party affiliation might play only a small role in the individual's decision to join an exempt company.

Demand for wartime information stimulated the start of a fresh newspaper in New York City. Samuel Woodworth, who later established a reputation as a poet, playwright, and novelist, was an avid supporter of the administration. In June, he published *The War*, a four-page weekly paper. *The War* reported on diplomatic and political activities as well as news from battlefield and naval actions. Interestingly, unlike most newspapers of the day, *The War* carried little advertising. Woodworth continued publishing throughout the conflict.[9]

On July 31, Col. Jonathan Williams, chief engineer of the army and the person most responsible for the design and construction of the defenses of New York City, resigned his commission in the regular army. Capt. George Armistead's arrival at Bedloe's Island in April prompted this unfortunate act. Armistead, who would command Fort McHenry during the September 1814 crisis, complained that a recently implemented policy from Eustis was illegal. Secretary of War Eustis, having Williams in mind, had given Gen. Bloomfield permission to place an officer of the Corps of Engineers in command of a fortification. Armistead represented eighteen other officers of the regular army and argued that an engineer could not command line units. Eustis relented, prompting Williams to resign in protest. New York then immediately hired Williams to oversee construction of state fortifications.

On August 11, Brig. Gen. John Armstrong replaced Bloomfield as commander at New York City. Bloomfield took command of a brigade in Plattsburgh. Armstrong had been an aide to Gen. Horatio Gates in the Revolution and was the purported author of the notorious letter that launched the Newburgh

Conspiracy. Armstrong married into the politically and socially prominent Livingston family. Armstrong had been a U.S. senator and Minister to France. While generally capable, Armstrong had the odor of intrigue about him. He reentered the army at the outbreak of the war as a brigadier general and he brought with him Capt. Charles K. Gardner, a New Yorker and staunch Republican. The ever-capable Gardner served Armstrong as brigade inspector. Tompkins, to ensure a smooth transition between Bloomfield and Armstrong, sent the new commander a detailed analysis of the work required on fortifications to defend the city. He also alerted Armstrong that Robert Fulton had proposed a steam-powered gunboat for harbor defense.[10]

Some of the troops in the city chafed at the monotony of duty and wanted to experience the excitement of battle. Francis McClure requested orders for his volunteer regiment of riflemen to participate in the invasion of Canada. The governor was happy to grant this request and, in September, McClure's troops moved by boat to Albany and then marched on to the Niagara frontier. Stationed at Buffalo and Black Rock under Alexander Smyth, the riflemen missed the Battle of Queenston Heights. However, McClure and some of his soldiers participated in the early battles of 1813.

When Chauncey departed for Sackett's Harbor, Secretary of the Navy Hamilton gave temporary command of the New York Navy Yard to Master Commandant Charles Ludlow. However, on October 10, he ordered Capt. Isaac Hull to assume command of all naval forces in the city and to be subject to orders from General Armstrong. Hull, now a national hero for his sensational victory over HMS *Guerriere*, was in New York to settle the affairs of his recently deceased brother. Hull immediately expressed his dissatisfaction with Hamilton's orders. "I cannot suppose it is your intention that I receive orders from General Armstrong as to the disposition or equipment of the force placed by you under my Command." Pleading the need for time to accommodate his brother's family, Hull went on to request transfer to Boston or to be granted a furlough of a few months' duration.[11] Hamilton relented, and command of the Navy Yard returned to Ludlow.

While the national government's main efforts were the military campaigns to seize the major cities of Canada, a secondary effort was on the high seas. Thomas Jefferson well understood that the British had it in their power to destroy the U.S. Navy. However, he predicted decisive results from the privateering effort. This was the second arm of the national strategy to inflict enough pain on Britain to persuade the giant to grant concessions. Hundreds of privateers set sail to seize British merchants laden with valuable cargoes.[12]

This was war for profit. As soon as war was declared, shipowners in every American port signed on large crews to sail armed vessels and sent off to the

national capital to secure commissions as privateers. Shippers had to post a
bond to ensure that their captains would not become pirates, seizing vessels
from countries other than Britain. Once at sea, the fast privateers sought British
merchantmen and threatened to fire upon them if they did not yield. Typically,
the merchant captain stopped and allowed his pursuers to take the ship to an
American port. Once there, a federal judge ruled on whether the capture met
the requirements of international law. Once the ship was judged a "good prize,"
the owner of the privateer could auction off the ship and its cargo. The federal
government collected duties on the cargo and court fees. The privateer owner
then shared the net profit with the privateer's captain and crew.[13]

Commercial interests quickly invested in privateers. By October 1812,
twenty-six privateers crewed by more than 2,200 men and carrying more than
two hundred guns called New York home port. With fewer merchant vessels
sailing, seamen scrambled to sign on to the privateers. *The War* noted, "Sailors repair to the recruiting rendezvous in such crowds that the commanders
have, in many instances, been obliged to *draw lots* [to select] who should go
on board." Eventually, New York City was home to forty-four privateers. These
vessels found open sea by sailing up the East River into Long Island Sound. The
Royal Navy focused its effort in the Lower Bay; thus, the sound offered a more
secure transit to the Atlantic.[14] The Federal District Court in New York City
was a prize court, and it handled seizures taken on Lake Champlain and the St.
Lawrence River as well as those brought into New York City.[15]

The owners of privateers assumed considerable financial risk. Voyages were
expensive, and sometimes the ships returned empty-handed. Even after a successful capture, the privateer crew had to evade the Royal Navy while returning
to a friendly port. British warships recaptured hundreds of their commercial
ships. The U.S. Navy captured 257 merchant vessels; American privateers
captured nearly 2,000. Despite these impressive numbers, privateering hardly
made a dent in British trade, certainly not enough to persuade the government
to make concessions in negotiations.

While the owner took on the financial risk, the crewmen were subject to
physical peril. Thousands found themselves in prison. In August 1812, fifteen
captains from New York, Boston, and other ports sent a letter to the State
Department from their prison in Halifax to report on the cruel treatment
received during their capture and imprisonment. They charged their captors
with firing at their crews after surrender and in some cases striking them with
cutlasses "without the least provocation for such inhumanity." Some British
robbed them of clothing and other possessions and fed them insufficiently.
"Every art has been practiced by the English officers to excite disaffection
in our men to the American Government, and to induce them to enter into

English service." These skippers estimated about 1,200 American crewmen were imprisoned with them.[16]

The plight of thousands of captured soldiers and seamen and defeats at Detroit and Queenston Heights demonstrated a failing war effort. The presidential election in November was widely seen as a referendum on Madison's administration. This was DeWitt Clinton's opportunity to gain the presidency. Clinton did not support the declaration of war, yet he had been tireless in preparing New York City's defenses. The Federalist-controlled Council of Appointment gave Clinton the rank of major general in August 1812, although Tompkins did not give him a field command. Tompkins remained Madison's firm supporter. New York Federalists in the Assembly joined Clinton's Republican supporters in giving New York's electoral votes to Clinton. Clinton's strongest supporter in the legislature was political newcomer Martin Van Buren.

Because Clinton was the anti-war candidate, he drew substantial numbers of Federalist votes. The Electoral College gave the election to Madison by a vote of 128 to 89. However, the popular vote was much closer—50.4 percent to 47.6 percent. The nation remained split on the war, but Madison retained enough political strength to continue. While Tompkins supported Madison's nomination for a second term, most New York Republicans had lined up under Clinton.

While Clinton was occupied in his presidential campaign, the governor completed his visits to militia on the frontier and returned to Albany around November 11. There, he gave a speech to the legislature proposing that the state loan $500,000 to the federal government. This proposal passed the Senate but failed in the Federalist-controlled Assembly. Tompkins reported to the legislature that 8,600 militiamen were still in service. These included one-year volunteers and detached and common militia. When all army forces were in place, the troops committed to the defense of the city and vicinity numbered approximately 2,200 New York militia, five hundred militiamen from New Jersey, and eight hundred regulars. The governor then returned to New York City, arriving around November 17 to preside over one of the city's most acclaimed observances, Evacuation Day, on November 25.[17]

That year, the city surpassed previous celebrations of the anniversary of Evacuation Day. On November 25, 1783, the British and many loyalists departed the city at the end of the Revolution.[18] In 1812, the city celebrated with a major military parade reviewed by Tompkins and Armstrong, followed by banquets conducted throughout the city. While there had been no raids made upon the city, the occasion served to remind New Yorkers that they were very much at war. The event was timed perfectly, as the first requisition of detached militia completed their tour of duty to be replaced by the next group of militiamen.

At the end of the year, the city outdid itself celebrating America's naval heroes. About September 1, news of Capt. Isaac Hull's victory over the frigate *Guerriere* reached New York. Following soon came word of Commodore Stephen Decatur's capture of HMS *Macedonian* and Master Commandant Jacob Jones's victory over His Majesty's Sloop *Frolic*. The city common council awarded these heroes the freedom of the city, the highest honor that the council could bestow. A bipartisan group of prominent citizens organized a banquet in honor of the captains and crews of the frigates *Constitution* and *United States*, and the sloop *Wasp*. Nearly five hundred guests attended the banquet on December 29. Thirteen scheduled toasts and twenty-three impromptu toasts punctuated the six-hour-long event.

As the year ended, the governor could reflect on the unsatisfactory status of the war effort. Despite the best efforts of the governor and other state officials, mobilization proceeded shakily at best. Many of the problems were the result of friction between federal and state authorities. The War Department was slow in getting federal officials such as quartermasters, commissary officers, and paymasters into the state to provide for the thousands of militiamen brought under federal authority. As early as September 9, Tompkins complained to Eustis about the refusal of the army paymaster to transfer funds directly to state paymasters. Federal funds, therefore, were given directly to Tompkins for dispersal. The governor complained that he had not agreed to handle the myriad vouchers and receipts, especially since the War Department would not pay for accountants to assist. As a result, pay arrived late for the detached militiamen. The failure to pay off the men upon discharge imposed unnecessary hardships on those who had spent months away from home and family.[19]

Tompkins selected six militia paymasters to accept funds from him and to disburse them to militiamen in detached regiments and volunteers. The federal government gave Tompkins more than $569,000. The six paymasters disbursed all but $23,191.98 that Tompkins had personally paid out.[20] Questions arose about travel expenses, chaplain's pay, remuneration for rations, and death benefits. Ambiguous pay policy plagued the governor and inconvenienced the militia. Tompkins pressed the War Department for answers, often without success.[21]

A glimpse into the militia units assigned to defend Ogdensburg illustrates the difficulties brought about when funds were not in the hands of the local commanders. In the spring of 1812, when the state called out ninety-day militia, Lt. Col. Thomas Benedict noted that the seventy-three soldiers under Lt. Elisha Griffin stationed at DeKalb had no rations. Benedict paid for rations for ten days out of his own pocket, approximately $150. The detachment was then sent to Ogdensburg. Griffin informed Benedict that the hospital had no blankets.

Benedict bought blankets, again out of his own funds. In June, Benedict commanded the Fifteenth Detached Militia Regiment at Ogdensburg. He bought shoes and axes at his own expense. The regiment was mustered out on December 28, 1812. Benedict was in Albany in the following February and met with Tompkins on the matter. Tompkins thanked Benedict for advancing the money to meet these needs and authorized immediate reimbursement.[22]

While the state reimbursed Benedict, other commanders were less fortunate. James McMahan of Pomfret Township, Chautauqua County, was captain in the regiment commanded by Col. John McMahan. In July 1812, General Van Rensselaer ordered James McMahan to protect Portland Harbor (now Barcelona) and the inhabitants there. McMahan bought provisions at his own expense for two weeks. In September, he paid for lumber to build a barracks. His troops were never paid. James Mahan claimed that the cost of feeding his company came to $332.52. In 1813, McMahan sent his petition for reimbursement and supporting vouchers and muster rolls to his assemblyman, Archibald Clark, who submitted them to the appropriate legislative committee. Clark took sick and died, and the paperwork was subsequently lost. McMahan recovered the lost documents in 1822 and his assemblyman, Thomas Campbell, took up the issue.

State authorities initially denied the petition, claiming that the regimental paymaster had drawn sufficient funds in 1813 to settle this claim. McMahan's regimental commander, John McMahan, wrote an affidavit certifying the veracity of James's claim that he never received payment. The committee again refused to approve the claim on the grounds that at this point, it was the business of the federal government to pay. McMahan sent his petition to Congress, only to have it returned to him. He was counseled that he must seek redress through the state, and afterward the state could submit its own claim to the federal government.

In 1830, James McMahan resubmitted his petition, tacking on additional personal expenses from 1814. For all his missed pay, expenses, and interest accrued, McMahan claimed a total of $771.39. Finally, the Committee on Militia and Public Defence of the State Assembly recommended that the state reimburse Captain McMahan for feeding fifty soldiers and some other expenses. In 1831, the Assembly authorized a payment of $209.50 plus interest of $117.04, for a total reimbursement of $326.54. Clearly, militia officers who cared for their men assumed a financial risk in supporting their government.[23]

Understandably, the war wreaked havoc upon state property. As militia units marched to the frontiers, those men without personal weapons drew arms and ammunition, signing a receipt at an arsenal. When the unit mustered out of service, the men returned what they had. A complete set of arms and equipment was valued at $18.75, not an inconsiderable sum given that monthly pay was $8.

The soldier was expected to pay for missing equipment. The process of mustering out was messy. Many soldiers were casualties, prisoners, ill in a hospital, or had been released from service early and therefore were not present when their unit mustered out. The state's Western District saw the brunt of fighting. Twelve arsenals or gunhouses stretched from Sackett's Harbor to the Niagara frontier. During 1812, these sites issued twenty-one artillery pieces, over 11,000 firearms, 438 kettles, and 176 tents. By the end of 1812, most of the militiamen had been mustered out or otherwise accounted for. These same arsenals reported holding only 478 muskets and twenty kettles; no tents or artillery remained.[24]

The arsenal at Batavia serves as a typical example of the wastage. In June 1815, Isaac Spencer, the third superintendent of the Batavia arsenal since the war began, reported that he had receipts from only eight companies that returned from the 1812 Niagara campaign. No doubt other companies returned weapons at Batavia, but the vouchers for those companies were missing. The militiamen eventually returned 1,446 muskets, 18 rifles, and 848 bayonets and assorted canteens and cartridge boxes. "Of the articles received in the arsenal, the muskets, rifles, bayonet belts and cartridge boxes were in the worst order. The muskets were without bayonets fitted generally." Before the development of interchangeable parts, each bayonet socket was filed to fit snugly to a specific weapon. Apparently, the arsenal workers had accepted muskets and bayonets turned in separately. In 1813, more units returned weapons and equipment. On July 1, 1813, the arsenal inventory consisted of 1,709 muskets and twenty rifles, "all foul, broken & in bad order." Additionally, the arsenal held 1,394 bayonets "some bent, all foul." Bayonets were useful tools, and it would be no surprise that a militiaman would damage his bayonet in a task other than combat. Spencer noted that these weapons were sent out to various armorers for repair "at heavy expense." Leather goods such as cartridge boxes, belts, and bayonet scabbards all required extensive cleaning, blacking, and oiling to restore them to serviceable condition. Over one hundred belts and scabbards were unrepairable. Had the war been won in 1812, the state's preparations would have been amply rewarded. However, much fighting was to come.[25]

After the failed foray into Lower Canada, General Dearborn wrote to Madison recommending that the federal government raise fifteen to twenty additional regiments. He further suggested that the focal point of the 1813 campaign should be Montreal, and if the campaign started by the first of March "would not require a very large force." Dearborn equivocated a bit, stating he thought it "more advisable to act on the defensive the next campaign than to attempt more than the strength of our regular force would be fully competent to." Dearborn rejected the notion of using militia troops for an invasion. Congress agreed with Dearborn and on January 29, 1813, authorized the creation of twenty new infantry regiments. The new recruits would enlist for a single year. Dearborn closed his letter stating it was "equally agreeable" to him to continue in service or to retire. For reasons best known to himself, the president retained Dearborn to lead the next campaign season.[26]

Activities in New York City and Albany and indeed throughout the state in 1812 highlighted the varied results of federal–state cooperation. Perhaps the most glaring disappointment of collaboration was the state Assembly's refusal to support a loan to the federal government. This was obstructionist politics pure and simple. Furthermore, ambiguous or non-existent federal pay policies hurt militiamen and their families. A citizen left his home to live and work in potentially grim circumstances for a number of months, only to return home with partial or perhaps no remuneration. During his tour of duty, his family got on as best they could without his contribution. While James McMahan's seventeen-year wait to receive reimbursement for feeding and sheltering his soldiers was an exceptional example, to a citizen-soldier living a subsistence existence, the lack of pay could be a devastating hardship. On the positive side, federal–state cooperation in erecting and manning the fortifications protecting the nation's largest city was smooth and judicious.

In 1813, the residents of New York were to witness yet another year of military activity and most of that was failure. That year marked continued suffering for soldiers, sailors, and civilians with little progress in advancing the national war goals. The year 1813 would end in utter catastrophe for thousands of residents on the Niagara frontier and in the western counties.

1813

CHAPTER 7

THE RAID ON YORK AND
THE BATTLE FOR FORT GEORGE

E arly in 1813, President Madison made two important changes to his cabinet. He replaced Secretary of the Navy Paul Hamilton with William Jones. Jones wrote to Commodore Isaac Chauncey, "It is impossible to attach too much importance to our naval operations on the Lakes—the success of the ensuing campaign will depend absolutely upon our superiority on all the lakes—& every effort, & resource, must be directed to that object." This affirmation must have delighted Chauncey, who had been tireless in his efforts to build up the naval forces on Lakes Ontario and Erie.[1]

Madison also realized that William Eustis was overwhelmed in directing the army. He offered the position of secretary of war to James Monroe, Henry Dearborn, and William Crawford in turn. All declined. Madison then considered Daniel Tompkins and John Armstrong. Madison distrusted Armstrong, yet Secretary of the Treasury Albert Gallatin believed him to be the better choice. As for Tompkins, Gallatin wrote, "No person thinks him equal to the place at such time as this. The office requires first abilities & frightens those who know best its difficulties." Gallatin pointed out the obvious political issue. It was better to leave Tompkins in the governorship "than to throw the immediate Government in the hands of DeWitt Clinton & to lose the only chance of a Republican Governor at the April election." The president replaced Eustis with Brigadier General Armstrong. Col. Henry Burbeck replaced Armstrong as commander of the defenses of New York City. Although Armstrong was decidedly more competent than Eustis, he would not be up to the formidable task of directing strategy or dealing with difficult generals.[2]

Madison nominated Morgan Lewis, a past governor of New York and the current army quartermaster general, to the rank of major general. The Senate confirmed the nomination on March 2 by a vote of twenty to seven. New

John Armstrong, by John Wesley Jarvis, c. 1812. Courtesy National Portrait Gallery, Smithsonian Institution.

York's two Republican senators split their vote, with John Smith voting yea and Obadiah German voting nay. Robert Fulton, a strong supporter of Lewis, wrote to Madison that Lewis was a man "with much energy and ambition to distinguish himself." Lewis took as his aide-de-camp Lt. William Jenkins Worth, a New Yorker who had served as Lewis's private secretary. Madison's changes in leadership had a moderately positive effect on the prosecution of the war. However, in New York state, opposition to the war effort created a friction that would prove crippling.[3]

The federal government, even with state assistance, was never able to quell illegal trade. British forces depended upon American foodstuffs for survival, and smuggling was rampant, particularly across the St. Lawrence River. After the British raid on Ogdensburg, that village effectively became an open city and a haven for smugglers. Brig. Gen. Zebulon Pike at Sackett's Harbor sent two officers and a detachment of soldiers to arrest persons conducting these treasonous activities. The soldiers arrested nine men and sent them to Sackett's Harbor. Civil authorities arrested the two officers for false imprisonment and held them with bail set at $180,000. Pike freed the nine, but a state court convicted the officers, who were assessed $13,685 in damages. Congress eventually paid the damages. The British continued to feast on New York meat and flour throughout the war.[4]

Despite his best efforts, Governor Daniel Tompkins was unable to harness all of the state's resources to prosecute the war. The Federalists had a majority in the Assembly, and the Senate remained in Republican hands when the legislative session opened in January. The Council of Appointment proceeded to displace many Republican incumbents in state office, and reappointed DeWitt Clinton as mayor of New York.

The gubernatorial election of April 1813 was largely about the war and was hotly contested. The Republican members of the legislature unanimously nominated Tompkins for re-election. DeWitt Clinton was currently the lieutenant governor. However, his influence in the state Republican Party was all but destroyed because of his role in opposing Madison in the 1812 presidential election and his continuing flirtation with state Federalists. The party bypassed this anti-war incumbent and nominated John Tayler of Albany for lieutenant governor. The Federalist caucus selected Stephen Van Rensselaer and George Huntington for governor and lieutenant governor respectively.[5]

Stephen Van Rensselaer was the unsuccessful general at the Battle of Queenston Heights. A small number of Federalists tried to prevent Van Rensselaer's candidacy because as general he had ordered militiamen to cross into Canada. Yet he remained popular, especially in counties less exposed to the fighting. The Federalists charged Tompkins with deliberately withholding support from Van Rensselaer's forces at Lewiston and snubbing the wounded Solomon Van Rensselaer when Tompkins visited Buffalo after the battle.

Federalists condemned Tompkins for sending thousands of militiamen away from their homes for months on end. For their part, Republicans extolled Tompkins's patriotic support for the war. They portrayed the immensely rich Van Rensselaer as a friend of the wealthy, while Tompkins worked for all classes. Nativist Federalists alienated Irish voters, who flocked to the Republican Party. While the conflict had dislocated the economy and established trade patterns, all was not disadvantageous. Farmers in the western counties, who expected the war to reduce their markets, were pleased to discover that the military was buying grain and meat at good prices. Waggoneers and boatmen had continuous employment moving food, artillery, and military stores to distant posts.

When the results came in, Tompkins and Tayler won by a narrow margin, 52 percent of the vote to 48 percent. Voters returned the Senate to the Republicans; however, the Assembly remained in Federalist hands. While the newly elected officials took office on July 1, the next legislative session would not begin until January 25, 1814. Federalists could still stymie Republican measures to prosecute the war.[6]

While this election campaign played out in New York, the Madison administration faced the business of winning the war. In early February, Madison met with his cabinet to develop the campaign plan for the year. Armstrong noted that as many as 12,000 soldiers, about five-sixths of which were regulars, defended Montreal. The new secretary of war understood that the country could not generate enough combat power to seize Montreal early in the campaign season, so he developed an alternate strategy to make some headway while the recruiting effort continued. Madison approved Armstrong's plan—a series of operations that would seize Kingston, York, and Forts George and Erie, in that order.[7]

On February 10, Armstrong sent the plan to Dearborn at Albany. Armstrong identified 7,000 regulars earmarked for the invasion, including John Chandler's and Zebulon Pike's brigades on Lake Champlain. The secretary of war ordered Dearborn to put these two brigades on the road to Sackett's Harbor quickly; Armstrong would replace these soldiers with "some new raised regiments." Dearborn ordered Pike to bring his brigade to Sackett's Harbor but did not order Chandler westward until March 14. Unfortunately, Chauncey was still in New York City requisitioning the massive amounts of materiel for the large frigate being built at Sackett's Harbor. Dearborn would not develop the campaign plan further without the commander of naval forces. Early in March, Dearborn arrived at Sackett's Harbor, to be joined a few days later by Chauncey. Dearborn estimated that there were 6,000 to 8,000 British troops at Kingston whom he expected to attack the American naval base imminently. This attack did not materialize, but Dearborn was convinced that Kingston was too well-defended to attack successfully.[8] Chauncey agreed.

Given their understanding of the location of British forces and aware that harbors would not be ice-free until mid-April, Chauncey and Dearborn came up with an alternative plan. They proposed raiding York first. Chauncey believed that capturing or destroying the warships there would tip the balance of naval power. Dearborn and Chauncey would then seize Fort George, while the forces at Buffalo would simultaneously attack Fort Erie. If Fort Erie fell, then the navy would move five vessels then at Black Rock to Presque Isle in Pennsylvania to join Master Commandant Oliver Hazard Perry's squadron. Finally, the land and naval forces would move on Kingston. On March 29, Armstrong approved the new plan, but he cautioned Dearborn to use overwhelming force. "If our first step in the campaign . . . should fail, the disgrace of our arms will be complete. The public will lose all confidence in us, and we shall even cease to have any in ourselves." Then Armstrong, who prided himself as a strategist, made a statement that demonstrated his incapacity. Urging Dearborn to take all the regulars from Sackett's Harbor, he proclaimed, "When the fleet and army are gone, we have nothing at Sackett's Harbor to guard, nor will the place present an object to the enemy." Armstrong saw little value in the facilities and stores at Sackett's Harbor necessary to support the squadron.[9]

Dearborn requested that Tompkins alert militia units to be ready to march on short notice to the Niagara frontier. Tompkins obliged, ordering Gen. Timothy Hopkins to make the arrangements. Dearborn also organized his command structure for the raid on York. Although Brig. Gen. John Chandler was senior to Pike, Dearborn selected Pike to command the landing force.[10]

Ensign Joseph Hawley Dwight of the Thirteenth Infantry recorded that Chandler appeared to be "a man of very ordinary abilities and totally unfit for the command of an army." Born in Massachusetts, Dwight moved to Bridge-water in Oneida County. When war broke out six years later, he received a commission. Dwight also wrote that half of the 4,000 soldiers gathered at Sackett's Harbor were "in very bad fighting condition" and that "upwards of 500 men" had already been buried at that post.[11] The army and militia had suffered terribly, and their travails would continue in the upcoming campaign.

Dearborn and Chauncey determined to attack York as soon as the ice cleared sufficiently to allow egress from Black River Bay. On April 22, Pike's brigade crammed onto *Madison* and *Oneida* and eleven other warships as well as bateaux towed by the squadron. Soldiers crowded the decks such that sailors had hardly enough space to perform their duties. A storm forced the squadron back into port, and it wasn't until April 25 that the weather cooperated. The soldiers, wet, cold, and seasick, were eager to set foot on dry land.[12]

The village of York sat on the northern shore of York Harbor, a protected bay formed by a long, low peninsula extending from the mainland.[13] Upper Canada's Parliament buildings stood in the village. The partially completed warship, *Sir Isaac Brock*, was in the dockyard. The battle was fought along a four-mile stretch through a series of gun batteries and fortifications lying west of the village.

Major General Sir Roger Hale Sheaffe, Isaac Brock's successor as president and administrator of Upper Canada, defended his capital with about 1,050 men, including 477 militiamen and fifty Indian warriors. The Americans arrived on the morning of April 27. Chauncey commanded about eight hundred sailors and marines while Dearborn brought nearly 1,800 regulars and volunteers. Among the army troops was the Sixth U.S. Infantry, raised largely in New York, and Capt. James Maher's company of Albany Greens, one of the ten companies of Francis McClure's volunteer regiment. Another New Yorker present at the battle was Lt. Melancthon Woolsey, commanding *Oneida*.[14]

The amphibious landing at York demonstrated nearly flawless cooperation between the U.S. Army and the U.S. Navy. This was the first time that the two services had conducted an opposed landing. Chauncey's seamen put Pike's troops into landing boats and rowed for shore. Several American schooners cruised eastward in the harbor, exchanging cannon fire with British guns. The first soldiers to arrive on the narrow beach were riflemen from Maj. Benjamin Forsyth's U.S. Regiment of Rifles. Forsyth pushed inland through forest, overwhelming a company of British grenadiers and Indian warriors. Infantrymen followed the riflemen in rapid order. Pike pushed his troops relentlessly toward a clearing that held the ruins of an old French fort. Sheaffe formed his regulars at the opposite side of the clearing. The two sides exchanged fire, and after a few minutes, it became apparent to Sheaffe that the more numerous Americans were slowly destroying his valuable regulars. The British commander ordered a withdrawal to a British battery closer to the village.

As the Americans moved toward the battery, a British gunner accidentally ignited a box of artillery ammunition. The explosion killed or wounded thirty British regulars and militiamen. Many militiamen, in shock from the explosion, simply departed the field. The regulars fell back to the garrison, a position protected by an earthen wall. Pike slowly drew his men together in a column, with the Sixth U.S. Infantry in the fore about three hundred yards west of the British position. Seeing no evidence of a British presence, Pike assumed that the British were in cover behind the earthworks. Pike ordered his artillery to fire into the British position while he made plans to assault with his infantry.

Sheaffe, however, had decided to abandon York in order to preserve the strength of his regular force. He could neither hold York in the face of overwhelming numbers nor put his irreplaceable regulars at risk. To his mind, the defense of Upper Canada depended upon his too few professional soldiers. He directed his indignant militia leaders to surrender the village, seeking the best terms possible. Sheaffe also ordered a captain to set an explosion in the magazine, a stone structure piled high with three hundred barrels of gunpowder and crates of ammunition.[15]

General Pike was interrogating a captured British sergeant when a roar, inferno, and shock dislocated all human senses. An immense column of smoke, fire, stone, and timber—a veritable holocaust—rose hundreds of feet. The stunned soldiers had but seconds to shelter themselves as the wind, heat, and shower of debris struck them. The wreckage of the magazine and its contents of iron shot and shell fell in a circular pattern five hundred yards in radius. The eruption killed about forty Americans outright and wounded more than two hundred, many of whom subsequently died of their wounds. The Sixth Infantry suffered the worst, losing over 104 casualties. Among the mortally wounded was Pike. To their very great credit, the Americans quickly responded to their officers, and the column moved forward to seize the abandoned garrison.[16]

As Sheaffe pushed his men eastward to Kingston, he ordered the burning of *Sir Isaac Brock* and the naval stores and facilities. Meanwhile, the Americans negotiated a surrender with the militia leaders. They paroled the Canadian militiamen, many of whom were heartened that they could not be called back into service until exchanged, a process that could take months. The Americans evacuated their wounded and loaded immense stores of public property onto vessels returning to Sackett's Harbor. Dearborn sent Pike's body to Sackett's Harbor. Chauncey declared Pike's untimely death to be a "national" loss. Burial parties laid to rest the many dead. While American officers posted guards around public buildings, many of their soldiers and sailors took the opportunity to loot homes of food, liquor, and valuables. The miscreants were joined by Canadians, some of whom the Americans freed from jail soon after the battle. On the third night of occupation, an unidentified individual or party set fire to the two Parliament buildings, an act in violation of the surrender. There were no witnesses nor did any American officers give orders to commit the arson. York was home to a number of disaffected citizens, any of whom might have set the fire; these persons would not be troubled by a British defeat.[17]

Dearborn and Chauncey had planned to make quick work of York and to immediately move on to attack Fort George. This was not to be. The Americans dealt with horrendous numbers of casualties. Surgeon's Mate William Beaumont recalled working forty-eight hours straight without food or sleep. The surgeons, he wrote, were "wading in blood, cutting off arms, legs, & trepanning heads to rescue their fellow creatures from untimely deaths."[18]

After the squadron had transported tons of captured supplies, it began moving soldiers. A week after the battle, the troops embarked and awaited the weather to clear for the short voyage across the lake to Four Mile Creek near Fort Niagara. Dysentery spread through the crowded ships, making the soldiers' wait particularly wretched. Heavy rains increased their misery as the ships rolled in the waves. The weather broke on May 8, and the troops crossed the lake. At Four Mile Creek, the disembarking troops found neither tents nor food awaiting them. The ground was sodden. Their ordeal continued.[19]

Dearborn and Chauncey had arrived at Fort Niagara on May 2 and met with Generals Morgan Lewis, John Boyd, and William Winder. Dearborn gave command of Pike's brigade to Boyd. Dearborn's intent was to follow up the raid on York with an attack on Fort George. However, preparations were disappointingly incomplete. The general discovered that no one was building barges to carry cannon and horses, and the boats that were built had not been moved to Four Mile Creek. Dearborn had directed the invasion force to concentrate at Four Mile Creek, yet Winder's brigade was still encamped at Black Rock.[20] Fortunately, Col. Winfield Scott arrived on May 12. Dearborn designated him as adjutant general and gave him the task of planning the operation to seize Fort George and to destroy the British troops under Brigadier General John

Vincent. Chauncey took most of the squadron back to Sackett's Harbor, where it embarked Chandler's brigade and quickly returned to Four Mile Creek.

As the invasion drew closer, Chauncey became increasingly fearful for the security of Sackett's Harbor, particularly as word arrived of the growing Royal Navy presence on the lake. He placed his brother, Lt. Wolcott Chauncey, in charge of the naval base while embarking most of Col. Alexander Macomb's Third Artillery Regiment for the last trip to Four Mile Creek. There, Chauncey met with Oliver Hazard Perry, who had left his Lake Erie squadron at Presque Isle in order to participate in the coming battle. Chauncey and Perry dropped buoys off the landing beach to mark positions for the schooners that would provide close-in fire support. Scott's objective was to destroy or capture the British forces defending Fort George. To that end, the plan included a landing of Col. James Burn's dragoons near Queenston to cut off Brigadier General John Vincent's retreat, should he decide to abandon Fort George. Dearborn, who had been ill for weeks, gave nominal command to Morgan Lewis.[21]

In the early hours of May 27, about 2,500 American troops embarked on nearly 140 small craft. Chauncey's ships towed the landing boats in the dark toward the landing area west of Fort George. Shortly after daybreak, American guns from Fort Niagara opened fire on Fort George. The cannonade was so intense that several buildings caught fire. As the sun rose and the fog lifted, Vincent saw waves of American boats pulling for shore. Soon, Chauncey's schooners anchored at their assigned buoys, within musket range of shore, and blasted away at the British defenders. Winfield Scott led the advance force, a body of four hundred selected soldiers. Scott's men hit the narrow beach and started clambering up the steep banks. Waiting for them were British regulars firing at close range as the Americans peered over the embankment. Scott dodged a bayonet thrust, lost his footing, and toppled unceremoniously backward onto the beach. Watching from a nearby ship, Dearborn exclaimed that Scott was killed. Scott picked himself up and started once again up the embankment. The second wave under Boyd landed, adding weight to the American assault. The exchange of musketry was fierce and deadly. Outnumbered and decimated, the British withdrew under orders toward the fort.

Surgeon's Mate Beaumont was with the Sixth Infantry in Boyd's Brigade. In a letter to his brother he stated, "at ½ past 11 A.M. we effected a landing immediately under a most tremendous fire of the enemy, at their chosen & most possible advantageous situation being concealed in a hallow behind an elevation of the banks, directly where our boats struck the shore & commencing an incessant fire, as soon as our boats came within reach of their shott; could not seemingly miss their aim in shooting us all dead in the boats before we could gain the shore; but our men commencing firing at the same time; pressed for the shore with undaunted fury with the loss of very few indeed."[22]

Meanwhile, Vincent organized a defensive line between the village of Newark and the fort. Colonel Christopher Myers commanded this portion of the British force until he received three wounds and could no longer command. Vincent understood that keeping his force of regulars intact was more important than defending the stockade fort. At about noon, he put his troops on the move south toward Queenston. He also sent out riders with orders for all troops along the Niagara River to withdraw and concentrate atop the escarpment at Beaver Dams. Finally, he issued orders to spike the guns and blow up the magazine and the six earthen bastions of the fort.

Winfield Scott appeared more intent upon capturing a token of victory than in pursuing the withdrawing British. Having taken a British officer's horse, he approached the fort at the head of two companies of men. An explosion inside the fort unhorsed Scott. Breaking his collarbone, the undaunted American colonel entered the fortification. There, he found an ax and started chopping at the flagpole while his officers began cutting the fuses to the stores of ammunition. With the British flag gone, it was obvious to all that the fort had fallen. Once he had his flag, Scott took up the pursuit.[23]

Vincent and his men made good their escape as Colonel Burn failed to cross the river in time to intercept them. Scott pushed his troops hard but could not close in on the British column before it disappeared from sight. Scott ignored written orders to break off the pursuit. Finally, General Boyd personally gave Scott General Lewis's direct order to return to Fort George. Dearborn later reported to Armstrong, "The troops having been under arms from one o'clock in the morning were too much exhausted for any further pursuit."[24] There was no reason to believe that the Americans were any more exhausted than the British. In a letter to his friend, Maj. Charles K. Gardner, Scott lamented, "It is now universally acknowledged, that if we had been permitted to pursue, we might have defeated the enemy at Queenston where he had collected his force or at any rate have saved immense magazines which were burned at his leisure."[25] Capt. Mordecai Myers recalled, "There was no necessity for stopping at Newark except the Generals having been hungry, and Mrs. Black having had a good dinner. I suppose they thought they had glory enough for one day without following up the enemy." The failure to destroy Vincent's force would cause Dearborn untold future calamities.[26]

Vincent linked up with Lieutenant Colonel Cecil Bisshopp's troops from Fort Erie, and the two groups headed for Burlington Heights. Vincent reported nearly one hundred casualties and over 250 missing. Many of those reported missing were casualties left on the battlefield or militiamen who chose not to remain with the colors. The Americans suffered nearly two hundred casualties. However, Dearborn was satisfied to grant parole to about five hundred Canadian militiamen who voluntarily sought the opportunity to return to their homes and enjoy the status that parole afforded. Militiamen on both sides of the border took legal means to avoid the dangers inherent in the fighting.[27]

With Fort Erie abandoned, the Americans removed the vessels from Black Rock. On May 28, Chauncey sent Perry, along with fifty-five seamen and about two hundred soldiers, to Black Rock. Fighting the wind and the Niagara River current, the men, aided by a few oxen, hauled each vessel upriver and into Lake Erie. After a week of brutal labor, Perry sailed the brig *Caledonia* and the smaller warships—*Somers*, *Trippe*, *Ohio*, and *Amelia*—to Presque Isle to join his squadron. The capture of Fort George made the American victory on Lake Erie possible.[28]

In addition to taking over 1,000 regulars and militiamen out of the British order of battle and decisively augmenting Perry's squadron, the raid on York and the capture of Fort George deprived British land and naval forces on the upper Great Lakes of tons of food, ammunition, and equipment. These losses contributed in no small part to the ultimately successful American campaign in the Old Northwest. The war would not, could not, be won in the West. Dearborn and Chauncey needed to focus on Montreal and eventually Quebec. As for federal–state cooperation, Dearborn did not use available militia forces. Tompkins had responded to Dearborn's request for militiamen, but given the increase in numbers of regulars and volunteers, Dearborn was satisfied in relegating the militia to a purely defensive role.

Two days after the incomplete victory at Fort George, Chauncey's worst nightmare came true. Word arrived that the British were back on the lake in force. The commodore restocked ammunition while waiting for favorable winds. Determined to defend his base, he was growing increasingly uneasy for the delay. Unfortunately for the naval and land forces at Sackett's Harbor, they would have to fight without assistance from the squadron. No one knew at the time, but the easy cooperation between American land and sea forces was eroding.

CHAPTER 8

THE RAID ON
SACKETT'S HARBOR

As early as February, Governor Tompkins bolstered the defenses of Sack-ett's Harbor. He gave orders to furnish Commodore Chauncey with a brass nine-pounder for a pilot boat then under construction. He also provided weapons and ammunition to the citizens of Henderson on Henderson Harbor. "As any attack which may be made upon the harbour [Sackett's Harbor], will probably be made by troops landing near Horse Island or in Henderson's harbor. It is particularly proper that the inhabitants of that town [Henderson], should be ready to aid in repelling such attack."[1]

Gen. Richard Dodge resigned his command at the end of January, and the detached militiamen under his command were discharged on February 24. That left only Col. Alexander Macomb's artillerymen and Chauncey's sailors and marines to defend the vital shipyard and warships. Tompkins alerted Gen. Jacob Brown to direct the men of his brigade of common militia to prepare to respond to a call for assistance from the commandant at Sackett's Harbor. In his note to Brown, Tompkins remarked that Gen. Henry Dearborn had specifically asked for Brown's services in an emergency. "You will perceive a very considerable compliment paid to you in the General's request."[2] Dearborn had brought the major operations of the campaign season westward to Fort George. He wanted the best commander available to watch over Sackett's Harbor.

Dearborn left about 1,300 regulars and volunteers at Sackett's Harbor. The volunteers, whom Dearborn estimated at three hundred in number, were built around the Albany Volunteers, recruited for a twelve-month term of service. Tompkins authorized the Albany Volunteers the previous October. This unit, about 160 soldiers, subsequently came into federal service and was uni-formed from federal stocks; they looked like regulars. Dearborn also ordered the patients in the army hospital to be moved to a new, temporary facility in

Major General Jacob Jennings Brown, by James Herring. Courtesy New-York Historical Society.

Watertown. Thus, many of the ill and convalescent were not at the post when the British attacked.[3]

Macomb was the senior army officer of the garrison. He developed a defensive plan that capitalized on the inherent strengths of the regulars, volunteers, and militia. It was possible, although unlikely, that the British would assault the naval base directly. The guns of Forts Tompkins and Volunteer, on either side of the harbor, would have easy work against landing boats. Macomb assumed that any raiders would land about one mile west of the base, using Horse Island to shelter their boats from the guns of the forts. The island also provided space for the troops to assemble before continuing the attack. Therefore, Macomb's plan posted riflemen to use the extensive woods on the mainland as concealment while taking the landing boats under fire. He cautioned the riflemen not to become decisively engaged but to maintain contact with the British as they moved toward the harbor. In the probable event that the riflemen became dispersed, they would use the commandant's quarters as a rally point. Col. Francis McClure's regiment of rifle volunteers arrived at Sackett's Harbor on February 27. They, along with Major Benjamin Forsyth's veterans, gave the defenders a large number of soldiers with highly accurate long-range weapons.

Sackett's Harbor on Lake Ontario. Courtesy Naval Historical Foundation, NH-1696.

Macomb placed his militiamen between Horse Island and the barracks at the western end of the village. He positioned his dismounted dragoons near the barracks. They would take up the battle as the militiamen withdrew, as Macomb expected they would. Macomb explained to Dearborn his plan for using his militiamen. They were "to watch the Enemy and endeavor by individual exertions to kill one man each and then I shall be perfectly satisfied and they may consider themselves as having done their duty." "I have impressed on their minds the importance of their harassing the enemy by gauling [*sic*] their flanks, picking off distinguished persons and of returning to the fight notwithstanding they may be beaten off occasionally. That they will run I have not the least doubt but I request them to return when they have got themselves warm." Macomb's plan did not depend upon the militia. These citizen-soldiers would supplement the fire of the regulars within their ability.[4]

Macomb ordered West Point graduate Lt. John Bliss to take overall command of the blockhouse at Fort Tompkins. He further directed that Bliss place a number of additional loaded muskets in the blockhouse and to cover his ammunition with blankets to protect them from fire. "You will command notwithstanding your commission may be junior to other officers. All officers or men that you may permit to enter you will consider as volunteers for there must be but one commanding officer. You will not surrender on any account." Thus, Macomb assured that a higher-ranking officer could not order Bliss to surrender this key defensive work.[5]

Macomb stationed most of his artillerymen in the two forts to man the guns. However, excess artillerymen would fight as infantry under Maj. George

Mitchell. He directed Capt. Ichabod Crane to take two light guns and crews from Fort Volunteer. Mitchell and Crane would act as circumstances allowed to bring the attackers under fire as they approached the harbor. He stationed the marines in Fort Tompkins to act as a reserve. As troops moved in and out of the garrison at Sackett's Harbor, Macomb adjusted the defensive plan, assigning specific tasks to new units. Moreover, he rehearsed the plan so that soldiers and marines would know where to go when the alarm bells tolled.

Over the winter, Chauncey and his officers and men had made giant strides in preparing the squadron for the spring campaign. On the Canadian side, Prevost, too, had taken steps to improve the Provincial Marine while awaiting the arrival of the Royal Navy. He gave orders for the construction of three new ships, one each at Amherstburg on the Detroit River, York, and Kingston. While the construction was a good enterprise to match the intense work going on at Sackett's Harbor, two aspects of Prevost's guidance degraded the effect. First, he appointed Thomas Plunknett to superintend shipbuilding. Plunknett was technically incompetent, and he lacked the energy and administrative talent to push construction to completion. Second, the decision to operate two shipbuilding sites on Lake Ontario used British resources inefficiently. It proved nearly impossible to share materiel and shipbuilding expertise between the two sites.[6]

In May, the arrival of Commodore Sir James Yeo with 450 Royal Navy officers and seamen at Kingston changed the trajectory of the war on the Great Lakes and Lake Champlain. Yeo was thirty years old and eager; his rise in the navy had been rapid. His career demonstrated inspired leadership and numerous acts of personal heroism. However, he had no experience commanding a squadron in combat. The Admiralty gave Yeo command of the warships and other vessels on the lakes of Canada with the mission to protect the provinces of Upper and Lower Canada. The new commodore understood the gravity of his appointment. He decided initially to give battle to the Americans soon rather than allow them to outbuild the British squadron. In his first report back to the Admiralty, he stated, "I am therefore about to proceed to Sea to meet them, as the possession of upper Canada must depend on whoever can maintain the Naval Superiority on Lake Ontario."[7]

Yeo quickly took charge and appointed Royal Navy officers to command vessels of the Provincial Marine. Yeo dispatched Acting Commander Robert Barclay to command the Lake Erie Squadron. In July, Yeo ordered Acting Commander Daniel Pring to lead the squadron operating on Lake Champlain and the Richelieu River. Like Yeo, these officers had no experience leading a squadron in a fight. Yeo retained the talented and audacious William Howe Mulcaster with the Lake Ontario squadron as captain of the *Royal George*. Yeo also assessed naval capabilities and discovered that he needed more of everything if he was to maintain control of the vital inland seas. Or, he must degrade the capabilities of Chauncey's squadron. Thus, he was alert for an opportunity to attack the American naval base.[8]

In May, as Americans shifted forces to attack Fort George, Chauncey understood that his squadron's absence from the eastern end of the lake put his base in jeopardy. Dearborn increased the risk by ordering Macomb's Third Artillery to depart Sackett's Harbor and join the attack upon Fort George. The Third Artillery was the hard core of the defenses of the naval base. Chauncey's fears were allayed by the arrival of a few hundred dismounted troopers of the First Light Dragoons with their commander, New Yorker Lt. Col. Electus Backus. Before the war, Backus had commanded the militia's Fourth Regiment of Cavalry. Chauncey expected about 250 infantrymen to arrive at Sackett's Harbor within days. He planned for the possibility of a British attack, giving command and responsibility for the security of the naval base and the safety of the new ship, eventually named for Zebulon Pike, to his brother, navy Lt. Wolcott Chauncey.[9]

Before Macomb left Sackett's Harbor, he briefed Backus in detail on the defensive plans so meticulously worked out. After Macomb departed with his men for Niagara, Dearborn had second thoughts about the security of Sackett's Harbor. He sent an order back to Macomb for himself and his men to remain there. However, Macomb's ship and the schooner carrying the orders apparently passed in the night and Macomb joined the attack on Fort George while Backus commanded the regulars defending Sackett's Harbor.

When Prevost, in Kingston, learned of the bombardment of Fort George, he rightfully assumed that the campaign season had opened on the Niagara peninsula. On May 26, Yeo himself took a fast vessel to scout out Sackett's Harbor. The following day, Prevost received Yeo's report—the American squadron had indeed departed its base. Prevost, Yeo, and other key leaders met to develop plans to raid the American base. About eight hundred regulars, fencibles, and Indian warriors loaded onto large vessels and bateaux, and as darkness fell on May 27, the squadron sailed out of Kingston Harbor.

Prevost gave command of the landing party to his adjutant, Colonel Edward Baynes. At noon on May 28, American lookouts sighted the British squadron and fired alarm guns to call troops and sailors to their battle stations and to call in the militia. Baynes ordered the troops into ships' boats and bateaux. The wind had died down, and it was a few hours later before the landing vessels began pulling toward shore, more than five miles away. Soon, heavy winds drove a rain shower over the squadron, and Prevost recalled the troops to the ships. However, the Indian warriors continued on in their canoes and chased a number of bateaux carrying regular troops to Sackett's Harbor. The Americans panicked and put to shore, where they fought briefly with the Indians. Fearing a massacre, the soldiers loaded into their craft and rowed out to Yeo's squadron to surrender. The British bagged about 115 recruits. Prevost's decision, opposed by Yeo, to postpone the attack until the weather improved gave the Americans plenty of time to ready their defenses.[10]

When they saw the British squadron, Lieutenant Colonel Backus, Lieutenant Chauncey, and Gen. Jacob Brown met to coordinate their defense. Fortunately, they had Macomb's plan in hand. While the Third Artillery and the rifle units were away at Fort George, sufficient regulars and volunteers were still able to fall in on the defensive scheme. Brown dispatched riders to alert the local militia, who streamed into the village. Parts of two militia regiments were present, those of Colonels William Sprague and Gershom Tuttle, about five hundred men in all. Brown placed the Albany Volunteers under Col. John Mills on Horse Island, the anticipated landing site. He settled the militia behind a low embankment on the mainland where they could engage the British as the volunteers withdrew. When the invaders left Horse Island, they would have to approach the base a half mile away either through the woods or along the lake road. As they drew near the Basswood Cantonment and Fort Tompkins, Backus and his regulars would present a stout defense. Meanwhile, about two hundred sailors, marines, shipwrights, and some artillerymen stood ready manning guns around the harbor. Vessels approaching to support the attack would encounter a storm of artillery fire.

The battle unfolded pretty much as Macomb and Brown had foreseen. After midnight, Commander Mulcaster led the landing force on its approach to shore. As the sun rose on May 29, British gunboats fired onto Horse Island while the heavy guns at Fort Tompkins engaged the landing boats. The Americans scored at least one hit, sinking a boat close to shore. The Albany Volunteers opened fire on the approaching boats, inflicting a number of casualties. Before the British could engage them, the volunteers withdrew across the narrow causeway connecting Horse Island to the mainland. They then fell in with Brown and his militia. British regulars landed, fixed bayonets, and charged down the causeway. Brown expected the militiamen to put up a stronger fight, but after they fired a few ragged volleys, many of them scattered. Brown wrote to Armstrong that, "to my utter astonishment my men arose from their cover broke & before I could realize the disgraceful scene, there was scarcely a man within several rods of where I stood." A furious Brown chased after them in an attempt to bring his men back into the fight. Colonel Mills died in the firefight.[11]

The volunteers and the few militiamen still in the fight sniped at the British regulars forming up on the mainland. Baynes ordered the advance, and Prevost and Yeo accompanied the attack. The British advanced both along the lake road and on a path through the woods. The Albany Volunteers withdrew firing and joined up with the regulars. Militia Capt. Samuel McNitt rallied between eighty and one hundred militiamen from Jefferson County and fired into the flank of the British advance. The schooner *Lord Beresford* was the only vessel of the squadron that managed to approach the harbor, where it exchanged cannon fire with the guns of Fort Tompkins.

It was nearly 8 A.M. when Baynes consolidated his force in a wood line looking across the open field to the American barracks, Fort Tompkins, and the big prize, the navy yard. Baynes ordered an assault into the strongest part of the American defenses. In the ensuing firefight, the British advance faltered and recoiled. Backus took the opportunity to consolidate his defense in the Basswood Cantonment and Fort Tompkins. Baynes ordered another assault. British infantry swirled around the American barracks but made little progress. Late in the battle, Backus received a mortal wound and fell, leaving Majors Thomas Aspinwall and Jacint Laval in command of the regulars bearing the brunt of the battle. Brown eventually managed to send about two hundred militiamen back toward the fight, although they arrived too late to participate.[12]

Amidst clouds of smoke billowing over the battle, navy Lt. John Drury in the shipyard made a most regrettable decision. Wolcott Chauncey placed Drury in charge of the defense of the base, while he went aboard the *Fair American* to bring that schooner and the *Pert* into the upcoming fight. At the harbor, Drury heard distressing reports that Fort Tompkins had fallen, and he feared that the British would continue on to drive the defenders out of the shipyard. Some reported seeing a flag on *Fair American* ordering destruction of the shipyard. Rather than allowing the British to seize the new ship and sails, rigging, guns, and stores, Drury sent his men to set fire to the warehouses. For some reason, no one succeeded in torching the new ship.[13]

The crisis, however, had passed. Baynes and Prevost saw how badly their landing force had been cut up. Unable to break into the barracks or Fort Tompkins, but seeing smoke rising from the shipyard, the British leaders signaled a withdrawal to their boats. Many of the attackers, officers and men, could hardly believe that Prevost broke off the assault. To many it appeared as if victory were awaiting them. Nonetheless, by 10 A.M. the battle was over.[14]

As Americans realized the British were withdrawing, they pitched in to extinguish the several fires, but the damage was done. Without sails and rigging, the *Pike* would not be ready to take its place in the squadron until mid-July, about a month later than anticipated. Brown, who had missed much of the fighting, wrote the official report to Dearborn. However, in a letter to Governor Tompkins, Brown was justifiably critical of the militia, except for McNitt and his men.[15] The Americans suffered 156 dead, wounded, and missing, of whom no more than twenty-five were militiamen.

Brown visited Backus in the hospital and presented him with the sword of a British officer killed not far from where Backus had been wounded. Backus died on June 7. His wife received a widow's pension of half pay, $37.50 monthly. Their son graduated from West Point in 1824. Governor Tompkins was in Washington when the news of the battle arrived. He sent a congratulatory letter to Brown and added that "your popularity there [Washington] was deservedly high." Madison and Armstrong agreed. Brown received his appointment as brigadier general in the regular army on July 19, 1813.[16]

The British had suffered heavy casualties—forty-six killed, nearly two hundred wounded, and sixteen missing. Many British, military and civilian, blamed Prevost for calling off the assault. Royal Navy Midshipman David Wingfield commanded a boat carrying members of the landing party. He was captured at Plattsburgh the following year. He recalled, "I was informed by several officers of the American Army and Navy . . . that had the attack commenced immediately after we hove in sight the day before, so far from defending themselves, the number of men in the garrison would have scarcely been sufficient to destroy the public works."[17] The battle marked the beginning of the split between Yeo and Prevost. Yeo had accompanied the landing party when his proper place was with the squadron. Had he done so, perhaps he could have brought more vessels closer to support the fight.[18]

Chauncey, returning on June 1 from the western end of the lake, was horrified that he had come so very close to losing his new ship. He decided that he would not take his squadron onto the lake until he could sail with the *General Pike*. Chauncey sent to New York City for sail canvas and other necessary items. The commodore kept foremost in mind his mission to gain control of Lake Ontario. The squadron would no longer support army operations if doing so detracted from his primary task. The days of successful army-navy cooperation in major operations, as evidenced by the amphibious assaults at York and Fort George, had largely come to an end. Thus, the British came out ahead strategically in this battle, although they could not perceive this at the time.[19]

Operations around Lake Ontario in the spring of 1813 demonstrated the limits of federal–state cooperation in war making. Tompkins ensured that sufficient numbers of armed militia were available to assist in the defense of the vitally important naval base at Sackett's Harbor. He also complied with Dearborn's request to assign important duties to Jacob Brown. Macomb's winning battle plan did not rely on the militia for success. Nevertheless, Macomb integrated militia forces into the plan so that militiamen could contribute to battlefield success within their capabilities. Perhaps the most important aspect of federal–state cooperation was the willingness on the part of the president and the secretary of war to bring a militia officer into the regular army as a general officer based on merit, even though this action deprived some regular army colonel of the promotion. Brown would validate Madison's decision in the upcoming campaigns.

The successful defense of Sackett Harbor's naval facilities was key to enabling the continuation of the 1813 campaign. Ultimately, the initial successes at the western end of Lake Ontario would yield little of strategic value. Ill-fated events on the Niagara peninsula in the summer of 1813 provoked a change in command and strategy.

CHAPTER 9

THE NIAGARA PENINSULA

Pitched battles and raids marked the summer of 1813 on the Niagara peninsula and Lake Ontario. Yet the American offensive could make no progress. The land campaign underscored weakness in American generalship, while the naval war proved indecisive.

On June 1, Commodore Isaac Chauncey brought his squadron back to home port and set about recovering from the British raid. He requested more sailors to man his new frigate, *General Pike*. Chauncey believed, not without reason, that he could hardly send sailors to Oliver Hazard Perry on Lake Erie until the secretary of the navy could replace them in the Lake Ontario squadron. Intelligence from Kingston convinced Chauncey that Commodore Yeo's squadron heavily outgunned his own. Therefore, he decided not to seek battle with the Royal Navy until *Pike* was ready. The immediate impact of the raid on Sackett's Harbor was that Maj. Gen. Henry Dearborn's operations on the Niagara peninsula were placed at a decided disadvantage. Whatever course Dearborn chose would be without naval assistance.[1]

Dearborn took ill shortly after the capture of Fort George, and his infirmity contributed to the botched pursuit of newly promoted Major General John Vincent's British forces. In early June, Dearborn decided to send two of his brigades to attack Vincent, who had made his camp at the supply depot on Burlington Heights. This geographical feature was not part of the Niagara escarpment. It was a ridge separating Coote's Paradise from Little Lake (now Hamilton Harbor). The ridge is nearly three miles long, a few hundred yards wide, and about one hundred feet above the surrounding waters. The road to York passed over the heights and a garrison there could protect the supply line to British-occupied Detroit, thus giving possession of the heights considerable operational importance.[2]

Dearborn's two brigade commanders were both political appointees. William Winder was a Marylander and a Republican. He was also the nephew of Levin Winder, the Federalist governor of Maryland. In March 1812, Madison commissioned him a lieutenant colonel. Three months later, the president promoted him to colonel and commander of the Fourteenth Infantry. In March 1813, he became a brigadier general. Winder would go on to notoriety as the general who lost the national capital, but he demonstrated shortcomings well before that debacle. John Chandler was a common man from the District of Maine. He rose quickly in the Republican Party, largely as Henry Dearborn's protégé. Chandler was a major general in the Massachusetts Militia, giving Madison some rationale to commission him a brigadier general in the regular army in July 1812.

The evening of June 5 found 2,200 American soldiers camped west of Stoney Creek and about three miles away from Vincent on Burlington Heights. Another eight hundred Americans were two miles away on the lakeshore guarding supply boats. Chandler, senior to Winder, was in overall command. Chandler set out pickets and posted a battery of guns where the main road bisected the American position and rose over an embankment that ran perpendicular to the road. However, here Chandler's preparations stopped. He issued no orders in the event of a British attack. He allowed each of his regimental commanders to position their men as they saw fit. Thus, one regiment, the Twenty-Fifth Infantry, encamped in a meadow west of the embankment while the other commanders chose campsites on the higher ground to the east. British scouts, including Lieutenant Colonel John Harvey, saw a haphazard and inherently weak encampment. Harvey also saw opportunity.

Harvey's commander, General Vincent, faced a dilemma. He was outnumbered two to one. If he gave battle on Burlington Heights, it was likely that he would lose. Given the nature of the land, it would be difficult to withdraw his troops once battle was joined. Withdrawal before the battle preserved his men but uncovered the supply line. Harvey provided a third option—a surprise bayonet assault in the night. Vincent ordered about eight hundred of his best troops to remove the flints from their muskets and stealthily approach the American camp. No accidental discharge would warn the Americans.

Fortunately for the Americans, rumors that the British had seen their encampment prompted a response. Without Chandler's involvement, each of the regimental commanders drew their soldiers up to the brim of the embankment and had the men rest in battle line with weapons within reach. The Twenty-Fifth Infantry did not extinguish their campfires when they relocated, a fortunate decision. The British advanced, Harvey in the lead, and bayonetted or captured many of the Americans on picket duty. As they approached the campfires, some of the over-eager British officers raised a yell. The Americans rose in their ranks and saw their opponents, now backlit by the fires. The Americans opened with volleys of musketry.

An unnamed officer of the 49th Regiment of Foot recalled that "the first volley of the enemy coming from a spot as 'dark as Erebus' seemed like the bursting forth of a volcano. Then again all was dark and still save the moans of the wounded, the confused click! Click! Noise made by our men in adjusting their flints and the ring of the enemy's ramrods in reloading. Again the flash and the roar of the musketry, the whistling of the bullets and the crash of the cannon—Chaos had come again!"[3]

Capt. Ephraim Shaler of the Twenty-Fifth Infantry recalled the confusion of the fight in pitch dark.

> At the commencement of the attack, the whole brigade was immediately under arms, ready to act as occasion might require: but no one knew where to go in the darkness of night, surrounded (as one might suppose from their yells) by all the Indians in Canada—there being, as I have before said, no rallying point designated, none could distinguish friend from foe; consequently all concert of action was lost, and confusion ensued:—our men often firing upon each other by mistake. The brigade was composed of gallant men and officers who were ready and willing to engage the enemy if they had known where to begin the work of death.[4]

John Norton was present with his Indian warriors, but probably no more than a dozen men. Indians allied to the British presented a psychological threat to Americans far in excess of their numbers.

With soldiers falling all about him, British Major Charles Plenderleath discovered that he was only yards away from the American guns. He gathered about thirty of his men about him and charged the guns. The American gunners had laid their muskets aside while they worked the cannon. The British overwhelmed them, bayonetting several. Soon after, Chandler rushed to his artillery wondering why the guns had fallen silent. The British captured him and sent him under guard back to their camp. Minutes later, Winder and his staff rode up to the guns, also curious at the lack of cannon fire. Winder met Chandler's fate. Vincent saw that his men had made no impression upon the American line. He ordered a withdrawal, believing his risky attack to have been a failure. The American commanders were unaware that their generals had been captured and remained frozen in place awaiting orders as their opponents escaped.

As dawn broke, the army learned that the attackers had captured Chandler and Winder. Colonel James Burn, the dragoon commander, discovered that he was now in charge. Despite strong voices, particularly Lt. Col. John Chrystie, arguing for an immediate attack on Burlington Heights, Burn lacked the confidence to do so. Instead, he ordered a withdrawal to Forty-Mile Creek. Capt. Mordecai Myers of the Thirteenth Infantry had been with the party guarding the boats. He recorded his opinion of the failure to reengage the British: "We might have retaken our two generals, and, perhaps, many prisoners, for General Winder told me, when he returned on parole, that at twelve o'clock [noon] that the enemy had not collected five hundred men; they were not three miles from us, and they expected an attack every moment."[5]

Later that day, Dearborn learned of the night battle. Still quite ill, Dearborn ordered Maj. Gen. Morgan Lewis to take command of the two brigades that had lost their commanders and to attack "as soon as practicable." Lewis arrived at 5 P.M. the next day. However, a new player entered the game and tipped the scales even further in the favor of the British. Dearborn felt the full impact of Chauncey's return to Sackett's Harbor. Commodore Sir James Yeo was at the head of the lake with reinforcements and supplies for Vincent. Soon, Lewis received new orders from Dearborn. The American commander at Fort George had seen sails. Once he was convinced that it was the Royal Navy, he feared imminent attack, countermanded his earlier order, and hurried Lewis back to Fort George.

Dearborn had persuaded himself that Yeo was carrying a large body of troops directly to Fort George to attack while most of the American army was forty miles away. Actually, Yeo had only 220 soldiers, and he dropped them off with Vincent, who was following Lewis back to Fort George. The British squadron captured the American supply bateaux, providing more reason for hasty retreat. In the final analysis, Dearborn, who in his younger days stormed into Quebec and led elite troops at Saratoga, was now more concerned with not losing than with winning. After a week of marching and fighting, the Americans were back where they started from.[6]

Lt. Joseph Hawley Dwight reflected the frustration of many when he commented on the lack of skill and resolve of the army's senior leaders. Referring specifically to Chandler, Dwight wrote, "Here we saw the blessed effects of having plough joggers for generals whose greatest merits consist in being warm partisans and supporting administration right or wrong."[7] New Yorker Dwight was representative of the younger officers, who were ready for a fight and contemptuous of many of their senior leaders, who appeared cautious to a fault.

General Dearborn attributed the loss at Stoney Creek to "some strange fatality." He was mortified that Colonel Burn had not pressed the fight on to Burlington Heights. "If either of the general officers had remained in command, the enemy would have been pursued and cut up, or if Colonel Burn had been an officer of infantry." Morgan Lewis, who seldom agreed with Dearborn, did so in this instance. "Could he [the enemy] have been pressed the next morning, his destruction was inevitable." Dearborn complained to Armstrong that his "ill state of health renders it extremely painful to attend to the current duties."

He was disappointed with Morgan Lewis and appealed to the secretary of war, "I hope General Hampton will repair here as soon as possible."[8]

While the two generals happily placed primary blame on their dragoon commander, other factors were at work. The attack on Sackett's Harbor had convinced Chauncey to leave Dearborn's army at Fort George in order to secure his home port. Thus, the army was without vital naval support and any appearance by Royal Navy warships would have a disproportionate, even decisive, effect. The initial layout of the American camp seemed to be the major factor in John Harvey's audacious recommendation to conduct a night attack. However, the repositioning of forces contributed greatly to stopping the British assault. Chandler's general incompetence and his disregard for security in particular resulted in the artillery being on its own to defend itself. Thus, Plenderleath, refusing to accept defeat, had an easier go at overrunning the center of the American line. The general fear among American troops of being tomahawked and scalped probably curbed any enthusiasm to counterattack in the dark and no doubt was accountable for some soldiers skulking in the rear of the lines.

Dearborn resigned his command soon afterward to regain his health. Morgan Lewis acceded to temporary command and unkindly wrote to Armstrong that he doubted Dearborn would "ever again be fit for service. He has been repeatedly in a state of convalescence, but relapses on the least agitation of mind." The former governor of New York may have believed his command to be permanent, but sometime over the next few days, Dearborn reassumed command and sent Lewis to Sackett's Harbor. Dearborn gave Armstrong several reasons for the army's inactivity besides the absence of Chauncey's squadron. Many regimental officers had resigned. Two hundred sick and wounded had been evacuated to a temporary hospital east of Lewiston; this number grew to 1,000 by year's end. The rains rendered the roads largely impassable. Without naval transport, an advancing column would be unsupportable. Yet, the old general made one last stab to seize the initiative.[9]

Dearborn approved Brig. Gen. John Boyd's plan to attack a contingent of British troops that was harassing American patrols. On the evening of June 23, Boyd ordered Col. Charles Boerstler to take his regiment, the Fourteenth Infantry, augmented by artillery, dragoons, and Dr. Cyrenius Chapin's mounted volunteers, to attack a British force encamped at Beaver Dams. Boerstler's column passed through Queenston, ascended the escarpment, and moved westward toward the objective. In the way was Lieutenant James FitzGibbon's special command, fifty Irish soldiers of the 49th Regiment of Foot, now mounted. FitzGibbon's men had been sparring with Chapin's raiders for several weeks. The two groups were well-matched in skill and audacity. Chapin's men, referred to by Canadians as the Forty Thieves, had achieved widespread notoriety. The

Montreal Gazette stated that around June 20, "Lieut. FitzGibbon went in pursuit of 46 vagabonds, volunteer cavalry, brought over by Doctor Chapin from Buffalo, and who had been plundering for some time the inhabitants round Fort Erie and Chippawa." FitzGibbon learned of the approaching Americans from several sources, including Laura Secord, who achieved fame for her twenty-mile nighttime cross-country walk. However, FitzGibbon could not have achieved any level of success without the arrival of approximately 450 Indian warriors.[10]

On the morning of June 24, Boerstler's column was about two miles east of Beaver Dams at a place the locals called the Beechwoods. Indian warriors appeared behind the American column. The Americans formed in an open field surrounded by woods. For nearly three hours, the fight raged while the Indian worked their way around the Americans, eventually surrounding them loosely. Boerstler was wounded twice. FitzGibbon appeared and proposed that Boerstler surrender. He was bluffing when he stated that the Americans were outnumbered by both Indians and British regulars. FitzGibbon went on to declare that it would be difficult to control the Indian warriors. Boerstler was reported to exclaim, "For God's sake, keep the Indians from us!" Boerstler was convinced that he could not break out and take his wounded with him. He thus surrendered 462 men, including his wounded.[11]

FitzGibbon's articles of capitulation granted parole to the militia and volunteers; however, upon learning that Chapin and his raiders were among the surrendered soldiers, he reneged. FitzGibbon sent Chapin and his men into captivity. Nineteen days later, two boats carrying Chapin, his men, and their guards were crossing Lake Ontario heading to Kingston. Chapin surreptitiously organized his men to overpower their guards. On his signal, the prisoners in both boats took control after a brief scuffle. The next day, Chapin, his raiders, and their prisoners docked at Fort Niagara.[12] Boerstler was a captive at Quebec until paroled five months later. A court of inquiry conducted in 1815 found Boerstler justified in ordering the surrender.

The British ended the American offensive campaign at Beaver Dams. Thereafter, fighting on the Niagara peninsula devolved into a cruel stalemate. Dearborn's service in the field was over. In a terse and cold note, Armstrong conveyed to the Revolutionary veteran that Madison had removed him from command of the Ninth Military District "until your health be re-established, and until further orders." On July 15, Dearborn transferred temporary command to General Boyd and began his lonely travels home. Armstrong sent Boyd orders to limit his activities to training his command and to "engage in no affair with the enemy that can be avoided."[13]

Major General Sir Roger Hale Sheaffe was also a victim of the 1813 campaign. After the battle at York, Sheaffe's critics complained to Prevost that

Sheaffe was responsible for the loss of the provincial capital. Prevost was happy to scapegoat Sheaffe and, on June 6, sacked the unfortunate general. Taking his place was Major General Baron Francis de Rottenburg. After serving eight years in the French army, de Rottenburg received a commission in the British army. Because he was Polish by birth and left French service early in the French Revolution, a change in allegiance was not unseemly. He was in command at Montreal when Prevost named him commander of forces in Upper Canada. De Rottenburg followed up the victory at Beaver Dams by establishing a loose blockade around Fort George. He also planned a series of raids to further weaken the American position.

The war was drawing closer to the Iroquois on the Niagara River. In April, President Madison, through Secretary of War Armstrong, sent word to the Iroquois acknowledging the Indians' unease with the proximity of British forces and declared, "Should the enemy cross the Niagara River you will be removed." He invited them to relocate to the Allegany reservation. The Iroquois would have none of that patronizing palaver. In any case, events were moving too fast for presidential control.[14]

After the battle at Stoney Creek, General Dearborn asked for 150 Iroquois warriors to join with American forces at Fort George. The men gathered and began their trek, but Dearborn cancelled his request. Needless to say, the Indians were annoyed. Cornplanter and others signed a letter to Granger: "We feel ourselves injured with the treatment we receive at your hand, and shall return home to our business, and there remain until we receive some explanation of the cause of such trouble and disappointment. We feel ourselves ready to turn out and defend our Country but cannot be treated this way."[15] Shortly thereafter, Dearborn received the orders from Armstrong relieving him of command. The New York Indians would soon find themselves in combat.

Before dawn on July 5, Lieutenant Colonel Thomas Clark led a party of forty-four Canadian militiamen and British regulars across the Niagara River to raid the supply point at Fort Schlosser. Clark's men surprised the small guard and seized a cannon, weapons, three small vessels, ammunition, tobacco, and food. They damaged or destroyed what they could not bring back across the river—a dozen small craft and tons of artillery ammunition. The British followed up the attack on Fort Schlosser with a larger raid on Black Rock.[16]

However, between these two events, American and British patrols fought a major skirmish west of Fort George on the farm of Peter Ball. On July 8, a company of British light infantry accompanied by approximately 150 Indian warriors engaged an American picket. An American relief force of about two hundred joined the swirling battle. The Indians fought fiercely and killed or captured about thirty Americans, suffering three wounded themselves. The next day, an American patrol found scalped and hideously maimed bodies, which they buried in a common grave. American morale plummeted.[17]

About this time, Brig. Gen. Peter B. Porter received word that the British planned to follow the raid on Fort Schlosser with an attack on the supplies at Black Rock and that Porter himself was also a target. Porter invited Farmer's Brother to bring a contingent of warriors to respond to an attack. The Seneca chief brought thirty-six warriors late on the evening of July 10. Maj. William King of the Fifteenth Infantry arrived at Porter's home at sunrise to report that the British had landed. Farmer's Brother told his band that it was time to "show their friendship for their brethren of the United States not only in words but in deeds."[18]

Lieutenant Colonel Cecil Bisshopp led the raiding party of about 220 regulars and militiamen. Although quite wealthy, Bisshopp dedicated his life to military service. Landing before daylight, Bisshopp's raiders overran the gun batteries and burned the barracks and a schooner near Black Rock. As the British were loading captured ammunition into their boats, Porter's men counterattacked. British surgeon William Hackett described the engagement. The Indian warriors fired from the woods while the Americans attacked along the road from Buffalo. The British were surprised to discover that the Indians had entered the fight, as the Iroquois in Upper Canada had been assured by those from New York that they would remain neutral. Hackett wrote, "Indeed as the poor Col. Expressed himself to me he would as soon have expected to see a body of Cossacks, as this force [Indians] opposed to us. Bisshopp ordered his men to retreat while he led a small band of soldiers to cover the withdrawal. An American shot Bisshopp in the thigh, breaking the femur. Soldiers carried Bisshopp to a waiting boat where he received two more bullet wounds before the crew reached safety at Chippawa. Bisshopp died three days later, lamented by his men.[19]

As a young boy, James Aigun watched the skirmish at Black Rock. Aigun was a civilian and son of a militiaman. He followed his father toward the engagement, keeping far enough away not to be discovered. In 1871, he recalled Porter leading an assault that caught the British raiders unprepared to receive the attack. The British rushed for their boats while the Americans and Seneca followed to the riverbank and fired into the vessels. As often happens after the passage of many years, Aigun's recollection did not match reality. Aigun exaggerated, writing, "The river was full of dead men. They must have lost 300 men or more. The Indians stripped the dead. I saw nine bodies lying alongside of each other as naked as they were born. I believe we lost not more than one or two killed, some eight or nine wounded. Among the wounded I saw the Indian, Young King, wounded in the foot, and a man by the name of Groosebeck who had his teeth shot out in front." Young King was the Seneca hereditary chief. In his report to Armstrong, Porter noted of the Seneca, "Their personal bravery greatly contributed in routing and defeating the enemy." The British reported fourteen dead and twenty-eight wounded or missing.[20]

Tompkins wanted to ensure his militia generals that they had authority under the Militia Law of 1809 to call out local militia units in order to repel invasion without the formality of requesting such authority from the governor. Following Bisshopp's raid, militia leaders at Buffalo and Black Rock anticipated subsequent attacks and sent a request directly to Tompkins to call out their units. Tompkins fired a note to Generals Amos Hall and Caleb Hopkins, the two closest militia commanders, that they had full authority to respond to emergencies and not to wait "till the blow be struck."[21] In this and other situations, Tompkins cut red tape that seemed to slow the response time of the local militia.

After the raid on Black Rock, the New York Iroquois formally declared a defensive alliance with the United States. Leaders from as far away as the settlements on the Genesee River pledged warriors if called for by white authorities. The chiefs, speaking in turn, requested pay, ammunition, shoes, and shirts for the warriors who would camp near Buffalo. Red Jacket asked that the Americans return to the New York Iroquois any Indian prisoners from the Six Nations of Canada. In reciprocity, the New York Indians would turn over white prisoners. Cornplanter requested that the Americans ensure that no liquor would be given to the warriors. "We can not stand [liquor] in battle. You can drink and fight. Our forefathers fought without liquor." Iroquois temperance was demonstrated in an earlier meeting at Fort Niagara. Red Jacket and twelve Seneca stayed overnight waiting for a meeting with Morgan Lewis. Their host, Lt. Col. George McFeely, offered his visitors a bottle of whiskey. "The whole thirteen did not drink the one wineglassful the whole evening although they would all take up the glass and put it to their lips as often as invited." Boyd organized about four hundred volunteer warriors who were paid and received rations. He appointed Farmer's Brother as their colonel.[22]

The Iroquois joined Porter's brigade of volunteers providing security to the American picket lines around Fort George. On August 17, Porter and Maj. Cyrenius Chapin led an attack upon the British pickets at Peter Ball's farm. The back-and-forth confusion brought John Norton's Grand River Iroquois in deadly close combat with the New York warriors. The New Yorkers, volunteers and Indians, had the better part of the day. Col. Winfield Scott recalled the "roars of delight" from the regulars as their Iroquois allies marched a dozen prisoners into Fort George. General de Rottenburg protested the barbarous treatment of the dead, wounded, and captured by the New York warriors.[23]

While the fighting continued in and around Fort George, the Royal Navy was enjoying success out on the lake. Chauncey remained in port, so Yeo had a free hand. His captains seized six merchant vessels and their sizeable cargoes. On June 15, the British raided Charlotte at the mouth of the Genesee River, capturing a sloop with a large cargo of grain. No guards were there to oppose the landing. On June 19, Yeo's squadron approached Oswego, but gunfire from land-based batteries and gunboats persuaded Yeo to seek a softer target.[24]

When he learned of the raid on Charlotte, militia Brig. Gen. William Burnet anticipated a raid at Sodus Bay. Burnet ordered out local militia units, including Philetus Swift's regiment and Captain Dorsey's company of exempts. Many of the local men were then serving at Lewiston on the Niagara. Swift's men removed the public stores, about eight hundred barrels of flour and pork, to safety. Burnet dismissed the militiamen on the morning of June 19. However, when Yeo and his squadron arrived just hours later, riders set off to recall them. A young boy, John P. Terry, recalled seeing a horseman riding fast past his house, "blowing a horn, and shouting 'The British are landing.'" Only about sixty militiamen under Capt. Elias Hull returned in time to oppose the night landing, and these men conducted a fighting withdrawal back to the location of the food stores. The New Yorkers suffered four casualties, the British about ten. The British shore party reembarked but returned early the following morning. Unopposed this time, the raiders took 230 barrels of flour, largely private property. Perhaps because the militia had opposed the landing, the British plundered homes and burned all the buildings in Sodus Point save one. After the British departed, swarms of local militia arrived. Burnet deployed a number of his men to Pultneyville to guard against an expected raid. In his report to Tompkins, Burnet praised the speed at which the local militia had answered the alarm and their success in removing public property.[25]

Operations at the western end of Lake Ontario picked up when the frigate *General Pike* finally sailed on July 22. Commodore Chauncey now believed that he had the advantage over Yeo's squadron. Secretary of the Navy William Jones prodded the commodore into action: "The moment is critical, and the issue of our contest, for ascendency on Lake Ontario, must ere this be decided; every thing that can inspire confidence and rational hope, is on our side." Chauncey arrived at Fort George on July 28, picked up Col. Winfield Scott and a detachment of regulars, and sailed toward Burlington Bay with the goal of seizing stores on Burlington Heights. Scott landed five hundred soldiers, marines, and sailors on the narrow neck of land that separates Burlington Bay from Little Lake. Scouting Burlington Heights, Scott discovered to his dismay that the position was too strong to assault. Chauncey agreed and the squadron sailed eastward to York, where they learned that the capital of Upper Canada was defenseless. Most of the militiamen had given their parole after the battle on April 27 and could not bear arms until they were exchanged. On July 31, Scott's landing party burned public buildings, seized four hundred barrels of flour and hard bread, and returned to Fort George. Chauncey regarded the raid as retaliation for the attack on Sodus Point.[26]

Chauncey and Boyd were planning to relieve the siege of Fort George when Yeo arrived at the head of the lake on August 7. The two squadrons were asymmetric in their armament, a condition that perhaps more than any other forestalled the naval battle that Chauncey needed. Yeo's squadron was armed predominately with carronades, artillery that packed a big wallop but had a limited range. The American fleet, in contrast, had a mix of carronades and long-range guns. Both commodores, of course, sought battle with the weather gauge to their advantage. A naval leader would attempt to approach the opposing vessels from an upwind position, the weather gauge, thus enjoying significant advantage in sailing capabilities. The squadron with the weather gauge controlled when and how the battle might unfold. Chauncey would choose to maintain a distance from Yeo, thus allowing his dominance in long-range gunnery to tell. Yeo, however, would want to close quickly to give his carronades greater effect. The weather gauge might give him this opportunity.

Another issue, this one strategic, influenced the thinking of the two naval commanders as well.[27] Yeo could lose the war in an afternoon. If the Royal Navy squadron was eliminated or if the Kingston shipyard fell, the government could not keep army or navy elements supplied. Without British weapons and ammunition, the allied Indians would very likely make peace with the Americans. If Chauncey lost the decisive battle, the Americans still had the option of invasion north along the Lake Champlain–Richelieu River corridor or down the Saint Lawrence River. The war would be won with the fall of Quebec. Britain would be forced, or so thought Madison, to either fight to retake the city and everything to the west or agree to the American war aims in return for the provinces.

Yeo understood this dynamic as he pushed his squadron toward Chauncey on the morning of August 7. Chauncey was eager to engage. This was the first time that the two commodores would meet with the majority of their fleets. On the shores around Newark and Fort Niagara, hundreds gathered to witness the clash of nineteen magnificent warships. However, the clash was not to be. While the wind favored Yeo, it was not enough to meet the requirement to close quickly. The lead warships of the two squadrons approached no closer than a mile and a half, well out of range. Both commodores changed course, sailing away from one another. No doubt, the crowds were disappointed. Yeo headed north toward York, while Chauncey settled in closer to the southern shore as the wind died away.[28]

Chauncey's squadron soon suffered two setbacks. The first occurred in the very early hours of August 8 when two former merchant schooners, the *Hamilton* and the *Scourge*, sank in a very sudden storm with the loss of about eighty-four souls. One of the handful of survivors of the *Scourge*, Ned Myers, had before the war been a shipmate of James Fenimore Cooper. Cooper later wrote of Myers's adventures in *Ned Myers: Or, a Life Before the Mast*. Two days later, the Royal Navy captured the former lakers, *Julia* and *Growler*. Seaman Myers, who survived the sinking of the *Scourge*, was among the captives on the *Julia*. His war was over, and he spent the remainder of the conflict as a prisoner in Halifax. Chauncey's attempt to bring Yeo to battle was over for the time being. The Americans lost four schooners and the British gained two—not an inconsiderable shift in the naval balance. On August 11, Yeo sailed toward York, and Chauncey brought the squadron back to Sackett's Harbor to take on provisions.[29]

On August 18, the American shipyard launched the schooner *Sylph*, a 330-ton purpose-built warship. Armed with four long 32-pounder guns on pivots and six six-pounders as broadsides, the Sylph more than made up for the loss of the four converted merchantmen. Melancthon Woolsey, now promoted to master commandant, skippered the new vessel. On the evening of August 29, Chauncey brought the squadron onto the lake in search of Yeo. The two squadrons met up about three miles north of the Genesee River on September 11. The *Sylph* and *Pike* opened up with their long-range guns, damaging the rigging of their targets but inflicting few casualties among the crews. Because the winds were light, Yeo could neither close nor escape the unequal cannonading of long guns. Eventually the wind picked up, and Yeo moved his squadron to safety. The day prior, Commodore Perry and the Lake Erie squadron defeated their Royal Navy counterparts, opening up the American land campaign in the west. Perry became a national hero while his superior, Isaac Chauncey, was still unable to destroy the British Lake Ontario squadron. Perry wrote to the secretary of the navy requesting transfer to Newport, Rhode Island. Secretary Jones approved the action. Mackinac Island remained in British hands, and Chauncey fumed at losing Perry before that officer had completed his work on the upper lakes.[30]

Later in September, both commodores received orders that brought the squadrons to the western part of Lake Ontario. Yeo was escorting a convoy of supply ships for de Rottenburg, and Chauncey moved to pick up troops at Fort George to carry them to Sackett's Harbor. On the morning of September 28, the two squadrons caught sight of one another south of York. The Americans enjoyed the wind at their back as Chauncey approached the British squadron. It must have appeared to the seamen of both fleets that their day of decision had arrived. The engagement began at about 1:15 P.M. and in minutes, fire from the *Pike* crippled Yeo's flagship, *Wolfe*. Commander William Howe Mulcaster saved the *Wolfe* by interposing his ship, the *Royal George*, between the *Wolfe* and the *Pike*.

Yeo ordered the damaged *Wolfe* to escape westward toward Burlington Bay. Those British warships that could, pounded the *Pike*, which soon suffered serious hits and a burst gun. The winds rose to gale force and Yeo's squadron raced toward safety with the Americans in pursuit. The storm threatened both fleets, and Chauncey wisely broke contact. This action, known as the Burlington Races, demonstrated competent seamanship and aggressiveness by both squadrons. Over the next two days, the storm raged, and the American squadron gathered at Four Mile Creek. Chauncey, erroneously believing that Yeo was heading eastward to capture the American transports carrying more than 3,000 soldiers, raced to protect them. Instead, he came upon an unescorted British troop convoy. The Americans bagged five of the seven schooners. While Chauncey had not destroyed the Royal Navy squadron, he and his crews had clearly come out on top.[31]

Meanwhile, the situation of the army at Fort George was serious, if not desperate. Firing between the American pickets and the British and Indian patrols was a near daily occurrence. Late in August, Prevost visited the Niagara frontier to see for himself what might be done. On August 24, he ordered a demonstration to induce the Americans to come out of their fortifications and give battle. Boyd declined the invitation. Prevost believed that he would require more troops, a battering train, and the cooperation of the Royal Navy. Without ready prospect of these resources, Prevost gave up the notion of reducing Fort George.[32]

General Boyd maintained a high state of vigilance in the garrison, an effort that took its toll on his division's morale and health. Surgeon James Mann maintained that poor sanitation in the camp, bad rations, and hot, wet weather, were responsible for extensive numbers of cases of diarrhea, dysentery, and typhus. In August, more than one-third of the garrison was on the sick list and half of the medical staff was sick or otherwise not able to do their duties. General Boyd directed that regimental commanders improve camp sanitation, and this action achieved some good results.[33]

Unfortunately for the American cause, James Wilkinson arrived on the Niagara frontier on September 4. Wilkinson had been the senior general in the army before the war. He had a well-deserved reputation as an intriguer and would demonstrate his general incompetence in the coming months. In the spring of 1813, the Senate confirmed his promotion to major general, and Secretary of War Armstrong ordered Wilkinson to join Dearborn's staff. However, with Dearborn's departure in July, Wilkinson acceded to command of the Ninth Military District.[34]

Armstrong needed to reenergize the 1813 campaign, and he discussed three options with Wilkinson. The first was to clear British forces from the Niagara peninsula. The second was to attack Kingston. Wilkinson eventually chose the third option, the capture of Montreal in conjunction with forces stationed around Lake Champlain. Wilkinson's bitter enemy, Maj. Gen. Wade Hampton, commanded the division on Lake Champlain.

Skirmishing continued sporadically outside Fort George through September and into early October. De Rottenburg decided that there was no point in continuing the loose blockade, and he pulled his troops back to quieter quarters on Burlington Heights. Meanwhile, Wilkinson directed his attention toward the upcoming operation to capture Montreal.

The 1813 campaign had begun with much promise. While the raid on York was expensive in human life, it also demonstrated the successful results of close army–navy cooperation. The capture of Fort George, another product of interservice cooperation, exhibited glimmers of military improvements. The raid on Sackett's Harbor illustrated an essential axiom: Chauncey would cooperate fully with the army only when his base was secure and Royal Navy power was diminished. However, his efforts to bring Yeo to decisive battle came to naught. Strategically, the Battle of Stoney Creek was the turning point in the campaign. Without naval support, no operation to clear the Niagara peninsula was likely to enjoy success. Operations directed against Montreal did not require Chauncey's warships, and thus were essentially army matters. For the state of New York, however, the defense of New York City commanded considerable attention.

CHAPTER 10

NEW YORK CITY REDUX

Governor Daniel Tompkins administered the state's militia organization efficiently. He rotated detached militia regiments, kept the rolls of the officer corps complete, and brought new companies of volunteers and exempts into service. Yet, in all of this, he was disappointed that Madison had not given him a command, an act that he thought "ought" to occur. In a letter to George Fleming he wrote, "I have never yet been requested, authorized, or permitted, by the President to take any command. Perhaps he thought it would deprive some of his Great Generals of the Army, of opportunities for collecting ungathered laurels." As a general in federal service, Tompkins would command both regulars and state forces. Such a position would give Tompkins the opportunity to reduce federal–state administrative friction that was crippling efficiency. However, he had no military experience. If Madison was aware of Tompkins's ambitions, he did not see a reason to confer stars on the governor in 1813.[1]

While Maj. Gen. Henry Dearborn and Commodore Isaac Chauncey readied their commands for the 1813 campaign, Tompkins turned his attention to the state's largest city. On March 15, and before the gubernatorial election, Tompkins informed the Assembly on the defense of New York City.[2] He reported that guns were emplaced on the islands in the Upper Bay and Staten Island. Construction of barracks and furnaces to heat shot continued at Fort Richmond on Staten Island. The fortifications on Manhattan Island were ready except no guns were yet mounted in Fort Gansevoort on the Hudson. While the land underwater on Hendrick's Reef on the Long Island side of the Narrows was in the possession of the federal government, the owner of the adjacent land would not sell. Thus, work there commenced slowly. New Jersey was erecting fortifications at Sandy Hook guarding the Lower Bay.[3]

The War Department took its time replacing Col. Jonathan Williams, who had resigned as the chief engineer in New York City. Lt. Col. Joseph Gardner Swift was the next in line for appointment to chief of engineers and superintendent of the military academy at West Point. Swift had been designated the first graduate of West Point. Alexander Macomb had taken the curriculum along with Swift; however, Macomb was already commissioned. The War Department nominated Swift to the rank of colonel in July, but the Senate did not get around to confirming the promotion until December, which it did unanimously. After consultation with Williams, Swift reported to New York City in April 1813 to superintend construction. Williams and Swift drew heavily upon the graduates of West Point to assist them in superintending the many projects associated with fortifying the city and its environs. Of West Point's ninety-seven graduates who served in the war, seventeen of them, all engineers, worked on the city's defenses.[4]

Tompkins reported to the legislature that the federal government maintained over forty field guns and 10,000 muskets in the federal arsenal in the city or on Governor's Island. Tompkins further noted that about 3,500 soldiers, nearly all volunteers, were present for duty in the city's defenses. This number included only 250 regulars. In March, Lt. Thomas Randall passed through the city while marching his company from Baltimore to Greenbush. He wrote to his father, "New York has a military appearance, bodies of troops continually passing the streets." Nevertheless, Tompkins considered the number "very inadequate." He estimated that defenses required 8,450 full-time soldiers— regulars and federal and state volunteers. In an emergency, this number could be supplemented with 4,000 local militia and seaman. He readily acknowledged that the federal government probably would not increase the numbers of regulars assigned to the defense of the city. The secretary of war deployed most regulars to invade Canada. Tompkins recommended that the legislature authorize funds to construct a number of supporting fortifications to protect the approach to the city from Long Island Sound. In all, Tompkins challenged the legislature with a reasoned plan to prepare the city's defenses to meet any likely contingency. Partisan politics, as much as any other reason, prevented the state from achieving the governor's vision.[5]

As the war moved into its second year, Congress and the War Department took steps to bring weaponry closer to the fighting front. During 1813, the newly created Ordnance Department built new manufacturing sites and arsenals. In July, James Gibbons sold the federal government twelve acres of land north of Albany. Workers initially produced musket cartridges and later fabricated gun carriages and all the paraphernalia associated with equipping a train of artillery. Initially known as the Arsenal at Gibbonsville, after the war this facility was called the Arsenal at Watervliet.

On May 1, the War Department rationalized the command structure with the establishment of nine, later ten, military districts. The Third Military

District comprised New York from the ocean north to the Highlands and eastern New Jersey. Newly promoted Brig. Gen. George Izard took temporary command from Brig. Gen. Henry Burbeck until Secretary of War John Armstrong assigned Izard to command a brigade at Plattsburgh. Izard was born in London of a rich South Carolinian father and a mother from New York's prominent DeLancey family. With the patronage of James Monroe, minister to France, Izard attended a military college in Metz, France. Izard served in the regular army from 1794 until he resigned in 1803. Because Izard was an officer of Federalist sympathies, it was noteworthy that the Madison administration recommissioned him in March 1812 as a colonel.[6]

Armstrong appointed Maj. Gen. Henry Dearborn to command the Third Military District. Dearborn had been cooling his heels at his home in Massachusetts since Armstrong relieved him of command of the Northern Army in June. The elderly general arrived in New York City in October. The secretary of war commissioned Nicholas Gray as a colonel and inspector general of the district. Gray had provided artillery and engineering expertise the previous year to Maj. Gen. Stephen Van Rensselaer. As the inspector general, Gray's duties were to oversee discipline, conduct inspections, and improve training.

In 1813, the War Department raised federal volunteers and regulars to defend New York City. Armstrong understood the difficulties associated with repeated calls for detached militia for ninety-day tours of duty. Fewer militiamen volunteered for detached service, which disrupted their lives for small economic gain. The earlier call for United States Volunteers for one-year service had seen modest results. The War Department then eased the requirements of volunteer units and realized some success. Responding to the governor's concerns, the War Department raised the Second and Third Regiments of United States Volunteers for one-year service exclusively for the defense of New York City. The U.S. Volunteers received the same pay as regulars but without a land bounty. However, if a soldier served faithfully and returned his weapon in good repair, he received ten dollars at the end of service. One year of continual employment appealed to many of the city's working poor. Col. Samuel Hawkins, from Ulster County, commanded the Second Regiment and Lt. Col. Alexander Denniston, from Newburgh, commanded the Third Regiment. Denniston was a veteran of the 1798 Irish Rebellion and, before the war, had commanded a company of volunteer light infantry familiarly known as the Irish Blues. These two regiments recruited quickly and replaced militia units in the garrisons on Staten Island in early 1813.

In July, the Forty-First U.S. Infantry recruited in the city and absorbed large numbers of men who had served in volunteer militia units. Militia Gen. Robert Bogardus resigned his state commission to accept appointment in the regular army as a colonel. Later in the summer, the Forty-Second U.S. Infantry recruited in Pennsylvania and New York City. The War Department assigned this regiment, under Lt. Col. James G. Forbes, to the city's defenses. Forbes had served in the state's volunteer militia. The Thirty-Second U.S. Infantry, recruited in Pennsylvania and Delaware, sent most of its newly recruited companies to New York City. The commander of the Thirty-Second was Col. Stephen E. Fotterall, a Pennsylvanian. The Third U.S. Artillery had companies scattered in several commands. Lt. Col. James House, a skilled artillerist as well as an accomplished portrait painter, commanded a few companies of the Third on Governor's Island. The regular soldiers joined the two regiments of U.S. Volunteers, thus adding a level of permanency to the city's garrison.[7]

The increase in regular and volunteer units assigned to the city's defense was particularly opportune because the mechanisms for bringing militiamen into service in an emergency were inefficient. In early September, British warships proceeded up Long Island Sound. The local militia commander at New Rochelle called up his regiment. Maj. Gen. Ebenezer Stevens, a veteran of the Revolution and the militia commander in southern New York state, asked Col. John R. Fenwick, the adjutant general of the Third Military District, to approve the call-up. Fenwick responded that he had no orders to do so. This meant that there would be no rations or pay. Stevens had no advance authority granted by the state legislature, so he appealed to the mayor of New York City, DeWitt Clinton, to pay the militiamen. Fortunately, the warships departed. However, this event illustrated the problem of responding to a surprise attack.[8]

Fenwick himself was disappointed with the time required to summon, assemble, arm, and transport militiamen to posts on the Narrows should an invasion fleet appear in the Lower Bay. Stevens pointed to the challenge of assembling sufficient boats and rowers to move the men from lower Manhattan. Stevens noted that in the absence of an actual invasion, a general mobilization would be difficult.

> For if the minds of the Citizens are not alarmed it would be difficult to furnish the troops within the time before mentioned [six hours]. An order to Citizens to go into the service is not always with alacrity obeyed. No forfeitures or penalties, whether than from the deficiency of the U. States laws or a neglect in executing them, having been enforced on the delinquents under the former requisition in this Place. A general belief exists among the Militia that they cannot be compelled to go into the Service.[9]

The state and federal governments never achieved a practical solution in forcing militiamen to respond to a call-up. However, they continued to cooperate in arming the militia. The state received 2,000 stands of arms from the federal arsenal at Springfield, Massachusetts. Tompkins directed these weapons be sent to the state arsenal in Albany. Additionally, the last five hundred muskets from Eli Whitney's factory in Connecticut arrived in the fall and went to the state arsenal in New York City. By October, however, with arms issued to the brigades on the frontiers, only 3,250 state muskets remained for the militiamen guarding the city.[10]

While Federalists in the city generally supported defensive efforts, evidence of partisanship still existed. In one example, Capt. William Hawley of the common militia issued an order stating, "We condemn the administration for their weakness and folly in plunging us unprepared into this Quixotic war." Hawley's regimental commander court-martialed the captain on a charge of "endeavoring to excite dissension and insubordination among the members of his command." The court met and acquitted Hawley. However, General Bogardus disapproved the court's findings and convicted the captain. Hawley resigned his commission in 1814.[11] Many soldiers were well aware of the case. Such events diminished the morale and cohesion of the militia units charged with the defense of the city.

Tompkins responded to a War Department requisition for 5,000 detached militia. On the last day of July, the governor issued a general order for thirteen of his brigade commanders to select citizens for up to three months' duty starting in early September. The counties involved were all on the eastern side of the state, from Dutchess and Orange Counties in the south to Franklin and Clinton Counties on the Canadian border. The governor gave command of these detached units to Maj. Gen. Benjamin Mooers and directed him to organize the men into ten regiments to be combined into three brigades. Tompkins selected the regimental commanders but allowed commanders supplying the troops to choose the other officers.[12]

New York City celebrated America's successes on the high seas. On March 1, 1813, the Common Council awarded Commodore William Bainbridge of the frigate *Constitution* the freedom of the city in recognition of his victory over the frigate *Java*.[13] Within weeks, word arrived that Master Commandant James Lawrence of the sloop *Hornet* had defeated HM Sloop *Peacock*. Lawrence was a darling of New Yorkers as he maintained his household in the city. The Common Council recognized his achievement with freedom of the city and a dinner for Lawrence and his crew.[14] The Navy Department gave Lawrence command of the *Chesapeake* and he fell, mortally wounded, in battle with HMS *Shannon* on June 1. As he was carried below deck, he admonished the crew with the timeless exhortation "Don't give up the ship." The British did not return his body to American control until September.

As the year unfolded, the threat to the city's commerce increased measurably. Late in March, First Lord of the Admiralty Robert Melville ordered a strict blockade of the American coast south of Rhode Island. Admiral Sir John Borlase Warren implemented the blockade as warships became available. On April 11, word arrived that a large British squadron including ships of the line and frigates was sighted off Sandy Hook.[15] The British watched the Narrows closely to ensure that no vessel could escape the Upper Bay. If the British captured a vessel, the captain demanded a ransom, the amount being relative to the value of the craft and its cargo. However, British captains allowed vessels carrying Admiralty licenses to pass in either direction. Congress had passed several bills outlawing trade with Britain, and thus American merchant ships carrying these licenses were breaking American laws and therefore subject to capture by American privateers.

A small flotilla of gunboats defended the waters around New York City. The Department of the Navy commissioned Jacob Lewis, former captain of the privateer *Bunker Hill*, as a master commandant and gave him command of the gunboats with the honorific title of commodore. Commodore Lewis kept his gunboats actively engaged in protecting the coastal trade. Lewis maintained most of his gunboats near Sandy Hook, where they could observe the blockading squadron yet were protected to some extent from deep-draft vessels by sandbars and shoals. On occasion, his gunboats exchanged long-range shots with blockading vessels, with little damage inflicted on either side. He also maintained gunboats in Long Island Sound to challenge warships approaching the city from that quarter.

In February, before Melville had announced the blockade, Secretary of the Navy William Jones reduced the number of gunboats to fifteen as a cost-cutting measure. Jones stipulated that Lewis could bring the excess gunboats back into temporary service in an emergency, crewed by volunteers. With the appearance of the Royal Navy squadron off Sandy Hook, Lewis returned the surplus gunboats to service and requested the Department of the Navy to pay for crews. This request brought a strong rebuke from Jones, who reminded Lewis that he was to find volunteers to crew the excess gunboats and that Lewis could be held personally responsible for any costs his actions had incurred. Jones ordered Lewis to take the gunboats out of service unless the British should attack. Nicholas Fish, the Federalist chairman of the city's Committee of Defense, asked Jones to authorize a number of additional gunboats for which the city would pay for the crews. Jones agreed to this compromise and told Lewis to bring up to fifteen additional gunboats into service. This situation was a successful example of sharing defense responsibilities between the federal and state governments.[16]

In the darkness of May 29, a number of ship's boats silently approached Sandy Hook on a reconnaissance. The picket guard discovered the British attempt to land and opened fire. The boats reversed course and returned to the squadron.[17] On July 6, Captain Thomas Hardy transmitted to city officials that Admiral Warren declared a "strict and vigorous" blockade of the port of New York.[18] Hardy had been Admiral Lord Horatio Nelson's friend and had been with him at his death at Trafalgar in 1805. Now Hardy commanded the blockading vessels. He established his headquarters in Gardiner's Bay at the eastern end of Long Island. The local populace fed his crews for the duration of the war, despite laws prohibiting trade with the enemy. In July, a small British raiding force landed at night at Sag Harbor and set fire to a sloop. However, the militia stationed there was alert and fired upon the raiders, who withdrew.[19] This was the largest action on Long Island during the war.

British captains continued to stop and check passing merchant ships for proper trading licenses. Still, many neutral vessels managed to deliver their cargoes to the city. The British found that it was more difficult to stop vessels transiting Long Island Sound than those attempting to sail through the channel at Sandy Hook. Thus, the city was not entirely cut off from the coastal trade with New England, although the British would include that region within its blockade in 1814. Nonetheless, many of the city's large merchant vessels remained idle.[20]

The arrival of the Royal Navy squadron was the cause of increased vigilance on the part of land forces and anxiety on the part of the citizenry. Series of telegraphs consisting of spheres on ropes suspended from the arms of poles enabled signalers to transmit messages, weather-dependent, from Sandy Hook, Staten Island, and Governor's Island to Third Military District headquarters at the Southwest Battery. When warships approached, signalers informed headquarters. Depending on the strength of the enemy, headquarters would raise an alarm that summoned the volunteer and common militia to their assembly areas. Alarms interrupted daily life, yet served to exercise the city's response to a real emergency.

In June, Governor Tompkins wrote to Secretary of the Navy Jones recommending the creation of a regiment of Sea Fencibles dedicated to the defense of New York City. Tompkins reasoned that seamen were more capable than land forces because they could crew artillery in shore fortifications as well as serve in the flotilla. These forces would serve under the navy's authority. Tompkins added that mariners, by the nature of their experience, were "better prepared to submit to subordination & discipline."[21] On July 26, 1813, Congress authorized the formation of ten companies of Sea Fencibles. The companies assigned to New York City, about 1,000 sailors, came under the command of Commodore Lewis.

In November, Admiral Warren proclaimed a strict blockade of the entire American coast from Long Island Sound to the Gulf of Mexico. In December, Commodore Hardy, with his flagship *Ramillies*, moved to the Sound to add emphasis to the expanded blockade. The net effect was to further constrain the rights of neutral merchant vessels attempting to trade at these American ports. The British did not formally blockade New England in order to encourage popular anti-war sentiments and to allow some trade beneficial to the British, such as the export of food for ports under British control. Typically, farmers or intermediaries took flour to New England ports to be loaded onto neutral ships and then transported to Halifax to feed British troops. Congress attempted to close this loophole in December. Starting on the first of the new year, no American vessel could carry cargo of any kind to a foreign port, and no neutral vessel could depart an American port carrying provisions or military or naval stores. Smuggling continued; however, the federal government now had a clear policy for enforcement.

The supply of goods entering the city diminished, and farmers lost foreign markets for flour and other foodstuffs. With the coming of winter, the loss of a steady supply of Virginian or European coal distressed the population, especially the poor. Households became dependent upon firewood from Long Island and the Hudson Valley. Concerned citizens raised funds to supply firewood to the needy, assisting about 3,000 households.[22] Various social groups solicited funds to distribute to the poor, and the City Council voted funds that aldermen could use to distribute as they thought best. The war's negative effects were widely felt throughout the city.

The Madison administration had big expectations for the contributions of privateers to the war effort, but by 1813, conditions had changed. The expansion of the British blockade had a deleterious effect on privateers. It became more difficult to slip a captured prize into New York harbor. Privateer captains responded by taking captured merchant vessels into compliant European ports. Some captains offered the skipper of the captured vessel an opportunity to ransom his ship and cargo with an immediate cash payment. If the cargo was of insufficient value to justify the risk of sending a prize crew into a friendly port, the captain might sink the vessel. In all of these cases, the federal government was denied the duties that would have been assessed in an American court.

As the profits collected by privateers dropped off, captains and merchants in New York and Baltimore complained to Congress and recommended steps to make privateering more advantageous. In June, Congress reduced duties on captured cargoes and also offered privateer owners a bounty for every British sailor brought to America. As the Royal Navy increased its anti-privateering efforts, more American seamen became incarcerated as prisoners of war. The

U.S. government needed British sailors to exchange for Americans held captive.[23] Privateering continued, but not at a pace that would persuade the British government to give in to American demands.

In April, *General Armstrong* returned to port after an encounter with a British warship off the coast of Surinam. The stockholders of the privateer voted its captain, Guy Champlin, a sword in recognition of his gallantry in avoiding capture. The *General Armstrong* eventually captured twenty-three ships, but only two made it back to a prize court. However, more typical of the privateering enterprise was the *Governor Tompkins*. This ship captured twenty-one vessels, but only five arrived at a prize court. The owners of *Governor Tompkins* took her out of privateering service in September and sold her at auction for a heavy loss.[24]

Perhaps the most famous New York privateer was the legendary sloop *Young Teazer*. The story starts with the capture of its predecessor, *Teazer*, seized in December 1812. Frederick Johnson, the captain of that vessel, accepted parole, vowing not to return to the war until he was exchanged. However, Johnson reneged on his agreement and sailed on *Young Teazer* as the vessel's first lieutenant. The privateer took a dozen prizes until it was cornered on June 27, 1813, in Mahone Bay near Halifax, Nova Scotia. As the crew were preparing to fight off half a dozen ship's boats approaching them, Johnson disappeared below deck. He knew what was in store for him when the British discovered that he had broken parole. Moments later, the ship's magazine exploded, killing twenty-nine crewmen. The eight survivors surrendered. Since that time, viewers have recorded mysterious lights in the night sky of Mahone Bay.[25]

Congress prompted experimentation to develop new weapons and methods of naval combat. Congress passed the Torpedo Act in March, granting one-half the value of a warship to an individual who destroyed it. Robert Fulton and Commodore Lewis cooperated in developing torpedoes and underwater gunnery. In the early nineteenth century, a torpedo was an explosive charge detonated against the side of its target. Typically, a small vessel rammed the enemy warship below the waterline with a torpedo mounted on a forward spar. Also, a submarine could attach the torpedo to the target under water. Fulton and Lewis demonstrated the potential of an underwater cannon. They placed a one hundred-pounder columbiad with a ten-pound powder charge below the surface of the water. The firing mechanism of the cannon was dry inside the attacking boat while the muzzle extended into the water. Upon firing, the cannon could drive the massive ball through three feet of solid oak at a range of six feet. The British decision not to attack New York City precluded the use of this cannon under combat conditions.[26]

Fulton's creativity seemingly knew no bounds. While working on torpedoes and underwater cannon, he conceived of a steam-powered warship carrying guns sufficient to challenge anything the Royal Navy could sail into the Upper Bay. This vessel would be the world's first steam-powered warship. Fulton asked Thomas Jefferson to petition Congress for an appropriation for the warship and the Navy Department came up with $95,000. During the summer, Fulton worked with Stephen Decatur to establish the functionality and specifications of his warship. The vessel sailed the following year.[27]

The Americans experienced limited success in a less technical method of naval warfare. Commodore Lewis assisted a civilian in an attempt to win the bounty authorized by the Torpedo Act. The civilian crew brought a small schooner loaded with foodstuffs within range of Admiral Hardy's flagship *Ramillies*. They connected one of the barrels to a charge of gunpowder. Lewis anticipated that the British would capture the vessel and bring it alongside *Ramillies* to be unloaded. Removing the barrel would trigger the detonation. As predicted, the warship sent boats to capture the schooner. However, winds prevented the British sailors from bringing the schooner to the *Ramillies*. Instead, they unloaded the cargo into a ship's boat. The resulting explosion killed an officer and ten seamen. Afterward, Royal Navy captains exercised greater caution in dealing with captured vessels.[28]

The war also affected city politics. Indian combat activities as allies of the British caused general revulsion. The killing of wounded Americans after the Battle of the River Raisin angered the country. In response, the Republican Tammany Society dropped its traditional Indian trappings, such as titles and symbols of office. This was a divisive issue within the club, and several traditionalists dropped their membership. Typically, when the society marched in the Fourth of July parade, its members wore Indian garb. Choosing not to provoke a negative response, members of the Tammany Society dressed in civilian attire in the 1813 parade. The marching units represented not only political clubs, but also every sort of social and ethnic group or trade guild. The uniformed companies marched, and artillery units fired national salutes from the Southwest Battery and the harbor islands. After the parade, clubs moved to separate venues for dinners, at which time participants made toasts that reflected party differences.

In September, the people of New York City united in mourning when the British returned James Lawrence's body to the U.S. Navy for burial. On September 16, the city staged a funeral procession of over six thousand military and civilians who accompanied the casket to a burial site at Trinity Church on Broadway. A few days later, the joyous news of Oliver Hazard Perry's decisive victory on Lake Erie arrived. Perry's flagship, *Lawrence*, had flown a battle flag inscribed "Don't Give Up the Ship." The city's mood changed from gloom to ecstasy, amplified by the news of William Henry Harrison's unequivocal triumph at the Battle of the

Thames on October 5, 1813, in Upper Canada. City officials had discouraged illuminations in the past for fear of accidental fires. However, this time the citizenry would not be denied. On the evening of October 23, City Hall was decked out with hundreds of candles and lamps, as were dozens of other public buildings and private clubs and homes. Church bells rang. In the harbor, Commodore Lewis decked out two of his gunboats with colored lamps while other vessels fired rockets. It was a year since the debacle at Queenston Heights, and the city was disposed to celebrate these new naval and military victories.

General Harrison passed through New York City in late November en route to Washington. The month prior, Republican aldermen in the Common Council offered a resolution to award Harrison a sword and Freedom of the City. The Federalist majority on the council voted down the resolution, ostensibly on the grounds that the city had not awarded swords to the naval heroes. Republicans used the negative vote against the Federalists in the city elections in mid-November. Notwithstanding the effort, the Federalists maintained a slender majority on the Common Council. The Republicans honored Harrison with a magnificent dinner attended by Governor Tompkins, Major Generals Dearborn and Hampton, and Commodore Perry. Mayor DeWitt Clinton did not attend; it was doubtful that he would be welcomed in the midst of ardent Republicans.[29]

Defensive activities in New York City continued as a model of federal–state cooperation. The entities shared a common focus—the defense of a city vital to the national economy. State and federal governments shared responsibility for building and garrisoning harbor fortifications. The War Department raised both regular and volunteer regiments for dedicated service in the city and its environs. Recruiting went more easily as new soldiers had good prospects of avoiding service on the frontiers. Still, issues of responsibility and authority remained. Lieutenant Colonel Fenwick's refusal to authorize the call-up of common militia in a potentially critical situation demonstrated the need for the War Department to devolve such authority to lower levels of command in response to an emergency. Doing so would require a change in military culture that was not fully resolved during the war. The state and city governments were generally much more responsive to the war's demands. The City Council's unique and generous offer to pay for the crews of federal gunboats stands out as an example.

Despite the growing presence of the Royal Navy, the year 1813 passed without an attack on New York City. However, in the fall of that year the focus of the war shifted north with two ill-fated invasions of Canada.

CHAPTER 11

THE BATTLE OF CHATEAUGUAY

Secretary of War John Armstrong had given in to Maj. Gen. Henry Dearborn and Commodore Isaac Chauncey in developing the 1813 campaign in March. However, that plan was overturned at Stoney Creek. Armstrong saw an opportunity to restart the campaign in July. With the temporary dominance of Chauncey's squadron, Armstrong proposed to Maj. Gen. Morgan Lewis at Sackett's Harbor to move on Kingston on the next occasion that Yeo withdrew his squadron to his base there. "Could a successful attack be made here, the fate of the campaign is decided—perhaps that of the war." Armstrong outlined a two-pronged plan—simultaneous attacks on Kingston and Montreal. In support of this venture, a large body of militia would assemble at Ogdensburg to draw British attention.[1]

However, it was not Morgan Lewis who led the second act of the 1813 campaign, but James Wilkinson. Wilkinson earned a well-deserved reputation as a devious intriguer whose skill at shifting blame to others allowed him to keep his career intact despite inquiry and court-martial. Congress approved Wilkinson's promotion to major general on March 2, along with Wade Hampton and Morgan Lewis. Wilkinson was the senior of this trio. With the removal of Dearborn in July, Wilkinson was the commander of the Ninth Military District.

Armstrong had to negotiate a very serious personality conflict between his two division commanders, Wilkinson and Hampton, the latter in command on Lake Champlain. Like Wilkinson, Hampton was also a Revolutionary veteran. Following that war, he became an extremely wealthy South Carolina planter and a member of Southern aristocracy. Hampton rejoined the army as a colonel of dragoons in 1808. From that time forward, the officer corps divided into two camps, those seeking favor with Wilkinson and those currying the patronage of Hampton, Wilkinson's hated foe. Now in 1813, Armstrong attempted to resolve the issue by allowing Hampton to receive orders directly from the secretary himself rather than, more properly, from Wilkinson.

Hampton arrived at Burlington, Vermont, on July 3. His task was formidable. Col. Robert Purdy, who had served in Mad Anthony Wayne's Legion of the United States, joined Hampton's division in mid-September to command a brigade. In a report to Wilkinson, Purdy related that "the army, consisting of about four thousand men, was composed principally of recruits who had been but a short time in service, and had not been exercised with that rigid discipline so essentially necessary to constitute the soldier. They had indeed, been taught various evolutions, but a spirit of subordination was foreign to their views."[2] Brig. Gen. George Izard, who would not arrive until October 16, would command Hampton's Second Brigade.

On August 5, Armstrong communicated his first analysis of the upcoming campaign to Wilkinson, who had finally arrived at the nation's capital. Armstrong rightly dismissed continuing operations on the Niagara peninsula as indecisive. The secretary offered Wilkinson two courses of action. The first was to attack Kingston when Chauncey had seized ascendency on Lake Ontario. The British would be expected to defend their major naval base "with great obstinacy." "That it may be taken by a joint application of our naval and military means is not, however, to be questioned." The second course of action was an advance down the St. Lawrence River to seize Montreal. In either event, Hampton would move north toward Montreal to pin down enemy forces. Both courses of action required Wilkinson's division to concentrate at Sackett's Harbor, an action that would lead to tragedy on the Niagara River in December. Armstrong left the decision of attacking either Kingston or Montreal to Wilkinson, depending on that general's operational judgment.[3]

Wilkinson's response the following day demonstrated his incompetence. He maintained that clearing the Niagara peninsula should take priority "to increase our own confidence, to diminish that of the enemy, and to popularize the war." He would then continue the operation by moving on Kingston "like lightning." Finally, if the weather held, both he and Hampton would attack Montreal. Given the lateness of the campaign season and the mountain of work necessary to prepare his forces, it is astonishing that Wilkinson thought his plan was feasible. He presented the secretary of war with a list of demands. Among these, Wilkinson insisted that "no order, of whatever nature, will be passed to any officer under my command, but through my hands." He then doubled down on his transparent effort to subordinate Hampton. "I hope I may be expressly authorized to detach from my command all persons who may manifest a temper or disposition to excite discontents, to generate factions, or embitter the service."[4]

Armstrong disabused Wilkinson of the notion of operating first on the Niagara peninsula. An attack west of Kingston "but wounds the tail of the lion, and of course is not calculated to hasten the termination of the war. Kingston, therefore . . . presents the first and great object of the campaign." The secretary of war again offered Wilkinson the option of moving directly on Kingston or indirectly, by seizing Montreal and thereby cutting logistical support to the naval base. Armstrong's basic understanding of strategy was sound; however, he failed to rein in Wilkinson's animus toward Hampton, whose impending operations would support the overall campaign. In fact, he seemingly granted the authority that Wilkinson demanded. Armstrong declared that orders to subordinate officers would pass through the commander of the military district—Wilkinson. Furthermore, he stated that "no specific permission is necessary for removing factious or disorderly men."[5]

Armstrong went to Albany, arriving on August 22, to plan and resource operations. He met with Governor Tompkins, who pressed upon the secretary his concern for the defenses of the state. In a letter recalling the meeting, Tompkins noted that Armstrong did "not seem to feel so much apprehension of any attack on New York as I do."[6] Armstrong then moved to Sackett's Harbor, Wilkinson's last known location, and arrived there on September 5. However, he missed Wilkinson, who was heading to Fort George.

Tompkins moved quickly to raise militia forces to support the new offenses. He ordered the muster of 1,500 militiamen and appointed Brig. Gen. Reuben Hopkins to command the militia brigade assigned to General Hampton's division at Plattsburgh. Sixty-seven year-old Hopkins had fought at Bunker Hill and had also served as a state senator for four years. The governor also moved to establish penalties for citizens who refused to report for militia duty. Tompkins gave detailed orders to Hopkins to "organize as speedily as possible a Court Martial for the trial of those persons . . . who have failed to rendezvous & enter service, according to orders for that purpose." Tompkins wrote to the secretary of war to recommend that Armstrong direct Tompkins to establish military courts specifically to bring delinquent militiamen to justice. Both regular and militia commanders knew that the legal issue was a militiaman who failed to attend muster was not in federal service and not subject to court-martial by the regular army. Tompkins wanted to close that loophole by getting a legal reading from the federal authorities. The Assembly was in Federalist hands, and Tompkins could not expect that body to change the state's militia laws. Tompkins also ordered Hopkins to conduct "rigorous & constant" training of the brigade.[7]

On September 22, Armstrong was still at Sackett's Harbor. He wrote to Maj. Gen. William Henry Harrison that in the wake of Perry's victory, Harrison should move eastward and clear the Niagara peninsula. This operation was preferable rather, "than to pursue the Indians into their woody and distant recesses." Harrison never received the order. He reoccupied Detroit and shattered Indian and British forces at the Battle of the Thames. Tecumseh died, along with his confederation. Over the next few weeks Harrison brought 1,300 regulars to Buffalo, arriving on October 24. His veterans remained on the Niagara frontier until ordered to Sackett's Harbor—too late to reinforce either division moving on Montreal.[8]

The final offensive movements of 1813 jumped off late in the year from Sackett's Harbor and Plattsburgh respectively. The year also saw the expansion of the U.S. Navy on Lake Champlain and the Royal Navy on the Richelieu River. In April, naval Lt. Thomas Macdonough moved his base of operations from Burlington, Vermont, to Plattsburgh. His squadron consisted of three sloops and two gunboats, though he did not have enough sailors to crew the gunboats.[9]

In June, Macdonough sent two of his sloops, *Growler* and *Eagle*, to patrol the northern end of the lake to deter activity by British gunboats. Lt. Sydney Smith rashly led the two craft into the narrow Richelieu River toward the British base at Isle aux Noix, where they were captured on June 3. The Americans lost one killed and ninety-nine taken prisoner. The loss of the two warships left Macdonough with only a sloop and two gunboats. Macdonough purchased two commercial sloops, but he had no guns to mount on them. When Secretary of the Navy William Jones learned of the loss, he gave Macdonough a blank check to rebuild. "You are to understand, that upon no account are you to suffer the enemy to gain the ascendency on Lake Champlain, and as you have now unlimited authority, to procure the necessary resources of men, materials, and munitions for that purpose, I rely upon your efficient and prudent use of the authority vested in you." Nevertheless, for the time being, the balance of naval power had shifted to the Royal Navy.[10]

At the end of July, the British at Isle aux Noix took advantage of their dominance and launched a series of raids. The purpose was to cause sufficient alarm to persuade the Americans to maintain troops on the lake rather than to shift them westward to Lake Ontario. Lieutenant Colonel John Murray led a raid on Plattsburgh on July 31, burning barracks, storehouses, and a blockhouse. The handful of militiamen stationed at Plattsburgh scattered at the approach of the British. Samuel Beaumont Jr., brother of Surgeon's Mate William Beaumont, lamented that despite boasts that Canada would be conquered by "a few men," that event was "now further off than when the war was declared." The following day, the British raided Cumberland Head and Point au Roche, in New York, and Swanton on the Vermont side. On August 2, the British raiders appeared offshore of Burlington, firing from long range at American shore batteries. Brig. Gen. Thomas Parker guarded the base with his brigade. Unable to engage the American squadron with any effect, the British burned four private vessels before withdrawing. Macdonough did not have enough men to properly crew more than a single schooner, the *President*, and he wisely chose not to pursue the raiding party.[11]

In September, General Hampton began his movement toward Montreal, one prong of the two-sided invasion. He was not optimistic of success, reporting to Armstrong that he was short of ordnance and ammunition and had no more than 4,000 men. The last two regular regiments arrived, "with mumps and measles upon them, and totally destitute of the least instruction." In searching for a route to Montreal, Hampton categorically rejected following the traditional Richelieu River axis. Commodore Macdonough concurred on this point; his few vessels would be hindered in sailing the narrow waters.[12] Instead, Hampton would take a land route that ran parallel to and west of the Richelieu River.

Starting on September 8, Macdonough shuttled Hampton's division across Lake Champlain from Burlington to Cumberland Head. On September 19, Hampton crossed the international border and fought a skirmish at Odelltown. Here, Hampton was surprised by "an insurmountable difficulty." A recent drought resulted in dry wells along the planned route. Hampton gathered his senior officers and gained unanimous agreement to drop back south and pick up a line of march westward to the settlement at Chateaugay, a distance of forty miles. Chateaugay sat at the intersection of two roads, and the location was widely referred to as Four Corners. From there, the division would march another fifty miles down the Chateauguay River to the St. Lawrence River.[13]

Armstrong approved this move but cautioned Hampton to time his advance with that of Wilkinson. "In the present state of the campaign we ought to run no risks by separate attacks, when combined ones are practical and sure." As it turned out, Hampton's offensive set off for Montreal several weeks before General Wilkinson departed Sackett's Harbor. The failure to deliver a coordinated invasion contributed to the failure of the 1813 campaign.[14]

Once at Four Corners, Hampton set about improving the road back to Plattsburgh to ease the transit of artillery, ammunition, and food. Of the 1,500 militiamen Tompkins ordered Hopkins to muster, only about 250 arrived at Hampton's camp. Of these, fewer than sixty agreed to cross into Canada.[15]

Hampton was increasingly apprehensive of coordinating his advance with Wilkinson's. On October 12, he wrote to Armstrong, "My solicitude to know your progress, and the real state of the grand army, is extreme." Armstrong responded that Wilkinson's division was consolidating on Grenadier Island, and from there would strike either Kingston or Montreal. He ordered Hampton to start advancing to the mouth of the Chateauguay River and there to await further guidance.[16] General Izard finally arrived in camp on October 16 and took command of the Second Brigade. Hampton set off on October 21. The roads along the river could not support wagons and artillery, so Hampton employed work parties to improve them. Izard commanded a body of troops to contest the Indian warriors and British light troops in front of the American main body.

Having progressed about thirty-three miles, Hampton's division on the left bank of the river discovered that the river road passed through an extensive forest. Here was the British main defensive line. Hampton described the woods as "an entire abbatis." The competent British commander Lieutenant Colonel Charles de Salaberry led a force of Canadian fencibles, militia, and about 170 Indian warriors. He ordered his militia to barricade the road where five streams entered the Chateauguay River. The streams served as ditches fronting each defensive position. Indians and light troops filled the woods. The opposite side of the river was also wooded but trafficable by infantry. Hampton's guides informed him of a ford behind the British lines. Hampton was disappointed at the perceived strength of the British position. Why hadn't Wilkinson's offensive caused the enemy to position itself closer to Montreal? Hampton reasoned that with the British gaining strength hourly an immediate attack was called for.[17]

Hampton's plan was theoretically solid, although it depended on knowledgeable guides and steadier officers and troops than were with him. His division was composed of two infantry brigades. Hampton directed Colonel Purdy's brigade to cross the Chateauguay River to the right side during the early evening on October 25 and to move through the woods to seize the ford in the morning. Once across the ford, Purdy would be in the rear of the British position and could continue the attack. The sound of Purdy's assault would be the signal for Izard's brigade to attack down the river road. The American forces would be divided by a river in the face of the enemy, a risky proposition to be sure. However, if Hampton's bold plan worked, his division would defeat the immediate opposition and have a clear path to the St. Lawrence River.

The guides repeatedly apprised Hampton that they were unfamiliar with the wooded area on the right bank of the river, where Purdy was to lead his men during the night. Hampton brushed aside their protests–a fatal mistake.[18]

The New York troops present were the Twenty-Ninth U.S. Infantry, recently recruited in Albany, and the few militiamen who had volunteered to accompany the offensive. Col. Melancton Smith Jr. commanded the Twenty-Ninth. Born in New York City and son of a Revolutionary colonel, Smith had been in the army only nine months. Also present was Maj. John Wool, who had scaled Queenston Heights one year earlier. Wool commanded a detachment of three light infantry companies. Fellow New Yorker Capt. James McKeon led his company of the Third Artillery. McKeon had been a participant in the failed Irish Rebellion of 1798 and fled to New York City to escape the fate of rebels. There, he recruited his artillery company. The Twenty-Ninth and Wool's detachment served in Izard's brigade. McKeon and his men served in the division's small artillery detachment.

As the sun set on October 25, Purdy and about 1,500 soldiers started out in a drizzle. The column had already departed when Hampton received a letter from the secretary of war. Armstrong directed the quartermaster to construct huts for winter quarters just south of the border in New York. Hampton reported that "this paper sunk my hopes." Apparently, Armstrong did not expect to seize Montreal. Too late to recall Purdy, Hampton decided he "could only go forward." Throughout the night, Purdy's brigade wandered through thickets and marshy ground. The guides were unable to conduct them and as a result, Purdy's men became lost and confused, a state that would devolve into fear and panic.[19]

When the sun rose, Purdy sent forward an advance guard of two companies. Moving in single file through the thick woods, this party ran into a company of Canadian militia. In the confusion of the firefight, both groups fell back. The Canadians rallied around another militia company, and the two units posted themselves to defend the ford. The Canadians numbered fewer than one hundred. Purdy's 1,500 troops vastly outnumbered his opponents, but he and his officers could not get their men organized to continue the attack.

When Hampton heard firing from the direction of Purdy's advance, he ordered Izard to engage de Salaberry's position. Neither general was aware of Purdy's precarious state across the river. Izard moved forward with the Tenth Infantry in the lead. The Americans approached a deep ravine. The forest began about one hundred yards beyond the ravine. De Salaberry's men had emplaced a thick abatis in front of the woods, and here was where they manned their first line of defense. The Tenth Infantry formed a firing line, and the two sides exchanged musketry for about twenty minutes.

Across the river, all was in confusion. Men in the rear of Purdy's command shouted to Hampton that the ford remained in British hands. Hampton's plan had fallen apart. Frustrated, he ordered Purdy to withdraw and to cross the river so as to reunite with the rest of the division. Hampton decided to press his attack with Izard's men. Izard formed his entire brigade into a solid line and began firing by volleys. The British troops, in the cover of trees and the abatis, returned fire individually. De Salaberry ordered his buglers to sound the advance, thus sowing confusion, and apprehension, in the American ranks. In mid-afternoon, Hampton decided that it was unlikely that Izard could prevail since his men had thus far failed to dent the British defenses. Thwarted and discouraged, he ordered the Second Brigade to break off the attack and to withdraw.

All discipline collapsed in Purdy's brigade. Some officers abandoned their men and attempted to cross the river on their own. The two Canadian militia companies bravely advanced through the woods and fired upon some of

Purdy's men before being driven back. Purdy ordered a general withdrawal in thankful obedience to Hampton's orders. He managed to evacuate his wounded to the left bank, but he and his men spent the night east of the river. Indian warriors fired into Purdy's encampment, keeping the tired and hungry Americans awake. At two A.M., the sky opened up in torrents of rain.

Casualties were minimal on both sides, about twenty-two British and as many as eighty Americans killed, wounded, and missing. Hampton brought more than 3,500 men into action while fewer than four hundred of de Salaberry's 1,700 troops were actively engaged. In the final analysis, British professionalism and leadership far exceeded that of Hampton's officers. The results of the battle were disgraceful to American arms.[20]

Hampton received no word at all of Wilkinson's advance. He once again held a council of his senior officers, who unanimously agreed to return to Four Corners and await events. This would place the army closer to its source of supplies. On November 7, Hampton received a letter from Wilkinson, who was only then approaching Ogdensburg. Wilkinson urged Hampton to meet him at St. Regis along the route to Montreal and to forward food and musket ammunition. Citing the current lack of food in both divisions, Hampton declined to move directly to St. Regis, about a thirty-five-mile march from Four Corners. Instead, he would fall back on his supply line to Plattsburgh and attempt to move north from there, linking up with Wilkinson closer to Montreal. Hampton noted that his troops were raw, ill, and exhausted, but, "With these means, what can be accomplished by human exertion I will attempt."[21]

By November 12, Hampton was in Plattsburgh, and he wrote to Armstrong analyzing the potential for his division to aid Wilkinson's advance toward Montreal. Of course, he was unaware of Wilkinson's engagement at Crysler's Farm the day prior. Hampton signaled that his division would be of little service. "But I should be uncandid not to own that many circumstances are unpropitious." Nearly half of the division was sick and almost all the men demoralized. He confessed, "What is more discouraging, the officers, with a few honorable exceptions, are sank as low as the soldiers, and endure hardship and privation as badly." What Hampton did not say was that much of the demoralization was a result of his not pressing the fight on the day of battle. The last of the troops arrived at Plattsburgh on November 15, the last of their march through a snowstorm. The men threw up barracks as fast as the quartermaster could provide lumber. Despite the protestations of Doctor James Mann, senior surgeon in the Ninth Military District, lumber went first to the erection of barracks, not hospitals for the hundreds of sick.[22]

Hampton's offensive failed for a number of reasons, but primary among them was the lack of leadership and competence of the officers. The untrained and unmotivated state of the soldiers falls directly to the responsibility of their leaders. Apparently, the company officers did not know either where their duty lay or even the basics of their profession. That officers would abandon their men in battle is inexcusable. A good leader shows his troops how to endure privation and fear. Hampton was unable to improve or motivate his officers, and the results were foreordained. The quality of Hampton's regular regiments was only a notch above that of the detached militia.

Armstrong and Tompkins had attempted to create prospects for success. While Armstrong was laying out his plans for the move on Montreal, he had proposed using the state's militia to draw British attention to Ogdensburg. This demonstration of force was a task within the militia's ability since it did not include crossing the border. For his part, Tompkins directed that the militia train using the same doctrinal manual as the regulars so that battlefield maneuvers might be mutually understandable. However, the militia again proved recalcitrant. Despite the governor's orders to bring 1,500 men into Hampton's camp, militia leaders managed to mobilize only about 250 in time for Hampton's forward movement. Of these men, fewer than sixty agreed to cross into Lower Canada. Tompkins unsuccessfully tried to harmonize federal and state policies to bring charges and try citizens who refused to muster into federal service. This failure crippled the governor's ability to mobilize the full resources of the state. Federal–state cooperation was inherently weak despite Tompkins's best efforts.

Knowing that Wilkinson would blame him for the campaign's failure, Hampton resigned from the service. His departure was timely, as an arrest order from Wilkinson was speeding its way to Plattsburgh. Hampton turned over command to Izard but not before granting leave to "almost every efficient officer of the division." Izard took ill, and, in early January 1814, relinquished command to Purdy. Izard went to Philadelphia to convalesce at his home.[23]

As Gen. Wade Hampton's prong of the 1813 campaign sputtered to an inglorious end, Gen. James Wilkinson's attempt was still in motion.

CHAPTER 12

THE BATTLE OF
CRYSLER'S FARM

Maj. Gen. James Wilkinson commanded the more potent of the two prongs of attack into Canada in the fall of 1813. Military operations were at a stalemate on the Niagara Peninsula and the strategic focus shifted eastward to the St. Lawrence River, where events had not been entirely quiet.

While privateering was most typical on the oceans, it also occurred on the St. Lawrence River. On July 19, 1813, two privateers out of Sackett's Harbor, crewed by about sixty men, captured a British gunboat and the fifteen bateaux it was escorting. The Americans seized sixty-nine prisoners, munitions, and more than five hundred barrels of pork and hard bread. The Americans moved up Cranberry Creek on the New York shore and prepared to receive a British attack. Regular and militia reinforcements arrived, bringing American strength to about ninety-six. They drove off four British gunboats and nearly 250 soldiers intent on retaking the bateaux. The British lost twenty-two casualties, the Americans fewer than ten. The *Buffalo Gazette* reported the crews were "composed chiefly of volunteers who have been injured by the depredations of the British." The district court awarded the intrepid Americans $3,422.80 for the captured vessels alone. In the midst of war, enterprising people could make a profit.[1]

Wilkinson departed Washington after conferring with Secretary of War John Armstrong and arrived at Sackett's Harbor on August 20. He consulted with Commodore Isaac Chauncey, discussing the two options of attacking Kingston directly or moving down the St. Lawrence River to seize Montreal. Unsurprisingly, Chauncey favored a direct attack to reduce Kingston. Wilkinson intended to travel to Fort George to prepare that post to defend itself and to select troops Chauncey would move to Sackett's Harbor for the major offensive. Wilkinson proposed departing the Niagara on September 15 and either to seize Kingston or move on Montreal by September 26. He complained to Armstrong that he had heard nothing from Hampton and further declared, "I hope he does not mean to take the stud; but if so, we can do without him, and he should be sent home." Clearly, the man charged with the major effort of 1813 seriously underestimated the time required to put this operation into effect. However, another interpretation is supportable, given Wilkinson's prior behavior. The commanding general was perhaps displaying his unqualified support of Armstrong's operation so when things went wrong, he would be more believable in assigning failure to the lack of support or duplicity of others.[2]

Wilkinson saw "the necessity of settling the point of naval superiority" before beginning movement. If Commodore James Yeo continued to refuse battle, then Chauncey would need to bottle him up in Kingston before the army pressed forward. By the end of August, Wilkinson was still at Sackett's Harbor and offering Armstrong reasons for his delay. Chauncey did not take the squadron out of his base to challenge Yeo until August 29. Also, there were too few transports to move even one thousand troops. "If I could have mustered three thousand combatants on this ground, with transport to bear them, I would now have been before Kingston."[3]

In late August, Wilkinson requested 1,500 militiamen to backfill those at Oswego and Sackett's Harbor whose time of service was nearing completion and to bolster defenses as regulars were about to move on Kingston or Montreal. Governor Daniel Tompkins supported the upcoming campaign by calling into service 2,000 militia from the state's central counties for a period of three months. These detached militiamen formed a brigade commanded by Brig. Gen. Oliver Collins of Utica. Tompkins designated September 14 as the day to commence their tour of duty.[4]

The president promoted eleven promising officers to brigadier general in 1813. Two of these were New Yorkers. Robert Swartwout, a militia colonel, received his commission to general in March. Swartwout replaced Morgan Lewis as the army's quartermaster general when Lewis received his second star. Jacob Brown, a militia brigadier general, became a brigadier general in the regular army in July. Brown took charge at Sackett's Harbor while waiting for Wilkinson to arrive. First Lieutenant Thomas Powers had arrived at Sackett's Harbor from Fort George. He wrote to Republican Congressman Charles J. Ingersoll that he was "gratified beyond description to find regulation so different from what it was at Fort George under Genls. Dearborn and Lewis." Powers credited Jacob Brown for the transformation. He declared the garrison to be "the best disciplined I have seen in service, a more industrious officer than Genl. Brown could not be."[5]

After requesting militia support, Wilkinson moved to Fort George. Arriving on September 4, he fell ill, "baffled by a severe and unremitting malady." He sent Brig. Gen. Peter B. Porter to recruit volunteers from the militia to augment the Indian warriors already mustered into service. However, as of September 18, Wilkinson was still unable to meet with Brig. Gen. George McClure, who was in command of the militia that would backfill the regulars when they departed. Wilkinson wrote to Armstrong complaining of the militia's tardiness and forlornly whined, "The season, I fear, be lost." However, demonstrating his commitment to the endeavor, he stated he would "not abandon the prospect while a ray of hope remains." When the campaign failed, Wilkinson would have ample reasons amassed to deflect blame from himself.[6]

On September 20, Wilkinson was still at Fort George and still providing Armstrong with more reasons why preparations were going slowly. He offered that it was a "herculean task to extract order from chaos." Reinforcements were arriving at Sackett's Harbor at a "snail's pace." He requested the secretary's help in causing gunboats to be built and reinforcements to be hurried along. As for Fort George itself, "This place neither stops a gap, extends our possessions, nor covers or protects a country; it is good for naught, but to command the ground it occupies, and therefore, I shall dismantle and abandon it."[7] Truly, the fort would be difficult to defend once the regulars departed, but possession of Fort George offered three advantages. First, along with Fort Niagara, it protected the mouth of the Niagara River as a useful harbor. Second, it served as a jumping-off point for offensive movements. Third, any possession in British territory served as a chip in peace negotiations.

On October 1, Wilkinson dispatched about 3,500 regulars in bateaux toward Sackett's Harbor. The general left eight hundred regulars and 690 militiamen to defend Fort George. Arriving at Sackett's Harbor three days later, Wilkinson met with Armstrong and "remonstrated freely and warmly against making an attack on Kingston" and instead to move directly on Montreal. Armstrong countered that no more than 1,000 troops were defending Kingston and Yeo was at the western end of Lake Ontario. "The time necessary to reduce the place will not exceed a single day." However, the troops from Fort George only completed their movement to Sackett's Harbor on October 18, and by then, Yeo's squadron had returned to Kingston. Armstrong believed that 1,500 troops had augmented the Kingston garrison while the American troops from the Niagara had been slowly moving to Sackett's Harbor.[8]

To Armstrong's mind, the window of opportunity to seize Kingston had closed. Yet, Wilkinson now changed his mind and argued to attack Kingston first. Armstrong lost all patience and all but ordered Wilkinson to proceed against Montreal. On October 19, Wilkinson threw responsibility for the direct attack on Montreal to Armstrong, writing "It is necessary to my justification that you should, by authority of the President, direct the operations of the army under my command particularly against Montreal." Armstrong countered by quoting his letter of August 8, in which he explicitly gave Wilkinson the choice of how Kingston would be reduced, either by direct attack or indirectly by joining with Hampton in seizing Montreal. Armstrong was aware of Wilkinson's slippery ways and was not about to assume accountability for the campaign, already late in the season. With this, the secretary of war returned to Albany.[9]

Wilkinson organized his 7,000 soldiers into four brigades and a large reserve corps. New Yorkers Jacob Brown, Robert Swartwout, and Alexander Macomb commanded three of the five elements. Generals Leonard Covington and John Boyd commanded the other two. Of the thirteen regular infantry regiments composing Wilkinson's division, only two, the Sixth and the Thirteenth, were recruited largely in New York. One small volunteer battalion, the Albany Volunteers, was also part of the invasion force and assigned to Macomb's reserve corps. Wilkinson had been ill intermittently since early September. His subordinates commanded in the battles to follow.[10]

While reinforcements were arriving at Sackett's Harbor, Chauncey's squadron began shuttling the troops to Grenadier Island, at the mouth of the St. Lawrence River. From this staging area, Wilkinson could direct his attacks at either Kingston or Montreal. The weather was cold and windy, and the troops suffered accordingly. In the movement to Grenadier Island, 196 troops took ill and were returned to the naval base. Many small craft and their cargoes were lost on the shores as boats' pilots attempted to escape the storms by seeking landfall. About ten inches of snow covered Grenadier Island. Chauncey met with Wilkinson on October 29 to learn for the first time that the army was moving on Montreal, not Kingston. Chauncey was furious. He had expected that an attack on Kingston would force Yeo to accept a decisive battle. Now, Chauncey would be required to keep the supply line open along the St. Lawrence River, a difficult task at best. While doing so, he still had to defend Sackett's Harbor.[11]

Wilkinson sent ahead a large advance guard under General Brown to clear the path to French Creek (now Clayton, New York), where the invasion force would disembark and rest. Brown's troops entered the cove where French Creek flowed into the St. Lawrence River on November 1. Brown placed two eighteen-pounders on shore. Late in the day, William Mulcaster, now a Royal Navy post captain, took three gunboats into the cove. In an exchange of artillery, Mulcaster decided to break contact and to try again the following morning. The cannonading continued shortly after dawn, the Americans now firing hot shot at the British gunboats. Unable to destroy any American boats, Mulcaster wisely broke off the fight and returned to Kingston. The main body of Americans departed Grenadier Island on November 3 and were soon arriving at French Creek.[12]

Jacob Brown's advance guard brigade continued downriver. Wilkinson reinforced Brown with Colonel Macomb's reserve corps. The two officers worked exceptionally well together. Wilkinson was unaware that the enemy was following his division. On November 6, a body of nearly nine hundred British regulars led by the highly competent Lieutenant Colonel Joseph Morrison departed Kingston with the task of keeping an eye on the Americans. Captain Mulcaster transported Morrison's men. This slender body of soldiers would contribute to the end of the American campaign just five days later.

On November 6, Wilkinson ordered a night passage of the British batteries at Prescott. The troops disembarked and marched along the New York shore while the vessels, protected by fog, rowed past seventeen British guns. The British fired when an American vessel came into view but sank none. Also on that day, Col. Winfield Scott joined Wilkinson's division. He had left Fort George on a questionable interpretation of his orders. Wilkinson assigned him to Macomb's reserve corps in the advance guard.

Brown cleared the way, engaging Canadian militiamen along the river. Trailing Brown, Wilkinson's main body arrived upriver from the Long Sault Rapids. The troops disembarked as the boat pilots prepared to negotiate the water obstacles. Three brigades encamped on John Crysler's land. On November 11, Lieutenant Colonel Morrison approached the Americans with about 1,200 regulars, militia, and Indian warriors. Wilkinson, from his sickbed, ordered Boyd to drive off the British. Boyd ordered Swartwout's Brigade to attack while his and Leonard Covington's brigades supported. About 2,200 American troops were committed to the fight. However, the American artillery was still aboard ship and would not join the battle for two hours.

The American attack soon became disjointed as Swartwout's battalions strained through woods on their approach to the British line. Harassed by Mohawk warriors, the ill-disciplined soldiers fired despite the shouted orders to withhold fire. As the troops exited the woods, their officers struggled to reform them into a firing line. Boyd's brigade avoided the woods and confronted the British more directly. Covington's brigade crossed a deep ravine and emerged disordered. Covington was mortally wounded in the action. The Americans conducted a piecemeal attack, battalions seemingly operating independently of one another. In stark contrast, Morrison's men fired controlled volleys and maneuvered smartly. The American artillery, four guns, fired into the British line, stabilizing the fight. One by one the American battalions disintegrated with many soldiers withdrawing from the fight without orders. Boyd ordered a tactical withdrawal to reorganize and resupply his troops with ammunition. This movement away from the British established Morrison's claim to victory.[13]

Second Lt. Reynold M. Kirby and many others were angry at the battle's outcome and blamed their senior leaders. "We had repulsed the enemy in his attack, but still everything was the appearance of defeat. We had left our killed & many of our wounded on the field of battle." Maj. Charles K. Gardner professed that the army "had no advantage of a commander—we would have done better without any, for there was no concert. The individuals who fought, need not regret it." Col. William Clay Cumming pronounced a more brutal analysis. "The action was fought, on our part, without plan, system, or concert. No points of attack were designated; the line was not correctly formed—there was no reserve on hand, were long unsupported by artillery & worst of all, no provision was made for supplying us with ammunition, till too late. The consequence was we were obliged to retire."[14]

The day after battle, Wilkinson received Hampton's note of November 8. He used Hampton's decision not to join Wilkinson's division at St. Regis as his excuse to call off the advance on Montreal, "as such resolution defeats the grand objects of the campaign in this quarter, which before the receipt of your letter, were thought to be completely within our power, no suspicion being entertained that you would decline the junction directed." Wilkinson convened a council of his senior officers, who sanctioned the decision to move to winter quarters at French Mills on the Salmon River.

Wilkinson confidently reported to the secretary of war that the engagement on November 11 was not the cause of the termination of the move to Montreal. He assigned blame for the failure of the campaign entirely on Hampton. He declared his "unspeakable mortification and surprise" upon learning that Hampton refused to meet at St. Regis. Maintaining that only six hundred British defenders were in Montreal, Wilkinson wrote, "What a golden opportunity has been lost by the caprice of Major General Hampton"[15] Wade Hampton's refusal provided Wilkinson with a golden opportunity to concurrently call off a problematic campaign and to shame his personal enemy. The British had suffered twenty-two killed, 148 wounded, and about nine missing. For their part, the Americans reported 102 killed, 237 wounded, and about one hundred captured. The lopsided tally and British possession of the battlefield were proof of American defeat despite Wilkinson's assertions otherwise. The protracted suffering of the American soldiers continued.

On November 13, Wilkinson put his men on the move to French Mills. The disheartened men rode their small craft eight miles up the Salmon River and arrived at the campsite just south of the international border that would be their wintry home. The men set about erecting tents or other rude shelters to protect them from the worst of the elements while they built permanent wooden huts. The men completed the huts and occupied them on Christmas day. At peak strength, over 6,000 soldiers wintered at French Mills.[16]

Armstrong directed Wilkinson to retain "a full complement of your most efficient officers" to command the soldiers in winter quarters and to order surplus officers on recruiting duty.[17] Generals Boyd and Lewis took leave. Major Gardner wrote to his mother, "Numbers of officers have left their men before they knew what would become of them and some on furlough, or orders of accommodation, given (contrary to regulation) by Gen. Wilkinson so as to leave a young brigadier in command of the Army—colonels in command of brigades and a major in command of one." He concluded his letter, "Boyd, the great General of Sepoys . . . Summer Birds!!! Gone!"[18]

Col. James Miller wrote to his spouse, "The Army has been in a state of starvation ever since we landed here." He noted that when flour arrived, half of it was damaged. "The men were obliged to pound it up with axes and mauls before they could make it into any kind of bread." Lieutenant Kirby recorded an incident in the early hours of New Year's Day: "About 3 o'clock this morning I was awakened by an alarm gun & the beat of the long roll. A firing apparently upon pickett No. 1 was heard distinctly. The whole army was under arms until morning. The alarm was occasioned by some citizens of the vicinity firing in the New Year."[19]

The ill and wounded suffered the most. From their arrival in mid-November until late December, these unfortunates sheltered in tents. Much personal clothing, blankets, and medical stores were lost on campaign. Dysentery, typhus, pneumonia, and frostbite ravaged the division. A senior medical officer reported that the nearest medical stores had to come from Albany. He went on to note the near total lack of nutritious food. "The poor subsistence, which the bread of the worst quality afforded, was almost the only support which could be had for nearly seven weeks." Wilkinson ordered public and private buildings in Malone be converted into hospital wards, enough for 250 beds. Before the winter encampment broke up, the hospital served more than 450 patients.[20]

With Hampton gone, Wilkinson directly commanded the troops at French Mills as well as the remains of Hampton's Division at Plattsburgh. Apparently in an attempt to salvage his badly damaged reputation, Wilkinson dispatched Lt. Col. George McFeely and 250 men north to Chazy to distract the British. McFeely's men dutifully set off in sleighs and remained overnight at Chazy. McFeely recorded that the "night was intensely cold; the thermometer was 30 degrees below zero." The next day, McFeely received a message from Wilkinson ordering the soldiers back to Plattsburgh. The men bundled up in their sleighs and travelled forty-two miles back to Plattsburgh. McFeely wrote, "We had fourteen men so frozen that they were put into the hospital, two of whom died, and some of the others were cripples, no doubt for the remainder of their lives." War is cruel, crueler still when the senior commander is callous.[21]

The 1813 campaign to seize Montreal ended in abject failure. However, the year was not yet over. Wilkinson had denuded the Niagara frontier of regulars. This decision led directly to one of the greatest human tragedies of the war in New York.

CHAPTER 13

THE BURNING OF
THE NIAGARA FRONTIER

The military disaster and civilian tragedy that befell the Niagara frontier in December 1813 emanated from the departure of the regulars to support the failed campaign against Montreal as well as the unfortunate handling of the rotation of militia to guard the western frontier. As in most tragedies, human failings such as pride, lack of judgment, incompetence, and hardheartedness contributed to the catastrophe.

Governor Daniel Tompkins issued a general order on August 25 calling for 2,100 citizens for three months service as detached militia. The commanders of five brigades of the common militia situated in the western portion of the state selected the men to serve. No one who had served previously was obliged to do duty. Tompkins directed the units to muster between September 6 and 9; thus their service would end in early December. The governor appointed Brig. Gen. George McClure of Steuben County to command the brigade. His mission was to defend the Niagara frontier, including Fort George. In anticipation of the two infantry regiments of the brigade serving in several locations, Tompkins ordered that each regiment be commanded by two lieutenant colonels. He assigned the commands to Lieutenant Colonels Henry Bloom, Hugh Dobbin, Philetus Swift, and Caleb Hopkins, all experienced commanders.[1]

McClure emigrated from Ireland as a twenty-year-old and settled near Bath. He served as a judge and sheriff and also in the State Assembly. Like many upwardly mobile men, McClure joined the militia and rose in rank. Tompkins sent McClure detailed instructions, warning him the regular units might depart to support Maj. Gen. James Wilkinson's campaign to the eastward. "Your command will then become doubly delicate & responsible, & will require the exertion of your utmost vigilance & talents." Tompkins noted that the British could easily cross the Niagara and isolate McClure. He suggested that McClure erect redoubts or blockhouses at key points to secure his supply lines. In 1813, at the age of fifty-two, McClure found himself in the unenviable position of defending Fort George with too few soldiers, an impossible task.[2]

Tompkins was disappointed that "no two Commanding Generals during the year 1812 agreed upon the same mode of proceeding against delinquents of Militia." Most militiamen who failed to show up at muster suffered no consequences. The governor wrote to Gen. James Wilkinson asking that he establish courts to bring justice to citizens evading militia service. "The impunity of those of the Militia who neglected to rendezvous, or who put the laws at defiance in 1812, has had a most injurious effect, & has afforded a subject of great murmuring to those who under great hardships endured the service which the good of their Country exacted from them."[3] A citizen could not fall under military jurisdiction until he had been mustered into service. Wilkinson took no action. The substantial numbers of militiamen who evaded onerous service away from home reflected the general unpopularity of the war and the legislature's reluctance to force military service in the face of potential political backlash.

On the Niagara frontier, militia officers Peter B. Porter and Cyrenius Chapin were troubled when they heard rumors that the regulars at Fort George might be called to support operations elsewhere. On September 17, they offered Wilkinson to raise a force of 1,000 to 1,200 by October 1 and to conduct offensive operations. Porter and Chapin closed with an extraordinary promise: "We pledge our lives, that, before the close of the season, we will occupy the whole of the valuable and populous peninsula, opposite this river, and either capture, destroy, or disperse, all the enemy's force in this quarter." Wilkinson responded that he did not have the authority to accept this force into federal service, but he would refer the request to Secretary of War John Armstrong at Sackett's Harbor. Five days later, Armstrong gave his assent to the proposal to raise the force, although he did not clearly give approval to act offensively.[4]

Wilkinson's troops began movement eastward on October 1, and the general departed the following day. Wilkinson turned command over to McClure and ordered Winfield Scott and his eight hundred regulars to remain. However, Scott and McClure understood Wilkinson's guidance differently. Scott understood that he had discretionary orders to move to Sackett's Harbor if the British pulled back from Fort George. McClure's understanding was that Scott should not depart until McClure considered his force "sufficient to hold the fort without them." This misunderstanding contributed to the coming disaster, as did Armstrong's guidance to McClure. On October 4 he wrote, "Understanding that the defense of the post committed to your charge may render it proper to destroy the town of Newark, you are hereby directed to apprise its inhabitants of this circumstance and advise them to remove themselves and their effects to some place of greater safety."[5]

Potential assistance to defend the Niagara frontier was available from Indian warriors at Buffalo Creek. In early September, Little Billy offered Indian agent Erastus Granger a defensive alliance in the event that the British and their Indian allies crossed the Niagara River. The chief stressed, "We volunteer [but] we must have our customs; be at liberty to take our own course in fighting." For example, the Indians would not fire on parties displaying a white flag. They also warned, "We wish you not to place us in forts. We can not act. You know what took place at Detroit; an army was sold. We wish not to be sold." Initially, Indian warriors supported operations, but when the British offensive unfolded in December, their assistance was sporadic and uncoordinated.[6]

About October 9, the British began withdrawing toward Burlington Heights. On the 10th, Cyrenius Chapin led about a hundred men on a reconnaissance. McClure and Porter set out the next day with about a thousand militiamen and Indian warriors and advanced as far as Twelve Mile Creek. In a letter to Wilkinson, Winfield Scott proclaimed that the British had "abandoned this whole peninsula" and as for McClure and Porter, "There is no danger of their coming up with the enemy, or they would be in great danger of a total annihilation." Lt. William B. Rochester, McClure's aide, wrote the Americans had "about 800 militia here, who are completely raw, untrained and lawless." McClure received a note from Scott requesting that McClure return to Fort George. Scott was about to depart the Niagara frontier, taking his regulars with him to Sackett's Harbor. McClure duly returned to Fort George. At the time, he had the services of approximately 1,000 militia and 250 Indian warriors.[7]

In mid-November, McClure led about 1,500 troops and one hundred Iroquois westward as far as Twenty Mile Creek to imbue his men with an offensive spirit after weeks of inactivity penned up in Fort George. They had no significant contact with the British; General John Vincent's furthest outpost was at Stoney Creek. However, on this expedition McClure's men gave in to wanton destruction. Chapin was leading the advance guard when he heard shooting to his rear. Believing that the main body with McClure was under attack, Chapin rode to the sound of gunfire. He discovered the militiamen shooting at livestock. Porter joined Chapin in putting an end to the malicious slaughter. Apparently, McClure had allowed these excesses. After this expedition, the Iroquois departed for their homes. They had received no pay for their months of service. On November 16, Chauncey began transporting 1,100 regulars from Maj. Gen. William Henry Harrison's western army to Sackett's Harbor. Storms wracked the squadron, and the last of the cold and terrified troops arrived at

Sackett's Harbor eleven days later. Harrison's experienced regulars were unable to support the move on Montreal or protect the Niagara frontier.[8]

In his final orders to McClure, General Harrison specifically addressed the potential of the commander of the Canadian Volunteers. This unit was raised from residents of Upper Canada, most of whom had originally been Americans. "I recommend that you make use of the zeal, activity, and local knowledge, which Colonel Willcocks certainly possesses, to counteract the machinations of our enemy, and ensure the confidence of our friends amongst the inhabitants." Harrison also praised the new commander at Fort George. "Your conduct appears to me to have been extremely judicious and proper throughout, and your troops exhibit a state of improvement and subordination which is at once honorable to your officers and themselves." As it turned out, Joseph Willcocks was certainly instrumental in influencing McClure to make the most disastrous decision of his career.[9]

About this time, the medical department ordered the hospital at Lewiston to close. Doctors sent 250 of the sick and wounded by boat and wagon to Black Rock with a final destination at Williamsville, eight miles away. While the men were at Black Rock, a severe storm struck, washing away personal baggage, about 200 blankets, and much of the medical stores. Six soldiers died before the contingent arrived at Williamsville. After three weeks, attending surgeons declared about fifty soldiers fit for duty. These men were ordered to Fort Niagara, where most were killed or captured when that fortress fell.[10]

In late November, Armstrong and Tompkins anticipated that the militia currently at Forts George and Niagara would need replacing. With a requisition in hand from Armstrong, Tompkins directed McClure to remain on duty over the winter. He also told McClure to request volunteers to garrison the forts for three or four months. If too few militiamen volunteered for winter service, Tompkins authorized McClure to issue a general order calling out the common militia. The order left blank the number to be called out. Tompkins instructed his general to fill in the number based upon McClure's judgment and to forward the completed order to Maj. Gen. Amos Hall for implementation. In Armstrong's requisition, he stated, "As the garrison force will not be called upon to perform any other duty than that of mere protection to our frontier, I have sufficient confidence in the patriotism of the Western District to believe that a competent number of volunteers will offer for that purpose." Tompkins agreed the duty would not be onerous. Both men would be shaken by the events of the next month.[11]

George McClure's name entered the annals of infamy for his next act. Virtually all of the militia had departed at the end of their service. The paymaster

Fort Niagara as seen from Fort George. Courtesy Library and Archives Canada, John Elliott Woolford Collection/C-099561.

issued only one month's pay, not the three that were due. McClure wrote to Armstrong, "The best and most subordinate militia that have yet been on this frontier, finding that their wages were not ready for them, became, with some meritorious exceptions, a disaffected and ungovernable multitude." Only one hundred regulars and volunteers remained to defend the post. A scouting party of Canadian Volunteers made contact with a force of British near Twelve Mile Creek and lost one killed and four taken prisoner. The British were at the gates. Efforts to raise volunteers from the militia were unavailing. McClure held a council of officers, who agreed that Fort George was no longer tenable.[12]

Before withdrawing his troops to the New York side of the river, McClure destroyed Newark, the village near Fort George, to deprive the British of winter quarters. In this decision, he willfully misinterpreted his orders and was influenced by Willcocks. McClure burned more than eighty houses, leaving several hundred persons without shelter. Some of McClure's men removed a bedridden woman from her home before destroying it. Cyrenius Chapin, who had conducted partisan warfare along the river earlier in the year, opposed the wanton destruction. Referring to McClure, Chapin later recalled, "Women and children were turned out of doors in a cold and stormy night; the cries of infants, the decrepitude of age, the debility of sickness, had no impression upon this monster in human shape." The inhabitants walked in a snowstorm seeking shelter with neighbors. McClure reported to Armstrong, "The village of Newark is now in flames; the few remaining inhabitants of it, having been notified of our intention, were enabled to remove their property."[13]

As public outrage grew on both sides of the river, McClure addressed the event. "This act, however distressing to the inhabitants and my feelings, was by order of the Secretary of War, and I believe at the same time proper. The inhabitants had twelve hours notice to remove their effects, and such as chose to come across the river were provided with all the necessities of life."[14]

After burning Newark, the Americans burned the magazine at Fort George, but left "an immense quantity" of ammunition. McClure departed Canada in haste, leaving tents standing and throwing seven cannon in the ditches surrounding the palisaded walls rather than transporting these items across the river.[15]

McClure was aware of the extreme danger of a British retaliatory attack. The detached militia had departed, and their replacements had not yet arrived. McClure wrote to Armstrong, "The enemy is much exasperated, and will make a descent on this frontier, if possible." McClure ordered Capt. Nathaniel Leonard to prepare Fort Niagara for attack "as soon as possible" by having hand bombs placed in the redoubts and the mess. "Much is expected from Captain Leonard from his long experience and knowledge of duty." McClure and the inhabitants of the frontier would be severely disappointed in Leonard's performance of that duty. McClure was reluctant to give command of the fort to Leonard, but the artillery captain outranked all other available officers. Believing that he had done all that he could for the safety of Fort Niagara, McClure moved his headquarters to Buffalo to see to the defenses there. On December 11, Erastus Granger wrote to McClure seeking permission to raise as many as two hundred Indian volunteers. However, events moved too quickly and the few Iroquois present were unable to contribute substantially to the defense of Black Rock or Buffalo.[16]

Lieutenant General Sir Gordon Drummond, the new commander of forces in Upper Canada, arrived on the Niagara peninsula on December 16. He brought with him Major General Phineas Riall, who replaced John Vincent. The absence of an appreciable number of American regulars provided the British with an unparalleled opportunity. Drummond planned to seize Fort Niagara and retaliate for the illegal burning of Newark. The new commander ordered Colonel John Murray to cross the river with about 562 regulars to seize Fort Niagara. Drummond ordered Riall to cross after Fort Niagara fell in order to secure the fort. Drummond planned to follow the capture of Fort Niagara with an attack on Lewiston to destroy artillery positions there.

Drummond provided enough bateaux to cross over half of Murray's force at a time. He directed Murray to ensure that the troops had scaling ladders and enough axes to remove any picketing barring the way. The men's weapons were to be unloaded in order not to accidentally discharge a musket and inadvertently warn the Americans. Drummond ordered, "It should be impressed on the mind of every man, that the bayonet is the weapon on which the success of the attack must depend."[17]

Belatedly, McClure warned the citizenry that a British attack on Fort Niagara was imminent and if the British succeeded in taking the fort, they would "lay waste to our whole frontier." He called out the common militia of Niagara, Genesee, and Chautauqua Counties to report immediately to Lewiston, Fort Schlosser, or Buffalo. These militiamen, as well as the citizens and Iroquois, would pay heavily for McClure's shocking lack of judgment in callously destroying Newark.[18]

Laundress Betsy Doyle, who had served the guns courageously the year prior, was aware that some of the Fort Niagara garrison was growing increasingly fearful of British reprisal. To inspire or perhaps to shame the men, Betsy donned soldier's garb and a musket and joined the guard detail. She "stood her turn through a very dark & rainy night." The British struck the following evening.[19]

The attackers embarked in the evening darkness on December 18. The troops landed south of the fort at Five Mile Meadow. As the British advance guard approached Youngstown, it came upon a small building that sheltered the American pickets. The British surrounded the building. Some Americans were playing cards and a British soldier overheard a player ask, "What are trumps?" A British soldier replied, "Bayonets are trumps!" The British broke into the building and bayoneted every American. No shots were fired; no warning was given. The British column moved on.[20]

The American guards were snug in their sentry boxes outside the gate. British Sergeant Andrew Spearman saw the gate ajar and, moving quickly, threw his body inside. As the American sentry attempted to yell a warning, Spearman bayoneted him. The British infantry flooded through the gate. They raised a yell that aroused the defenders. The gun crew atop the south redoubt fired their cannon. Lieutenant Maurice Nolan rushed into the redoubt, leading by courageous example. His men were too far behind to save him. An American plunged a bayonet into the lieutenant and fired his musket. Nolan died; his men went wild. Lieutenant Henry Driscoll recalled, "This resistance exasperated our men, who rushed wildly about into every building, bayonetting every American they met."[21] The convalescents in the hospital made the most determined defense. Many were bayonetted, some while begging for quarter. The British assailants were faithful to Drummond's explicit order. In less than thirty minutes, the entire fort was taken. The British officers eventually stopped the wanton killing.

Robert Lee, a civilian captured at the fall of Fort Niagara, reported that he and about eighty other civilians were moved to Upper Canada until they were eventually freed. He recalled that while he was a prisoner, his guards bragged "that the Americans cried out and begged for quarter, but that they bayonetted or in their language, skewered them, notwithstanding."[22]

The British suffered only five men killed and five wounded. Drummond boasted in his official report, "The Enemy's loss amounted to 65 killed; and but 12 in wounded; which clearly proves how irresistible a weapon the Bayonet is in the hands of British Soldiers." The British took more than three hundred prisoners. The attackers captured twenty-seven guns of various sizes and more than 3,000 stands of arms. These firearms belonged to both the state and the federal government. Drummond forwarded the captured flags to Lieutenant General Sir George Prevost.[23]

Betsy Doyle was at her home outside the fort when the noise awakened her. Before the British and their Indian allies arrived, she took her four children and began a trek of 310 miles across the state to Greenbush. There she joined dozens of wives and children of soldiers who were refugees from the fighting. As she was on the rolls of her husband's company, she received rations. Betsy continued to wait for her husband, Andrew, who was a prisoner at Dartmoor Prison in England.

In his report, McClure blamed Captain Leonard's failure to prepare and to keep his men vigilant. More than three hundred fit regulars were in Fort Niagara, enough to defend the post. The fall of this proud fortress was due to the "gross neglect in the commanding officer of the fort." McClure believed that he had issued sufficient orders to Leonard to prepare for the inevitable assault, but "the commandant did not in any respect comply with those orders." McClure believed that Leonard was drunk and that he departed the fort before the assault.[24] Indeed, the artillery captain was in his home four miles away. When he learned of the circumstances of the loss of Fort Niagara, Armstrong ordered Leonard's arrest. The British assault surprised the garrison despite days of warnings. Only about twenty regulars managed to escape.

After the capture of Fort Niagara, Drummond ordered raids that resulted in the destruction of nearly every dwelling, barn, and warehouse on the Niagara frontier and the hurried evacuation of the citizenry to safety. General Riall led 1,000 regulars and four hundred western Indian warriors and captured Lewiston without loss. The Indians were refugees from Tecumseh's defeat at the Battle of the Thames in October. Drummond included them in the attacks because they would surely incite terror among the Americans. The Indians arrived at the village first, surprising the citizenry and slaying a number of them. The regulars followed and occupied the village. The raiders continued on to capture Fort Gray and the Tuscarora village atop Lewiston Heights. The defenders, an assortment of militiamen, Tuscarora, and Canadian Volunteers, put up a strong enough fight to create time for many of the civilians to flee but insufficient to prevent the raiders from destroying homes.[25]

Drummond ordered the burning of Lewiston not only as retaliation, but also "to deprive the Enemy of cover for Troops which might be sent for the purpose of destroying the opposite Town of Queenstown." Despite orders to the contrary, the Indian warriors committed acts of violence against civilians. Drummond acknowledged Indian misconduct to Prevost. However, he did not omit the western Indians from his future attacks.[26]

Fifteen-year-old Eber Howe was with the terrorized refugees. He recalled that riders spread the alarm along the single road heading eastward toward Batavia and the Genesee River. Settlers along that road joined the throng of refugees. "By this time the road was getting pretty well filled up with men, women and children, horses, oxen, carts, wagons, sleds, in fine, everything that could facilitate the movement of women and children; and after filling up all these, many were carried in the arms of those most able to endure fatigue." Howe recollected that he could not see the front or rear of the column "resembling somewhat the serpentine movements of a huge black snake—rendered more distinctly visible by the snow on the ground."[27]

Drummond had sufficiently retaliated for the burning of Newark; nevertheless, he chose to bring the scourge of war heavily upon the citizenry. Riall followed up this raid with an attack two days later on the small settlement of Manchester at the falls. Drummond then ordered his troops to destroy every dwelling from Manchester north to Fort Niagara. Many of the soldiers and Indians, fortified with captured liquor, performed their arson thoroughly.

Drummond ordered soldiers to move along the shores of Lake Ontario as far east as Eighteen Mile Creek to destroy mills and burn homes. No Indians accompanied this mission. To the credit of the British, these soldiers assisted occupants in removing necessary items before torching the dwellings. The refugees fled eastward. Settlers along the route fell in with them to escape the Indians they thought were surely following the long columns of exiles. Some even crossed the Genesee River seventy-five miles away looking for safety. Hamlet Scrantom wrote from Rochester on December 26, "Daily are passing here in sleighs and wagons, families deprived of their all. Not a cent of money, no provision, no bedding; children barefoot, etc., all depending on the charity of the people." The people were suffering grievously for McClure's folly.[28]

On Christmas Eve, Governor Tompkins returned to Albany from New York City, only to learn of the British raids along the Niagara frontier. He fired off a letter to McClure reminding him that he had authority to requisition militia from General Hall's division to replace the militiamen leaving service. He wrote that he was unaware that Armstrong had given McClure authority to

destroy Newark. Had the governor known of that possibility, he insisted he
would "most assuredly" have provided for a much larger force in anticipation of British retaliation. In an order to General Hall, the governor stated he
was "much surprised . . . to learn the weak & disastrous state of that frontier."
Tompkins ordered Hall to take command on the Niagara frontier, to muster
his militia, and to expel the British from New York soil. "You will consider
yourself vested with liberal powers & authority to effect that object & you will
doubtless be zealous to accomplish it." Hall had already hurried hundreds of
volunteers toward the frontier, and he stitched together a command structure
for the disparate elements responding to the emergency.[29]

On December 26, before the governor's letter arrived granting him extensive
authority, General Hall replaced the discredited McClure. Hall commanded
about 1,800 militiamen, one hundred Iroquois warriors, and one hundred
Canadian Volunteers under Maj. Benajah Mallory. Hall had only a few days
to organize the assembled mass and to prepare a defense. Ammunition was in
desperately short supply. McClure departed Buffalo and headed to Batavia. He
wrote Armstrong scapegoating Chapin for much of the catastrophe: "To him
in great measure, ought all our disasters to be imputed. . . . I have found him
an unprincipled disorganizer. Since dismissing him and his marauding corps,
he has been guilty of the most outrageous acts of mutiny, if not of treason."
Chapin gave leadership and voice to the many local citizens who saw McClure's
order to burn Newark as the catalyst of the ongoing destruction, devastation
that was not yet completed.[30]

Encouraged by the easy success north of the falls and determined to make
the Americans pay even more for the unnecessary and therefore criminal
destruction of Newark, Drummond ordered attacks on Black Rock and Buffalo. He purposefully anticipated burning homes and buildings "in order to
deprive the Enemy of the cover which these places afford." In the early hours
of December 30, General Riall led a force of 1,000 regulars and 400 Indian
warriors across the Niagara River, landing north of Black Rock. The British and
their Indian allies burned a schooner and two sloops of the Lake Erie squadron
as they moved southward. As dawn broke, an additional force of about 350
regulars crossed the river closer to Black Rock.[31]

Hall deployed his troops against the attackers. In his report to the governor, Hall wrote, "The whole force now opposed to the enemy was, at most, not
over six hundred men, the remainder having fled, in spite of the exertions of
their officers. These few but brave men, disputed every inch of ground, with
the steady coolness of veterans, at the expense of many valuable lives."[32] The
American defense eventually collapsed, and the British advanced toward Buffalo preceded by Indian warriors. A gun crew discharged a few rounds from a

twelve-pounder cannon; however, the fire had no appreciable effect upon the British advance.

Cyrenius Chapin, who was not then in federal service, sought out Riall to surrender Buffalo. Riall agreed to respect private property; however, all public property was now spoils of war. During this negotiation, most of the citizenry abandoned their homes. They left in haste, many with nothing more than the clothing they wore. Most travelled eastward toward Batavia. Others, including the residents of the Seneca Village, travelled southwest along the lake shore. At this point, a number of convalescent soldiers from the hospital in Williamsville who were unaware that the village had surrendered now appeared. Some British, perceiving a breaking of the negotiated surrender, began setting fire to private homes. Riall, upon learning that Chapin was not then in federal service, decided he was therefore incompetent to negotiate the surrender. Riall, believing that every house in Buffalo had at one time or another been used to shelter American soldiers, condoned the conflagration. Drummond had anticipated the wholesale destruction of houses and any building capable of providing shelter. The British spared only the home of the widow St. John. Indian warriors killed a few citizens, including one woman who had chosen not to leave the village. The British took others prisoner, including Chapin. Chapin was sent to Quebec and not exchanged until the following June.[33]

The defense of Black Rock and Buffalo on December 30 was costly to the militia, who had gathered only days prior. Thirty-five militiamen died, including Lt. Col. Seymour Boughton of the dragoons and Maj. Samuel Dudley, who was tomahawked and scalped. Additionally, twenty-six militiamen were wounded and nearly seventy taken prisoner.[34]

Daniel Brayman, a Buffalo resident, recalled, "I saw that day thirteen bodies of the killed laying at Reese's blacksmith shop. It was a bitter cold day and the bodies were frozen stiff just as the men had died. They were in all conceivable postures. Legs and arms twisted around in all shapes; the gaping wounds, the mangled heads torn by the ruthless scalping knife; all formed a sight horrible to behold."[35]

After Buffalo burned, many militiamen saw no point in remaining. As an example, John McMahan brought 354 men with him from Chautauqua County. After the battle, only seventeen officers and 118 enlisted men remained. The militiamen guarded the American camp, a duty McMahan recalled as "fatiguing and arduous. . . . The officers were frequently compelled to take the place and perform the duties of private soldiers." With no buildings remaining to shelter the soldiers, the penetrating cold was hard to bear.[36]

Governor Tompkins unleashed his frustration upon the secretary of war. Had he known that Armstrong had sanctioned the destruction of Newark, Tompkins would have evacuated state-owned weapons and equipment from Fort Niagara. "You may remember that I pressed upon you the probability of winter expeditions by the British on that frontier." Tompkins also criticized Armstrong for the regular officers who passed through Albany "in shoals" going on leave for the winter. "At any rate the absence of so many of them at this particular juncture creates great apprehension & dissatisfaction in the public mind." The impression created in the public mind was that the federal government had abandoned New Yorkers to their fate. Tompkins forcefully warned Armstrong that Governor General Prevost was actively recruiting Indian warriors to support further winter raids. He summarized with a stark warning: "Something must be done soon, or more mortification & disgrace will be the consequence."[37]

Armstrong vociferously denied that his guidance to McClure envisioned burning Newark if it did not contribute to the immediate defense of Fort George. He went on to say that no regulars were available to retake Fort Niagara. Speaking frankly as a New Yorker, Armstrong went on to write, "The invaders must be expelled by the militia of the west and, if it not be done, shame light upon them! Why should Virginia, Georgia, Tennessee and Kentucky men so far outact and outshine us?"[38] Armstrong's proposition missed the mark. Much of the cause of the debacle lay at the feet of federal officers. Wilkinson drew most of the regulars away to support his move on Montreal. Winfield Scott, in a search for glory, stretched his orders to allow his departure from Fort George. Finally, Captain Leonard's gross neglect in preparing his garrison and his personal absence made him primarily culpable for the loss of Fort Niagara.

When word reached Albany that the British had burned Lewiston, federal and state officials cooperated to transport 1,500 muskets and ammunition to the Niagara frontier. However, camp kettles and axes were lacking. These necessities for hundreds of militiamen who would soon be marching westward to a region devoid of shelter and civilian support were simply unavailable.

On December 31, General Hall's initial report arrived at Albany. This report gave Tompkins "reason to hope, that farther depredations of the enemy would be prevented." However, news of the catastrophe at Buffalo arrived on January 2. Tompkins dispatched one of his aides, Col. Anthony Lamb, to the Niagara frontier with instructions giving Hall full command of all militia forces west of Onondaga for the duration of the emergency. The governor implored his general to stabilize the situation. "I beg that you will endeavor to check that panic which I am informed exists amongst the Militia and inhabitants, and endeavor to animate them with feelings and courage more worthy of their profession and of the character of the Militia of the State of New York." The governor mobilized a brigade of detached militia under Brig. Gen. William Burnet for immediate service on the Niagara. Burnet assembled nearly 1,200 men who remained along the Niagara frontier for three months. When Colonel Lamb reached Batavia, he reported to Tompkins that the crisis had passed; the British and their native allies had returned to Upper Canada.[39]

Brig. Gen. Lewis Cass passed through Buffalo on January 12 and sent his assessment to Secretary Armstrong. He concluded the loss of Fort Niagara resulted from "the most criminal negligence." Cass reported that three of the commanders of regular army companies were absent from the fort when the British attacked. He continued his report strongly criticizing the militia's combat performance at Black Rock. "All except a very few of them, behaved in the most cowardly manner. They fled without discharging a musket."[40]

Tompkins, in his January 1814 address to the legislature, called the surrender of Fort Niagara "extraordinary." He castigated the British for unleashing the brutality of Indian warriors on civilians. "The conduct of the enemy during that invasion was marked by a disregard of the rules of civilized warfare, and by a malignant ferocity. Many of our fellow citizens, who were at peace with their families, were murdered and scalped. The bodies of many of those who were wounded or taken prisoners in the engagement at Black Rock, have been found mangled in the most shocking manner by the tomahawk and the scalping knife."[41]

British authorities took a different view. Sir George Prevost issued a proclamation from Quebec on January 12, 1814. He stated forthrightly that it was a matter "of imperious duty to retaliate on America the miseries which the unfortunate inhabitants of Newark had been made to suffer on the evacuation of Fort George." He blamed the start of the vicious cycle of abuse against civilians and their property with Brig. Gen. William Hull's invasion across the Detroit River in 1812. Prevost charged that it was here that the American forces began "marking out as objects of their resentment the loyal subjects of His Majesty and in dooming their property to plunder and conflagration." Thus, acting out of a sense of honor and justice, General Drummond exacted "a full measure of retaliation." The Governor General concluded, stating he would not pursue further retaliation unless the Americans did so. In McClure's senseless and foolhardy actions at Newark, no one died, but British retaliation included Indian warriors making war against civilians.[42]

Some few brave citizens returned to the remains of their homes as early as January to begin the slow process of rebuilding. The *Buffalo Gazette* resumed publishing on January 24. Assistance for the returning civilians arrived slowly and from numerous sources. At Canandaigua, concerned citizens formed the Committee of Safety and Relief. This group sent requests throughout the state for funds to meet the needs of the victims along the Niagara River. In a circular letter, the committee reported as many as 12,000 refugees. "The fugitives from Niagara County especially were dispersed under circumstances of so much terror that in some cases, mothers find themselves wandering with strange children, and children are seen accompanied by such as have no other sympathies with them than those of common sufferings." On January 24, the Common Council of New York City voted $3,000 from the city treasury. The churches and private benefactors raised a total of $6,500 and turned this over to city officials, who forwarded the money to the committee at Canandaigua. The Common Council of Albany appropriated $1,000 to the relief effort as well.[43]

In February, the state legislature passed a law entitled "An Act for the Relief of the Late Sufferers on the Western Frontier of this State." The state formed a commission to distribute $50,000 in grants. The commissioners drew the funds on May 19, 1814. This deputation invited persons to request money and required evidence of the value of the losses. The commissioners gave the Tuscarora Nation $1,500 and distributed the remainder in amounts ranging from $10 to $300 to approximately 325 individuals and families who signed receipts for the cash. In their report back to the state comptroller, the commissioners noted that their investigation "was rendered extremely difficult by the dispersed state of the inhabitants and by the desire to procure such evidence of the losses of the inhabitants as would prevent unjust claimants from participating in the fund." However, the state comptroller, Archibald McIntyre, examined the receipts delivered to him by the commissioners and in July, 1818, declared that receipts amounting to $16,455 were considered defective for various reasons. In 1821, the state legislature passed an act allowing the defective receipts, and the commissioners were no longer held liable. Over the next two decades, citizens left out of the initial settlement submitted their claims as well.[44]

In addition to grants, the state also made loans to fifty-nine persons totaling $49,800. Judge Samuel Tupper directed the loan program starting in August 1815. Persons typically secured their loan by offering their land as collateral. By 1822, only three persons had repaid their loan in full.[45]

As for the brigade of detached militia called to the frontier, they spent their ninety-day term of service in camp at Williamsville. Their days were filled with patrols, guard duty, and work details. Desertion was punished leniently with forfeiture of a month's pay. One unfortunate soldier was convicted of intoxication. The court awarded him an imaginative sentence. The miscreant was to march across the front of the assembled brigade "having his arms extended and lashed to a five-feet pole, with a bottle in each hand, one of which is to be empty and the other filled." In late March and early April, the companies mustered out of service. There was no money to pay them. They trudged to their homes, no doubt gravely disappointed with their treatment.[46]

The tragedy that befell the civilian population on the Niagara frontier in December ranks among the worst of the war. Gen. James Wilkinson denuded the region of regulars, leaving defense to the militia. The inability of federal officials to pay militiamen and Indian warriors quelled any desire to continue service voluntarily. Lack of volunteers contributed to McClure's criminal decision to burn Newark. The destruction of this village gave Drummond the excuse to destroy all structures along the river in the name of retaliation. Drummond's retaliation was vastly disproportionate for the loss of Newark. His use of Indian warriors was unnecessary, and once he learned of their excesses at Lewiston, the continued commitment of Indians at Black Rock and Buffalo was unconscionable. The unfolding catastrophe severely tested the limits of federal–state cooperation. The governor and the secretary of war bickered over the causes, although there certainly was much blame to go around. The repercussions of the needless suffering of civilians, Canadians as well as Americans, echoed into the 1814 campaign and beyond.

1814

CHAPTER 14

STRATEGIC CONFUSION

Congress declared war in 1812 with the understanding that Britain was fully committed to war with France. A window of opportunity of uncertain duration might allow a quick seizure of Canada's major cities. Such a circumstance might provide the chance for a negotiated settlement. However, in February 1814, the allied armies were within striking distance of Paris. Napoleon's days seemed numbered. His defeat would free huge numbers of veteran British troops and hundreds of warships for use against the United States. President James Madison received intelligence from sources in France and Britain to "be prepared for the worst the Enemy may be able to effect against us." The country that had declared war less than two years prior was bracing for the inevitable hammer blows to follow.[1]

Madison and the Congress acted to increase the size of the regular army. The current regiments were understrength, so there was little use in increasing the number of units. In January 1814, Congress decided to enhance the bounty to $124 for soldiers who would enlist or reenlist for five years or the duration of the war. This was an astounding increase. Prior to the war, the enlistment bounty was $12. Just months before the declaration of war, Congress increased the bounty to $31 ($16 upon enlistment and three months' pay upon completion of the term of service). Under the new law, the army paid $100 when a soldier joined his unit and $24 upon completion of his service. Similarly, Congress increased the land bounty from 160 acres to 320 acres.[2]

This new law saw results. The War Department estimated that approximately 8,740 new soldiers enlisted between February 1 and September 30. While War Department numbers were incomplete, about 20 percent of the new soldiers entered the ranks in New York state. This number is corroborated by the paymaster's report that of the nearly $2 million paid in bounties during that period, 24 percent went to recruits in New York state. By 1814, of the forty-six infantry regiments and four rifle regiments, three recruited in New York City and two each in Albany and Utica. Clearly, New Yorkers were responding to the approaching emergency. However, nationally new enlistments and reenlistments served only to make up for losses from death, injury, capture, or soldiers simply leaving at the end of their term of service.[3]

On January 2, Governor Tompkins wrote to Secretary of War Armstrong of the tragic loss of the Niagara frontier and urging immediate retaliation. "Be assured, Dear Sir that something must be done & that speedily and effectually, or the confidence of the Citizens of this quarter of the United States, in the government, will be lost." Tompkins pledged to raise five thousand volunteers, if the War Department will "unite with them 2,500 regulars." One week later, Tompkins recommended that Brig. Gen. Peter B. Porter be placed in command of volunteers and militia if the federal government anticipated operations on the Niagara frontier. Tompkins followed with another letter on January 16 claiming, "The inhabitants of the Western District, without distinction of party, would now cooperate with zeal and usefulness in any plan of penetrating into Canada as far as Burlington and York, provided transportation, provisions and military equipments were furnished by the government of the United States." However, neither the War Department nor the president was yet prepared to launch the 1814 campaign.[4]

The British offered to meet directly with American emissaries to discuss peace, and in December 1813, War Hawk Henry Clay led a negotiating team to Europe. However, it was not until August 1814 that the negotiators met in Ghent, United Netherlands, to begin active negotiations. Both sides continued to prosecute the war while they simultaneously considered a settlement. With the forces now available for use in North America, the British contemplated a strategic shift to the offensive.

British goals were twofold. The first was to push America's northern boundary southward to the Ohio River and perhaps below Lake Champlain as well. The second was to seize New Orleans. British land and sea forces could strike other targets, such as New York, Boston, Philadelphia, Baltimore, and Washington. In April 1814, Lord Bathurst planned to create a force of two divisions under Sir Rowland Hill to operate independently against the American coast. Roughly half of these forces had served under Lord Wellington on the Iberian Peninsula. However, on May 18, Bathurst changed strategic direction. He ordered two brigades under Major Generals Manley Power and Frederick Robinson to reinforce Canada under George Prevost's command. Bathurst designated a single brigade, Robert Ross's, to operate with Admiral Sir Alexander Cochrane against the Atlantic coast.

Admiral Cochrane anticipated commanding as many as 20,000 troops to raid America's Atlantic and Gulf coasts. He estimated that he would require at least 12,000 soldiers landing on Long Island to seize New York City. After he learned that only one brigade was allocated for attacks on the coast, Cochrane had to choose targets within his means. He focused his attention on Washington and Baltimore. Leaders preparing the defenses of New York City were unaware that their city would be safe in 1814. Nevertheless, they proceeded with passion and energy to prepare for an attack. Cochrane was anxious to inflict grievous damage. "I have it much at heart to give them a complete drubbing before Peace is made—when I trust their Northern limits will be circumscribed and the Command of the Mississippi wrested from them." Britain's heaviest offensives of 1814 would fall upon Plattsburgh and New Orleans.[5]

The Admiralty expanded shipbuilding on the Great Lakes, largely in response to the unprecedented loss of a squadron on Lake Erie the previous September. The shipyard at Kingston produced two frigates, *Princess Charlotte* and *Prince Regent*, both of which outstripped the twenty-eight-gun frigate *General Pike* in armament. The new frigates also carried a balance of long guns and carronades, thus diminishing Yeo's disadvantage in long-range engagements. Yeo and Prevost decided to build a first-rate ship, the *St. Lawrence*. With over one hundred guns, it would outclass anything the Americans had to offer.

When Commodore Isaac Chauncey learned three new vessels were going up at Kingston, he gained permission from Secretary of the Navy William Jones to start work on more warships. Jones insisted, "Every possible resource and effort must be directed to the creation of such a force at Sacketts Harbour as will enable you to meet the enemy on the Lake the moment he may appear, and with means competent to ensure success." Chauncey replaced the converted lakers that had performed poorly in 1813 with larger craft. Shipbuilder Henry Eckford laid out two brigs, *Jefferson* and *Jones*, and two frigates, *Mohawk* and *Superior*, at Sackett's Harbor. Jones transferred hundreds of officers and seamen from idle vessels on the Atlantic to Lake Ontario. The naval arms race picked up momentum.[6]

The remnants of the two divisions that saw defeat the previous year at Chateauguay and Chrysler's Farm were languishing in Plattsburgh and French Mills, respectively. Maj. Gen. James Wilkinson retained command of these divisions as well as all federal forces in the Ninth Military District. When Maj. Gen. Wade Hampton left his division in December after the failed Chateauguay campaign, he put Brig. Gen. George Izard in command. Izard sent Wilkinson, then at his headquarters in Malone, New York, a note stating, "Almost every officer is either sick, or was furloughed by Major General Hampton, at the moment of his own departure; those that remain, are barely enough to perform the routine of duty in this cantonment." Izard himself was desperately ill, and he eventually moved to Philadelphia to recover.[7]

On February 13, Maj. Gen. Wilkinson broke winter quarters at French Mills. Troops burned or scuttled over three hundred batteaux and other vessels that had carried Wilkinson's division only two months prior. Maj. Gen. Jacob Brown led troops through the snow to Sackett's Harbor while Brig. Gen. Alexander Macomb's soldiers began their trek to Plattsburgh. Wilkinson and his staff headed for Plattsburgh. On February 17, British raiders entered the abandoned camp and proceeded to Malone and Chateaugay, plundering public and private property as they went. The British withdrew before Wilkinson could launch a pursuit.[8]

Wilkinson ordered the sick and convalescents to move to Sackett's Harbor, Plattsburgh, and the hospital at Burlington, Vermont. Over 450 hospital patients made the miserable journey seventy miles in sleighs through thinly populated country to Lake Champlain. Dr. James Mann with this group noted that it snowed or rained "during the whole journey" and that accommodations were "wretched." He recorded, "The inhabitants, although kind, were not under circumstances to furnish means to render the situation of sick men even comfortable." Lt. Col. George McFeely recalled that his soldiers marching to Plattsburgh "lay three nights around fires in deep snows and without covering and many men had their noses, ears, and hands and feet frozen." The soldiers, who initiated the 1814 campaign, were hardly recovered from the ordeal at French Mills.[9]

The early months of 1814 showed an increase in the sick and wounded at the Burlington hospital. The movement from French Mills increased the number of patients in Burlington to 671, and by the end of March, the number reached 931. In the first three months of 1814, fifty-three patients died at the hospital. These numbers do not include battlefield deaths, the twenty who died at the hospital in Malone in January, or patients retained in the regimental hospitals. Sickness and wounds substantially degraded the strength of American forces on Lake Champlain.[10]

Wilkinson well understood that after the defeat at Crysler's Farm his days in command were numbered. In an attempt to reestablish his reputation, he ordered an advance northward and parallel to the Richelieu River. Four thousand regulars marched off; Wilkinson brought no militia with him. On March 30, the Americans passed through Odelltown in Lower Canada, about thirty miles north of Plattsburgh. The British had felled trees across the main road toward the Lacolle River five miles away. The Lacolle flows eastward into the Richelieu. A large stone mill guarded the crossing point. The British garrisoned the mill and surrounding defenses with about 250 troops and another 650 soldiers within seven miles.

Wilkinson surrounded the mill on three sides and opened fire with three artillery pieces. The cannon fire was ineffective against stone masonry. An

American attack was thrown back, as was a British counterattack. Seeing no way around or through the determined defense, Wilkinson withdrew through a heavy, cold rainfall back to Lake Champlain. Each side had suffered fewer than seventy casualties.[11] That same month, Armstrong removed Wilkinson from command and preferred charges, the principal being neglect of duty. The court-martial did not sit until the following year. Although the jury acquitted Wilkinson, the War Department dropped him from the rolls of the postwar army.

With the departure of Wilkinson, Madison promoted George Izard to major general. After a lengthy convalescence in Philadelphia, Izard returned to Plattsburgh on May 1, 1814. There he found "the wretched and ragged remnant of what had undergone the fatigues of the last winter's deplorable attempts on the Enemy's Frontier." He methodically went about the arduous task of rebuilding his forces. The War Department designated Izard's command as the Right Division to distinguish it from Maj. Gen. Jacob Brown's Left Division. Macomb noted of the new recruits, "The men are of the first quality, but like their officers are destitute of military ideas or feelings." Izard set high expectations for his officers and began a grueling training regimen. He chose Baron von Steuben's *Blue Book* as the standard drill manual. Izard's condescension offended several of the officers serving close to him. His inspector general, Col. William Cumming, wrote that Izard "treated me like he treated others, with Bashaw-like superiority." Yet, over the following months the transformation of the force was remarkable. The Right Division was ready for whatever would come.[12]

While Izard prepared the land forces, Commodore Thomas Macdonough strengthened the naval contingent. In December 1813, Macdonough put the vessels into winter quarters at Otter Creek, near Vergennes, Vermont. He started 1814 with a squadron consisting of four sloops and four row galleys carrying a total of thirty-seven guns and carronades. Secretary of the Navy Jones offered Macdonough a choice of building programs. Jones would authorize the construction of fifteen galleys or a ship of twenty-four guns and three or four galleys. The galleys carried a gun and a carronade and were shallow-draft and excellent for maneuvering when winds were light or nonexistent. However, fifteen galleys required many more crewmen than a ship, and seamen were scarce. Sailors generally preferred service on a privateer, where prize money was possible, rather than service on the lakes. Given the configuration of the shoreline and the shifting winds on Lake Champlain, Macdonough preferred the galleys. He thought it possible to recruit soldiers to row, while sailors manned the galley guns. In the end, however, Macdonough engaged shipbuilder Noah Brown to construct a corvette of twenty-six guns, the *Saratoga*, which was the squadron's flagship. Macdonough also began construction of six galleys, although he had no guns to arm them nor crewmen to serve them. Governor Tompkins recommended that the navy purchase a steamboat then under construction by the Steamboat Company of Lake Champlain. Macdonough acquired the vessel and had it completed as the fourteen-gun schooner *Ticonderoga*. The commodore rightly believed the steam engine to be unreliable in battle and therefore dispensed with it on *Ticonderoga*. Eventually, Macdonough added a brig to the fleet, the twenty-gun *Eagle*.[13]

As early as April 1814, Tompkins received warnings that the Royal Navy squadron on the Richelieu River might conduct raids into Lake Champlain before the American warships could respond. The governor sent two of his brigade commanders to assess the situation. Brigadier Generals Micajah Pettit and Simon De Ridder, both of Washington County, conducted their reconnaissance and as a result, alerted three regiments of the common militia to respond if a British squadron passed south of Crown Point.[14]

The British were the first on the lake. Commander Daniel Pring led an expedition to capture or destroy the American vessels on Otter Creek. The Royal Navy squadron attempted to force entry into Otter Creek on May 14. The Americans opened fire from a shore battery named Fort Cassin. Unable to silence the American fire, Pring withdrew. Twelve days after the engagement, Macdonough brought the American squadron out onto the lake, dominating the waters and suppressing smuggling. On June 7, sailors destroyed four large spars that American smugglers were attempting to bring to Isle aux Noix for use as masts on the newest British ship. Macdonough continued preparations to ensure the American fleet on Lake Champlain would be sufficiently ready for its climactic battle in September.[15]

Izard conducted vigorous small-scale operations along the border with Lower Canada to keep the British at bay and to prevent spies or scouts from approaching too close to the American camps. In one of these raids, Maj. Benjamin Forsyth and his riflemen captured a notorious spy at his home in Odelltown in British territory. This violated Izard's orders to arrest Canadian civilians only when they were on the American side of the border. The British retaliated by holding an American citizen hostage for the return of theirs. Forsyth paid for his indiscretion. Returning to Odelltown a few days later, Forsyth was leading a patrol from the front as he often did. An Indian warrior shot and killed him. Izard reported, "On our side none has fallen besides the gallant, but eccentric and irregular Forsyth." The civilian hostages were soon returned.[16]

The prospect of a major British counteroffensive impelled Governor Tompkins and the Republicans to bolster the state's preparedness for whatever would come. In January, Tompkins delivered his annual address to the legislature reviewing the events of 1813 and setting goals for the current year. Tompkins rendered a balanced account of the military situation, noting that the battles of York and Fort George and the defense of Sackett's Harbor "were honorable to our arms and have exhibited traits of conduct and intrepidity in the army that justify high expectations." He noted that Wilkinson's and Hampton's campaigns were "disappointments and disasters."[17] The Republican-controlled Senate validated the governor's report; however, the Federalist-majority Assembly panned Tompkins's assessment. The Federalist caucus responded, "Despots may boast of the success of their arms—they may to obtain honor and fame sport with the feelings and property & lives of their subjects, but the greatest honor of a republic is, to protect the property, defend the lives and maintain the liberty of the people."[18]

The Assembly appointed only two Federalist senators to the Council of Appointment. Thus, the governor and two Republican senators, one of whom was former governor and now Maj. Gen. Morgan Lewis, controlled the council and with it the selection of civil officials and militia officers. However, the Federalist majority in the Assembly passed virtually none of the governor's recommendations to strengthen the state's military capacity.[19]

Tompkins dispassionately assessed the effectiveness of the common militia in responding to British raids into the state. Although over 97,000 men were enrolled in the militia, these citizen-soldiers were unable to prevent destruction or loss of life and property. In this opinion, he was supported by many of the senior militia officers from the western counties.[20] Tompkins was frustrated by the number of persons who failed to answer the intermittent calls for militia service and only paid a fine, if that, for their evasion of service.[21] Tompkins knew the state could not count on regulars to defend it. The nation's offensive arm was concentrated at a few strategic locations. That left hundreds of miles of frontier exposed to attack. Tompkins asked the legislature to create a brigade-sized force of volunteers "to take the field upon any emergency, without the tedious process of detaching, assembling and organizing men from remote districts, and would perform any actual service which might legally be required more usefully than detached militia."[22]

As more news of the destruction of the Niagara frontier arrived in Albany, Tompkins pushed his agenda, and on January 31, he sent the legislature a detailed design of the brigade. Tompkins requested two infantry regiments of 1,000 volunteers each, as well as a mounted battalion of four hundred men. He added that the legislature should authorize monthly pay of $10, much higher than that of regulars. He confirmed that sufficient state equipment "for twice the number of Volunteers before mentioned" was available.[23]

Tompkins had requested that the legislature authorize volunteer regiments in 1812 and 1813 as well. The Federalist-controlled Assembly ignored Tompkins's request a third time, but incongruously remarked, "Your Excellency must be convinced from what has happened upon our Frontier that if the State of New York is to be defended from the incursions of the enemy, it must be by a force of her own providing and not one provided for her by the General Government."[24] In a note to Secretary of War Armstrong, the governor wrote, "The Assembly has too much of the Massachusetts leaven in it, to do anything favorable to the support of the Country."[25]

In April, state elections saw record voter turnout and gave Republicans control of both houses of the legislature. Nine Senate seats came open and the election produced eight Republicans and a single Federalist. Voters gave Republicans a two-to-one majority in the Assembly and filled twenty-one of the state's twenty-eight congressional seats with Republicans. A small minority of Federalists had adopted a pro-war stance, diluting the Federalists' anti-war platform. It appeared that voters responded to the British burning of the Niagara frontier. The enemy had gone too far by not stopping their Indian allies from killing civilians. The defense of the state was safer in Republican hands. Voters also apparently responded to the repeal of the onerous embargo that Congress had approved in December 1813. This act had prohibited American ships from departing American ports and also banned importation of any commodities customarily produced in the British Empire. Additionally, the market for grain grown in the western part of the state rose with increased demand from the army. Perhaps voter backlash to the fierce and unrelenting resistance to the war tipped the election in favor of the Republican candidates. Now, Tompkins would enjoy freedom of action in directing the state's defensive efforts when the legislature met in the fall.[26]

This change in the balance of state politics came none too soon. On February 15, Commodore Chauncey departed New York City, where he had been honored with a dinner by city Federalists. He returned to Sackett's Harbor with a hundred more seamen. The shipyard launched two twenty-gun brigs, the *Jefferson* and the *Jones*, in April. Work started on two frigates. Learning from his spies of the feverish activity at Sackett's Harbor, British Commodore Sir James Yeo complained to Admiral John Borlase Warren that "The Roads from Albany, Boston, and New York, are covered with Ordnance, and Stores for these Vessels, and which, when added to their old Squadron, will be far Superior to any thing I can bring against them." Yeo was exaggerating; shipwrights at Kingston were industriously constructing two large frigates, the *Princess Charlotte* and the *Prince Regent*. The arms race continued unabated.[27]

Chauncey and Yeo both understood that their relative strengths would be substantially adjusted should either Sackett's Harbor or Kingston be successfully attacked. Chauncey complained to Secretary Jones about Kingston, "It really appears strange that the whole Military force of the Nation aided with the Naval force here cannot take that small place." However, it was the British who first took action. In April, Lieutenant General Gordon Drummond and Commodore Yeo collaborated on a plan to destroy the naval base at Sackett's Harbor. Yeo was convinced that the Royal Navy could not win a shipbuilding competition. "The only way completely to secure the tranquility of the Upper Province is a vigorous combined attack of Army and Navy against the Enemy's chief means of annoyance, their Fleet & Stores, at Sackett's Harbour." However, Governor General George Prevost would not provide the necessary numbers of troops. Yeo settled for an attack on the transshipment facilities and stores at Oswego. Success at Oswego would delay the American shipbuilding effort and perhaps throw a decisive advantage to Yeo's squadron.[28]

In mid-April, warnings of impending British raids along the shore of Lake Ontario arrived in Albany. Tompkins took decisive action. He ordered the brigade commanders supporting Sackett's Harbor, Oswego, and Sodus to prepare their militiamen to march at a moment's notice. He informed Commodore Isaac Chauncey and Brig. Gen. Edmund P. Gaines, then commanding army forces at Sackett's Harbor, that these brigade commanders would respond immediately to requisitions for the militia without waiting for confirmation from their militia superiors. The governor thus effectively reduced militia response time. Tompkins understood that Oswego and the dilapidated Fort Ontario would be difficult, if not impossible, to defend. In his letter to Gaines, he stated that if a British raid on Oswego seized Fort Ontario, "it will be impossible to expel them from it with Militia only." Tompkins informed Chauncey that there were about 750 state muskets in Oswego or nearby Oswego Falls ready to issue to militia. However, there was no state artillery to send to Fort Ontario.[29]

Lt. Col. George Mitchell, commanding about three hundred artillerists fighting as infantry, and Master Commandant Melancthon Woolsey, with twenty-five seamen, were determined to defend the guns, rigging, and provisions awaiting shipment from Oswego. Larger numbers of guns, cable, and supplies were located about twelve miles to the south at Oswego Falls. Mitchell reported, "The corroding hand of time had destroyed every Picket around the Fort and at several points it was as accessible as through an open Gateway." The Americans found five condemned guns, and the artillerists prepared these for action. The Americans erected tents on the western side of the river, and militia occupied these grounds. Mitchell hoped that the sight of the camp would create the semblance of a large defensive force. Mitchell's troops had been improving the defenses at the fort for five days when Yeo and Drummond arrived early on May 5.[30]

British warships exchanged fire with American cannon until late in the afternoon. Colonel Victor Fischer commanded the landing party of 750 seamen,

Royal Marines, and infantrymen. Adverse winds prompted Yeo to postpone the amphibious assault. Early on the morning of May 6, the Royal Navy squadron bombarded the fort and militia camp in earnest, eventually forcing the militiamen to abandon their position. After hours of unequal pounding, the landing party made its way to shore. Mitchell formed his men into a firing line to oppose the British, who were advancing on the fort. After about thirty minutes of a lopsided firefight, Mitchell gave the order to withdraw. The Americans had lost sixty-nine killed, wounded, and captured. The British seized seven naval guns, a couple of small schooners, and massive amounts of food and salt at the high cost of ninety casualties. Yeo's squadron departed Oswego the following morning. Drummond declared that the attack constituted a "compleat success." The losses suffered in the attack as well as a general lack of troops persuaded Drummond and Yeo to drop their plans for attacking Chauncey's base.[31]

Meanwhile, Mitchell and Woolsey had pulled their survivors back to Oswego Falls, fully expecting Yeo and Drummond to exploit their success by attempting to seize the guns and naval stores piled up there. Brig. Gen. John Ellis, commander of the Twenty-Seventh Militia Brigade, called out more than 2,000 men. Mitchell became aware that the British had returned to Kingston; no attack at the falls was forthcoming. Although the militia had not participated in the fight, Mitchell noted in his report to Jacob Brown, "It would be injustice not to acknowledge and report to you the patriotism evinced by the Militia officers and soldiers who arrived at a very short notice and were anxious to be useful."[32]

After the battle, young boys collected the British cannonballs that lay about the ground and sold them to a local doctor. The doctor in turn sold five tons of iron balls to the owner of a local forge, who sold them to the army. The British balls were admittedly "much better" than those cast locally. Those same youth collected musket cartridges scattered about and exploded them "to the infinite gratification of themselves, and the terror of their small sisters."[33]

After dropping off the captured materiel at Kingston, Yeo cruised along the southern shores of the lake, and on May 14 the squadron anchored off the Genesee River near the settlement of Charlotte. Thirty-three American militiamen gathered on shore to oppose any landing. Yeo sent a party under a flag of truce. The British officer demanded that the militiamen deliver public provisions and military stores. Failing that, the officer promised to destroy the settlement. Col. Isaac Stone sent his official response: "Go back and tell them that the public property is in the hands of those who will defend it." After receiving the response, Yeo ordered a sloop to fire at the visible storehouses. After about fifteen to twenty shots, only one of which hit a storehouse, the sloop broke contact. Yeo sent a second officer to repeat his threat, this time adding that there would be four hundred Indians with the shore party. By this time Gen. Peter Porter had arrived. He replied that he was ready to face both soldiers and Indians and, if the British sent another flag of truce, the Americans would fire at it. By then, hundreds of militiamen were streaming into the American camp. Yeo decided not to land but to proceed eastward and look for an easier target. The previous year the British squadron had raided the Genesee River without opposition. This time the American response was different. Porter wrote to the governor, "We saved the town and our credit by fairly outbullying John Bull."[34]

The following day, the squadron approached Pultneyville, located nine miles west of Sodus Point. About one hundred barrels of damaged flour—government property—was stored there. Militiamen had moved three hundred barrels of good flour to safety a mile away. The villagers notified Brig. Gen. John Swift of Palmyra of the British presence. Swift called out the local militia. Swift had served in the Revolution, and he was the older brother of militia leader Philetus Swift. The general brought 130 men with him, arriving after dark. The next morning, Yeo sent an officer to the village demanding all public property. Refusal would result in destruction of the village. Swift reluctantly agreed to allow the British to seize all the flour in the storehouse—the damaged flour.

The shore party, consisting of several hundred men, arrived and loaded the flour. What happened next has never been firmly established. Several British soldiers apparently went into various buildings, in violation of the terms of the agreement. An American fired his weapon, and a firefight exploded throughout the village. The raiders withdrew with the flour and one dead soldier. Gun crews on the warships opened fire, holing a few houses. Soon, however, Yeo departed, and the Americans celebrated their victory.[35]

On May 19, Yeo and his squadron appeared off Sackett's Harbor, effectively bottling up the American fleet. Yeo sent ships up and down the American coast looking for opportunities to raid. When Brown recalled Mitchell and his artillerymen to Sackett's Harbor after the battle at Oswego, he left Capt. Daniel Appling and 150 riflemen at Oswego Falls. On May 25, Appling responded to a British raid east of Oswego and requested that General Ellis send three hundred infantrymen to Oswego Falls. The militiamen arrived two days later and guarded the naval stores then being loaded on boats and sent downriver to Oswego and on to Sackett's Harbor once the coast was clear. Ellis then marched his battalion to Oswego, remaining there until he mustered his men out of service on June 4.[36]

Believing (erroneously as it turned out) that Yeo had broken off the blockade of Sackett's Harbor, Chauncey ordered Woolsey to send some guns from Oswego Falls to the naval base. On May 28, Woolsey dutifully responded and started thirty-four naval guns and a number of large cables eastward in nineteen bateaux. The convoy travelled in hours of darkness accompanied by 130 of Appling's riflemen. About 150 Oneida Indians travelled by land paralleling the water route. At about noon the next day, the convoy entered Sandy Creek and moved about two miles up the winding, narrow watercourse.[37]

Yeo received a report of the American movement and sent Captain Stephen Popham with two gunboats and three smaller craft to intercept the valuable cargo. The British managed to seize one of the nineteen bateaux. Yeo later sent Captain Francis Spilsbury with two boatloads of troops to reinforce Popham. Sighting the masts of the American vessels above the intervening trees, the British incautiously entered Sandy Creek. Popham found the chance of depriving the new American frigates of their armament overpowering. Woolsey and Appling had become aware of their pursuers and laid an ambush. The creek narrowed continuously and Popham sent sailors and his Royal Marines ashore to better secure him in the lead gunboat. Appling sprung the ambush; the opening volleys felled more than sixty British tars and marines. Popham surrendered, recognizing that there was no hope in continuing the uneven exchange. The British lost eighteen killed. Lt. Col. Clark Allen's regiment of Jefferson County militia marched over 170 prisoners into captivity at Sackett's Harbor, including the two naval captains. The Americans lost one killed and two wounded. Yeo was furious at the loss of the senior officers and so many crewmen as well as the small boats. He pulled back his blockading force and returned to anchorage near the Bay of Quinte, close to the head of the Saint Lawrence River.[38]

The Americans had captured two large guns, a sixty-eight-pounder carronade, and quite a bit of weaponry and ammunition. These items, as well as the contents of the eighteen remaining bateaux, had to be taken to Sackett's Harbor. Most of the captured material moved by water, but much was loaded on wagons acquired from the local populace. However, one very thick and long cable presented a challenge. It was too big to fit entirely on any of the wagons. Someone proposed having men follow the wagon while carrying the excess cable on their shoulders. The volunteers worked in two shifts. Militiaman N. W. Hibbard recalled that "every man's shoulders were bruised until they were black and blue—larger than the palm of a man's hand." This strange convoy moved about twenty miles to the naval base, arriving the day after the battle. The soldiers and sailors at Sackett's Harbor met the expedition with cheers, relieved the tired civilians, and completed the move. Chauncey gave the militiamen who had carried the cable $2 each.[39]

The shipbuilding war continued at Sackett's Harbor. Chauncey had his shipwrights construct fifteen large armed barges to transport troops. American naval officers and seamen arrived at Sackett's Harbor in numbers large enough to crew the new ships. Chauncey would be ready for an amphibious assault on

Kingston. The naval squadron was also the beneficiary of a promising technological advance. The Navy Department had purchased a number of Chambers
repeating weapons and shipped them to Chauncey. Inventor Samuel G. Chambers developed a fairly reliable repeater in three variants. The seven-barrel
swivel gun could fire 175 rounds of .75 caliber cylindrical bullets at roughly one
round every second from each barrel. The purpose was to mount two or more
of these weapons in the fore and mainmast fighting tops to fire down upon
an opposing ship's deck at close range. Chambers also developed a repeating
musket that fired eleven rounds with one in reserve. The third variant was a
boarding pistol. One of his officers reported to Commodore Yeo in July that
a reliable spy reported there were twelve swivel guns, fifty muskets, and two
hundred boarding pistols then at Sackett's Harbor, with more expected daily.
No conclusive evidence exists that these specialized weapons were ever used in
combat during the war.[40]

As military and naval forces on the frontiers made ready for a fateful
campaign season, similar preparations unfolded in New York City. The city's
defenses improved markedly on February 18, when Commodore John Rodgers
completed a lengthy voyage and ran the blockade to bring *President* into the
Lower Bay. He anchored the fifty-four-gun frigate near Sandy Hook, where it
could challenge any warship attempting to cross the sandbar and enter the bay.
In addition to *President*, the naval warships at New York City included *Alert* and
Peacock, each with eighteen guns. The flotilla of thirty-one gunboats crewed by
five hundred seamen did yeoman service patrolling the two approaches to the
city—Long Island Sound and Sandy Hook.

In March, *Peacock* made a nighttime crossing of the sandbar at Sandy Hook.
It was difficult but not impossible to evade the British blockade. *Peacock* sailed
along the eastern seaboard, capturing over $110,000 in gold specie. On April
25, Admiral Sir Alexander Cochrane, who had succeeded John Borlase Warren, extended the blockade to the entire American coast. With many warships
released from European blockade duty, the British no longer excluded the New
England coast.

In March 1814, Congress authorized two more infantry regiments, the
Forty-Sixth and the Forty-Seventh, to add to the garrison of New York City.
These formations joined the Thirty-Second, Forty-First, and Forty-Second
regiments. In May, the War Department consolidated a number of regiments
and redesignated the Forty-Seventh as the Twenty-Seventh Infantry. The Second and Third U.S. Volunteers had mustered out of service in January 1814,
and many of the men reenlisted in the new formations. These trained soldiers
took advantage of the increased enlistment bounty by reenlisting in the regular
army. Col. Stephen E. Fotterall resigned from command of the Thirty-Second

Infantry to command the Forty-Sixth. Colonel James Mullany, who had fought at Queenston Heights, assumed command of the Thirty-Second. The Senate negated Fotterall's appointment in November. Lt. Col. William S. Tallmadge, a New Yorker who had served as a major in the Second U.S. Volunteers, assumed command of the Forty-Sixth. Lt. Col. Alexander Denniston, an Irish veteran of the 1798 uprising who had recently commanded the Third U.S. Volunteers, now commanded the Twenty-Seventh Infantry.[41]

Tompkins tweaked the land defenses of the city and Long Island. Starting in December 1813 and continuing into the spring, the commander in chief converted several militia cavalry units into horse artillery, as these would be more useful in battle. He also mobilized a small militia force of infantry and horse artillery to replace the militiamen at Sag Harbor as their ninety-day service drew to a close.[42] Work on harbor defenses as well as land defenses around Brooklyn and Harlem Heights progressed steadily. By and large, the city's defensive posture was better than it had ever been.

Robert Fulton introduced a revolutionary approach to harbor defense. He built a model of a steam vessel armed with twenty-four heavy guns and with the ability to heat shot red-hot to burn wooden vessels. At the time, sailing vessels were not equipped with furnaces for that purpose because these would present a fire hazard. Stephen Decatur assisted in developing the requirements of such a harbor-defense warship that Fulton incorporated into the design. The ship's wooden sides were particularly thick and the paddle wheel was positioned inside, thus making it difficult for enemy guns to damage. A steam-powered warship had the ability to move when wind was light or absent, while sailing vessels would be rendered immobile or very slow. Thus, Fulton's warship could position itself advantageously to engage the enemy.

Decatur, Oliver Hazard Perry, Jacob Lewis, and James Biddle, among other naval officers, wrote letters praising the practicality and utility of Fulton's design. Congress authorized the president to acquire one or more working steam batteries, and Fulton proceeded to build his project.[43] A few entrepreneurs, including Maj. Gen. Henry Dearborn, formed the Society for Coast and Harbor Defence specifically to build Fulton's warship. Shipbuilders at the yard of Adam and Noah Brown laid the keel in June.

Secretary of War Armstrong relieved General Dearborn of command of the Third Military District, and Maj. Gen. Morgan Lewis assumed command in mid-June. Armstrong gave Dearborn command of the tranquil First Military District, with headquarters in Boston. Dearborn's health and energy had played out over two years of war. Nevertheless, he was able to refurbish the image of the federal government in Massachusetts, a decidedly anti-war state.[44]

Now that the state legislature was controlled by Republicans, Governor Tompkins was in a better position to lead an emergency program to fully mobilize state resources to protect the citizenry and to support the efforts of the federal government. With the end of the war in Europe in sight, the strategic balance was shifting rapidly in favor of Britain. Hoping to achieve worthy results, the Madison administration would launch the longest and most deadly campaign of the war along the Niagara River.

CHAPTER 15

THE BATTLES OF CHIPPAWA
AND LUNDY'S LANE

When the winter cantonment at French Mills broke up, Secretary of War John Armstrong directed Maj. Gen. Jacob Brown to take 2,000 troops to Sackett's Harbor. His soldiers, now designated the Left Division, arrived there in mid-February. With the fall of Wilkinson following the aborted operation at Lacolle Mill, Maj. Gen. George Izard commanded the bulk of the army in the Ninth Military District (the Right Division) on Lake Champlain. Brown was responsible for operations from St. Regis to the border with Pennsylvania. In early April, Armstrong issued guidance to Brown that confused him and ultimately led to the major campaign of 1814 being directed away from decisive objectives such as Kingston or Montreal. Armstrong's instruction appeared in two letters. One directed Brown to consider attacking Kingston across the ice if practicable. Armstrong suggested using the second letter to mask Brown's attack on Kingston. This spurious second letter ordered Brown to move to the Niagara frontier to retake Fort Niagara. The secretary of war offered Brown the opportunity to leak the information on the second letter to British authorities, thus directing them away from an attack on Kingston. However, Armstrong had not made his intention clear. Brown consulted with Commodore Isaac Chauncey and decided that an attack across the ice was too risky. However, the commodore persuaded Brown that Armstrong intended the second letter to take effect if Brown decided against attacking Kingston.[1]

Armstrong assigned three newly promoted brigadier generals to the Left Division: Winfield Scott, Eleazar Ripley, and Edmund P. Gaines. Brown gave Gaines the responsibility to defend Sackett's Harbor in his absence. He gave brigade commands to Scott and Ripley. Brown and Scott were both aggressive, willing to give battle and trust the valor of their men for victory. Ripley was clearly out of step with them. While personally brave, he was more cautious and unwilling to commit to battle without a substantial advantage over his adversary.

Brown put his troops on the march toward the Niagara frontier. Along the way, Gaines persuaded Brown that he had misunderstood the secretary of war's guidance. Brown turned the column around and he himself sped back to Sackett's Harbor. Once there, Chauncey argued again that the second letter was operative; Brown was to conduct an offensive on the Niagara frontier. Brown sent orders to the column to reverse its course again and continue its trek across cold, muddy roads toward Batavia, thirty-five miles east of Buffalo. However, Brown and Chauncey had indeed misunderstood Armstrong's intent. When he learned that Brown was moving the Left Division to the Niagara frontier, Armstrong acquiesced, urging him to "go on and prosper. Good consequences are sometimes the result of mistakes." With thousands of British troops receiving orders to sail to North America, Madison had but a narrow window to gain a strategic objective. Armstrong unintentionally placed the Left Division where it could strike only secondary goals.

As the three-month tour of duty for the militia on the Niagara frontier was about to expire, Tompkins issued a call for volunteers to form a brigade of two regiments commanded by Brig. Gen. Peter B. Porter. The newly elected legislature, dominated by Republicans, would take office in July but not meet to make laws until October. Therefore, the new brigade would not be state volunteers subject to the governor's command. Instead, the volunteers would be mustered into federal service for a term of six months. Federal volunteers had no constitutional protection to disobey orders to deploy outside of the national boundaries. Citing the "late ravages and barbarities of the enemy on the Niagara frontier," Tompkins appealed to patriotism to fill the ranks. In democratic fashion, Tompkins directed the men of each company to select their officers and the officers of each battalion to select their commander. However, it would take months to recruit and equip the brigade. Tompkins gave command of the first regiment to be formed to Col. Philetus Swift, an experienced and competent officer.[2]

Winfield Scott spent several weeks in Albany before moving to the Niagara frontier. During this time, he coordinated with Maj. George Bomford at the Albany arsenal for the ordnance to support operations on the Niagara River. Bomford graduated from West Point in 1804 and was a gifted specialist in artillery. At Madison's direction, Scott also met several times with Governor Tompkins and Judge Ambrose Spencer. In his memoirs, Scott pronounced, "At this dark period of the war, Albany, rather than Washington, was the watchtower of the nation."[3]

Scott joined his brigade several miles east of Buffalo and brought them into camp. Here began the epic tale of Scott and his storied brigade. Starting on

April 22, Scott conducted a rigorous training program at Buffalo. Except for bad weather, the soldiers drilled for seven to ten hours daily for six days a week. As units arrived, Scott, and later Brown, included them in the training routine. Scott used the drill book written by defamed Brig. Gen. Alexander Smyth. Every Sunday, the officers inspected their men's weapons and equipment. The troops had to be ready to march on a moment's notice. The Left Division was blessed by the quality of its field officers. Experienced leaders such as Thomas Jesup, Jacob Hindman, Henry Leavenworth, Eleazar Wood, and others added their talents in creating an excellent fighting force.[4]

Scott took steps to ensure the success of the campaign. He enforced high standards of camp and personal sanitation, which reduced illness. Surgeon Joseph Lovell reported "only one or two deaths occurring before they crossed the Niagara, on the 3rd of July—even the demon diarrhea appeared to have been exorcised by the mystical power of strict discipline and rigid police."[5] Scott also collected useful information. Maj. Azor Orne, the assistant inspector general, interviewed recent travelers and assembled data from the Niagara peninsula and as far away as Lake Simcoe and York.[6]

To augment the troops assembling to fight the upcoming campaign, the Seneca and other Iroquois decided that their interests were best served by actively supporting the American cause. Porter sent his interpreter, Jasper Parrish, to recruit from the Oneida and Onondaga. While in Herkimer County waiting for the Oneida to return from the engagement at Sandy Creek, Parrish sent Porter an update: "I find the white people in this country are using every exertion to keep the Indians in this part of the country [at home] stating the necessity of them being here on account of so many alarms." This assessment speaks to the trust between white and Indian communities even after the events on the Niagara River the previous December.[7]

In 1813, Cornplanter commanded the Iroquois contingent. However, in the forthcoming invasion, Indian Agent Erastus Granger would command the battalion. Granger had white officers serving on his staff. The company commanders were all Indians. When the Iroquois battalion appeared on the battlefield, Granger turned over field command to Captain Pollard, the Seneca war chief. The aging tribal spokesman Red Jacket provided moral strength and confidence to the expedition.

The War Department also ordered a regiment of Pennsylvania Volunteers to join the Left Division. This unit was initially stationed at Erie. On May 15, Col. John B. Campbell led a body of regulars and some of the Pennsylvanians forty-five miles across Lake Erie to raid Port Dover, a settlement directly north of Erie. Once there, they shamefully burned private homes and killed livestock.

No doubt many of Campbell's raiders were motivated to retaliate for the burning of the Niagara frontier a few months earlier.

Winfield Scott was notoriously prejudiced against militia. In a letter to Jacob Brown, he wrote "Col. Fenton and his militia are already in march for this place. I am sorry for this circumstance, for I had rather be without that species of force, than have the whole population of New York & Pennsylvania at my heels. I now give it as my opinion that we shall be disgraced if we admit a militia force either into our camp or order of battle."[8] The Pennsylvania troops joined the Left Division in late June, receiving no more than ten days of training under Scott's rigorous regimen. Swift's New Yorkers arrived too late to benefit from the training program. The small group of Canadian Volunteers, under the command of Lt. Col. Joseph Willcocks, rounded out the American forces at Buffalo.[9]

Despite strenuous exertions across the state to prepare for what would be the most decisive year of the war, the national campaign plans were slow to emerge. President Madison had been sick, and until June 7, he had not met with his cabinet to develop goals for the year. No one could know where the British might strike. Formal negotiations did not open in Ghent until August; yet American negotiators were well aware that the British were intransigent on American demands concerning neutral trading rights and impressment.[10] Secretary of the Treasury George Campbell reported that insufficient funds were available for a major campaign, such as one aimed at Montreal. After much haggling, Madison decided on four limited goals, the successful accomplishment of which might improve the American position in peace negotiations. Clearly, it would be best to secure these goals before British reinforcements arrived in strength.

First, a joint navy-army force would retake Mackinac Island at the confluence of Lakes Michigan and Huron, which had fallen to the British on July 17, 1812. Second, General Brown would cross Lake Erie and move to seize Burlington Heights. Commodore Chauncey would have to cooperate to supply the Left Division. This meant controlling Lake Ontario prior to Brown's move. Third, fifteen large gunboats from Sackett's Harbor would operate from a base on the St. Lawrence River to choke off the British supply line. Fourth, Izard, who commanded the largest army force, would make a demonstration of force by moving toward Montreal to divert British attention away from Burlington Heights.[11]

Generally, Armstrong had positioned troops appropriately in anticipation of Madison's choice of specific objectives. By the summer of 1814, 28 percent of the regular army was positioned in Military Districts 3 and 9 (all of New York and Vermont and eastern New Jersey) or moving to reinforce critical areas in New York and Vermont. The next highest concentration of regular troops, 8 percent, was assigned to Military District 8 and largely positioned in Michigan Territory. The War Department requisitioned the states for 93,500 detached militia.[12]

In transmitting Madison's guidance to Brown, Armstrong sent his analysis. He could not see the possibility of Brown establishing himself at Burlington Heights until Chauncey controlled Lake Ontario. "The conclusion from all this is, that though the expedition [to Burlington Heights] be approved, its execution must be suspended till Chauncey shall have gained the command of the lake." He added, "To give however immediate occupation to your troops & to prevent their blood from stagnating—Why not take Fort Erie & it's garrison, stated at 3 or 400 men?" Brown was eager to comply.[13]

As time for the invasion approached, Brown organized his troops into three brigades. Scott commanded the First Brigade and Ripley the Second Brigade, both formations of regulars. Brown gave Porter the Third Brigade, composed of the Iroquois Battalion, the Pennsylvania Volunteers, and a company of New York mounted riflemen. Colonel Swift's volunteers were still drawing equipment from state arsenals and would miss the opening battle. Brown maintained direct command of a battalion of artillery and a company of dragoons.

Brown adjusted his plans after learning that Commodore Arthur Sinclair, at Erie, would be unable to transport the Left Division across the lake because the expedition to Mackinac Island required too many vessels of the Lake Erie squadron. In accordance with Armstrong's instructions, Brown decided to seize Fort Erie. Once in Upper Canada, Brown could move on Burlington Heights, assuming Chauncey would support the advance. He contacted Chauncey to arrange for naval assistance. On June 25, Chauncey responded that he expected to sail in the first week of July. However, he made it clear that fighting Yeo to a conclusion was his first goal. Only after a naval victory yielding control of the lake would Chauncey assist the Left Division.[14] This plan was consistent with Armstrong's guidance. Judging that his quartermasters could supply the Left Division if it remained close to the Niagara River, Brown decided to attack Fort Erie and move northward along the river, seeking opportunities as he moved.

Brown's immediate opponent was Major General Phineas Riall, commander of the British Right Division and responsible for the defense of the Niagara peninsula. Having overrun New York militia the previous December, Riall held American forces in low regard bordering on contempt; therefore, he was prone to take risks. He and his superior, Lieutenant General Gordon Drummond, overestimated Brown's strength at 7,000. Brown commanded no more than 4,000 regulars and volunteers and about five hundred Iroquois. Riall had nearly 3,000 regulars and eight hundred Indian warriors on the Niagara peninsula. The four-month-long Niagara 1814 campaign was about to commence.

In the very early hours of July 3, 1814, Scott's First Brigade and Ripley's Second Brigade embarked. Ripley was to move a portion of his brigade in four vessels from Buffalo to land west of Fort Erie while Scott crossed from Black Rock and landed north of the British fort. The two brigades would converge on Fort Erie, thus cutting off all escape. Ripley balked and offered his resignation because he sensed that his brigade would land amidst British troops on the beach. Brown was unmoved. This confrontation marked the start of the friction between Brown and Ripley.

When the Americans appeared at Fort Erie, the British commander judged that the fort could survive neither a siege nor an assault. He surrendered the fort and 137 soldiers. After the fall of Fort Erie, about 150 Iroquois departed Porter's Brigade, leaving Erastus Granger with about 350 warriors.[15]

On Independence Day, Scott's Brigade led the Left Division north along the river. Riall was unaware that Fort Erie had fallen. He sent Lieutenant Colonel Thomas Pearson, an exceptionally competent officer, to delay the American advance. Pearson's troops destroyed bridges and fired upon Scott's men as they pushed on toward the Chippawa River, a major obstacle. The British had blockhouses, barracks, and artillery batteries on the north side of the Chippawa. Scott arrived at the river and realized that he lacked the artillery and the numbers to force a crossing. He withdrew his brigade south of Street's Creek to bivouac. Ripley's Brigade closed later in the evening.[16]

The battlefield at Chippawa was bounded on the north by the Chippawa River, on the east by the Niagara, and on the south by Street's Creek. A flat meadow extended between a primeval forest on the west and the Niagara River. A tongue of the forest on the north side of the meadow extended to within a quarter mile of the Niagara River. This portion of woods blocked the line of sight between the bridge over the Chippawa River and the bridge across Street's Creek two miles to the south.

During the night of July 4–5, Porter's Brigade crossed the Niagara River. A number of Pennsylvanians refused to cross. The brigade arrived at the American camp at noon. Porter had with him 350 Iroquois and about five hundred Pennsylvania volunteers. Brown described for Porter the troublesome situation of Indian warriors firing from the forest into the camp. Brown sent Porter to "scour the adjoining woods, & drive the enemy across the Chippewa, handling them in such a manner as would prevent a renewal of this kind of warfare." The warriors in the forest were the vestiges of Tecumseh's confederacy who sought refuge in Upper Canada following the Battle of the Thames fought on October 5, 1813. Tecumseh's brother, Tenskwatawa, the Prophet, was their leader.[17]

Porter began his attack at 3 P.M. Red Jacket led the Iroquois in single file into the forest, followed by three hundred Pennsylvanians. Between the two battalions marched Porter, his aide, Lt. Donald Fraser, Seneca chief Captain Pollard, Maj. Roger Jones, the assistant adjutant general, and brevet Maj. Eleazar Wood of the engineer corps. Wood won his brevet promotion for distinguished service at Fort Meigs in northwestern Ohio the prior year. All these officers, except the Virginian Jones, were New Yorkers.[18]

Once Porter's men had entered the woods, each Indian warrior and volunteer faced to the right and moved forward. The brigade engaged Britain's Indian allies along Street's Creek. Porter's men overran their opponents amidst "savage yells" and pursued them about a mile through the thick forest, which was cluttered with deadfall. The Iroquois and Pennsylvanians assaulted "through scenes of frightful havoc & slaughter—few only of the fugitives offering to surrender as prisoners, while others, believing that no quarter would be given, suffered themselves to be cut down by the tomahawk, or, turning upon their pursuers, fought hand to hand to the last."[19]

As they moved forward, the Iroquois outdistanced the volunteers and arrived at the northern edge of the forest. There, British light infantry, Canadian militia, and John Norton's Grand River Indians confronted the New York Iroquois. British fire drove back the Iroquois. Still in the forest, Porter rallied his forces and advanced once again. At the margins of the forest a tremendous fight ensued. While the Canadian militia suffered greatly, it was the exhausted Americans and Iroquois who fell back. Seeing his lines disintegrating, Porter ordered a general withdrawal. Retracing their steps, the broken brigade emerged from the southern edge of the forest, where Porter and his officers rallied and reformed them. Although they had quit the forest, Porter's Brigade had inflicted about one hundred casualties while suffering only thirty-five losses themselves.

Believing that he confronted only a portion of the Left Division, General Riall decided to attack the Americans in their camp. He believed the American formations to be brittle and easily shattered with a strong blow. While the fighting was going on in the forest, three battalions of British regulars, accompanied by artillery and some dragoons, crossed the Chippawa bridge. They marched around the tongue of the forest and, once on the meadow began deploying in line. When Brown realized that Riall was on the march, he ordered Scott to give battle. Scott, incredulous that the British would give up their strong defensive position, nonetheless quickly put his men on the move.

The two sides were quite evenly matched. Riall's forces consisted of about 1,400 infantrymen and six guns. Scott's Brigade was comprised of 1,350 infantry and seven guns. Henry Leavenworth, leader of one of Scott's battalions, led his men across the bridge as shot and grape flew overhead. Scott's other two battalions followed. Scott saw the Iroquois and Pennsylvanians withdrawing through the forest, so he ordered Thomas Jesup to take his battalion, the Twenty-Fifth Infantry, into the forest to secure Scott's left flank. With both sides now in lines facing one another, a terrific firefight commenced. Riall saw the gray uniforms of Scott's men and surmised that they were militia. However, as the Americans deployed steadily through artillery fire, he reportedly remarked, "These are regulars!"[20]

The two sides traded volleys, with neither willing to give an inch. Once Jesup had stabilized the situation in the forest, he brought the Twenty-Fifth onto the British right flank. Jesup's men fired three volleys and advanced. The British line cracked despite the best efforts of Riall's officers to keep their soldiers in line. Riall directed an orderly withdrawal covered by his dragoons. The British fell back across the bridge, removing the decking as they went. The battle was over. The British suffered about five hundred killed, wounded, or captured; the Americans about 325.[21]

Historian Henry Adams wrote, "The Battle of Chippawa was the only occasion during the war when equal bodies of regular troops met face to face, in extended lines on an open plain in broad daylight, without advantage of position; and never again after that combat was an army of American regulars beaten by British troops. Small as the affair was, and unimportant in military results, it gave to the United States army a character and pride it had never before possessed."[22]

Porter claimed that one result of the forest fight was that the warriors of Tecumseh's confederacy withdrew from the war, "thus giving a practical & decisive proof that they held the prowess of their red brethren, the American Indians, in much higher estimation than some of the allies of the latter were disposed to accord them." Porter confirmed that the battle gave Americans "confidence in the courage and officering of their army, & the latter confidence in themselves." Porter generally criticized the officers commissioned in 1812: "A great blunder had been committed at the commencement of the war, in the appointment of incompetent & unworthy characters, taken perhaps from the gambling table or the race courses, as officers of the army & owing their places to the importunities of influential friends."[23] However, by 1814 most of the incompetents had resigned, and the remainder had learned their trade.

The morning after the battle, about twenty Iroquois visited Porter carrying the scalps taken in the forest fight. These warriors were badly disappointed when the general refused to pay for the scalps. The Iroquois returned to the forest, recovered the bodies of fifteen of their own, and buried their comrades "with the honors of war." The search parties discovered three of the enemy mortally wounded yet still alive. The Iroquois cut the throats of two of the western Indians but recognized the third as having been "a late member of one of their own villages." They left the dying warrior with a full canteen. Porter reproached the natives for killing the two. In response, a contrite native responded "That it did seem hard to take the lives of these men, but that we ought to recollect that these were very hard times."[24]

While the Left Division was advancing to Queenston, Red Jacket suggested to Porter that the Iroquois send two chiefs to the western Indians near Burlington Heights to offer a mutual withdrawal from the campaign. The British allies were receptive to the proposal, and most of the Indian warriors on both sides quit the fight. A small number, however, remained with their respective armies. Red Jacket had achieved his goal of gaining the good will of Brown and others while not expending lives in further battle. Porter remembered the Indian warriors as worth double their number in white troops when fighting in their own manner.[25]

Even after the New York Iroquois departed Brown's army, they supported the war effort closer to home. A militia officer, Asa Warren, recalled an incident on the streets of Buffalo in late July. He witnessed a crowd of Seneca that included Farmer's Brother, Captain Pollard, and Young King. They were standing around a Canadian Indian, an alleged spy, who had been boasting of taking American scalps and those of Indians fighting alongside them. Farmer's Brother put a gun to the man's chest and shot him. The Indians took the body away, and the sheriff chose not to investigate the murder.[26]

Arriving at Queenston Heights on July 10, Brown looked for the sails of the American squadron. None were visible; Chauncey was not on the lake. Impatient to achieve some worthy goals before the British could react in strength, Brown wrote to Chauncey on July 13 conveying a sense of urgency and optimism. He argued that Kingston was lightly garrisoned and that Yeo would not fight Chauncey. He promised that acting together the Left Division and Chauncey's squadron could "break the power of the Enemy in Upper Canada." His annoyance with Chauncey was thinly veiled: "At all events have the politeness to let me know, what aid I am to expect from the Fleet of Lake Ontario." Chauncey was too ill to command the squadron, but he chose not to transfer temporary command to Captain Jacob Jones, his second-in-command. Furthermore, Chauncey maintained that destruction of Yeo's squadron was a prerequisite for a successful campaign.[27]

Brown pursued the British to Fort George. Major Eleazar Wood, an engineer, examined the fort and judged that the walls were too difficult to breach with the few heavy guns available. While Brown considered laying siege to Fort George, a general officer of the New York militia was killed in action. Brig. Gen. John Swift of Palmyra, who had defended the village of Pultneyville from a British raid just two months earlier, had volunteered to serve with Porter's

Brigade. One of the members of the brigade described the general "as a sort of fearless, care-for-nothing guerilla." On July 12, General Swift led a force of about 120 men to capture a small British picket guard. One of the British soldiers, after his squad had surrendered, shot the general in the abdomen. Col. Philetus Swift accompanied his brother's body back to Palmyra and turned command of the regiment over to Lt. Col. Hugh Dobbin.[28]

Swift's obituary in the *Ontario Messenger* praised the general's patriotism, which overcame partisan politics. "As it is, he has exhibited an example which will have its effects: that of a warm and decided opponent of the present administration coming forward to support and engage in a war which he was convinced required and demanded the united exertions of all true Americans, to preserve their independence and to maintain their rights."[29]

On July 20, Brown formed the Left Division outside of Fort George, hoping that Riall would leave the fort and give battle. The British commander would not accept the invitation. Two days later, Brown withdrew to Queenston to assess his options. There he received a message from Gaines that Chauncey was too ill to sail, and that Yeo was blockading Sackett's Harbor. Gaines could not bring siege guns to break into Fort George. The American general planned a bold move. He withdrew the division to its camp south of the Chippawa River, where it would resupply and move directly on Burlington Heights. Brown hoped that Riall would react to reopen his supply line and in doing so bring about a general battle. It did, although not as intended.

On July 25, Col. Philetus Swift reported British troops atop Queenston Heights and British warships anchored near Fort Niagara. He also reported smaller craft moving south on the river. Soon thereafter, Brown received another report of British troops landing near Lewiston and threatening provisions at Fort Schlosser. Loss of the supplies would frustrate Brown's plan to march on Burlington Heights. Unable to quickly deploy a force across the river, Brown decided to threaten the British on his side of the Niagara. He directed Scott to take his brigade, along with dragoons and Brevet Maj. Nathan Towson's battery, and to move north toward Queenston Heights. Brown directed Scott to "report if the enemy appeared, and to call for assistance if that was necessary." Brown's orders to Scott, limited in scope, led to the bloodiest battle of the war up to that time.[30]

Scott's Brigade, more than 1100 strong, marched north on the portage road. Mrs. Willson, an American-born tavern keeper, told Scott that there were about 1,100 British on the other side of the woods at Lundy's Lane. Lundy's Lane ran east-west atop a low ridge. Without making a personal reconnaissance, Scott issued orders to advance through the woods toward Lundy's Lane. He sent word back to Brown, fully understanding that it would take Brown at least an hour to send reinforcements. When Scott passed through the woods, he saw the British Right Division drawn up on the high ground—far more than the 1100 troops that Mrs. Willson reported. Between Scott and the British position was a large expanse of field west of the portage road. This open area was bordered by woods on the west, south, and east. Despite being vastly outnumbered by a force along the high ground and within easy artillery range, Scott rashly chose to advance into the field. Years later, Scott rationalized his blunder writing that upon seeing the multitudes of British soldiers he could not "suppress his indignation at the blundering, stupid report made by the militia colonel to his confiding friend Major General Brown."[31]

The combat at Lundy's Lane falls into three phases. The first concerns Scott's Brigade's fight before the arrival of the rest of the Left Division at dark. The second encompasses the capture of the British artillery and the immediate attempts to recapture the guns. The third embraces Drummond's three determined counterattacks. Scott sent Jesup's battalion into the woods to the east to be "governed by circumstances." Scott then deployed the remaining three battalions in line at a distance of about 400 yards from the British line. Fifteen-year-old New Yorker Jarvis Frary Hanks was a drummer in Scott's Brigade. He recalled, "I remember, a trumpeter was riding back, furiously, wounded, with the blood streaming, profusely down his temples & cheeks. As I was also a musician, I felt much alarmed for my own safety, not knowing but I should be in as bad or a worse situation in a few minutes. There was no stopping, nor escape, into battle we must go."[32]

Brevet Major Nathan Towson positioned his three guns on the portage road.[33] In the artillery exchange, the five British guns held a notable advantage. Firing from a higher altitude, British shot bounded across the open field in low arcs making it nearly impossible not to strike the American line. Towson's artillerists had to elevate their guns and as a result, American rounds plunged into the soil, thus less effective in striking their intended targets.

Over the next hour, British artillery fire decimated Scott's Brigade while American musketry fire, delivered at long range, was largely ineffective. Col. Hugh Brady received a severe wound yet refused to leave his men. Soldiers carried the wounded to the woods behind the lines and sometimes sought shelter there from the uneven fight. Drummer Hanks was standing behind his regiment's color party. He recalled that, "During this engagement, nine different persons were shot down, under this flag, successively. At last, this Sergeant Festus Thompson took it and threw its folds to the breeze. He was wounded in the hip, and the staff was severed into splinters in his hand. But he again grasped it by the stump, and waved it triumphantly over his own, and his fellow soldiers' heads, until the close of the battle."[34]

Years later, Scott explained his decision for not withdrawing while waiting for Brown to arrive. "Being but half seasoned to war, some danger of confusion in its ranks, with a certainty of throwing the whole reserve [coming up] into a panic, were to be apprehended; for an extravagant opinion generally prevailed throughout the army in respect to the prowess—nay, invincibility of Scott's brigade." Hubris killed many brave men.[35]

While Scott blindly refused to take the three battalions under his direct control out of their exposed position, Jesup and his men achieved some notable success. In the failing light, the Twenty-Fifth Infantry surprised and drove off the battalion of Volunteer Incorporated Militia, a well-trained, well-led unit. Jesup sent Capt. Daniel Ketchum and his company to watch the intersection of Lundy's Lane and the portage road. Jesup with his five remaining companies remained close by in support. Within fifteen minutes, Riall and his staff fell into Ketchum's hands. General Gordon Drummond's aide, Captain Loring, was captured soon after as were dozens more. For his valor at Lundy's Lane, Ketchum received a brevet promotion to major.[36]

The second phase of the battle began as the rest of the Left Division entered the fight. Brown had been so convinced no sizable body of British troops was nearby that he failed to notify either Ripley or Porter to prepare to march to support Scott should that prove necessary. Hundreds of soldiers missed the fight as they were away from camp washing clothing or guarding supplies. When Brown arrived, he saw the gravely reduced numbers of Scott's Brigade. Brown also saw opportunity. He finally had the British Right Division out of their defenses and in his grasp. He ordered Ripley to position his brigade in front of Scott. Brown ordered Scott to place his remaining soldiers in reserve. Henry Leavenworth, the only unwounded battalion commander in Scott's Brigade, formed the troops in the fast fading light.[37]

Brown sent his senior engineer, Lt. Col. William McRee, to reconnoiter the British lines. McRee reported that capturing the British guns would break the integrity of the British line. Brown ordered Ripley to seize the guns. Ripley's attack was uncoordinated as the battalions were out of sight of one another in the dark and they stepped off at different times. British fire drove off the First Infantry and the Twenty-Third Infantry. The commander of the Twenty-Third, Maj. Daniel McFarland, died at the head of his troops. Col. James Miller led his battalion, the Twenty-First Infantry, stealthily forward to a position directly below the British guns. Miller ordered his men to stand, fire, and immediately attack with the bayonet. The Americans overran the battery. However, as Miller reformed his men, the British attempted to recapture the cannon.[38]

Drummond refused to accept the loss of his guns. He ordered Lieuten-ant Colonel Joseph Morrison, commander of the 89th Regiment of Foot, to recapture the guns. Morrison's men tramped forward up the slope. In the darkness, the two battalions opened fire at point blank range, the men aiming at the muzzle blasts of their opponents. In some places, the combat was hand-to-hand. The 89th withdrew. Drummond added reinforcements, and Morrison and his men surged forward again. This time, American fire wounded Morrison who was carried off the field. The British line receded down the slope a second time. Drummond led a third assault. Casualties were grievous on both sides, but the Americans refused to yield the guns. Drummond received a bullet through his neck. He refused medical attention. He understood that only an attack with all his forces would reestablish the British line atop the ridge.[39]

During the pause between the second and third phases of the battle, both sides received reinforcements. Ripley consolidated his brigade on the highest part of the ridge. Brown found Jesup's men and positioned them on the ridge to the right of Ripley. Porter brought what he had to the battlefield, fewer than 600 men. He positioned Hugh Dobbin's New York Volunteers and the Pennsylvania and Canadian Volunteers to the left of Ripley. Porter bent back his line, thus better protecting the left flank. Colonel Brady was too weak to lead Scott's men; that duty now fell to Leavenworth. Drummond commanded about 3,000 soldiers, and Brown had fewer than 1,600. Brown and his aide, nineteen-year-old Capt. Ambrose Spencer, Jr., rode between the lines. Brown's aide was the son of Judge Spencer, associate justice of the New York Supreme Court. Perceiving movement to their front, Spencer called out "What regiment is that?" The response, "The Royal Scots" was enough to prompt the two to return to their lines. The final phase of the battle began about 10:30 P.M.

Drummond sent virtually all of his infantry forward, uphill, in the dark stopping their men about forty yards away from the steadfast American line on higher ground. The opponents exchanged volleys. Sergeant Commins of the 8th Foot could think of only one reason why the Americans refused to yield. "The Yankees was loth to quit their position and being well fortified with whiskey made them stand longer than ever they did."[40] After twenty or thirty minutes, the British withdrew to regroup. The Americans knew that they would return.

After a lull of about thirty minutes, Drummond gave the order to advance yet again. Ignoring his wound, he was determined not to lose his guns or this battle. The firefight re-opened. Brown ordered Scott back into the action. Scott had Leavenworth form the brigade, down to about 250 men still on their feet, into an attack column. Scott led the column downhill toward the British. For unknown reasons, Scott's column did not make contact, but instead veered to its left heading between the opposing lines. Believing that the troops moving across their front were the enemy, both sides opened fire on Scott's unfortunate soldiers. Having done little if any damage to the British, Scott brought his men to a position to the left of Porter's small brigade. British fire slackened after about twenty minutes as Drummond withdrew his division.[41]

During a lull of about forty-five minutes, both sides re-formed and replenished ammunition. Jesup had to array his troops in a single rank in order to cover his portion of the line. Drummond ended the battle with a final assault. A wave of British infantry surged forward. This last action was brutal; several regiments reported being in close combat. Scott led the remnants of his brigade on another glorious but futile assault. The head of the column momentarily made contact before it was driven off with heavy casualties. Leavenworth withdrew the men while Scott galloped over to the far right of the line to see Jesup. While they conversed, British musketry wounded both officers. Scott was out of the battle and out of the war. Brown fell after being struck by two projectiles. Fortunately for the battered Americans, Drummond saw that British valor was unavailing. He ordered a withdrawal.[42]

The Americans did not fear another attack. Weak from loss of blood, Brown attempted to turn over command to Scott. When he learned that Scott had been evacuated, Brown retained command. He did not trust Ripley with command of the division. The regiments marched back to camp to get water and ammunition. Brown knew he was out of the fight. He directed Ripley to march the division back to the battlefield by dawn. For reasons known only to himself, Ripley failed to pass on Brown's order to the subordinate commanders. When the sun rose, Brown became aware that the men were still in camp. He sent staff officers to order each unit to return to the battlefield. When they came into view of the ridge, Ripley, Porter and Leavenworth saw that Drummond's troops had re-occupied the high ground and in large numbers. Ripley judged that the Americans would be unable to repeat their success of the prior evening. Porter agreed.

Brown was evacuated to the hospital in Williamsville and Ripley took command. Instead of positioning the division behind the security of the Chippawa River, Ripley ordered the troops to march back to the ferry site opposite Black Rock. Not understanding the import of his actions, Ripley was about to throw away the last opportunity to win the war. The government could not resource another attempt to seize Kingston or Montreal. When key officers perceived that Ripley intended to return to New York, they protested. Had they not just won a major battle? Ripley sought out Brown in the hospital to gain his permission to cross the Niagara. Brown was indignant. He ordered Ripley to fortify and defend Fort Erie. Although the initiative had passed to the British, much hard fighting was ahead.

The Battle of Lundy's Lane was the largest of the war up to that time. Casualties were roughly equal. The respective commanders reported:

	Killed	Wounded	Missing/Prisoner	Total
British	84	559	235	878
American	173	571	117	860

Porter brought about 546 men of his brigade onto the battlefield. Of these, Hugh Dobbin commanded about 250 New York Volunteers. The rest of the regiment was with Col. Philetus Swift near Lewiston. Captain Boughton's Volunteer Dragoons were fighting under Captain Harris with the regular light dragoons. Brown praised the contribution of Porter and his troops in his report to Armstrong. "It was with great pleasure I saw the good order and intrepidity of General Porter's volunteers from the moment of their arrival, but during the last charge of the enemy, those qualities were conspicuous." He added, "Under the command of General Porter, the militia volunteers of Pennsylvania and New York stood undismayed amidst the hottest fire, and repulsed the veterans opposed to them." This was one of a handful of occasions in which volunteers or militia stood toe-to-toe with British regulars and achieved some level of success.[43]

During the fighting, a spent musket ball struck Lieutenant Colonel Dobbin in the chest. Thinking himself badly wounded, he rode a short way back to camp where he checked himself for blood. Finding neither blood nor a wound, he returned to his battalion. "This caused some dry jokes among his fellow officers."[44]

After the battle, Porter wrote to Governor Tompkins that his brigade, "in proportion to the numbers engaged . . . lost more than any other corps, and I believe, small as we were, we actually lost more officers killed then either of the other brigades."[45] The brigade lost 65 casualties, or 12 percent of its battlefield strength. The Left Division's 860 casualties were 31 percent of the American battlefield strength.[46] By far, Scott's Brigade took the highest percentage of casualties, about 38 percent. Among those officers dying of wounds was Brown's young aide, Capt. Ambrose Spencer Jr. Brown reported to Armstrong, "I shall ever think of this young man with pride and regret; regret, that his career has been so short; pride, that it has been so noble and distinguished." While many of the American battalion commanders were wounded, only one was killed in action. Felled by British fire while leading the Twenty-Third Infantry, a unit raised largely of New Yorkers, was Maj. Daniel McFarland.[47]

In its report of the battle, the *Buffalo Gazette* declared, "Considering the numbers engaged, the history of modern wars will scarcely produce a parallel."

As for the American casualties, "their names will justly be added to that brilliant catalogue of worthies, the heroes of the revolution; and the battle of Bridgewater, will be remembered, by posterity, with the same sensations as those of Bunker Hill and Saratoga."[48] Americans initially called the clash the Battle of Bridgewater or Battle of Niagara; however, it is now universally known as the Battle of Lundy's Lane.

Secretary of the Navy William Jones learned of the impasse between Brown and Chauncey and altered Chauncey's instructions. Chauncey was to destroy the British squadron, if that end was possible; if not, Chauncey should blockade Yeo in port and render assistance to Brown within his means. Acknowledging the extreme "public anxiety" over Chauncey's failure to sail, Jones sent orders to Stephen Decatur in New York City to travel immediately to Sackett's Harbor and to take command if Chauncey was too ill to sail. Chauncey recovered quickly and sailed on August 1.

Furious at the tenor of Brown's letters and for provoking the controversy raging in the nation's capital, Chauncey addressed a scathing response directly to Brown on August 10. He argued that Brown understood all along that Chauncey could assist the army only after he had decisively dealt with Yeo. "That you might find the fleet somewhat of a convenience in the transportation of Provisions and Stores for the use of the Army and an agreeable appendage to attend its marches and counter marches I am ready to believe but Sir the Secretary of the Navy has honored us with a higher destiny—were are intended to Seek and fight the Enemy's fleet. . . ." Chauncey was also concerned that there were too few troops to guard his base should he depart it. In a letter to Secretary Jones, he noted that only 700 regulars were fit for duty. He further complained that "it is true a few militia had been called in, but little could be expected of them should an attack be made." However, Chauncey received a full measure of disapproval from both Jones and the president. Jones wrote, "I cannot withhold from you the knowledge of the extreme anxiety and astonishment which the protracted and fatal delay of the Squadron in port, has excited in the mind of the President." The spirit of cooperation between the services, so well demonstrated in the 1813 campaigns, was largely diminished in 1814.[49]

While the army and navy commanders bickered publicly, federal–state cooperation was finally reaching its stride. As always, Tompkins was proactive, ordering the formation of a volunteer brigade in March. Swift's regiment performed well at Lundy's Lane and more volunteers and common militia would join the Left Division in the coming weeks. While Madison and his cabinet discussed the conflict between the army and navy commanders, the major American campaign of 1814 moved to its brutal conclusion at Fort Erie.

CHAPTER 16

THE SIEGE OF FORT ERIE

The day following the battle at Lundy's Lane, Brig. Gen. Eleazar Ripley withdrew the Left Division southward toward the ferry site opposite Black Rock. Lt. David B. Douglass recalled that the British were nowhere to be seen. "There was no pursuit—no hanging upon our flanks or rear—no enemy visible, in any quarter. The march was as quiet as if it had passed through a portion of our own territory." British Lieutenant General Gordon Drummond had received a musket ball into his neck, and perhaps his wound had induced a measure of caution. Nevertheless, he eventually recovered his focus. In a letter to Sir George Prevost, he stated, "The great object at present is the defeat and expulsion of the Enemy's force which has taken Post at Fort Erie and to this object my sole attention must be given."[1]

Drummond slowly pursued the retreating Americans, allowing them to throw up earthen breastworks fronted by a ditch around their camp. Ripley anchored the extensive camp with Fort Erie on the north and a battery atop Snake Hill about 750 yards away at the southern end. The British established their siege camp about two miles north of Fort Erie. If the British could force their opponents to evacuate their camp, the Americans would face the daunting task of moving hundreds of soldiers by boat across the Niagara River. Drummond could force such a desperate move by a sustained bombardment or by a direct assault that might collapse the American defenses. It would take time to bring up heavy guns. Drummond also understood that an assault, even if it was successful, would be costly.[2]

Thus, the British general attempted to starve the Left Division by cutting its supply line to Buffalo. On August 2, Drummond ordered Colonel John Tucker to cross the Niagara with 380 men north of Squaw Island to destroy supplies and if possible, to turn the guns of American batteries against Fort Erie. Squaw Island lay in the Niagara River at the mouth of Conjocta Creek. Fortunately for the Americans, Maj. Ludowick Morgan, the charismatic leader of the First Rifle Regiment, caught sight of the British that evening as they were moving toward their embarkation point. Morgan commanded about 240 riflemen guarding Black Rock and the approaches to Buffalo from the north. His men fortified the southern bank of Conjocta Creek. The riflemen removed the planking from the south half of the bridge such that anyone attempting to cross might not see the missing boards until they were on the bridge itself.[3]

Before dawn on August 3, the British infantry were on the bridge when they discovered the missing timbers. Tucker's men withdrew as the riflemen opened accurate fire. For the next two hours, the British tried to repair the bridge well enough to cross. Rifle fire drove back each assault party. The British commander also attempted to ford the creek to outflank the defenders. Nothing worked. After suffering thirty-four casualties, Tucker called off the attack and withdrew to the Canadian shore. Drummond was livid at Tucker's failure.[4]

From his hospital bed in Buffalo, Maj. Gen. Jacob Brown organized support for the garrison across the river. As early as August 1, Brown called out 1,000 militiamen on his own authority and requested that Governor Tompkins call out three or four thousand. Brown was pessimistic: "I find the inhabitants of this frontier more disposed to skulk from the danger that threatens them, than to arise in defense of their country and her rights." No doubt the destruction of the Niagara frontier settlements the previous December discouraged the civilian populace throughout the western part of the state. To underscore the imperative need for manpower, Brown sent a request for militia directly to Secretary of War John Armstrong. Maj. Gen. Amos Hall called out 1,000 militiamen, but by August 18, only three hundred had appeared. On August 13, Tompkins sent one of his aides, Lt. Col. John B. Yates, to Buffalo to confer with Brown and Brig. Gen. Peter Porter. Tompkins gave Yates full authority to act in the governor's name to mobilize as many of the common militia as these generals deemed appropriate. The governor apologized for the lack of equipment. Tompkins cited "the wanton destruction and embezzlement of public property on the Niagara frontiers" over the preceding campaigns.[5]

The medical staff on both sides of the river reconfigured operations to serve the men at Fort Erie. Regimental surgeons retained some sick and wounded within the encampment. They sent those requiring hospitalization across the river at night on the returning supply vessels to a receiving hospital in Buffalo. Once there, patients who could be further evacuated went to the main hospital in Williamsville. During the siege, the total hospital population ranged between six and eight hundred men, the wounded somewhat outnumbering the sick.[6]

Brown feared that Ripley would fail to defend the toehold on the Canadian shore. Ripley had proven overcautious throughout the campaign. Brown sent for Brig. Gen. Edmund Pendleton Gaines at Sackett's Harbor. Gaines arrived

August 4. Brown wrote to Armstrong of his total confidence in Gaines and implying his lack of trust of Ripley. "Under his [Gaines's] command, this army will not permit the fair fame it has acquired to be sullied."[7]

The Americans suffered a setback on August 12 when a British raiding party in six small vessels surprised three schooners—*Porcupine, Somers,* and *Ohio*—anchored in the lake off Fort Erie. Royal Navy Commander Alexander Dobbs and his men cut a portage eight miles through the woods to bring the six craft from the Niagara River around Fort Erie and into Lake Erie. In the darkness, the raiders seized the *Somers* and *Ohio* in a bloody fight and towed them to Chippawa.[8]

General Gaines put pressure on the British as they constructed their siege batteries by sending skirmishers to fire upon the British picket guards protecting the work parties. On one of these engagements, the British killed Maj. Ludowick Morgan. At Morgan's side at the time of his death was Maj. Johnathan Kearsley of the Fourth Rifle Regiment, who had nothing good to say about these frequent skirmishes in no man's land:

> The truth is, that although no great or permanent good was to be attained, yet this enabled Genl. Gaines to issue daily an order on morning parade, which order no doubt reached the newspapers of the day, if not the War Department, setting forth the gallantry of his troops and showing that although closely besieged in Fort Erie, the Genl. was not only defending the place but constantly engaged offensively against the enemy. Thus many valuable lives were lost and the services of more lost to their country, when most needed by wounds.[9]

When Morgan was hit, Kearsley led five men to recover the body. The party suffered one killed and three wounded. Kearsley managed to bring in the two bodies and the wounded riflemen.

During the bombardment of August 13–14, Gaines reported nine soldiers killed and nineteen severely wounded. The deadly British bombardment sapped the spirits of the men. Work parties threw up earthen berms called traverses in the camp at right angles to the direction of British artillery fire to stop cannon balls from careening through the camp. Lt. Douglass recalled that cannonballs dropped between the traverses and could "knock over a whole range of tents at a single stroke."[10] Gaines anticipated a British attack sometime in the evening of August 14–15. He ordered that everyone who was not on guard would sleep by their assigned fighting position in their clothes and with their weapons at hand. Drummond had indeed ordered a surprise nighttime assault. He instructed the troops to remove the flints from their muskets so as not to warn the Americans should a weapon accidentally discharge. In the dark, the Americans would be identified by their return fire and their white trousers.

This would allow the attackers "to use the bayonet with effect which that valuable weapon has been ever found to possess in the hands of British soldiers."[11]

Drummond's plan was simple, but even simple plans could miscarry in the darkness. Lieutenant Colonel Viktor Fischer would lead the main attack, striking the American perimeter between Snake Hill and the lake. Reconnaissance determined, incorrectly, that the path was not blocked by breastworks or *abatis*. Once Drummond heard the noise from Fischer's assault, two supporting attacks would spring into action. Lieutenant Colonel William Drummond (no relation to the commanding general) would lead an assault of Fort Erie while Colonel Hercules Scott's troops would attempt to penetrate the line between the fort and the lake. These two attacks would pin down the defenders at the northern end of the camp while Fischer's forces, having entered the camp, would cause the collapse of the American defense.

As Fischer's columns approached the camp, American pickets opened fire. These shots brought the entire garrison to life and men sprang to their fighting positions. The pickets withdrew through a path in the *abatis* that closed the gap between Snake Hill and the lake. Brevet Lt. Col. Eleazar Wood ordered his small command of the Twenty-First Infantry to open fire over the tangle of sharpened tree limbs. Brevet Lt. Col. Nathan Towson's guns atop Snake Hill fired into the darkness below. The continuous flashes from the guns on Snake Hill lit up the darkness, and the position was known henceforth as Towson's Lighthouse. At the northern end of the camp, Lt. David Douglass recalled, "To the ear, the reports of musketry and artillery were blended together, in one continuous roar, somewhat like the close double drag of a drum, on a grand scale."[12]

The British onslaught failed and with near-catastrophic results. Towson's artillery fire, combined with that of Wood's musketry, stopped Fischer's attack cold. The British could not penetrate the *abatis*, and attempts to wade in the lake waters to outflank the defenses proved unsuccessful as well. Colonel Scott's assault could not reach the American lines through a hail of musketry and cannon fire. Scott died in the attempt. Lieutenant Colonel Drummond's attack on Fort Erie managed to enter the northeast demibastion. Three American officers, Capt. Alexander Williams and Lieutenants Patrick McDonough and John Watmough, were in the demibastion directing the fire of their gunners. The British climbed over the parapet. Williams and McDonough died in the ensuing melee. Williams was the son of Col. Jonathan Williams, former chief of the corps of engineers. Watmough was knocked down by a soldier using his musket like a club. He was then shot in the chest but managed to survive.

Lieutenant Colonel Drummond's men had seized the demibastion but could not continue their attack in the face of American fire coming from a stone barracks only yards away. Drummond died while assaulting the barracks. The two opponents were at a standoff. Then, large quantities of gunpowder in the demibastion exploded. Lieutenant Douglass recalled that the explosion was followed by "a jet of flame, mingled with fragments of timber, earth, stone, and bodies of men, rose to the height of one or two hundred feet, in the air, and fell, in a shower of ruins, to a great distance, all around."[13] The only British remaining in the American camp were the dead, wounded, or prisoners.

Drummer Jarvis Hanks was stationed at the northern end of the American camp. He remembered, "This explosion occurred just before daylight. During the forenoon, I inspected the awful scene. I counted 196 bodies lying in the ditch and about the fort, most of them dead; some dying. Their faces and hands were burned black, many of them were horribly mutilated. Here and there were legs, arms and heads, lying, in confusion, separated, by the concussion, from the trunks to which they had been attached."[14]

Eber Howe of Porter's Brigade was a hospital attendant. He recalled receiving the British wounded: "Some of their faces and hands were so crisped that the skin peeled off like a baked pig."[15] Sixteen-year-old Howe succeeded in nursing back to health a young British soldier who displayed no wounds but was apparently a victim of the concussive effects of the blast.

General Drummond blamed Fischer's troops who wavered in following the lead elements into the American defenses for the failure. He reported the loss of fifty-seven known killed, 309 wounded, and 539 missing and presumed dead or wounded. This was a lopsided victory for the Americans. Gaines reported a total of only seventy-nine casualties. However, unlike Gaines, Drummond was able to quickly replace British losses. Veterans of the war in Europe were arriving on the Niagara frontier.[16]

Life within the American camp consisted of construction of new traverses and improvements to the defensive works. British cannon fire and skirmishing between the lines continued for four more weeks. Casualties were a steady occurrence. Unsurprisingly, the men became callous to suffering and death. Each night, boats from Buffalo brought over food, ammunition, and supplies and returned with injured and sick destined for the hospital. Surgeon's Mate William E. Horner oversaw the general hospital in Buffalo. In his memoirs, he recalled an instance of dark humor:

> I remember, one day, in making my hospital rounds, a patient just arrived presented an amputated forearm, and in doing so could scarcely restrain a broad laugh; the titter was constantly on his face. "What's the matter? This does not strike me as a subject of laughter." "It is not, Doctor, but excuse me, I lost my arm in so funny a way, that I still laugh, whenever I look at it." "What way?" "Our first sergeant wanted shaving, and got me to attend to it, as I am a Corporal. We

went out together in front of his tent, I had lathered him, took him by the nose, and was just about applying the razor, when a cannon ball came, and that was the last I saw of his head and of my hand. Excuse me, doctor, for laughing so; I never saw such a thing before."[17]

President Madison was becoming increasingly uneasy with Secretary of War John Armstrong's direction of the campaign in and around New York. In late July, he reviewed correspondence between Armstrong and his two commanders on New York's frontier, Izard and Brown, and discovered no evidence that Izard and Brown were in direct communication with one another. Armstrong was attempting to direct the campaigns himself from hundreds of miles away in the nation's capital. Madison correctly criticized Armstrong for not having an overall commander closer to the scene of activity. Madison dug further to discover that Armstrong was assuming presidential powers himself without informing the president. Madison was losing confidence in the cabinet officer charged with winning the war before Britain could bring the entirety of its substantial power to North America.[18]

From his vantage point, the president dreaded the potential annihilation of the Left Division while Izard's Right Division stood by. Armstrong suggested to Izard to consider taking the Canadian village of Prescott on the St. Lawrence River or combining with Commodore Isaac Chauncey to make a move on Kingston. Izard received Armstrong's letter on August 10 replying that the British outnumbered his division. "I will make the movement you direct, if possible; but I shall do it with the apprehension of risking the force under my command, and with the certainty that everything in this vicinity, but the lately erected works at Plattsburgh and Cumberland Head, will, in less than three days after my departure, be in the possession of the enemy." Armstrong was not unmindful that he was taking trained troops away from an important region, yet he believed Prevost understood "his trade too well" to hazard an offensive against Plattsburgh or Burlington. The secretary of war authorized Izard to request militia from the governors of New York and Vermont. Izard was understandably reluctant to leave, but he dutifully began planning for the move that would, six weeks later, bring him to the Niagara River. He arrived too late to relieve the siege, and his absence opened up the Lake Champlain Valley to the largest invasion of the war.[19]

On August 28, a shell crashed through Gaines's headquarters inside Fort Erie, severely wounding the general. Young Eber Howe investigated the building shortly after the incident. "The floor and inside were shivered to atoms." Howe was told, "the general and his staff were sitting around the dinner table when a shell came down through the roof, through the table into the ground and there exploded." Gaines turned command over to Brevet Brig. Gen. James Miller. Brown was in Batavia recovering from his wounds when he learned that Gaines was unable to command. He immediately travelled to Fort Erie to personally take charge of the fight.[20]

Brown requested that Commodore Arthur Sinclair bring the Lake Erie squadron closer to Fort Erie to protect the camp on its open flank. Brown was particularly concerned about bringing over the militia or, if necessary, evacuating the garrison. Sinclair responded that no good anchorage was nearby, but he would do what he could. Sinclair fully understood what was at stake. He wrote to Secretary Jones that he would do all in his power to save the Left Division from destruction. "I shall risque [sic] every thing, for on the safety of this Army depends the whole Niagara Frontier and the Winter security of the Fleet."[21]

During the siege, General Porter worked tirelessly to gather the men selected for the detached militia, equip them, and persuade them to cross into Canada to reinforce the garrison in Fort Erie. Porter was fast becoming one of the most competent and accomplished militia generals of the war. Brown wrote to the governor on August 21 recommending that Tompkins award Porter with a brevet promotion to major general and continue Porter in command of all the militia in western New York. Brown needed Porter, and Porter met the challenge.[22]

When the militiamen arrived in Buffalo, General Porter paraded them in the center of town in a driving rain to persuade them to cross the Niagara to break the siege. He asked for volunteers and formed these men into a column. Porter then marched this group across the front of those militiamen who were not yet willing to cross. As the number of volunteers slowly increased, Porter led the column around the block so as to repeatedly pass the reluctant militiamen. Elijah Efner, a young merchant, watched as Porter eloquently solicited the militiamen to join the besieged garrison. "Every time they passed around, the volunteers would cheer, and jeer their comrades who were left, and this continued until nearly all of them had been brought in." Efner recalled of a colleague, John Richardson, that he was "the only Volunteer Captain whose whole company crossed to Fort Erie to engage in the sortie of Sept. 17, 1814. I saw them volunteer, every man passing around the square, during a tremendous rain-storm, General Porter leading, drenched meanwhile in rain."[23] These militiamen responded far differently than those who refused to get in the boats at Lewiston in October 1812.

The militiamen who crossed the Niagara numbered approximately 1,500. Brown wrote to the governor, "This reinforcement has been of immense importance to us; it doubled our effective strength." The new arrivals established an encampment surrounded by earthen breastworks west of Snake Hill along the lakeshore. Porter organized his headquarters inside this bivouac site. The militiamen who refused to cross into Upper Canada were organized as sentries and laborers and designated "Buffalo Guards."[24]

Brown planned to break the British siege and brought Porter into his confidence. Brown wrote to the secretary of war that he intended "to storm the batteries, destroy the cannon, and roughly handle the brigade upon duty before those in reserve could be brought into action."[25] On September 16, Porter sent his two aides, Brevet Captains Donald Frazer and David Riddle, along with one hundred axmen, into the forest to blaze two trails from the militia encampment to the vicinity of the third British battery. The British sentries failed to notice the Americans so close to their positions. Ironically, Drummond had decided to break off the siege. It was proving near impossible to sustain the flow of food, ammunition, and fresh troops from Kingston to the siege camp.

On the morning of September 17, Porter assembled his militiamen, most of whom were in civilian clothing. Officers directed the men to leave their hats in camp and to wrap red strips of cloth about their upper arm as a means of identification. An officer announced the electrifying news of the recent victory at Plattsburgh to the assembled men. Porter then divided the militiamen into two columns and merged them with the regulars and volunteers making the attack. Militia Brig. Gen. Daniel Davis led the left column, consisting of five hundred volunteers and militiamen. Davis was thirty-seven years old and a resident of Le Roy in Genesee County, where he commanded the Sixth Brigade of the common militia. Eleazar Wood, the intrepid engineer, led the right column. His formation was composed of four hundred regulars and five hundred militiamen. The whole was preceded by Col. James Gibson and two hundred regular riflemen and twenty Seneca warriors. Gibson graduated from West Point in 1808, and his rise to the rank of colonel had been meteoric.[26]

Brown's plan was simple. When Gen. James Miller heard the noise of Porter's men assaulting the right flank of the British lines, he would begin his attack with his regulars from a ravine north of Fort Erie. The two bodies of American forces would destroy or damage the British siege guns and withdraw before Drummond's relief force could intervene. Brown posted Ripley with a reserve to assist in the withdrawal. The plan almost worked.

Porter's columns moved covertly through the forest in a drizzle. The rain rendered some of the firearms inoperable. Swords and bayonets figured large in what devolved into a hand-to-hand brawl. Porter's men crashed into the British line, taking their opponents by surprise. Miller led his men forward into the melee. Fighting in a forest laced with trenches and *abatis*, the Americans managed to capture a blockhouse and destroy three artillery guns. Brevet Captain Riddle blew up the ammunition magazine and was severely wounded doing so.

The attackers worked their way through two batteries, became overconfident, and surged on toward the last battery. However, the British reserves entered the fray and the fight increased in intensity and brutality.

General Davis and Lt. Col. Wood fell assaulting the first battery and Colonel Gibson was killed at the second battery. Porter reported, "Brigadier General Davis, although a militia officer of little experience, conducted on this occasion with all the coolness and bravery of a veteran, and fell while advancing upon the enemy's entrenchments." Among the Americans slain was Capt. Lewis Armistead, who was unaware of his brother, Maj. George Armistead's, famous victory defending Fort McHenry just three days earlier. Porter praised his citizen-soldiers: "To the militia the compliment is justly due, and I could pay them no greater one than to say, that they were not surpassed by the heroes of Chippewa and Niagara in steadiness and bravery."[27] In the face of the spirited British counterattack, Porter and Miller ordered a withdrawal. Porter received a sword wound on his hand while evading capture. The Americans continued the fight as they pulled back and through Ripley's reserve. Private Amasiah Ford of the Twenty-third Infantry recalled: "At this crisis, General Ripley was shot down by a ball striking him in the neck & was carried from the field but his wound did not prove mortal. About this time I was in the act of discharging my piece at a Red Coat [when] a ball passed through my cap directly under my cockade. I discharged my piece at my mark at the same time & never saw my mark again." The Americans returned to their camp, leaving hundreds of slain, wounded, and prisoners in the wet forest.[28]

After the burning of Washington in August, Madison forced Secretary of War Armstrong to resign. Secretary of State James Monroe replaced the disgraced Armstrong. Brown reported to Monroe noting that victory came at a high cost. "In such a business we would not but expect to lose many valuable lives. They were offered up a voluntary sacrifice to the safety and honor of this Army and the Nation." Brown, who was gravely disappointed with the militia's performance at the defense of Sackett's Harbor the year prior, now praised the militia. He reported to Governor Tompkins, "The militia of New York have redeemed their character—they behaved gallantly." He continued, "The brave men deserve well of their country; and I flatter myself that the legislature about to convene will notice them as becomes the representatives of a generous people."[29]

Drummond claimed the victory, reporting to Governor General Prevost, "The Enemy being thus repulsed at every point was forced to retire with precipitation to their works leaving Prisoners and a number of their wounded in our hands." British casualties amounted to 579.[30] Brown likewise claimed victory; he believed, erroneously, that the sortie had broken the siege. The Americans suffered 511 killed, wounded, and missing. The hundreds of missing reported by both commanders were largely prisoners held by their opponents. Drummond, in accordance with his decision made prior to the sortie, continued removing guns from the siege lines and at dusk on September 21, the British evacuated their camp in a torrent of rain. The forty-nine-day siege was over.

After the sortie, dysentery and typhus unfortunately ravaged the ranks of the militia. Those who did not recover within two weeks were evacuated to the hospital in Williamsville. When Brown released the militia two months after the sortie, he ensured that those who had served at Fort Erie received a special recognition. As they mustered out, the men received a printed document that read:

HONOR TO THE BRAVE

This certifies that _____ being one of those who generously and bravely Volunteered their services and crossed the lake to Fort Erie in September last, for the relief of the American Garrison, then closely invested by a superior force, and having faithfully performed his term of service, is most honorably discharged.
Batavia, Nov _____ 1814

However, many of these volunteers did not receive their pay for this period of brutal service until 1819.[31]

The state Assembly was effusive in praise of the nation's newest heroes. In a response to the governor, the speaker of the Assembly wrote,

> Since the opening of the campaign in that quarter, a brilliant succession of skillful & heroic exploits has gilded our horizon & has shed beams of brightest effulgence upon the characters of Brown, Scott, Porter, Gaines & Ripley & the companions of their fame. They have manifested to the world, that the victorious legions of Lord Wellington cannot successfully contend with the prowess of our hardy freemen, nor defeat the well digested plans of our military commanders. And while they have gathered for themselves deathless & unfading laurels, they have retrieved & reestablished our character as a nation for deeds of martial heroism.[32]

Speaker of the Assembly Samuel Young repeated the common misperception that the British were largely veterans of the campaigns on the Iberian Peninsula. In December, the state legislature voted to award presentation swords to Generals Brown, Scott, Ripley, Gaines, and Miller.

Congress had awarded these general officers and Porter as well with gold medals in November. Scott was brevetted a major general for his distinguished service at Chippawa and Lundy's Lane. Ripley's brevet to major general recognized his gallant conduct at Lundy's Lane. Gaines received his brevet promotion to major general for gallantry during the night attack on Fort Erie. Col. James Miller, who led the decisive attack at Lundy's Lane, was brevetted to brigadier general for distinguished service at that pivotal battle. Unwilling to raise anyone to the rank that George Washington held, the president did not brevet Jacob Brown to lieutenant general.

Tompkins responded angrily to President Madison's message to Congress on September 20 lauding the federal troops and generals who participated in recent battles: "Yet whilst all others have been brevetted & complimented, Genl. Porter & his little band alone, are neglected & are not even mentioned by the President in his message." In his fiery letter to congressman Jonathan Fisk, Tompkins continued, "Nor is the patriotism, Volunteers nor Militia of the State mentioned, altho,' at the time the President penned his message, nearly thirty thousand of the yeomanry of this State were in the service of the United States, & without whom two of their armies would probably have been lost, & the metropolis of the State before this time have been in the possession of the enemy." In Madison's defense, he included a nod to the militia for their participation in the Battle of Plattsburgh, but was probably unaware of the details of the sortie conducted just days prior to his speech.[33] Tompkins recognized the valor of the two militia generals killed on the Niagara frontier. He presented swords to General Davis' son, Alfred, and General Swift's eldest son, Asa, noting their fathers' gallantry in combat.[34]

General Izard and the troops of the Right Division arrived at Sackett's Harbor on September 13 after a march of sixteen days. He believed Kingston was too well defended to attack with any probability of success. An urgent note from Brown written prior to the sortie stated that he considered "the fate of this army very doubtful unless speedy relief is afforded." Brown suggested that Izard join him on the Niagara frontier to defeat or destroy Drummond's forces. Commodore Chauncey had just broken off his blockade of Kingston. Royal Navy Commodore James Yeo's ship of the line, St. Lawrence, was about to sail, making an American victory on Lake Ontario problematic. Chauncey and Izard decided to move the Right Division to the Niagara frontier.[35]

Chauncey moved 3,000 of Izard's troops from Sackett's Harbor to the mouth of the Genesee River on September 21–22. Izard left a battalion of the Thirteenth Infantry, a veteran regiment raised in New York, at Sackett's Harbor. He also left a regiment newly raised in the Massachusetts District of Maine, the Forty-Fifth Infantry. Lt. Col. George Mitchell of the Third Artillery commanded the regulars at Sackett's Harbor. Chauncey lamented that too few regulars remained to defend his major base. The artillerists and the Thirteenth Infantry were veterans, but the Maine troops were recruits. Militia Brig. Gen. Oliver Collins called out the common militia of Herkimer, Lewis, Oneida, and Jefferson Counties. The lack of sufficient room to quarter the militiamen forced them to occupy every barn and many dwellings around the naval base. Chauncey reported that the militia, about 2,000 in number, "desert by companies." Chauncey believed Collins to be a good officer, but it was "out of his power to make Soldiers of Militia in the short space of a few Weeks." Eventually, as fears of a British attack diminished, Collins released the militiamen to their homes.[36]

From the Genesee River, Izard marched his men to Batavia. Once there, Izard met with Brown telling him that he intended to recapture Fort Niagara. Izard directed Brown to start moving his artillery northward from Fort Erie. Izard arrived at Lewiston on October 5 and received a letter from Secretary of War Monroe giving Izard command of the Ninth Military District. Izard promptly renamed his command the Northern Army. He referred to the division that had marched with him as the First Division, or the Right Wing. Brown's division became the Second Division, or the Left Wing. Brown and Porter met Izard at Lewiston and persuaded him to give up his plan to recapture Fort Niagara and instead to destroy Drummond's command.[37]

Brown and many of his officers were frustrated by Izard's lack of urgency. The weather was quickly growing colder and wetter. If the Northern Army, the largest and best-trained American force during the war, was to destroy Drummond's division, it would have to act quickly. Izard took what was to his mind a more strategic view. It was more important to preserve the fighting capability of the Northern Army into 1815 than to weaken it in what would be a costly battle with Drummond. For his part, Drummond was satisfied to avoid battle with a more numerous foe.[38]

Lacking sufficient boats to cross the First Division near Lewiston, Izard brought his men to Black Rock and crossed the Niagara into Upper Canada on October 10 and 11. On October 15, Izard had both divisions, about 6,300 regulars and volunteers, drawn up south of the Chippawa River. Brown's division was back where it started on July 5. The next day, Izard was discouraged to discover that Commodore Chauncey had returned with his squadron to Sackett's Harbor. Without the services of the Lake Ontario squadron, he believed there was no point in continuing the offensive. He wrote to Monroe, "I am greatly embarrassed. At the head of the most efficient army which the United States have possessed during this war, much must be expected from me, and yet I can discern no object which can be achieved at this point, worthy of the risk which will attend its attempt."[39]

On October 17, Izard dropped south behind Black Creek, about six miles from the Chippawa River. He hoped that Drummond might advance to battle once he had enough maneuver room to his front. The next day, the calculus of battle changed. Yeo's squadron appeared off the Niagara River led by the *St. Lawrence*, the most powerful warship on the Great Lakes. Drummond had no reason to give battle now that he had the full support of Yeo's squadron.

Izard learned that a large quantity of flour was located at Cook's Mill on Lyon's Creek, a tributary of the Chippawa River. Hoping to make Drummond's plight a bit more difficult, Izard sent Brig. Gen. Daniel Bissell to seize or destroy the foodstuffs. This order set up the last battle of the war along New York's border. Bissell marched about nine hundred soldiers, all regulars, twenty miles on miserable roads and arrived at the mill on the evening of October 18. Drummond learned of the American move and sent a mixed force, including a Congreve rocket launcher, to see what the Americans were up to.

The following morning, Colonel Christopher Myers formed his British troops north of Lyon's Creek and about one mile from the bridge at the mill. He sent a battalion of infantry to push in a screening force of Americans positioned north of the creek. The Americans conducted a fighting withdrawal back toward the bridge. Bissell leapt into action at the sound of musketry. He ordered three of his four well-trained regiments across the bridge with orders to push back the British. Bissell sent his remaining regiment eastward along the south bank of the creek to lend support.[40]

The British withdrew to their main line. The Americans opened an intense musketry fire, and the British responded with muskets, artillery, and rockets. Myers waited for an American attack that never came. He withdrew a few miles, leaving scouts to report on any American movement. Bissell believed that he had driven off the British. He reported sixty-seven casualties; Myers reported thirty-six. Both commanders had accomplished their mission. Myers reported the size of the American force and Bissell destroyed about two hundred barrels of flour. The battle was neither large nor decisive. Izard was convinced that Drummond would not willingly offer battle, and the Americans could not force the issue. Izard decided to end the campaign that started four months earlier.[41]

On October 20, Izard offered Brown the opportunity to take the Second Division back to Sackett's Harbor. Brown jumped at the suggestion. Brown's division began the seventeen-day trek eastward on October 28. Capt. Joseph Henderson recalled the miserable march through snow and rain: "We had to wade in mud and water to our knees and our baggage wagons breaking down or sinking in the snow[.] We had to pass the night without shelter or provisions, lying upon the hemlock branches which we spread under us to keep out the water, and which perhaps before morning was converted into ice." Upon their arrival at Sackett's Harbor, Chaplain Nathaniel Stacy recalled, "A more besmeared set of reptiles were never seen crawling out of the mud. They had marched from the Niagara frontier, through incessant rains, which covered the whole country with a bed of mortar, almost up to their knees; and their tattered and filthy garments looked more like the habiliments of beggars—much more, than like the neat uniform of regular troops." No barracks were waiting for them, and the men slept in the snowy fields for weeks until they could build enough shelters.[42]

While Brown's men marched to Sackett's Harbor, Porter brought his volunteers to Batavia, where he released them from federal service. Izard started moving the soldiers of the First Division across the Niagara River to Buffalo on October 25. Izard believed maintaining a garrison at Fort Erie served no purpose. It would be particularly difficult to keep a garrison fed and supplied from Buffalo over the winter. Izard ordered work parties to blow up the fort. Engineer and West Point graduate Lt. Col. Joseph Totten supervised the work. On November 5, workers lit the long fuses. The work parties were crossing to Buffalo as one by one the charges exploded. Snake Hill was returned to a mound of sand and the stone buildings and ramparts of the fort were reduced to a pile of rocks.

The four-month-long campaign generated huge numbers of sick and wounded. Hospital facilities at Williamsville expanded, and hundreds of soldiers were housed in tents during the increasingly cold weather. Izard ordered those who were able to move to Greenbush, and the hospital at Buffalo closed on December 23. Still, more than 2,000 sick and wounded remained at Williamsville over the winter of 1814–15.[43]

Izard's men constructed barracks in Buffalo and Black Rock. Second Lt. Jacob Porter Norton, a Bostonian, had nothing good to say about his new winter home: "Went to Buffaloe, the impression which I received from my visit is, that it is a nest of villains, rogues, rascals, pickpockets, knaves, & extortioners." Norton, an ardent supporter of the war, compared Massachusetts to New York. He wrote to his father that he heard "of the fuss in Boston about their fortification, Militia, Volunteers etc., and I believe their greatest operations are performed upon paper. Not so with New York. She says less. And does much."[44]

Izard was intent on preserving the strength of the Northern Army for the 1815 campaign. The 1814 Niagara campaign started with a misunderstanding of orders and ended back where it had begun. The British remained along the western banks of the Niagara River and held Fort Niagara as well. American soldiers demonstrated their vastly improved battle skills and won their share of military glory, both on the Niagara River and on Lake Champlain.

The United States had failed in its last attempt to achieve decisive results by invading Canadian soil. Nevertheless, the marked improvement in federal-state cooperation had contributed in no small part to the results of the campaign. Tompkins acted as early as August 13 to energize the call-up of militia.

These citizen-soldiers responded favorably as 1,500 of them put aside their constitutional prerogatives and crossed into Canada. In doing so, each of them risked death or capture. Undoubtedly, they responded to heroic leadership of men such as Jacob Brown and Peter B. Porter. The contrast with those who remained on New York's shores at the Battle of Queenston Heights was stark. The Left Division was in deadly peril, and New York's militiamen responded bravely and with effect.

CHAPTER 17

The Crisis

As Maj. Gen. Jacob Brown prepared to lead the nation's last major offensive of the war, state leaders braced to defend the borders against potentially powerful British counterstrokes. Contrary to Henry Clay's 1810 boast, "The militia of Kentucky are alone competent to place Montreal and Upper Canada at your feet," New Yorkers had seen two years of division, sacrifice, and suffering.[1]

Napoleon's defeat triggered an increase of political partisanship. Heedless that Napoleon's fall could bring the might of the British Empire into the war against America, New York City Federalists celebrated. They observed the "deliverance of Europe from the yoke of military despotism" with church services and a dinner in Washington Hall on June 29, 1814. During dinner, nearly two thousand protesters gathered outside and hurled epithets and stones. Peace officers arrived, breaking up the demonstration and arresting several alleged ringleaders.[2]

With the nation approaching a crisis, President Madison directed his secretary of war, John Armstrong, to assess the capabilities of seacoast cities to defend themselves. He further ordered Armstrong to move federal weapons to depots accessible to the defenders. On July 4, 1814, Armstrong requisitioned 93,500 militiamen and requested governors to hold them in readiness for immediate service. New York's allocation was 13,500 men. Armstrong asked New Jersey to mobilize 5,000 militiamen, half of whom he allocated to the Third Military District.[3]

Since the spring of 1812, Governor Daniel Tompkins had diligently rotated militiamen to defend New York City and more than four hundred miles of border. The militia had become jaded; citizens willing to serve away from their homes were few and far between. Yet, the threat was growing and with it the requirement for citizen-soldiers. On July 20, the governor doubled down on Armstrong's requisition. Tompkins issued a general order that selected the common militia formations that would provide the 13,500 detached militia. He

237

further directed "that all the residue of the militia of the State of New York be likewise kept in complete order of service, and ready to march at a moment's warning, to any part of the State which may be attacked, or in immediate danger of being attacked." The state's commander in chief was prepared to mobilize the entire manpower resources of New York. Militia leaders scurried to notify and inspect their citizen-soldiers. There were insufficient weapons and equipment to bring over 90,000 men into the field. However, with this order, Tompkins had clearly expressed to the citizenry the sense of crisis and urgency. On August 2, Tompkins ordered 3,000 detached militia to march to New York City. These troops came from as far north as Albany. While the detached militia was called up for three months' service, Tompkins reminded them that the President could extend the tour of duty to six months if "the public interest requires it."[4]

Interestingly, Maj. Gen. Morgan Lewis, commander of the Third Military District, wrote to Armstrong on July 28 asking whether a district commander could judge the "menace of invasion" and mobilize the militia, or whether such an action needed preapproval from the War Department. If the militia mobilized, all costs passed to the federal government. Armstrong referred the note to Madison, who responded in a common-sense manner that in an urgent situation the district commanders had authority to mobilize militia units. He added, "If New York be in danger at all, the danger is probably not very distant, and preparations for its safety therefore urgent."[5] This exchange reflected Lewis's caution and timidity.

State records provide a glimpse of the detached militia sent to defend New York City. The Twenty-Third Militia Brigade provided five companies. These companies mustered a total of 248 men; however, another 111 were absent for reasons not given. Even though state law required militiamen to maintain their own weapons, the 248 men brought only ninety-four firearms with them. Of these weapons, thirty-four were unfit for service. Twenty-three of these men, did, however, wear uniforms.[6]

On August 29, the governor called Maj. Gen. Ebenezer Steven's Detached Militia Division and a brigade of common militia into active service to defend the city. Stevens was a veteran of the Revolution and a highly respected leader. Tompkins also requested that any willing companies of exempts, sea fencibles, or "other associations of citizens" volunteer for immediate service. He completed his order by having each common militia brigade as far north as Saratoga County send a battalion of men immediately to New York City to reinforce the thousands of troops already there. The governor ensured the city would not go down without a titanic struggle.[7] New York City would be spared; however, the British were even then marching on Plattsburgh.

The officers, officials, and civilians around Lake Champlain were keenly aware of the growing threat. Capt. Sylvester Churchill of the Third Artillery Regiment was at the northern end of Lake Champlain negotiating a prisoner exchange. While Churchill and his counterpart conferred, a second British officer asked with much bluster, "Can you tell me, Sir, what is the distance from Whitehall to Albany?" Whitehall was at the southern end of Lake Champlain. Churchill surmised that Albany was the objective of the anticipated invasion. Churchill replied, "I do not know the exact distance but I have always understood that Saratoga is about midway between the two points." The reference to the place of British General John Burgoyne's surrender during the Revolution was not lost on the British officer; speechless, he departed the room.[8]

The British were indeed readying a large force to eliminate the American military and naval presence on Lake Champlain. On June 3, Secretary of State for War and the Colonies Earl Bathurst sent orders to Sir George Prevost, governor of British North America. Bathurst had dispatched more than 13,000 soldiers to Quebec. He gave Prevost two missions. The first was to give "immediate protection" to Canada, and the second to provide "ultimate security" to British North America. "The entire destruction of Sackets Harbor and the Naval Establishment on Lake Erie and Lake Champlain come under the first description. The maintenance of Fort Niagara and so much of the adjacent Territory as may be deemed necessary, and the occupation of Detroit and the Michigan Country came under the second."[9]

Bathurst also authorized Prevost to occupy "any advance position on that part of our frontier which extends towards Lake Champlain, the occupation of which would materially tend to the security of the province." Bathurst warned Prevost not to make any forward movements into the interior of New York. Clearly, he did not want a repeat of Burgoyne's campaign.[10]

A successful campaign that destroyed American naval power or seized American territory could go far to provide leverage in negotiations or even to push the international border permanently south. Prevost consulted with Commodore Sir James Yeo, who maintained that the Lake Ontario squadron would not be ready until the new first-rate ship, *St. Lawrence*, could sail in mid-October. October was too late in the campaign season, so Prevost directed his efforts toward Lake Champlain.

In a letter to the ministry, Prevost noted, "The State of Vermont having shewn a decided opposition to the War, and very large supplies of Specie daily coming in from thence, as well as the whole of Cattle required for the use of the Troops, I mean for the present to confine myself in any offensive Operations which may take place to the Western side of Lake Champlain."[11]

Meanwhile, at Plattsburgh, Maj. Gen. George Izard received Armstrong's order of July 27 to march westward to attack Kingston or Prescott. Izard warned Armstrong of the grave risk they were taking; large numbers of British troops were gathering for an imminent invasion. The secretary of war considered himself to be an able strategist; yet his order was reckless. Armstrong sought to address Izard's concerns by authorizing Izard to contact the governors of New York and Vermont directly for militia to backfill Izard's regulars "if in your opinion they will be necessary." However, it was not until August 23 that Izard called upon Brig. Gen. Benjamin Mooers to provide a regiment of infantry and a company of dragoons to replace the 4,000 regulars that Izard had earmarked for movement six days later. Nor did Izard contact Governor Tompkins for assistance.[12]

Considering Izard's fears of the looming British offensive, his omission is bewildering. Mooers was stunned to learn that Izard was leaving Plattsburgh, yet hesitated to comply with the request for militia, doubting the legality of the order. Tompkins quickly disabused his general of that notion and directed Mooers to take action immediately. As usual, Tompkins smoothed the process of cooperation between his officers and those of the federal government. Mooers ordered out the common militia from Clinton, Essex, and Franklin Counties. Tompkins feared a two-pronged invasion to sever the state along the traditional invasion route, a campaign the British had partially implemented in 1777. The governor declared an emergency and diverted militia units previously ordered to New York City to join General Mooers's command instead. Yet again, Tompkins was cleaning up behind federal ineptitude.[13]

Izard took more than 4,000 trained troops with him and placed Brig. Gen. Alexander Macomb in command of the regulars left behind. After Izard's departure on August 29, Macomb had four major tasks to prepare for the inevitable arrival of the British. First, he had to complete the fortification of the American camp. The second task was to coordinate the defensive plan with Commodore Thomas Macdonough. Third, Macomb had to integrate the militia coming into camp with the regulars. His fourth task was to develop a plan to slow down the invaders to allow more time for preparation.

Macomb decided to defend his base on the peninsula formed by Cumberland Bay and the Saranac River. This was a dangerous position because there would be no escape should a British attack prove successful. His first task, then, was to prepare defensive positions to give his outnumbered forces physical protection from British fire and a measure of confidence. Key to the fortifications was the line of three redoubts, Forts Brown, Moreau, and Scott, which sealed the southern end of the camp. Engineer Maj. Joseph Totten laid out the defenses, consisting of the three forts augmented by parapets and two blockhouses. The redoubts were staggered such that fire from each could cover the face of an adjacent fort. Macomb himself assisted in the hard work of digging ditches and moving timbers.[14]

Macomb conveyed his fierce determination to his soldiers. He ordered his officers to defend each redoubt, blockhouse, or fortified building to the extreme; they did not have authority to surrender. Every soldier understood that the fortified camp was a potential death trap if the redoubts fell. Even if the garrisons of the forts wanted to surrender, it would be nearly impossible for the British officers to call off the deadly assault once their soldiers entered the defensive works.

More than nine hundred sick and convalescents were within the American fortifications. Macomb retained those capable of light duty but removed more than seven hundred to Crab Island, where they sheltered in tents on the wet ground. These soldiers were eventually shuttled to the hospital at Burlington on vessels used to bring in the Vermont volunteers. By the end of the campaign, the Burlington hospital had more than eight hundred patients, of which about fifty were wounded.[15]

Macomb and Macdonough anticipated that the attack would come by land and water. They agreed on an integrated defense of the fortified peninsula, thus accomplishing Macomb's second task. Macdonough decided to anchor his four largest warships in a line across Plattsburgh Bay. The squadron's guns would keep British vessels too far away to support the land assault. Macomb sent Macdonough 250 soldiers, yet Macdonough still had too few men to man the guns. He compensated for this shortfall by the adroit use of cables and anchors that enabled his captains to rotate their warships 180 degrees. Thus, the Americans would assign gun crews only to the side of the vessel facing the British attack. If these guns became unusable, the captain could rotate his vessel while the gun crews moved to the opposite side. This movement would present an entire bank of fresh guns to continue the fight.

Macomb's third task was the coordination of the stream of militia entering the camp. On September 7, the call went out in Vermont for volunteers to defend Plattsburgh. While Federalist Governor Martin Chittenden believed that he had no authority to send his militia outside the state, he implicitly approved the formation of volunteer units. Men gathered and elected their officers. These in turn selected Brig. Gen. Samuel Strong of Vergennes to command all of the Vermont volunteers. The Vermonters crossed Lake Champlain on whatever vessels were available. They marched into the American camp, and the regulars issued weapons to any militiamen who had arrived unarmed. However, lacking tents meant the militiamen spent the cold nights gathered around their campfires.

The last of Macomb's tasks was to delay the British while preparations continued. He sent Majors Daniel Appling and John Sproull with soldiers to fell trees onto the road between Plattsburgh and Chazy. When the British appeared, the Americans would conduct a fighting withdrawal, hopefully buying time for the defenders on the peninsula.

Sir George Prevost personally led the invasion. British troops started crossing into New York from Canada on the last day of August, and eventually Prevost's invasion force numbered about 10,000. The roads were abysmal, and the columns were slowed correspondingly. Prevost assigned troops to secure his supply lines. Therefore, only about 8,000 arrived at Plattsburgh. The British issued a proclamation offering protection to peaceful inhabitants. Each American militiaman along the invasion route had to decide whether taking up arms was worth the risk of injury, death, or loss of farm and livestock. As it turned out, several militiamen reported for muster but drifted away as the campaign progressed. The story was different south of Plattsburgh. The number of militiamen mustering in Washington and Warren Counties was reportedly larger than any previous mobilization, with a number of exempts joining the ranks. The *Albany Argus* concluded, "A stronger evidence of the patriotism and valor of our countrymen cannot be evinced." However, events moved quickly, and these citizen-soldiers did not arrive in Plattsburgh until after the battle. By September 4, Prevost's advance party was about ten miles north of Plattsburgh. He divided the main body of troops into two wings advancing on parallel roads.[16]

Macomb needed time to complete his fortifications and for more militiamen to assemble. He sent Major Appling and about 110 riflemen north to contest the enemy advance. He also ordered Major Sproull, with two hundred infantrymen and two guns, to defend the bridge over Dead Creek, two miles north of Plattsburgh. Additionally, he directed General Mooers to take some militiamen to East Beekmantown, a small village about five miles north of Plattsburgh. Mooers's force included a detachment of volunteer cavalrymen uniformed in red jackets. The sight of them disturbed the militiamen, who reported seeing British cavalry all about them. Ironically, the only cavalry in red jackets were American; British light dragoons wore blue.

On about September 5, militia Capt. Martin J. Aiken and his lieutenant, Azariah C. Flagg, approached Macomb with an offer. Aiken had fifteen young men, all under eighteen years of age and several under sixteen, who volunteered to fight. Macomb accepted their services and ordered them to report to General Mooers. This company of teenagers moved to Beekmantown and harassed British pickets and forwarded information to Mooers. When the Americans fell back to Plattsburgh, Aiken's small company helped to defend the American camp. After the battle, Macomb promised each of them a 'handsome rifle' to recognize their valuable service.[17]

In the early hours of September 6, Macomb sent Maj. John E. Wool with 250 regulars and thirty militiamen north on the Beekmantown Road. About seven miles from Plattsburgh, Wool's party encountered the British. Wool's men fought a delaying action, firing from behind cover and withdrawing to new positions to fire again. At Culver's Hill, a British soldier shot Wool's horse out from under him. The assembled militiamen fired a volley and retired. In Wool's words, his battalion disputed "every foot of ground until it arrived on the right bank of the Saranac in the village of Plattsburgh." Meanwhile, Appling's riflemen skirmished with the British advance guard and fell back slowly to Dead Creek.[18]

West Point graduate Capt. Luther Leonard brought two guns and joined Wool a half mile from Plattsburgh. Wool claimed that these guns did 'great execution.' After Wool's men crossed the wooden bridge to enter the fortified peninsula, Wool ordered Capt. John C. Rochester and his company to pull up the decking. Rochester was the son of one of the founders of the city of that name. The British on the north side of the Saranac took Rochester's men under fire. Aiken's teenagers provided covering fire for the Rochester party. The infantrymen removed the planking, leaving only the timber piers and stringers. The British eventually withdrew behind the concealment of nearby houses.[19]

For the next several days, Prevost established battery positions to bring the American fortified area under fire while he waited impatiently for Commodore George Downie and his naval contingent to appear. Skirmishers from both sides kept up a brisk fire, joined intermittently by artillery rounds crashing into houses and parapets. Captain Rochester commanded his company and two guns in a bastion of Fort Moreau. He wrote to his father that he had either to "distinguish or extinguish" himself. He added, "The troops here are in high spirits—you would be amused to see me write this. I am now seated on the parapet of the fort with my paper on my knee & within plain sight of the whole British force. . . . I am now hearty & fearless of any danger from the enemy—as I was several times on the 6th in the midst of showers of musketry."[20]

Capt. George McGlassin volunteered from his sick bed to lead a raid on one of the British battery positions under construction. About midnight on September 9, his fifty soldiers forded the Saranac and surprised and drove off about 150 British troops working on the battery. McGlassin's raid boosted the morale of Plattsburgh's defenders, and the War Department brevetted him for his gallant conduct.

British snipers used the houses along the Saranac for cover. Macomb directed his guns to fire hot shot into these structures to burn them down. Prevost sent officers under a flag to ask that the Americans cease fire, thus allowing the British to put out the fires. The Americans refused; the British general now understood that his counterpart was willing to destroy civilian homes in order to defend his base. No one could question Macomb's grim determination.

On September 11, with the British naval squadron finally underway heading toward Plattsburgh, Prevost ordered Major General Frederick Robinson to assault the American fortifications from the south. Robinson led 4,400 troops toward Pike's Ford on the Saranac River. However, Mooers's men had disguised the direct path by emplacing fir trees and brush on the roadway while opening logging trails that led away from the ford. The assault force lost at least an hour finding their way to the ford. Mooers's militiamen and the Vermont volunteers fired upon the British as they crossed the Saranac. Macomb ordered them to contest the advance but not become decisively engaged. More Americans appeared and took up the fight as the whole body withdrew away from the American lines. Robinson reformed his men and prepared to assault the redoubts in the distance.

Meanwhile, Downie brought his squadron up the lake under a north wind. However, as the squadron rounded Cumberland Head and entered Plattsburgh Bay, the winds became light and variable. The British had an advantage in long-range guns, but for unknown reasons, Downie yielded this superiority. He ordered his warships and gunboats to move directly on the American line to cut it. He intended to take his largest vessel, *Confiance*, to pierce Macdonough's line, thereby firing broadsides both left and right down the long axis of *Eagle* and *Saratoga*. If done according to plan, Downie's move could be decisive. However, the winds failed to cooperate. Downie wanted a quick victory, but it was not to be. The British vessels approached the American line, but with a light wind they could not pass through. Both squadrons commenced firing at short range at about 9:30 A.M.

The American dominance in short-range carronades inflicted considerable damage on their opponent. Fifteen minutes into the furious fight, Downie was struck down, dying shortly thereafter. The warships battered one another mercilessly. Huge splinters broken loose by the impact of heavy shot tore into flesh. Sailors kept the deck clear by throwing overboard the dead and those believed to be fatally wounded. Seamen carried the wounded below deck to await the attention of the surgeons. Prodigious amounts of blood made the decks treacherous. Sailors pitched sand on the puddles of blood, restoring traction. Blinding white smoke swirled around the deck amid the cries of the wounded and barked orders of the gun captains. Loading and firing, every crew was caught up in its own private fight.

Nearing two hours of mutual pounding, all the guns on the starboard side of *Saratoga* were out of action. Macdonough gave the order to rotate the warship.

Battle of Lake Champlain, by Peter Rindlisbacher. Courtesy of the artist.

Soon he had fresh guns from his port side blasting into *Confiance*. Lieutenant James Robertson, who had replaced the unfortunate Downie, attempted the same maneuver, but his ship stalled at right angles to the American line. Robertson could not return the brutal fire relentlessly cutting down his crewmen. He struck his colors. The firing died away as the British surrender became apparent to all. The British suffered 170 casualties, the Americans 110.[21]

Watching the battle and confusing the warships, Vermonter Jonathan Stevens later wrote to his brother:

> We could see our ship the *Ticonderoga* made no fire till just as we got to the fort, she wheeled & gave a broadside that brought down the colours of the *Confiance*, the British frigate. The rest not long after followed suit. This was an hour in which the various feelings of my mind may have been felt by others but cannot be described by any for seeing our best vessels lay mute, hope was almost ready to take flight. The sequel, however, raised my feelings above any other hour of my life.[22]

Catherine Shute Mooers recalled that "when the people on Cumberland Head saw the British retreating they shouted and blew horns and showed signs of rejoicing so much that the British fired a cannon at them."[23]

Robinson, readying his men to assault the three American redoubts, received Prevost's order to break off the attack. This new order stunned Robinson and his men; they were confident of victory. Nevertheless, the soldiers returned to camp, no doubt cursing Prevost for his timidity. Prevost gave orders to withdraw back into Lower Canada. Without the naval squadron, it would be impossible to feed his men.[24] The American artillery fired at the British battery positions until darkness. As the guns fell silent, the men gave three cheers for the victory, and the bands played Yankee Doodle.[25]

Immediately after the battle, Macdonough sent a brief letter to William Jones, the secretary of the navy, announcing, "The Almighty has been pleased to grant us a signal victory." The Royal Navy was no longer a threat on Lake Champlain. The Americans sent 366 naval officers and seamen captured after the battle to Greenbush as prisoners and paroled forty-seven of the wounded. Two days later, Macdonough requested that Jones transfer him to Stephen Decatur's command, giving as his reason "the almost certain inactivity of future operations here." To Macdonough's mind, the focus of the war was moving to New York City.[26]

Macomb reported to Secretary of War James Monroe that "deserters are continually coming in, so that the loss of the British Army, in this enterprise will be considerable." He complimented the performance of his citizen-soldiers: "The Militia of New York and the Volunteers of Vermont have been exceedingly Serviceable and have evinced a degree of Patriotism and bravery worthy of themselves and the States to which they respectively belong." However, three days later in a more detailed report, Macomb criticized the militia's performance in support of Major Wool: "But the militia could not be prevailed upon to stand, notwithstanding the exertions of their general and staff officers; although the fields were divided by strong stone walls, and they were told that the enemy could not possibly cut them off."[27]

Macomb ordered the hundreds of wounded, both American and British, to be taken to Crab Island. Over the next few days, surgeons performed more than forty amputations and treated dozens of gunshot wounds.[28]

The New York State Assembly praised the efforts of the militia. Assemblyman August Wright stated, "We most cordially concur with your Excellency [Tompkins] in awarding to the patient endurance, good conduct, and patriotism of our militia the just tribute of our praise. The late battles at Plattsburgh and at Erie bear ample and honorable testimony to their usefulness and merits. They have hastened to scenes of danger, with an ardor and enthusiasm which belongs only to freemen."[29]

The governor had been surprised and disconcerted by Izard's movement from Plattsburgh to the Niagara frontier and the general's unfounded expectation that the militia would readily replace the regulars at that important post. Tompkins wrote to Secretary of War Monroe, "The happy turn which affairs have taken in that quarter has relieved my anxiety; but I must remonstrate against the propriety of transferring an army from one frontier of this state to another with an expectation of my supplying the deserted frontier with Militia, unless seasonable intimation of the intended movement be given."[30]

The victory at Plattsburgh saved the state and the national boundary; British negotiators could not claim territory by right of conquest. America's newest heroes received plenty of awards. Congress presented gold medals to both Macomb and Macdonough. Albany and New York City each gave Macdonough valuable lots of land and voted him Freedom of the City. New York City had Macdonough's and Macomb's portraits displayed in City Hall. The state awarded Macdonough a sword and 1,000 acres of land in Cayuga County. His home state of Delaware presented Macdonough with a sword and silver plate. Macomb named his newborn son Alexander Saranac Macomb. The state legislature awarded swords to Maj. Gen. Benjamin Mooers, Vermont's Maj. Gen. Samuel Strong, and Brigadier General Macomb.[31]

The regiment of detached militia that reported to Plattsburgh following the battle was a sad disappointment. Militiamen went into the village, with or without permission, and pilfered from orchards, barns, and homesteads. Some used "unbecoming language" in front of ladies. Unfortunately, typical of militiamen who didn't want to be there, some used disrespectful language to the regulars and even to their own officers. Maj. John Wool refused to complete an inspection because he found militiamen filthy and their weapons dirty and in disrepair. Macomb noted that work parties were shirking their duties. Fortunately for the villagers and regulars, the militiamen were released on December 12.[32]

With Plattsburgh and Brown's Left Division safe for the time, state officials shifted their attentions to defending New York City and Sackett's Harbor. When Madison fired John Armstrong as secretary of war, he had replaced him with James Monroe. This left a vacancy for the office of secretary of state. Madison wanted Tompkins. Tompkins responded in mid-October, refusing the invitation in light of the current crisis in New York. Tompkins was ambitious, and certainly had his sights on the presidency, but this was the wrong time to make a move in that direction.[33]

As the crisis continued, Tompkins bolstered the defenses of Sackett's Harbor. He issued instructions to his general officers in Herkimer, Madison, and Montgomery Counties to "comply immediately" to any requests for militia made by the commander of the vital naval base without forwarding the request to the governor for approval.[34]

The burning of Washington on August 24 had triggered a run on the banks of major cities. Banks hemorrhaged specie to panicky investors. New York City banks, and others on the east coast, suspended specie payments, seriously damaging credit. Commerce suffered accordingly.[35]

After learning of the burning of the national capital and perceiving the situation in New York was indeed a crisis, Washington Irving approached Tompkins with an offer to assist in the war effort. Irving was already the nation's foremost author. His satire, *A History of New York from the Beginning of the World to the End of the Dutch Dynasty*, by Diedrich Knickerbocker, was tremendously popular. Tompkins gladly appointed Irving as an aide-de-camp with the rank of lieutenant colonel. Of course, Irving had no particular military talent, yet his new position announced that in this time of crisis, all citizens could contribute.[36]

Col. Solomon Van Rensselaer also served as the governor's military aide-de-camp. While Irving was a national celebrity, Van Rensselaer was an experienced officer, wounded in two wars. After the Battle of Queenston Heights, Tompkins had stirred up political trouble by failing to visit the badly wounded Federalist colonel in Buffalo. Now that they were in daily proximity, relations warmed considerably. Van Rensselaer wrote to his spouse, Harriet, that when reviewing troops, "I am the right hand man of the Governor, who from my usefulness to him, grows daily more and more attached to me."[37] Both the governor and the colonel submerged partisan politics for the common cause of the state.

With a heightened fear of British attack, the officials charged with the defense of New York City turned their attentions to the all-around defense of Manhattan. This enterprise was a partnership between the regular army and navy, and between state and city government. The city was represented by the Committee of Defence, a body working as an agency of the Common Council. The committee mobilized volunteer laborers from all strata of society to erect fortifications under the direction of army engineers. While work continued on the harbor fortifications, additional effort prepared for an attack from the north.

As early as July 8, the Committee of Defence had sent a letter to Gen. Morgan Lewis noting that an invasion landing on Long Island was more to be feared than an attempt by naval forces to pass the Narrows and land troops directly at the city. The council recommended fortifying Brooklyn Heights, arming the militia immediately, establishing batteries to cover every bridge across the Harlem River, and fortifying Harlem Heights. (This defensive plan was similar to that employed by George Washington during the Revolution.) Approximately 2,700 regulars were assigned to General Lewis's command, and many of these were new recruits.[38]

On July 14, the Committee of Defence followed up the Common Council's letter to Lewis with a plan to improve the city's defensive posture. The committee noted that work at the Narrows and the close-by islands was progressing, yet little had been done to defend the land approaches to the city, particularly from a major incursion on Long Island. It would be beyond the city's resources to defend every potential landing site on Jamaica Bay. The plan revealed the deficient state of the defenders: "The inadequacy of the regular force is palpable, and we have no reason to believe that the regular militia can supply the deficiency." Recognizing that the federal government had authorized the mobilization of 13,500 militiamen, the report cautioned that these troops were untrained and would not be available for several weeks. Even then, the report noted that fewer than 3,400 muskets were available to issue in the city. The committee looked to the federal and state governments for assistance in the form of troops and new fortifications.[39]

Members of the committee called upon the president and secretary of war with their concerns. Armstrong, still serving as secretary of war at the time, responded that he would call into federal service 3,000 militiamen if the city would pay costs to be reimbursed later from federal funds. The federal government would also provide muskets to make up the expected deficiencies for the 3,000. The City Council agreed. City officials well remembered the British operation that seized the city in 1776 and dreaded its repetition.[40] The militiamen came from counties from Albany southward and were to serve for 90 days or 180 days if necessary. They gathered on the Hudson River for water transport to New York City. The farmers among them left crops to be harvested. New Jersey conducted a parallel if smaller mobilization. Twelve New Jersey volunteer companies offered to serve in the defense of New York City.[41]

On August 3, Mayor DeWitt Clinton issued a statement calling upon the citizenry to respond to the emergency: "Fellow-citizens, this city is in danger! We are threatened with invasion. It is the duty of all good citizens to prepare for the crisis! We must arm ourselves to aid the regular force of the government in a vigorous defence."[42] Clinton asked people to volunteer their labor to construct fortifications. Ward officials organized bands of volunteers at rallies. At one such gathering, Col. Marinus Willett, a former member of New York's Sons of Liberty, soldier of the Revolution, and city mayor, gave an impassioned speech: "Fifty-eight years are now passed since I was a witness of press gangs traversing these streets and dragging men from their houses on board of ships of war!" Willett pleaded for unity in a time of dire crisis. He reminded them of a common toast from the revolutionary past: "May every citizen be a soldier, and every soldier a citizen."[43]

The effect was electrifying. Over the next weeks, thousands volunteered to dig entrenchments and throw up earthen walls. On any given day, between five hundred and fifteen hundred people came as members of guilds and societies and as individuals—men and women, black and white. Blacks, both free and slave, answered the call. The *New York Herald* reported on August 24, "This morning between 800 and 1000 of the hardy and patriotic sons of Africa, accompanied by a delightful band of music and appropriate flags, crossed the ferry at Catherine slip, to work on the fortifications at Brooklyn Heights." Over fifteen hundred Irish immigrants, women as well as men, responded in the construction of ramparts at Fort Greene guarding Brooklyn. The Committee of Defence noted "their zeal, their industry . . . and their universally correct deportment."[44]

News of the fall of the national capital arrived in the city on August 26. Officials, newspapers, clergy, and others called on the citizenry to redouble their efforts. General Lewis asked Governor Tompkins to allocate all 13,500 detached militia to the city's defense. The Common Council, in recognition of the federal government's inability to feed or pay for more citizen-soldiers, authorized a loan of $1,000,000 to meet the emergency. In opening the loan to subscribers, the public notice stated, "In order to be safe we must rely upon our means—upon ourselves! Any other reliance in the present state of the country would be delusive and might be ruinous."[45] The people of New York rapidly raised the million dollars.

The governor had established a headquarters in the city in late August to more efficiently influence local preparations, and by August 22, he was issuing orders to state troops and coordinating the dispersal of state weapons and equipment. Tompkins ordered Col. Richard Platt, commissary general of military stores, to acquire musket cartridges and artillery ammunition and to deposit these at the New York City Arsenal. On August 27, Tompkins wrote to General Lewis noting the "alarming state of affairs" in the city and requesting that the district commander inform him of the operational plans to defend the city. In September, approximately 1,000 sea fencibles came into service. Tompkins sent them to man the blockhouses guarding landing sites on Gravesend Bay and to other water batteries. Tompkins coordinated directly with Governor William S. Pennington of New Jersey, who planned to move his headquarters to the vicinity of the city to coordinate his resources for the general defense. Tompkins moved between New York City and Albany to better direct resources to threatened points throughout the state.[46]

On August 27, Tompkins ordered the detached militia in the city to train three days each week, even though they had not yet been called into federal service. Two days later, Tompkins ordered the detached militia into active service.[47] Inspections revealed an insufficiency of arms for the detached militia. Tompkins requested that residents of the city who possessed cannon, pistols, and broadswords to offer them for sale to the state arsenal.[48] Tompkins also announced formation of a volunteer unit. He hoped to recruit up to two thousand men for a term of service from three months to the duration of the war. The specifics of the announcement as to pay and policy indicated that

Tompkins was preparing to offer this unit to the federal government to be accepted as U.S. volunteers.[49]

On August 29, New York's commander in chief ordered a large proportion of the common militia of the Hudson Valley as far north as Albany into service, with orders to march to the city. The first troops arrived on August 31. Tompkins issued a very strong statement assailing the failure of militia officers to ensure that every man possessed a musket and accoutrements. "The crisis has arrived when the culpable remissness which has hitherto prevailed among militia officers in respect to deficiencies of equipments among their men is seriously felt; all indulgence in this point must henceforth cease; it has always been pernicious, but now becomes criminal."[50]

General Lewis issued detailed orders to the troops arriving in the city that covered camp routine, sanitation, and picket guard. He ordered five hours of drill daily and directed that each brigade establish a school to instruct officers in drill. Presumably officers would instruct their soldiers in movements that the officers had themselves learned in the preceding days.[51] Lewis also ordered detached militia units from New Jersey to move closer to the city. Governor Pennington issued the orders to twenty-three company commanders to march their men to Powles' Hook (present Jersey City).

On September 5, Mayor DeWitt Clinton issued a rousing statement calling for a supreme effort, and he warned the citizenry to put aside all partisanship: "It is necessary, absolutely necessary, that there should be at least a truce to the animosities of party; that we should join hand in heart in the great work of patriotic exertion, and that we should merge all personal, all local, all party considerations in the great duties we owe to our country."[52]

Federalist Senator Rufus King was a political foe of both Clinton and Tompkins. Yet he met with the governor, urging a nonpartisan approach to the looming crisis. Tompkins later recorded that King declared, "The time had arrived when every good citizen was bound to put his all at the requisition of the government; that he was ready to do this; that the people of the state of New-York would, and must hold me [Tompkins] personally responsible for its defence and safety."[53] Federalist leaders encouraged their followers to support the massive defensive undertaking.

The newly elected state legislators had taken office on the first of July, and Tompkins called an early legislative session to start on September 26 in response to the burning of Washington and anticipation of further British attacks. Tompkins warned the legislature, "A predatory and wanton warfare, destitute of all generous principle, and disgraced by pillage and conflagration, has been carried on in our bays and rivers; and the enemy has openly avowed his intention of laying waste our cities, and of making a common ruin of public and private property."[54]

The new Republican-controlled legislature enabled Tompkins at last to get bills passed to support the war effort. In addition to providing $50,000 for the victims on the Niagara frontier, the lawmakers approved increased pay for the militia and support for their families. The legislature also passed a law authorizing the governor to raise a body of 12,000 militiamen for a two-year term of service, providing that the federal government pay for the new formation.[55] Looking to New York City, the legislature appropriated funding to complete the fortifications on Staten Island and authorized raising as many as twenty companies of sea fencibles for three years. By the middle of September, more than 17,000 state militia were armed, organized, and serving in the defense of New York City and its environs.[56] The congressional elections brought even more support for continued prosecution of the war. New York sent only six Federalist congressmen to Washington from the twenty-seven-member delegation.

In early October, the commanding officer at Sackett's Harbor wrote to Tompkins that the base was in imminent danger of attack. Tompkins ordered the troops of three brigades of common militia to march immediately to reinforce the hundreds of militiamen already at Sackett's Harbor. He also sent Lt. Col. Washington Irving there with discretionary authority to order out militia and to give any other orders necessary to defend the post.[57] Irving spent six days at Sackett's Harbor, meeting with Commodore Chauncey and other officers. These officials reassured Irving that the emergency had passed. During this time, it is very likely that Irving met Brevet Maj. Ichabod Crane of the regular artillery. The author tucked that peculiar name into his pocket, to reappear in 1820 with the publication of *The Legend of Sleepy Hollow*. No doubt, Crane was mortified to read his name associated with such an odd character. Nevertheless, the War Department saw Crane's obvious talents and promoted him to colonel after the war.

On October 1, the members of the Committee of Defence noted in a letter to Congressman William Irving that they felt "in common with every citizen, great anxiety for the safety of this metropolis, and being convinced from daily experience of the total incompetence of the present commander, as well as the entire want of confidence in him."[58] Morgan Lewis had to go. On October 14, Secretary of War Monroe replaced General Lewis with Governor Tompkins as commander of the Third Military District.[59]

Apparently, this move was not a surprise to the governor or his staff. In a letter to his congressman brother written on October 14, Washington Irving said, "Tompkins is absolutely one of the worthiest men I ever knew. I find him honest, candid, prompt, indefatigable, with a greater stock of practical good sense and ready talent than I had any idea he possessed, and of nerve to put into immediate execution any measure that he is satisfied is correct. I expect he will have the command here in a few days, in which case my situation will be everything I could wish."[60]

Tompkins assumed command on October 23 and arrived in New York City on October 28. General John Boyd continued in command of the regulars in the district. Tompkins remained a civilian; the president did not commission him a major general. Tompkins was in a novel situation. Half of New Jersey was within the Third Military District. Thus, several thousand New Jersey militiamen were now under the command of the governor of New York. Fortunately, this anomaly did not result in any loss of effectiveness.

Tompkins was now dual-hatted. He remained commander in chief of the state militia as well as commander of an important military district. Finally, he was in a position to cut through the bureaucratic barriers that had so often impeded the transfer of resources between federal and state organizations. As recently as September 29, he had complained of these inefficiencies to the secretary of war. It appeared that Monroe's appointment of Tompkins was in direct response to the governor's dissatisfaction as well as that of the city's Committee of Defence.[61]

Tompkins immediately addressed issues that his predecessor had neglected. The day after taking command, he wrote a letter to the secretary of war asking that Monroe replace the current deputy quartermaster general for incompetence and to complain that the contractor for rations was habitually providing bread that was "truly offensive & unhealthy."[62] Tompkins spent the following week consulting with Governor Pennington and Commodore Decatur and inspecting defenses.

Tompkins believed the war would continue into 1815. Of the reports arriving from Ghent, Tompkins remarked, "They furnish no hopes of a speedy peace. So far from it, there is reason to believe, that a very formidable armament is preparing to assail some point of our seaboard."[63] Monroe was of the same mind. He reported to the Senate that "there was reason to presume that it is the [British] intention to press the war from Canada on the adjoining States, while attempts are made of the city of New York, and other important points."[64]

Looking to the future, Tompkins and the state legislature passed an act authorizing two infantry regiments of African Americans, both free and slave. Tompkins intended that the state would pay the enlistment bounty, but the federal government would take the regiments into federal service. Slaveowners who agreed to release their men into service would receive the bounty and pay, but the soldier would receive his freedom upon completion of his service. No records exist as to the state of recruiting when the war ended.[65]

During one of his many inspection tours, the governor suffered a mishap. On November 3, Tompkins visited Fort Greene, on Brooklyn Heights. As he crossed the causeway leading to the fort on horseback, the soldiers guarding the gate gave a loud cheer. In the recollection of Washington Irving, the horse "gave a pirouette," throwing the governor into the ditch. Initially, Tompkins complained only of a sprained thumb and "a sudden sickness of the stomach." However, the injuries plagued Tompkins throughout the remainder of his life.[66]

Construction was proceeding on fortifications to challenge a naval attack on the city. At the Narrows, several forts and batteries mounted heavy guns to turn back or damage an attack by the Royal Navy. Nearly one hundred guns, from 18- through 32-pounder cannon, were positioned on Staten Island. Forts Hudson and Richmond were close to shore, and the defenders were concerned that the British would land a force to take these two defensive works before the attacking squadron entered the Narrows. Fort Tompkins guarded the land approaches to the shore defenses; however, by September, Fort Tompkins was only partially completed. On Long Island, the federal government erected Fort Diamond on Hendrick's Reef across the Narrows from Fort Richmond. An attacking squadron would pass through a crossfire.[67] In July, Mayor Clinton and other dignitaries had laid the cornerstone to Fort Stevens on the Long Island side of Hell Gate. It would take months to complete the fortification and mount the guns.

One of Tompkins's prerogatives was to name some of the new fortifications. He chose to honor two of the heroes of the Left Division, both of whom fell at the head of their soldiers in the sortie from Fort Erie on September 17. Tompkins named the Ellis Island fortification Fort Gibson after Col. James Gibson, commander of the Fourth Rifle Regiment. He honored fellow New Yorker Brevet Lt. Col. Eleazar Wood by naming the fortification on Bedloe's Island after him. Today, Fort Wood continues to serve as the base of the Statue of Liberty.

The U.S. Navy was also heavily committed to the defense of the state and New York City. In October, Secretary of the Navy William Jones reported to President Madison that 1,300 sailors were stationed in and around the city. Adding the crewmen on Lakes Ontario and Champlain, more than 4,100 seamen were operating around the state, 40 percent of the entire strength of the Navy Department.[68]

In 1814, work on Fulton's steam warship continued with energy in light of the perceived possibility of attack. The Department of the Navy provided $95,000 to build the steam-powered battery. However, $80,000 of that amount was in treasury notes, a medium of exchange not readily accepted by contractors or useful for workers' wages. City banks had loaned considerable currency for the city's defense, but by September they were unwilling to provide cash for treasury notes. Fortunately, the Common Council accepted the notes and provided cash from the city treasury to pay contractors and the 260 workers. Congress eventually appropriated $500,000 to hurry the project along. Fulton accepted no wages for superintending construction. The builders, Adam and Noah Brown, launched the vessel in October. The Navy gave command of the new ship, which the Navy named *Fulton the First*, to Capt. David Porter. Fulton preferred the name *Demologos*—Voice of the People. Workers mounted the 120-horsepower steam engine in November. The twenty heavy guns had not yet been cast, and the warship was not ready for deployment until the following May. One can only imagine the scale of combat and carnage had the British attempted an attack on the city in 1815.[69]

The privateering effort had failed to achieve the results Thomas Jefferson had once predicted. Two hundred and forty-six privateers sailed under the American flag and took nearly two thousand cargo ships. However, only 762 of the captured ships made it back to port and a prize court. The forty-four privateers home-ported in New York City took 401 ships, but only 149 were declared prizes by a court. Still, some of the captains and crews became heroes. On September 9, Capt. Samuel C. Reid sailed *General Armstrong* eastward through the blockade and into celebrity. On September 26, the privateer arrived in the Azores port of Fayal, under Portuguese governance. Noting the arrival of three Royal Navy vessels, Reid cautiously anchored under the guns of a Portuguese fort. Portugal was neutral in the war between Britain and the United States, and Reid expected protection from the Portuguese government. None was forthcoming. In the dark, about four hundred sailors and royal marines approached *General Armstrong* in several boats. In the resulting firefight, the crew of the privateer drove off the attackers, inflicting about 120 casualties and suffering very few in return. However, Reid decided to burn his badly damaged ship rather than allow it to fall into the hands of the British. Reid and his men escaped; however, the diplomatic furor over the charge that Portugal and Britain had both violated Portugal's neutrality lasted for twenty years. New York City and New York State recognized Reid and his men for the heroes they were and honored them the following year. Reid also achieved another sort of celebrity by originating the design for the American flag, allocating a star for each state but only thirteen stripes. This design was made official with the Flag Act of 1818.[70]

As summer faded into fall, the Royal Navy still had the power to raid the city. Based upon reports from Ghent, James Monroe warned Congress in October that Britain was intent "to diminish the importance, if not to destroy the political existence, of the United States." The British demands included creation of an Indian state north of the Ohio River, removing the American naval and military presence on the Great Lakes, the cession of a large part of Maine, and the right of navigation on the Mississippi River. Monroe continued, "There is also reason to presume that it is the intention to press the war from Canada on the adjoining States, while attempts are made on the city of New York, and other important points, with a view to the vain project of dismemberment or subjugation." Monroe pressed Congress to enlarge the army to 100,000 soldiers.[71]

Defensive preparations continued until mid-November. Volunteer citizens, militiamen, and military engineers ringed New York City with masonry and earthen fortifications and blockhouses. These fortifications mounted about 570 guns and mortars. Additionally, hundreds of cannon were assigned to artillery companies or fitted on vessels in the harbor.[72] The city was prepared to stand off any British assault from any direction.

Tompkins was justifiably proud of the contributions of the militia to the successful defense of the state during the crisis. He also recognized that leaders at all levels had overcome their party differences during the emergency. Tompkins reported to the legislature, "The present time will form a proud era in the history of this state. It will develop the vastness of her resources, the strength of her population, the intelligence and liberality of her legislative bodies, and the valor and patriotism of her citizens." Both houses of the Republican-dominated legislature validated Tompkins's leadership. In its response to the governor, the Senate noted "with great satisfaction the prompt & efficacious measures adopted by your Excellency, to avert the dangers which threatened the State." The Assembly found "ample cause for approbation of the measures pursued & the powers exercised by your Excellency to defeat the daring purposes of the arrogant invader."[73]

In late November, Tompkins ordered regular troops into winter quarters and began mustering approximately 25,000 militiamen out of federal service.[74] The military crisis had passed. With the national treasury empty, the issue of paying the militia remained. Tompkins approached the Common Council of New York City with a proposal. He requested that the council loan the federal government $400,000 to pay militiamen. Tompkins personally pledged to provide federal treasury notes within six months as collateral. Mayor DeWitt Clinton and the Common Council approved the transaction. Tompkins also negotiated loans totaling $200,000 from New York City banks and sent the details to Secretary of War Monroe for his approval.[75]

The city celebrated perhaps the most joyous Evacuation Day in years on November 25. Solomon Van Rensselaer wrote to his wife that ten thousand troops participated in the parade.[76] Shortly after the march, the militia began turning in weapons, tents, and camp equipment to the federal and state arsenals.

This undertaking was a challenge for the men, their officers, and the too-few quartermaster officers overseeing these activities. Once weapons were back in the arsenals, the armorers had a few months to repair weaponry for the anticipated reissue the following spring. The militiamen would be home by Christmas.

However, the threat to New York was not yet over. Rumors reached the president that Federalist delegates of the New England states would hold a convention in Hartford, Connecticut, to explore possible amendments to the federal constitution. Madison suspected a more sinister purpose. In a letter to Wilson Cary Nicholas, governor of Virginia, Madison declared the New England Federalists "the source of our greatest difficulties in carrying on the war, as it certainly is the greatest, if not the sole, inducement with the enemy to persevere in it." Moreover, were these disgruntled Federalists discussing secession? Madison warned Tompkins that 6,000 British troops had departed Canada with the intention of landing on Long Island, perhaps to assist New England's secession. Secretary of War Monroe directed Maj. Gen. Izard at Buffalo to send 1,000 troops to Greenbush to respond to a British invasion. Additionally, the secretary of war sent Brevet Col. Thomas Jesup to Hartford, ostensibly to recruit for his depleted regiment. However, Monroe actually sent him to spy upon the Federalist meeting. Monroe directed Jesup to coordinate with Tompkins for the use of militia to put down rebellion if such was in the offing. Madison had further taken the precaution to direct Jesup to coordinate his activities with Henry Leavenworth to secure the federal arsenal at Springfield in order to keep it out of Federalist hands.[77]

Madison's fears were not entirely unfounded. Governor Caleb Strong of Massachusetts sent an emissary to Lieutenant Governor Sir John Sherbrooke in Nova Scotia. Should the meeting of delegates at Hartford result in conflict, queried Strong, would the British lend military assistance? Strong was in essence testing the waters for a political secession of the New England states from the union and seeking a separate peace with Britain. Strong's actions were treasonous; however, they reflected the deep dissatisfaction of New England Federalists with the costly war. Sherbrooke sent the question to London. Bathurst was open to the possibilities, but treaty negotiations in Ghent rendered the proposal moot. Fortunately for the nation, the Hartford Convention broke up in early January without proposing secession.[78]

Tompkins departed New York City on Christmas Day to see his family and then go on to Lake Champlain. No one in America could have been aware that negotiators in Ghent had just signed the peace treaty. Tompkins placed General Boyd in acting command of the Third Military District.[79] Regular army troops were in winter quarters on the Niagara frontier, Sackett's Harbor, and Plattsburgh. Except for those at Fort Niagara, no British forces were in the state.

As the year rolled over, Stephen Decatur was determined to evade the blockade of New York City with his small squadron led by the frigate *President*. Many of the officers and crew were New Yorkers. While egressing the Lower Bay on January 14, 1815, Decatur's pilots missed the channel, and *President* stuck on the sandbar opposite Sandy Hook. This misfortune gave the British frigates *Endymion* and *Majestic* and two other blockading vessels time to confront *President*. With overwhelming odds against them, Decatur and his crew put up a fight. After suffering eighty dead and wounded, Decatur surrendered. The two other warships in Decatur's squadron escaped. Master Commandant James Biddle commanded the sloop *Hornet*. Biddle and his crew met and outfought H.M. Sloop *Penguin* on March 23, 1815, in the South Atlantic. Master Commandant Lewis Warrington of the sloop *Peacock* captured H.M. Brig *Nautilus* off Java in June. The captain of *Nautilus* attempted to convince Warrington that the war was over, but the American opened fire, nevertheless. This encounter was the last naval action of the war.

The crisis of 1814 prompted closer cooperation between state and federal authorities. Both Tompkins and Madison realized the potentially existential nature of the threat to the state and nation. Would the United States retain its sovereignty and its borders? In putting every militiaman on alert for immediate deployment, and granting authority to subordinate commanders to call out their men, Tompkins energized the populace. In a brilliant move, Madison gave Tompkins full authority over all troops—regulars, volunteers, and militia—to defend New York City. Tompkins also enjoyed a professional working relationship with the naval commanders. Finally, unity of command existed. Tompkins personally visited units, transmitting to the soldiers and sailors his fierce determination to prevail regardless of obstacles. Mayor Clinton, the Common Council, and even Federalist leaders were fully engaged in preparing the populace for what they anticipated to be the most important fight of the war. In December 1814, the conflict had moved on to the Gulf Coast. While no one knew it at the time, New York's war was over.

1815

CHAPTER 18

PEACE

In July 1814, Vice Admiral Sir Alexander Cochrane, in a letter to Secretary of State for War and the Colonies Earl Bathurst, proclaimed that he intended to give the Americans a "complete drubbing before peace was made." Cochrane was echoing a popular theme in Britain that America had stabbed Britain in the back while it was battling the ogre Napoleon. However, setbacks at Plattsburgh, the Niagara frontier, and Baltimore suggested that the war would continue into 1815. Dissatisfied with Governor General Sir George Prevost, Prime Minister Lord Liverpool tentatively offered command to the Duke of Wellington, then ambassador to France. Wellington responded on November 9 with a reasoned analysis. British forces could not carry the war deeper into America without "a Naval superiority on the Lakes." Wellington concluded that the negotiators in Ghent could not "on any principle of equality in negotiation, claim a cession of territory." The British cabinet studied Wellington's response and the deteriorating situation in Europe. Negotiations with European leaders in Vienna were not going in Britain's favor. Circumstances in defeated France were explosive. A war between the erstwhile coalition partners was not out of the question. Continuing the war in America would mean new and unpopular taxes. Liverpool sent instructions to his negotiating team in Ghent authorizing a move to a quick peace in which no territory changed hands. The negotiators signed a treaty on Christmas Eve. The American victories of September had proven decisive.[1]

In New York, word of the peace treaty had not reached the United States when the Republican-majority state legislature opened on January 31. The Assembly appointed four Republicans to the Council of Appointment, which proceeded to the replacement of hundreds of Federalist officials with Republicans. Among the members of the new council was Farrand Stranahan, regimental commander at the Battle of Queenston Heights. The council also perpetuated the split within the Republican Party by replacing DeWitt Clinton as mayor of New York with John Ferguson, grand sachem of the Tammany Society. The council also selected Brig. Gen. Peter B. Porter to be New York's secretary of state. The Council of Appointment furthermore confirmed Tompkins's nomination of Porter to be a major general in the militia. In a well-deserved action, the council appointed Col. Jonathan Williams to the rank of militia brigadier general. Williams had been at the center of design and construction of the defenses of New York City's waterways.[2]

On February 6, 1815, the city learned of Jackson's decisive victory at New Orleans. Five days later, British sloop of war *Favorite* passed the Narrows and sent a boat to shore carrying the unexpected news that a treaty had been signed. The city exploded spontaneously in celebration. Adelia Cooper of Brooklyn remembered, "People rushed into the streets in an ecstasy of delight, cannon thundered, bells rang, bonfires were lighted, houses illuminated, and flags were unfurled from steeple and dome, strong men wept and grasped each other by the hand—others fell upon their knees in heartfelt prayer." Peter B. Porter proclaimed the terms of the "peace of December 1814 honourable to both parties, and which it is to be hoped will not soon be again disturbed." People hoped for a quick return to normalcy and prosperity.[3]

City officials sent an express rider to Albany to inform the governor, reaching him on February 13. Like New York City, Albany erupted upon receiving the gratifying news. The *Albany Register* hailed "with joy indescribable the first glimmering of returning peace and prosperity to our suffering country." However, peace would not be official until the U.S. Senate ratified the treaty and the president signed it into law. Without a dissenting vote, the Senate approved the treaty on February 16 and President Madison signed it the following day. It was February 17; the war was officially over.[4]

Once word reached New York City that peace was formally approved by both belligerents, city officials planned a proper celebration to commence on Washington's birthday, February 22. However, a major storm arrived that forced the Common Council to postpone the celebration until February 27. A partisan storm had arrived as well. Federalists had appropriated Washington's birthday as their day of annual dinners and parades. Several city Republicans announced they would boycott the celebration on February 22. The snowstorm resolved the issue. At noon on February 27, soldiers fired artillery, and churchmen rang their bells for one hour. At 7 P.M., the citizenry illuminated homes, churches, government facilities, and businesses. Fireworks added to the light show, which ended at 10 P.M. Thousands of visitors ventured into the city for the festivities. City officials prohibited horses or carriages from the streets during these three hours of revelry. The Common Council encouraged everyone to attend church services that day to "offer up to the Great Ruler of nations their sincere thanksgivings for the restoration of peace to our country, and to humbly implore His blessings upon it."[5]

The state capital celebrated on Washington's birthday. The *Albany Argus* reported, "At least one hundred and thirty thousand lights, several transparencies, and a display of fire-works from the hills, combined to render the scene at once noble, brilliant and grand." The *Albany Register* recounted that Gen. Stephen Van Rensselaer sponsored a mural displayed at the Eagle Tavern of Britannia and America grasping hands. "On the ground lay their arms, whilst the genius of Peace directed their attention to that word, written in rays of glory, above her head."[6]

Governor Tompkins ordered the militia to join in the celebrations. As commander of the Third Military District, he directed his commanders in and around the harbor to fire artillery on February 25. In the general order announcing the peace, he stated that he could not "but hope that the accomplishment of an honorable peace, the smiles of an approving conscience and the gratitude of a virtuous and patriotic people will be regarded by them as an ample award for their many sacrifices." Of course, many hundreds of militiamen were still awaiting their pay, and federal paymasters had insufficient funds. DeWitt Clinton persuaded the Common Council to provide funds to pay off the militiamen. The *Albany Register* noted that despite the lion's share of the credit for the defense of the city falling to the governor, Clinton remained "one of the main pillars of the American cause."[7]

In the minds of Americans, the string of victories starting in September—Plattsburgh and Lake Champlain, Fort Erie, Baltimore, and now New Orleans—conflated with the news of peace, framed the enduring notion that America had won its second war with Britain. The Federalist Party had been slowly dying before the commencement of war. With war, the party became home for citizens protesting the conflict. The Federalist Party never rid itself entirely of the accusation of treason resulting from the Hartford Convention. New York Federalists did not send voting members to the convention; they had witnessed the transition of New York voters toward the Republicans in the spring elections. The 1815 state elections saw an increase in Federalists in the legislature; however, Republicans continued to enjoy majorities in both houses.

The war increased the number of New York City's impoverished. Between April 1, 1812, and April 1, 1813, the city provided some form of relief for 8,253 persons. For the year ending April 1, 1815, that number had jumped to 19,078, more than one-fifth of the city's population. With the news of peace, prices of food and merchandise in the city dropped precipitously in a matter of days. When soldiers of the regular army left the service in May 1815, they collected bonuses and land grants. Many sold their land grants to speculators for fast cash. Militiamen received no bonuses or grants of land.[8]

Tompkins requested relief from command of the Third Military District. The new secretary of war, A. J. Dallas, released Tompkins on April 10. In his brief note to Tompkins, Dallas wrote, "It is with great pleasure that I add an expression of the President's thanks for the patriotic, active, and able support which you have on all occasions given to the measures of the Government, during the late war."[9]

The fires that destroyed the settlements along the Niagara River had hardly burned out before the state and various nongovernment sources provided assistance and restitution. In April 1816, Congress passed an act to cover property losses due to the government's actions. Congress received 158 claims for restitution. British General Riall had openly proclaimed that he intended to destroy structures on the American side of the river. Thousands of militiamen arrived in Buffalo and Black Rock after the capture of Fort Niagara. Gen. Amos Hall had authorized militiamen to occupy private homes. Cyrenius Chapin recalled, "In most instances, the owners of the houses were compelled, against their wishes, to receive troops and public stores into their houses." The Committee of Claims recognized that the British had a right to destroy private buildings used as barracks. The question for the committee was to judge whether the buildings burned were done so legally. Unable to discriminate between homes that had been used as shelter for only a few days or not at all, or whether usage was the result of government action, the committee was unwilling to split hairs: "Although the claimants have no legal demands upon the government, the committee are of the opinion, that it would ill comport with the munificent character of the country, to entirely withhold relief in a case of such extreme suffering." However, the committee found the number of claims to be "enormously high." The committee recommended restitution of 50 percent claimed for buildings and 30 percent for personal property, but nothing for retail merchandise.[10]

Congressional action to provide relief ran parallel to state efforts. New York asked that the federal government assume responsibility for the grants and loans the state made, which amounted to $100,000. In 1825, Congress amended the 1816 act to do so. The victims had been generally slow to repay the loans, understandable in view of the postwar economy. The 1825 act opened up twenty years of accounting chaos between the U.S. Treasury and the New York Comptroller's Office. Although the U.S. Treasury made an initial wave of payments in 1827, it dragged its feet in reimbursing New York for getting cash to the victims to rebuild their homes, farms, and lives. Eventually, most claims were settled.[11]

As for the Six Nations, the president directed that the families of fallen warriors receive $200, with lesser amounts for disabled warriors. For the Tuscarora whose settlement was burned in 1813, Secretary of War Monroe ordered Erastus Granger to issue provisions until the 1815 crop was harvested. However, the 1815 and 1816 harvests were insufficient, and federal annuities arrived late. Writing of the plight of all the natives along the Niagara frontier, Granger reported to the War Department, "They are in fact in a state of starvation." In 1817, the War Department distributed $7,650 to the Tuscarora in compensation for their lost homes. Still, the Iroquois, whom Granger acknowledged gave loyal service to the United States, were left out of the general prosperity experienced by their white neighbors.[12]

Congress and the military services recognized military officers for their noteworthy achievements. Congress honored military service in three forms. In ascending order, these were the Thanks of Congress, a Congressional Sword, and the Gold Medal. Congress awarded twenty-seven gold medals for service during the war. Three of these went to New Yorkers: Generals Jacob Brown, Peter B. Porter, and Alexander Macomb. Congress awarded gold medals to fifteen naval officers, none of whom were New Yorkers.[13]

A more common recognition of exceptional service in the Army and the Marine Corps was brevet promotion. An officer who had been recognized with a brevet promotion wore the insignia of the brevet rank and was addressed as such. However, he continued to receive the lower pay of his permanent rank. The War Department awarded a total of 122 brevet promotions, most for instances of battlefield gallantry and a few for meritorious service over a period of time. Awards for gallantry had an effective date of the combat action, while the War Department selected the effective date for brevets for meritorious service. The Army awarded seventy-six brevet promotions for the campaign on the Niagara River and twelve more for the Battle of Plattsburgh.

Of the 122 brevetted officers, nineteen, or 16 percent, were officers from New York. Not all of these soldiers had been born in the state. For example, Patrick O'Flyng was born in Ireland, but he was a New Yorker when commissioned. Of all 122 officers, sixteen were awarded two brevets. A disproportionate number of New Yorkers— five—were among the courageous sixteen.[14]

Brig. Gen. Alexander Macomb received a brevet promotion to major general for "distinguished and gallant conduct in defeating the enemy at Plattsburgh."

Maj. George Bomford, who graduated from West Point in 1804, was brevetted to the rank of lieutenant colonel effective December 22, 1814, for "meritorious service in the ordnance department." Bomford invented the "Bomb Cannon" used during the war and more commonly known as the Columbiad Cannon.[15]

Maj. John E. Wool received his brevet promotion to lieutenant colonel for "gallant conduct" at Plattsburgh.

Maj. Henry Leavenworth received two brevets. The first was a brevet promotion to lieutenant colonel for "distinguished service" at Chippawa. The second was to the rank of brevet colonel for "distinguished service" at Lundy's Lane.

Capt. Ichabod B. Crane resigned his commission as first lieutenant in the Marine Corps in 1812 to accept a captaincy in the army. He received a brevet promotion to major, effective November 13, 1813, for "meritorious service and general good conduct."

Capt. White Youngs received his brevet promotion to major for "gallant conduct" at Plattsburgh.

Capt. Benjamin Birdsall was brevetted to the rank of major for "distinguished service in the defense of Fort Erie."

Capt. Gerard D. Smith received brevet promotion to major, effective July 25, 1814, for "distinguished service" at Lundy's Lane.

Lt. William Jenkins Worth received two brevet promotions. The first was to the brevet rank of captain for "gallant and distinguished conduct" at Chippawa. The second was a brevet promotion to major for "gallant and good conduct" at Lundy's Lane.

West Point graduate Capt. Eleazar D. Wood received two brevet promotions. The War Department brevetted him to major for "distinguished service in the defense of Fort Meigs" and to lieutenant colonel for "gallant conduct" at Lundy's Lane.

First Lt. Donald Fraser was also honored with two brevet promotions. The first promotion was to the rank of captain for "gallant conduct" at Lundy's Lane, and the second was to the rank of major for "gallant conduct" at the sortie from Fort Erie.

First Lt. René E. De Russey, of the West Point Class of 1812, received a brevet promotion to captain for "gallant conduct" at Plattsburgh. De Russey went on to serve as the superintendent of the Military Academy from 1833 to 1838.

First Lt. Chester Root earned his promotion to brevet captain for "gallant conduct" at Plattsburgh.

First Lt. John P. Livingston received his brevet promotion to captain for "distinguished service" at Lundy's Lane.

First Lt. David B. Douglass received a brevet promotion to captain for "distinguished and meritorious service during the siege of Fort Erie."

Second Lt. George Watts earned his brevet promotion to first lieutenant for "gallant and distinguished service" at the Battle of Chippawa.

Second Lt. John J. Cromwell received a brevet to first lieutenant for "gallant and good conduct in action at Plattsburgh."

Second Lt. John P. Dietrich was born in Germany. He received a brevet promotion to first lieutenant for "distinguished and meritorious service," effective on February 5, 1815.

Third Lt. Patrick O'Flyng, born in Ireland, was honored with two brevet promotions. The first was to second lieutenant for "distinguished conduct in defense of Fort Erie" and the other to first lieutenant for "gallant conduct in the sortie from Fort Erie."

Brevet promotion influenced retention as the army demobilized in 1815. Madison directed that the number of regular army officers, ensign through colonel, be reduced from 2,271 to 489, a 78 percent reduction. The board selecting officers for retention apparently saw brevet promotion as a discriminator. Of the 122 officers honored with brevets during the war, forty-nine were still in the army in 1822.[16]

The seven regular army infantry regiments raised wholly or largely in New York were amalgamated in the spring of 1815 into a much smaller army. New York, unsurprisingly, had raised the most of the forty-six infantry regiments in the United States. Massachusetts, with the second most, had raised six infantry regiments. New York provided a larger number of recruits for the regular army than any other state, and only Vermont provided proportionately more recruits based upon comparative populations.[17]

What was the comparative size of the contribution of the state militia during the war? Secretary of War John C. Calhoun reported to Congress in 1820 that the War Department had paid for 410,603 "periods of service" rendered during 1812–15. That is not to say that this was the number of militiamen who had served. Some citizens served multiple periods of service, while others never mustered into service. A period of service could range anywhere from a few days to a few months. New York militiamen served 76,668 periods of service, or 19 percent of the total. Included in the ranks of the militia were nearly 1,300 state sea fencibles called into federal service starting in August 1814. Only Virginia militiamen served more periods of service, with 88,584, or 22 percent of the total.[18]

Another metric to reflect the length of tours is payroll. The War Department paid $12,618,967 for militia service, of which 15 percent went to New York militiamen. Virginia militiamen received 20 percent of the payroll. Clearly, New York militiamen were much more likely to see fighting than their Virginia counterparts. Yet, why was the Virginia militia effort greater in terms of numbers and payroll? Virginia had a more vulnerable seacoast than New York, and the Royal Navy posed a very great threat of raids, especially in Chesapeake Bay. Given the Royal Navy's ability to strike pretty much at will, defense of the seacoast, bays, and rivers required a large number of militiamen on constant duty.[19]

What was the contribution of the militia to the war effort? New York State's militia organization provided a vast pool of potential recruits for volunteer and regular units. If a militiaman served a substantial period of service, then he was introduced to the hardships of service as well as the routines of camp life, military discipline, some level of training, and possibly combat. He could then better calculate the pros and cons of enlistment in a volunteer or regular unit. The vast number of officers in the new regular regiments had prior service as militia officers.

While the militia's combat record was mixed at best, on some occasions militiamen served admirably. The sortie from Fort Erie, where much of the fighting was at close range, was demonstrative of the willingness of hundreds of militiamen to cross the international border and to engage regular British soldiers. British authorities did not consider New York City to be a vulnerable target largely because of the extensive fortifications manned by thousands of militiamen as well as smaller numbers of regulars and volunteers. Moreover, the British generally considered American units to be brittle, and the militia to be the most fragile. Yet, British officers had to take into consideration that each engagement would cost the lives of their soldiers, sailors, and marines. It did not matter that the British might inflict far more casualties than they might receive. Unlike British regulars, Americans were available in endless numbers. In 1814, when Bathurst warned Prevost not to move too deeply into the interior of the state, the memory of Saratoga, in which the entire British force was captured and interned, was still fresh in London.

Militia service was symbolic of a free man's commitment to defend his hearth and home. All along the northern and western frontiers, large numbers of militiamen turned out on short notice to protect their communities from attack. British raiders were well aware that they could not remain too long on a mission; within a day hundreds of militiamen would arrive to drive them off. Those citizens who served would be elevated in stature by their neighbors long after the guns fell silent.

Many regular commanders preferred the services of volunteer units, as these soldiers were true volunteers, and many, if not most, had been members of uniformed companies prior to the war. Their period of service could be as long as twelve months, and federal generals could order volunteers to cross international borders. Nearly 4,100 New Yorkers served as federal volunteers during the war, most of them in artillery units. New York's contribution to the war effort in manpower—militia, federal volunteers, regular army—was impressive, and no doubt contributed meaningfully to the results of the war.[20]

Over the years, the state and New York City worked to recoup their expenditures from the national government. In its final report, in November 1815, the

Common Council's Committee of Defence noted that the Treasury Department had paid the city more than $1,150,000 for the city's expenses in fortifying the city and harbor. The committee was proud of the efforts of all concerned in preserving the city "probably from the unhappy fate of the seat of our National Government." The report claimed that had the British attacked, "they would have met with as gallant a repulse as they experienced at New Orleans."[21]

After the war, the lives of various New Yorkers moved along diverse trajectories:

Daniel D. Tompkins. In February 1816, Governor Tompkins addressed the legislature for the first time since the end of the war. Americans were well aware that their republic had made war upon a monarchy, and many speculated that fighting a monarchy had put the United States at a critical disadvantage. A monarchy consolidated power and authority and thus might be more efficient than a federation of eighteen states. Tompkins observed that the war "has presented, with some triumph to the world, the refutation of an opinion which denied to republics a capacity to resist the assaults of exterior hostility." Had Tompkins intentionally overlooked the number of outcomes in which a monarchy had vanquished a republic? No one knew better than he the inefficiencies of federal–state cooperation. More likely Tompkins was proudly validating Republican ideology.[22]

Turning his attention to the future, Tompkins urged the legislature to establish high-quality roads connecting rivers and lakes. The war had demonstrated the enormous costs in transporting supplies over inferior roads. Tompkins prevailed upon the lawmakers to support the expansion of manufacturing so that the state would become increasingly self-sufficient. The British blockade made evident the state's dependence upon foreign-made goods. Tompkins closed his address by recommending that the citizenry divest itself of "that spirit of party which has heretofore jeopardized the best interests of the country, and which, if persisted in, may ultimately involve us in those deplorable scenes, by which modern Europe has been convulsed and almost desolated." Tompkins gloried in American exceptionalism. He easily won reelection in April.[23]

While New York's Republican senators and congressmen lobbied for Tompkins's nomination to the presidency, his well-known opposition to slavery made him an unsatisfactory candidate. He was, however, the vice presidential candidate. He won alongside James Monroe in the fall of 1816 and resigned the governorship on February 24, 1817. One of his last political acts in Albany was to urge the state to abolish all slavery on July 4, 1827. The legislature passed an act to that effect. The State Assembly praised Tompkins for his tireless efforts to prepare for war: "Those borders, which, during our revolutionary struggle, were the seat of merciless warfare, and which, were again exposed to similar devastations, were rendered through your early solicitude, not only able to sustain the pressure of an enemy, but to retaliate upon him the ravages he might venture to perpetrate."[24]

In the postwar period, Tompkins was plagued by the injury sustained when he was thrown from his horse in 1814. As the pain worsened, he neglected his vice-presidential duties, preferring to remain at his grand home on Staten Island in a neighborhood now known as Tompkinsville. In July 1817, he wrote to an associate, "My present prospect is that kind of affliction and confinement for the residue of my life. I shall probably resign the office of Vice President at the next session, if not sooner, as there is very little hope of my ever being able to perform its duties hereafter."[25] However, his health improved sufficiently for him to return to public life in a limited way.

Tompkins was also caught up in a substantial and lingering financial scandal. Soon after Tompkins took office in Washington, the state comptroller, Archibald McIntyre, noted that the former governor was in default with the state treasury for $120,000. Tompkins had political enemies, particularly the supporters of DeWitt Clinton. They made the most of Tompkins's embarrassment. The federal government was responsible for feeding and paying the militia that was requisitioned by the War Department. However, since the federal treasury was all but empty, the state covered costs and expected reimbursement. Since Tompkins was the general disbursing officer, it was incumbent upon him to maintain accurate receipts or vouchers. In this duty, he had been careless.[26]

Tompkins could not produce vouchers for many of his disbursements of state funds. It is most likely that the governor simply failed to prepare or to acquire a receipt signature for many of his vouchers. He did not aggressively pursue subordinates who made disbursements, such as militia paymasters. Tompkins carried on a fierce defense of his finance activities with McIntyre, who just as fiercely attacked the vice president. Because the state comptroller would not clear Tompkins's account, the legislature stepped in. A joint committee of the Senate and the Assembly examined thousands of vouchers and reported that 257 vouchers were irregularly prepared. Nonetheless, in 1819, the committee recommended that the state settle the issue largely in Tompkins's favor, and in 1821, the legislature agreed.

With the support of the Tammany Club, Tompkins ran unsuccessfully against Governor DeWitt Clinton in the 1820 gubernatorial election. His financial difficulties had both cast a shadow on his reputation and ruined his credit. His drinking increased dramatically, due no doubt to his money worries and his loss to Clinton. In 1821, and while vice president, Tompkins was selected to serve as the president of New York's constitutional convention. He treasured this honor.[27]

Tompkins also had financial issues with the federal government over money he lent it while federal credit was at its lowest. He won a judgment in U.S. District Court in 1822 that vindicated his financial transactions. Now it was up to Congress and the president to make restitution. The House of Representatives formed a committee chaired by Louis McLane to resolve the issue. In his 1823 report, McLane stated, "We all know his services which at a very dark and gloomy period were exceedingly patriotic to his country and disinterested. We all know that at a moment when others were husbanding their funds or dealing them out with a very scanty hand, this man risked everything for the public cause and staked his private fortune in its support. It is to services thus rendered that his present embarrassment may be traced."[28] Tompkins received a partial payment to settle his most pressing debts. However, it was years after his death before the federal government paid all that it owed him.

Tompkins was physically and emotionally damaged, largely due to the stress of ten years of financial worry. He died in 1825 at the age of fifty and just three months after leaving the vice presidency. He is buried in Manhattan at St. Mark's Church in-the-Bowery. Tompkins was the only vice president in the nineteenth century to serve two terms under the same president.

Tompkins was the driving force that prepared the state for war and supported the federal government in its prosecution. Geography placed New York state at the center of the conflict. Over five years, Tompkins took deliberate steps to improve the militia and the fortification of America's largest city and commercial center. He navigated state politics to squeeze the most from a reluctant legislature. When conflict came, Tompkins was fiercely proactive, in stark contrast to a federal government that was shockingly incompetent to wage a war that it had brought upon itself. Tompkins spent state funds as well as his own personal money as federal resources repeatedly failed to meet the needs of war. Tompkins is a forgotten man today, but in his time, he was a selfless patriot and a magnanimous leader.

DeWitt Clinton. After the war, DeWitt Clinton was elected three times as governor. In his first reelection in 1820, he defeated Vice President Tompkins by a slender majority. He is best known for championing a bill to fund construction of the Erie Canal. Detractors derided the project as "DeWitt's Ditch" and "Clinton's Folly." However, once its 363 miles opened, Clinton basked in the glory of the canal's engineering and economic triumph. Perhaps no infrastructure in the state better served to lower the cost of transportation, open up the interior to development, and propagate commerce statewide. He died in office suddenly in 1828 at the age of fifty-eight. His final resting place is the Green-Wood Cemetery in Brooklyn.

Robert Fulton. The inventor was a hero to New Yorkers for his tireless work preparing the defenses of their city. In February 1815, Fulton and a friend were crossing to New Jersey on the ice. His friend broke through, and Fulton pulled him out. However, the inventor contracted a respiratory infection and died in a few days at the age of forty-nine. He left a widow and four children. New Yorkers held his funeral on February 25. His warship, *Demologos*, blew up in 1829 as a result of an explosion in the magazine. It was a total loss. Today, Fulton is remembered for his work in commercial steamboats; however, his contribution to naval warfare was immense.[29]

Stephen Van Rensselaer. The last Patroon of Rensselaerswyck continued to serve his nation following the war. He was a supporter of John Quincy Adams and was elected to the U.S. House of Representatives, where he served for seven years. Van Rensselaer was also a civic activist, supporter of the arts, and philanthropist. He was an avid supporter of the Erie Canal, having served many years on the Erie Canal Commission. In 1824, he founded the Rensselaer School, now known as Rensselaer Polytechnic Institute, in Troy, New York. He served twenty years as a member and then chancellor of the University of the State of New York Board of Regents. Stephen Van Rensselaer died in 1839 at the age of seventy-four. He is buried in Albany Rural Cemetery. At the time of his death, Van Rensselaer's net worth was over $100 billion in 2020 dollars.

Solomon Van Rensselaer. After the war, Solomon Van Rensselaer continued as the state's adjutant general. In 1818, he was elected to the U.S. House of Representatives as a Federalist. He resigned in 1822 to take an appointment as postmaster of Albany. When Andrew Jackson came to the presidency in 1829, he and his advisors sought to remove political opponents from appointive offices. Secretary of State Martin Van Buren pushed to oust Van Rensselaer. The postmaster got wind of the move, and he traveled to Washington and confronted Jackson in the White House. He pleaded for his job. When Jackson showed no sympathy, Van Rensselaer began removing his coat and shirt. Startled, the president asked what he was doing. The postmaster replied that he wanted to show the president his many wounds received defending his country. Jackson ordered Van Rensselaer to put his coat back on. The elderly man did so and departed. The following day when Jackson's advisors, who were unaware of the events of the prior evening, revisited the discussion to replace Van Rensselaer, the hero of New Orleans refused. "By the Eternal! I will not remove the old man. . . . Do you not know that he carries more than a pound of British lead in his body?"[30]

In 1836, Van Rensselaer published *A Narrative of the Affair of Queenston in the War of 1812* to refute John Armstrong's *Notices of the War of 1812.* Van

Rensselaer denounced *Notices* as a "deadly compound into which the apoth-
ecary has emptied his most malignant vials, expressly with a view to the production of as much individual suffering and distress as possible."[31]

Solomon Van Rensselaer served as postmaster from 1822 to 1839 and again
from 1841 until 1843. He died in 1852 at the age of seventy-seven, a hero of two
wars. He is buried in Albany Rural Cemetery.

Jacob Brown. New York City honored Jacob Brown with Freedom of the City
on February 4, 1815. The Common Council had Brown's portrait painted by
John Wesley Jarvis and ordered it hung in City Hall. Congress was anxious to
reduce the army as quickly as possible after the war. The new reorganization
cut the army to about 12,000 officers and men and allowed for only two major
generals and four brigadier generals. Madison retained Andrew Jackson as a
major general. The other five had achieved acclaim while serving in the Ninth
Military District: Maj. Gen. Jacob Brown and Brigadier Generals Alexander
Macomb, Winfield Scott, Edmund Pendleton Gaines, and Eleazar Ripley.
Brown commanded the Northern Division of the army, while Jackson commanded the Southern Division. Brown was intent on honoring Eleazar Wood,
who was killed at the sortie from Fort Erie. Brown collaborated with West
Point's superintendent, Joseph Gardner Swift, to erect a twenty-five-foot-tall
obelisk at West Point and at Brown's expense.

When John C. Calhoun joined Monroe's cabinet in December 1817 as
secretary of war, he began reforming and professionalizing the army. With
the economic panic of 1819 and the following depression, Congress acted yet
again to slash expenses by cutting the army. In 1821, the new reorganization
reduced the land force to a mere 6,000 officers and men and cut the number
of generals from six to three. Brown was retained and made the first Commanding General of the Army. Jackson resigned to accept the governorship
of Florida. Scott and Gaines remained, while Ripley resigned, and Macomb
was reduced in rank to colonel. Brown's new position and its relationship
with the secretary of war were ill-defined. Crippled by a stroke in October
of that year, Brown was able to discharge his duties as commanding general
after a year of recovery.

Brown was a strong advocate of unit training to overcome the worst aspects
of a small army fragmented in posts on the frontier or in coastal fortifications. He also recommended enlistment bonuses as well as increased pay for
noncommissioned officers to combat a flagging recruiting effort and the heavy
turnover in the enlisted strength of the army. Brown died in February, 1828, at
the age of fifty-two. He is buried in the Old Congressional Cemetery in Washington, D.C.[32]

Alexander Macomb. After the reorganization of 1815, Macomb was the ranking brigadier general. However, in 1821, President Monroe reduced him in rank to colonel and made him chief of the Corps of Engineers. The president granted that Macomb would continue to receive the pay of his brevet rank.

In succeeding years, Brigadier Generals Gaines and Scott quarreled publicly over their respective ranks. They had been promoted to brigadier general on the same day, but Scott's honorific brevet promotion was dated three weeks before that of Gaines. When Brown passed away in 1828, President John Quincy Adams decided to sidestep the quibbling over which rank took precedence. He made Colonel Macomb the commanding general with the permanent rank of major general. For several years, Scott pointedly refused orders coming from Macomb. During Macomb's tenure of thirteen years, he dealt with a number of issues that resulted in reforming the army, such as increasing the pay of enlisted soldiers. Macomb died in office in 1841 at the age of fifty-nine and is buried in the Old Congressional Cemetery in Washington, D.C.[33]

Morgan Lewis. The former governor accomplished little of note during the war. He was discharged in June 1815 along with all but six general officers. Lewis did not return to politics. He owned a large tract in Delaware County with numerous tenants. In 1816, he ordered his land agent to remit a year's rent to any of his tenants for each campaign in which they had served.[34] In 1831, he was one of the founders of the University of the City of New York, now known as New York University. Lewis served as president of the New-York Historical Society for four years. As a charter member of the Society of the Cincinnati, Lewis served as its president for the last five years of his life. An indifferent general, Morgan Lewis nonetheless contributed to his city and his country as a dedicated civic leader. Lewis died on April 7, 1844, and was buried in Saint James Episcopal churchyard in Hyde Park, New York.

Amos Hall. After the war, Gen. Amos Hall returned to his large farm near West Bloomfield. He was an innkeeper and ran a mill. Hall was typical of the landed gentry, who saw military service in time of war as a civic duty. Hall died in 1827 at the age of sixty-six and is buried in Pioneer Cemetery, West Bloomfield.

George McClure. The general who gave the order to burn Newark was appointed sheriff of Steuben County in 1816 and served for four years. In 1817, he published his apologia, entitled *Causes of the Destruction of the American Towns on the Niagara Frontier, and Failure of the Campaign of the Fall of 1813.* As might be expected, he heaped blame upon John Armstrong and Cyrenius Chapin. McClure continued in business, selling lumber and wheat. He also opened a mill that spun wool using water power. McClure relocated to Illinois, where he was one of the founders of Elgin. McClure died in 1851 at the age of eighty and is buried in Bluff City Cemetery in Elgin.[35]

Philetus Swift. Swift had spent much of the war in uniform, commanding regiments either of common militia, detached militia, or U.S. Volunteers. In 1814, Swift was elected a state senator for a four-year term. He served as president of the Senate in 1817. In 1815, he and Caleb Hopkins surveyed the Ridge Road, a major route connecting Lewiston on the Niagara River with Rochester on the Genesee River. This was the road used by the settlers of Lewiston to escape the British attack in December 1813. Swift represented Ontario County in the state constitutional convention of 1821, resulting in a much-needed update to the 1777 constitution. One of the provisions was jettisoning the Council of Appointment, a body that had institutionalized patronage. Swift died in 1828 in his hometown of Phelps in Ontario County at age sixty-five.

Peter B. Porter. Had the war continued into 1815, it was Madison's intention to commission Porter as a major general in the regular army. Just days after learning that a peace treaty had been signed, Porter assumed the office of New York's secretary of state. Congress awarded Porter a gold medal, the only militia general so honored. Voters in the western part of the state elected Porter their congressman. He served briefly, but left Congress to join the U.S.-Canadian Boundary Commission. Porter continued serving on the state's Erie Canal Commission.

In 1818, Porter ran for governor but was defeated by DeWitt Clinton. In May 1828, he joined the administration of John Quincy Adams as secretary of war but left after ten months, a tenure too short to enact meaningful reforms. Porter died in 1844 at the age of seventy-two at his home in Niagara Falls. He is buried in Forest Lawn Cemetery in Buffalo close by Flint Hill. Historians consider Peter B. Porter one of the most competent militia generals of the war.[36]

Melancthon Taylor Woolsey. When Congress declared war, Woolsey was the only naval officer on Lake Ontario. He commanded *Oneida* as well as the facilities at Sackett's Harbor until the arrival of Commodore Chauncey. Woolsey commanded Sackett's Harbor after the war and was promoted to captain in 1816. In 1824, the Navy Department gave him command of the frigate *Constellation.* Three years later, he commanded the Pensacola Navy Yard. The navy gave Woolsey command of the Brazilian Station in 1832 with the honorific title of commodore. Woolsey passed away in Utica in 1838 at the age of fifty-six, and he is buried in Utica's Forest Hill Cemetery.

Red Jacket. After the war, Red Jacket became one of the most recognized Indians among the white community, largely because widely published translations of his speeches addressed the issue of forcible Indian relocation. Red Jacket was also embroiled in internal Seneca conflicts over the question of whether Christian missionaries should be allowed permanent settlement on Seneca lands. Red Jacket vehemently opposed this prospect and for a year lost his status as a tribal chief. Eventually, Red Jacket realized that the Christians and the missionaries would remain, so he withdrew his hard opposition and various observers noted that he tried in his own way to make amends with missionaries and Christian Seneca.

In 1829, Red Jacket went on tour, giving presentations in Albany, New York City, Boston, and Washington. While in the national capital, he had a meeting with Andrew Jackson. Jackson, of course, was a strong advocate of Indian removal. Though no record exists of what either man said, Red Jacket undoubtedly expressed his opposition. When Congress met to deal with the issue of Cherokee removal, Congressman Davy Crockett quoted Red Jacket to express his opposition to Jackson's policy of Indian removal. Peter B. Porter, ten years after Red Jacket's death in 1830, recalled that he "was a man endowed with great intellectual powers, & more especially those of oratory, in which he was not only unsurpassed but unequalled . . . by any of his contemporaries."[37]

John E. Wool. In 1816, the secretary of war appointed Wool inspector general of the army with the rank of colonel. He served as inspector general for twenty-five years, reporting on the efficiency of army officers and the operations of army posts scattered across the country. The War Department brevetted Wool to the rank of brigadier general in 1826. Wool served as a division commander in Zachary Taylor's army in the war with Mexico, winning a brevet promotion to major general for gallant and meritorious conduct at the Battle of Buena Vista. Congress granted him the Thanks of Congress, and President Franklin Pierce presented him with a sword in 1854.

In 1856, as commander of the Department of the Pacific, Wool settled Indians into reservations to protect them from genocidal attacks by Oregon Territory volunteers that had resulted in the deaths of native women and children. When the Civil War exploded, Wool, then in his seventies, acted forcefully to keep Fort Monroe and the Norfolk Navy Yard in Union hands. President Lincoln rewarded him with a promotion to major general. In 1863, Wool led a force into New York City, pacifying the city after the recent deadly draft riots. A month later, in August 1863, Lincoln sorely disappointed Wool by retiring him from the service; Wool considered himself fit for duty. Wool retired to his home in Troy, where he passed away in November 1869 at the age of eighty-five. He is buried in Oakwood Cemetery in Troy.

Henry Leavenworth. With war's end, Brevet Col. Henry Leavenworth resumed his law practice and was elected to the State Assembly. The president offered Leavenworth the opportunity to remain in the army as a major with the Second Infantry, and he accepted. In 1818, he was promoted to lieutenant colonel and served in the Fifth Infantry in the garrison at Sackett's Harbor. In 1821, the secretary of war gave Leavenworth command of Fort Atkinson, on the upper Missouri River. Leavenworth learned the Sioux language and personally negotiated with the Plains Indians. In 1819, Leavenworth negotiated a peace between the Sioux and the Chippawa.

The Arikara War of 1823 was the first full-scale engagement between the Plains Indians and the U.S. Army. Leavenworth led a detachment of three hundred soldiers and found about eight hundred of the tribe's warriors in their palisaded village. After a demonstration of force, Leavenworth negotiated a treaty that ended the war. President Monroe commended Leavenworth's success in his annual message.

On July 25, 1824, the secretary of war awarded Leavenworth with a brevet promotion to brigadier general. A year later, Leavenworth was promoted to colonel and given command of the Third Infantry Regiment. In 1826, the War Department sent Leavenworth with his regiment to Jefferson Barracks near St. Louis to start a school for infantry units. The following year, Leavenworth led an expedition that founded Fort Leavenworth on the Missouri River.

In 1834, Leavenworth was leading a force of four hundred dragoons and infantry into Indian Territory (present-day Oklahoma) when his party came across a buffalo herd. Leavenworth was riding hard, chasing a buffalo calf, when his horse stepped into a gopher hole, throwing Leavenworth to the ground. Leavenworth never recovered. Within days, he developed a fever and on July 21, 1834, just four days short of the twentieth anniversary of the Battle of Lundy's Lane, Henry Leavenworth passed away. Orders promoting him to permanent brigadier general would have gone into effect four days later. In 1902, Leavenworth's body and that of his second wife, Electa, and their child were disinterred from their grave in Delhi, New York, and moved to Fort Leavenworth, Kansas.

William Jenkins Worth. Worth was very seriously wounded at the Battle of Lundy's Lane. For the rest of his life, he walked with a limp. After the war, Brevet Maj. Worth served as commandant of cadets at West Point for eight years. In July 1824, on the tenth anniversary of Lundy's Lane, Worth received a brevet promotion to lieutenant colonel. In 1836, he was promoted to colonel. Sometime during this period, Worth's anonymous memoir, *First Campaign of an A.D.C.*, appeared in print as a series of journal installments.

Worth commanded successfully in Florida in the Second Seminole War and was rewarded with brevet promotion to brigadier general in 1842 for gallant service. In the war with Mexico, Worth served under both Zachary Taylor and Winfield Scott. As a division commander in north Mexico, he received a brevet promotion to major general for gallant service in the battles around Monterrey. Landing in the first wave at Vera Cruz, Worth fought his division all the way into Mexico City. He personally removed the Mexican flag from atop the National Palace and replaced it with the American flag. Congress awarded him a sword for his gallant conduct.

Worth died of cholera in Texas in 1849 at the age of fifty-five. His remains are interred under an obelisk in Worth Square in Manhattan. The city of Fort Worth, Texas, is named after this hero of three wars.[38]

Jonathan Williams. The engineer most responsible for conceptualizing the harbor defenses of New York City, Jonathan Williams, resigned from the army at the outbreak of the war. He stayed on under the employment of the state for a while as Col. Joseph Gardner Swift assumed the post of chief engineer. Williams then moved to Philadelphia to assist in the design and construction of fortifications. The voters of Philadelphia elected Williams to the U.S. Congress. However, he died in May 1815 at the age of sixty-three before taking office.

Joseph Gardner Swift. Although born in Massachusetts, Swift was associated with New York as early as his cadet days at West Point. He replaced Jonathan Williams as the chief army engineer. Many New Yorkers believed that the British did not strike their city largely due to the extensive fortifications designed and built by Williams and Swift. The city awarded Swift the title "Benefactor of the City." His portrait, executed by John Wesley Jarvis, was hung in City Hall. Swift resigned from the army in 1818 and applied his talents to civil engineering, railroad construction, business, and education. In 1832, he was chief engineer of the New York and Harlem Railroad, one of the first rail lines in the United States. Soon after, Swift moved his family to Geneva, New York, where he passed away in 1865 at the age of eighty-two. He is buried in the Washington Street Cemetery in Geneva.[39]

Betsy Doyle. After the fall of Fort Niagara in December 1813, Doyle trekked across the state, arriving at Greenbush quite ill. Because she was on a company roster, she was allowed to continue her duties. She received rations for herself and her children but not the pay of her husband, Andrew, who was imprisoned at Dartmoor in England. In April 1814, the camp commandant unsuccessfully pleaded Doyle's case for her spouse's pay. After she recovered, she was employed in the camp hospital. She was waiting for Andrew until an erroneous report arrived of his death. In 1819, Doyle took ill and passed away. In reporting her death to the War Department, Lt. Henry Smith claimed that "her death was accelerated by the want of those necessities which her pay would have secured." Eventually, her daughter received Doyle's back pay as a nurse. Unknown to her, Andrew had returned to the United States in August 1815. He could not locate his wife or their children, and apparently presumed that his wife had died. Andrew married in 1819, just months before Doyle's passing. In 1871, Andrew applied for a pension. He died in 1875 at the age of eighty-seven.[40]

Washington Irving. After the war, Irving went to Britain on family business and remained in Europe for seventeen years. In 1819, he achieved international fame with the publication of *The Sketch Book of Geoffrey Crayon, Gent.* This collection of short stories included *The Legend of Sleepy Hollow* and *Rip Van Winkle.* While in Spain, he wrote a number of romantic histories, including a biography of Christopher Columbus. Returning to America, he travelled out West and wrote several books inspired by his journeys. He bought a small house on the Hudson River in Tarrytown and named it Sunnyside. Irving served as ambassador to Spain from 1842 to 1846. Returning to Sunnyside, Irving continued his prolific writing. He had just completed a five-volume biography of George Washington when he died of a heart attack in 1859 at age 76. Irving is buried at the Sleepy Hollow Cemetery in Westchester County, New York.

Hiram Silas Cronk. Cronk has the distinction of being the last surviving American veteran of the War of 1812. Born in the town of Frankfort in Herkimer County in 1800, he volunteered to serve in the common militia for the defense of Sackett's Harbor in October and November 1814. He was fourteen years old. Cronk served for a total of forty days and was awarded a monthly pension of $8. In later years, he was awarded land grants totaling 160 acres. In 1837, he moved to the town of Ava in Oneida County and lived out his 105 years there. Upon his death in 1905, Cronk lay in state in City Hall in Manhattan. Thousands lined the path of his cortege from City Hall across the Brooklyn Bridge to the Cypress Hills National Cemetery in Brooklyn.[41]

What were the results of the War of 1812 for New York state? The conflict lasted two and a half years, and much of the fighting occurred in the state or close by in Canada. Thousands of regulars and militiamen were maimed or lost their lives in combat or from sickness. While few civilians died from direct hostile action, thousands became temporary refugees and hundreds lost their homes. The embargos and blockade disrupted the economy and impoverished hundreds. Service in the militia for months at a time disrupted home life and imposed a hardship on the families.[42]

New York's biggest victories were the safety of New York City and the retention of the northern boundary. Federal and state cooperation and the immense contributions of the local residents of all races, ethnicities, and genders had created a fortress of America's largest city. The British did not consider the metropolis a vulnerable target, selecting Washington, D.C., and Baltimore instead. The threat to the state's boundaries was real. During peace negotiations at Ghent, the British proposed taking much of the American Northwest to form a buffer state for sole use of Indians. As many as 100,000 Americans would have had to relocate. The British further proposed taking a large segment of the District of Maine and removing all American warships and fortifications from the Great Lakes. The American victory at Plattsburgh and the British inability to destroy the naval squadron on Lake Ontario removed the possibility that any portion of the state would become part of British North America. In May 1815, the British evacuated Fort Niagara, the only piece of the state that had been occupied at the end of the war. The Rush-Bagot Treaty of 1818 limited warships on the Great Lakes and Lake Champlain, which furthered the security of the state.

The termination of the war marked the beginning of the end for the nation's first party system. The Federalist Party had acquired an odor of treason from its steadfast opposition to the conflict and its secret convention in Hartford, Connecticut. Although the Federalists did well in the April 1815 elections for the Assembly, the Federalists never again controlled either chamber of the state legislature. For all practical purposes, the party started disbanding in 1820. Without the war, no consequential issue remained to justify an opposition party. Former Federalists moved to support either Governor Clinton or his opponents within the Republican Party, the Bucktails. This latter group coalesced around Martin Van Buren and the Tammany organization in New York City.[43]

The war was a training ground for the regular army's leaders for the next decades. A disproportionally large number of the officers who had served in the Ninth Military District were retained as the army demobilized in 1815. Of course, only a minority of these men were New Yorkers. Yet, the state was well represented in the postwar leadership. Both Jacob Brown and Alexander Macomb rose to the very highest positions in the postwar army. They both lobbied, with some success, to correct the worst of the inefficiencies in the army that had come to light during the war. Their leadership helped the nation settle the West, secure the coast, and educate a new wave of officers who won the country's second foreign war – that with Mexico. John E. Wool and William Jenkins Worth rose to general officer rank and, along with Henry Leavenworth, contributed to the nation on the battlefield and off.

J. C. A. Stagg estimated that about 13 percent of enlisted soldiers serving in the war were foreign-born. Of these, more than half were Irish. The Irish in New York formed their own volunteer companies and went to war under their own officers, Francis McClure being foremost. The state's military operations were no doubt enhanced by refugees from the 1798 Rebellion in Ireland. Officers such as Nicholas Gray, Alexander Denniston, and James McKeon served competently in positions of responsibility and danger.[44]

It is difficult to estimate the extent to which the war advanced the status or circumstances of African Americans in the state. Generally, people accepted the notion that wartime service was the mark of citizenship in a republic. The War Department, however, was ambiguous as to the recruiting of African Americans into the regular army. Recruiting records did not specify race, but "black" was sometimes an entry under "complexion." Stagg offers that as many as 370 blacks may have served in the regular army. There were no restrictions on African Americans serving in naval forces or on privateers; therefore, thousands did. Estimates suggest that one out of seven prisoners at the infamous Dartmoor prison were black—about nine hundred men. These men were almost entirely taken from the crews of privateers. It is impossible to say how many of these soldiers and sailors came from New York. What is known is that Governor Tompkins was an avid opponent of slavery. He was the impetus behind the law that authorized the raising of two black regiments in 1814. In 1817, the legislature passed a law that would, in the year 1827, free slaves born before 1799. Slaves born after 1799 had already been moved to the status of indentured servants.[45]

With the demobilization of the regular army, hundreds of women lost their jobs as laundresses and nurses in the regiments and hospitals. Spouses of militiamen ran farms and households when their husbands left to serve for months at a time. Since these women were married to soldiers, they benefited from the land and bonuses earned by their spouses' service.

What presents a bit of a mystery, however, is why Betsy Doyle did not achieve the fame of women in the Revolution—Mary Ludwig Hays (Molly Pitcher) and Margaret Corbin? It is more puzzling why Laura Secord is a national hero in Canada, but Doyle has yet to appear on a postage stamp. Secord walked twenty miles to deliver a warning. Doyle served on a gun crew, showed frightened militiamen how to do their duty, and walked with three children across the state during the winter of 1813–14. As her biographer writes, her story "needs no embroidery to make exciting." New York should take notice of this woman's physical courage and her breaking of gender norms in the early nineteenth century.[46]

While historians continue to debate the issue of who won the war, agreement is widespread over who *lost* the war. Native Americans were forced to make treaties with the United States that resulted, over time, in their removal west of the Mississippi River. The Iroquois in New York resisted the removal policy legally and maintained six reservations. However, the pressure to relinquish the land of the Buffalo Creek Reservation was overpowering. Throughout the 1840s, the Seneca sold off their lands south of the expanding city of Buffalo. How much of their success in retaining traditional lands was derived from their active participation in the war on the American side is unmeasurable. Red Jacket's popularity with white audiences in the 1830s and his advocacy for native rights no doubt softened attitudes among some of the citizenry.

The war disrupted the state's economy and depressed the living conditions of thousands. Between the embargo and the blockade, trade moving in and out of the state plummeted. The war also deferred improvements within the state, most notably the Erie Canal. On the positive side of the ledger, upstate farmers found new markets feeding servicemen on the frontiers. Work increased for teamsters and shippers moving weapons and supplies. Many soldiers, sailors, and militiamen spent their bonuses and pay inside the state. After the war, many persons had difficulty collecting on vouchers for supplies or services rendered to the state or federal governments. The legislature enacted a law that established procedures to audit and pay these claims. The legislature also appointed officials to act on behalf of those making claims against the federal government.[47]

Certainly, the state was more secure. The boundary with Canada was largely de-militarized, and the defenses of New York City were substantial. The citizenry persuaded themselves that they had won a war against a premier military power. Perhaps the most widespread benefit of the conflict was intangible: a sense that the country had established its sovereignty as an equal among the nations of the world. This was not an inconsequential accomplishment. In assessing the results of the conflict, the *Albany Register* rejoiced "in the confidence that we shall hereafter be respected by the nations of the earth with a regard to our rights, and a deference to our valor, which will secure us for a long period from the necessity of again reverting to arms in support of our independence."[48]

The legislature did not fail to improve the militia laws based upon the lessons of the war. In April 1818, the legislature passed "An Act to organize the militia." This law clarified and adjusted the current militia act in a number of ways. The legislature organized and expanded the staff departments serving the state commander in chief, such as adjutant general, quartermaster department, commissary department, paymaster, and the hospital department. The new law raised the ranks of the officers heading the various staff offices and provided additional staff officers to the divisions and brigades. For example, the state's adjutant general had typically been a lieutenant colonel. That officer was now a brigadier general, adding stature to the position to match its responsibility. The net effect was to smooth administration throughout the militia organization. The state also adopted the latest federal tactical doctrine and issued the supporting manuals to all officers down to the rank of captain. At last, the state militia would be trained in the same tactical doctrine as the regular army.[49]

The new law mandated two days of annual training. On the first Monday of September, every militiaman went to his place of rendezvous for training. Division commanders would identify the second training day, and a third if necessary. Persons missing training were subject to fines and jail sentences from a court-martial, not a civilian judge. This change was a major improvement from the war years, when a judge opposed to the war could treat the crime lightly. In consideration of the greater threat of raid or invasion, the militia of New York County now had three mandatory days of training, except for the artillery. All artillery units on Manhattan were organized into the First Regiment of New York Artillery and trained for no fewer than twelve days annually. For their additional service, enlisted men and non-commissioned officers of the regiment were granted property tax reductions and exempted from jury duty. In April 1819, the legislature increased the number of days training for non-artillery units from three to five. The artillerists continued with their heavier requirements.[50]

The law clarified those persons who were exempt from militia service. Medical doctors and justices of the peace were still required to enroll in the militia but could miss a training day by paying two dollars. Sailors and firemen had been exempt from all militia service, but this exemption would no longer apply during war, insurrection, or invasion. Quakers and Shakers were exempt from service, but the lawmakers required these persons to pay four dollars annually for the exemption. Failure to pay this sum could result in a twenty-day jail sentence. Two years later, the payment was abolished and those persons "religiously or conscientiously opposed to the bearing of arms" could apply for an exemption. Members of religious communities, such as the Society of Friends, were required to provide evidence annually that they continued in good standing with their faith community.[51]

Eventually, the republican concept of the militia organization as the first line of national defense eroded. Along with many of the northern states, New York diluted requirements for the common militia by reducing mandatory training days. In 1846, the state dropped fines for missing training. In place of an organization of all persons subject to military service, New York encouraged the formation of volunteer companies that were subject to strict state standards. The men elected their own officers up to the position of regimental colonel. The governor and legislature retained the authority to commission the general officers.[52]

The War of 1812 was the first major test of war as a joint venture between the federal and state governments. The experiment clearly had mixed results. The Federalist governors of the New England states obstructed the war effort, refusing to mobilize their militias until British raids prompted a defensive response. States away from the frontiers, especially Tennessee, Ohio, and Kentucky, actively supported military operations with militia and volunteers. However, it was in New York, with an active front along hundreds of miles of border, that the war-sharing doctrine of federalism was most severely tested. The immediate challenge was the lack of policy and procedure to coordinate the federal–state effort. The federal government was unprepared to conduct three invasions of Canada in 1812 and was unprepared to assist in the arming and equipping of state forces. In short, no procedures were established prior to the war to integrate militia forces with regulars once the militia units were mustered into federal service. Daniel Tompkins was at the center of the state's efforts in preparing for and supporting the war. It was his effort and that of a few state officials and militia generals that managed to put thousands of reasonably armed, although poorly equipped, soldiers on the frontiers in strategic locations. The Battle of Queenston Heights was a disaster, yet there would not have been an attempt to invade Canada across the Niagara River had the state not made it possible.

The constitutional restriction on the use of the militia was an insurmountable challenge. Only militiamen volunteering to cross the international border could support invasion. Whether as a demonstration of opposition to the war or as an act of survival, militiamen volunteering to cross into Canada numbered in the hundreds, not thousands. Yet, thousands stood their ground to defend their communities on the shores of Lakes Ontario and Champlain and in New York City.

The last of the major challenges was financial. The federal government was entirely unprepared for a war lasting nearly three years and quickly ran out of money. Militiamen went unpaid for years. Fortunately, the state legislature and the New York City Common Council provided some emergency funding. However, the effort to account for invoices and claims was an accounting nightmare, and the people along the Niagara River and Tompkins himself were its foremost victims.

In the years that followed, the role of the states in supporting war efforts under the constitution was reduced largely to recruiting regiments of volunteers and sending them off to distant fronts in Mexico and the Confederacy. After 1815, no state faced the same challenges as New York during the last war with Britain. The federal government increasingly monopolized war-making.

During the Revolution, New Yorkers had suffered enormously. New York City was occupied, and much of it was destroyed by fire. Men died horribly in prison ships in the harbor. Settlers in the interior were the victims of unspeakable brutality. For many years the outcome was in doubt. New Yorkers knew war—its many terrors as well as the fruits of victory. Thirty years later, despite the many voices in opposition, war returned. There was no escape; the citizenry would have to endure to the end. The stakes were the same—death and destruction for some, sacrifice and suffering for all. Defeat might mean that many living on the periphery would find themselves the scorned residents of a foreign state. New Yorkers risked much more than most Americans. They met the challenge, paid the price in blood, sweat, and treasure, and they prevailed. It is long past the time when the Excelsior state proudly claims this conflict as its own. The War of 1812 is New York's War.

NOTES

Abbreviations

ASP:MA   *American State Papers: Military Affairs.* 7 vols. (Washington, D.C.: Gales and Seaton, 1832–1861).

BHM   Buffalo History Museum, Buffalo, N.Y.

DHNF   Ernest Cruikshank, ed., *Documentary History of the Campaigns upon the Niagara Frontier in 1812–1814.* 9 vols. (Welland, Ontario: Tribune Press, 1896–1908).

DHNF1814   Ernest Cruikshank, ed., *Documentary History of the Campaign on the Niagara Frontier in 1814* (Welland, Ontario: Lundy's Lane Historical Society, 1896).

LOC   Library of Congress, Washington, D.C.

NARA   National Archives and Records Administration, Washington, D.C.

NYSA/OSC   New York State Archives, Office of State Comptroller, Albany, N.Y.

Introduction

1. The claim of Tompkins's primacy among the governors rests upon an examination of the studies of James H. Ellis (New England), Victor A. Sapio (Pennsylvania), Alec R. Gilpin (Michigan Territory), Sarah M. Lemmon (North Carolina), and James W. Hammack Jr. and David Kirkpatrick (Kentucky).

2. Two sources are particularly valuable in placing the War of 1812 into a more global context. See Black, *The War of 1812 in the Age of Napoleon*, and Stagg, *The War of 1812: Conflict for a Continent.*

3. At the time, the term "Canada" generally referred to the provinces of Lower and Upper Canada, which were part of British North America. British North America also included Nova Scotia, New Brunswick, Prince Edward Island, Cape Breton Island, and Bermuda. British North America was administered from Quebec, Lower Canada, by Sir George Prevost.

4. An excellent analysis of Britain's goals and the evolution of its global strategy is found in Grodzinski, *Defender of Canada*, and more recently "American 'Independence is not threatened'," Grodzinsky, "American," 15–35. See also Hitsman, *The Incredible War of 1812.*

5. ASP:MA, 1:535, "A Report of the Army, its strength and distribution."

6. Tucker, *The Encyclopedia of the War of 1812*, 1:190–91.

7. Initial British negotiating demands were draconian and would have ripped thousands of square miles from United States territory. As negotiations proceeded, British demands mellowed, as did instructions to the military and naval leadership. See Bathurst to Prevost, June 3, 1814, Colonial Office Records, C.O. 43/23, National Archives of the United Kingdom, Kew, England. Bathurst, who was Secretary of State for War and the Colonies, allowed Prevost to retain a portion of the state. "Should there be any advance position on that part of our frontier which extends towards Lake Champlain, the occupation of which would materially tend to the security of the province, you will if you deem it expedient expel the Enemy from it, and occupy it by detachments of the Troops under your command." Bathurst also directed that Prevost retain Fort Niagara and some surrounding territory in order to provide security for Upper Canada.

8. Hastings, *Public Papers of Daniel D. Tompkins*, 1:3.

9. During the bicentennial of the War of 1812, in 2012–2015, the state government was unable to fully support commemorative activities, in contrast with Maryland's exemplary efforts.

Chapter 1

1. Emmons Clark, *History of the Seventh Regiment*, 44–46.

2. See Turner, *Pioneer History*, for conditions west of the Genesee River.

3. Erastus Granger took a census of natives living on reservations in 1816. See Snyder, *Red & White*, 30.

4. The Rome Canal was completed in 1797 and required four locks to manage the change in elevation. Engineers also cut several channels across the winding Wood Creek to ease passage of the long Durham boats.

5. Lampi, "Federalist Party Resurgence," 255–59.

6. New York Constitution of 1777; Mohl, *Poverty*, 5; Strum, "Saving Mr. Tompkins' War." For detailed results of various state elections, see "A New Nation Votes."

7. Irwin, *Daniel D. Tompkins*, 34–37.

8. Livingston was a founding father, having served on the committee to draft the Declaration of Independence. He was widely known as "The Chancellor" for his many years of service as the state's foremost justice official.

9. Prior to 1801, only the governor could nominate a candidate for office for those positions under the control of the Council of Appointment. However, a special election adjusted the constitution such that any member of the council could make nominations. Thus, the governor lost the exclusive power of patronage. Jenkins, *Lives of the Governors*, 162.

10. Irwin, *Daniel D. Tompkins*, 55–56. There are few biographies of Daniel D. Tompkins. An older yet still useful biography of Tompkins is a chapter in Jenkins, *Lives of the Governors*, 158–207. The chapter on Tompkins found in Mark Hatfield's *Vice Presidents of the United States* is largely derivative of Irwin.

11. Irwin, *Daniel D. Tompkins*, 5–6.

12. The fire in the state capitol in 1911 destroyed most of Tompkins's correspondence. However, many of the essays survived and were published in 1940 as *A Columbia College Student in the Eighteenth Century*.

13. Jenkins, *Lives of the Governors of the State of New York*, 160–61 and 165–67.

14. Jefferson operated from Republican ideology, with its aversion to a standing army and taxation. In doing so, he was largely responsible for gutting the nation's ability to conduct war. See Watson, "Trusting to 'the Chapter of Accidents'" for an indictment of Jeffersonian national security policy prior to war. The attack and the subsequent diplomatic activity became widely known as the Chesapeake Affair. The Embargo Act prohibited American ships from trading in foreign ports.

15. Tompkins to Pliny Moor, Samuel Hicks, and Ebenezer Dunning, October 6, 1807, in Irwin, *Daniel D. Tompkins*, 61–62.

16. Hastings, *Tompkins Papers*, 1:152–55; General Order dated December 10, 1807, in Hastings, *Tompkins Papers*, 1:161–65; "The Governor's First Address to the Legislature," January 26, 1808, in Hastings, *Tompkins Papers*, 2:18–28.

17. Granger to Dearborn, September 14, 1807, in Snyder, *Red & White*, 53–55. The most comprehensive study of the Six Nations in this conflict is Benn, *The Iroquois in the War of 1812*.

18. The Governor's First Address to the Legislature, January 26, 1808, in Hastings, *Tompkins Papers*, 2:19–20.

19. Ibid.

20. General Order dated November 15, 1808, and General Order dated May 6, 1809, in Hastings, *Tompkins Papers*, 1:203–7 and 1:220–21.

21. Jenkins, *Lives of the Governors*, 170; Hastings, *Military Minutes*, 1109–10 and 1171.

22. Harvey Strum has produced several meticulously detailed works that explain New York politics during the prewar years and the war years beginning with his dissertation "New York and the War of 1812." Three articles further expand his research. These are "New York Federalists and Opposition"; "Politics of the New York Antiwar Campaign"; and "A House Divided," 10–16.

23. Customs Collector to Department Chief, March 19, 1809, Hough. *Jefferson County*, 459.

24. General Order dated August 19, 1808, in Hastings, *Tompkins Papers* 1:194–97; Tompkins to Jefferson, August 22, 1808, in Hastings, *Tompkins Papers*, 2:104–6; Tompkins to Captains Cock, Brooks, and Townsend, September 15, 1808, in Hastings, *Tompkins Papers*, 2:119–21.

25. Bixby, *Peter Sailly*, 34.

26. Tompkins to Gallatin, December 1, 1808, in Hastings, *Tompkins Papers*, 2:165–67.

27. Tompkins to Mooers, February 2, 1809, in Hastings, *Tompkins Papers*, 2:189–92.

28. Irwin, *Daniel D. Tompkins*, 74–75; Lampi, "Federalist Party Resurgence," 260; Jenkins, *Lives of the Governors*, 170–72.

29. In 1814, New York reported 95,026 members of the state militia, ASP:MA, 1:679.

30. Tompkins to McClure, December 21, 1808, in Hastings, *Tompkins Papers*, 2:182. An examination of Irish-American participation in the war can be found in "Humbling the British Tyrant" in Wilson, *United Irishmen*.

31. Tompkins to Paulding, December 10, 1811, in Hastings, *Tompkins Papers*, 2:367–68; *The War*, July 11, 1812.

32. General Order dated June 6, 1812, in Hastings, *Tompkins Papers*, 1:329; Gero, *Excelsior's Citizen Soldiers*, 91–93.

33. Irwin, *Daniel D. Tompkins*, 137.

34. Kutolowski, "Commissions and Canvasses."
35. In a report to the War Department in 1812, New York reported 98,606 militia-men serving in the common militia. Only Pennsylvania, with 99,414 reported more citizen-soldiers. See Madison to Congress, February 13, 1813, ASP:MA, 1:332. Tompkins increased the number of regiments in the six months prior to the declaration of war. See Paulding to Tompkins, January 26, 1812, in Hastings, *Tompkins Papers*, 1:601–2; and Hastings, *Military Minutes*, 1400–1409.
36. In 1807 the two federal arsenals at Harpers Ferry and Springfield had produced 5,742 muskets. The federal government expanded production in 1808 to manufacture 8,921 muskets. Production continued to expand throughout the war. See ASP:MA, 1:679.
37. Jefferson to Tompkins, January 26, 1808, in Hastings, *Tompkins Papers*, 2:67–69; Tompkins to Dearborn, May 12, 1808, in Hastings, *Tompkins Papers*, 2:76–78; Eustis to Tompkins, April 29, 1809, and Tompkins to Eustis, December 30, 1811, in Hastings, *Tompkins Papers*, 2:395–96.
38. Tompkins to Committee of the County of Ontario, September 1, 1807, and Tompkins to Asa Ransom et al., October 7, 1807, and Tompkins to Peter B. Porter, et al., undated, in Hastings, *Tompkins Papers*, 2:10–16.
39. Jacob Brown et al. to Tompkins, undated, in Hastings, *Tompkins Papers*, 2:67–69.
40. Tompkins to McLean, May 9, 1808, in Hastings, *Tompkins Papers*, 2:72–76; Irwin, *Daniel D. Tompkins*, 133; NYSA/OSC, Record Series A0269, Ledgers, vol. 25, Ledger C.
41. Tompkins to Senate, November 4, 1808, in *Journal of the Senate, 1808*.
42. Irwin, *Daniel D. Tompkins*, 139; Tompkins to State Legislature, March 11, 1811, in Hastings, *Tompkins Papers*, 2:257–61; Tompkins to State Legislature, February 6, 1810, in Hastings, *Tompkins Papers*, 2: 242–43; Tompkins to Wolcott, September 21, 1812, in Hastings, *Tompkins Papers*, 3:136–37.
43. Report of John McLean, February 20, 1809, in Hastings, *Tompkins Papers*, 2:197–200.
44. Tompkins to State Legislature, March 11, 1811, in Hastings, *Tompkins Papers*, 2:257–61. Tompkins's proactive stance and success in equipping the militia is in stark contrast to that of Governor William Hawkins of North Carolina, who was entirely unable to secure funding as late as December 1811. In her study, Sarah McCulloh Lemmon cites the North Carolina legislature's jealousy of the governor's powers. As late as 1814, the legislature approved money for equipment, but stipulated that tents and camp equipment could not be allowed to exit the state. See *Frustrated Patriots*, 79–80.
45. Turner, *Pioneer History*, 585.
46. Shriver. "Brocken Locks," 355–56.
47. As an example, see General Order dated October 17, 1811, in Hastings, *Tompkins Papers*, 1:299–308.
48. Tompkins to Paulding, December 21, 1811, in Hastings, *Tompkins Papers*, 2:385–86; Graves, "Dry Books of Tactics."
49. Tompkins to Sage, September 9, 1811, in Hastings, *Tompkins Papers*, 2:354–55.
50. The tale of the loss of New York City and its occupation is told in Schecter, *Battle for New York*. Hastings, *Tompkins Papers*, 1:53–54; Arthur, *How Britain Won the War*, 145–46; Eustis to Cheves, December 3, 1811, ASP:MA, 1:87.

51. Paper dated July 1807, Jonathan Williams Papers, Lilly Library at the University of Indiana, Bloomington, Ind.
52. Griswold, "A Reasoned Approach." Williams to the Commissioner of Fortifications, May 28, 1814, in Hastings, *Tompkins Papers*, 3:472–77. See also Williams, "Old Fortifications of New York Harbor," 37.
53. NYSA/OSC Record Series A0802-78, 6:3–12; Mohl, *Poverty*, 112.
54. Hastings, *Tompkins Papers*, 1:74. The state turned over to the federal government a grant of land and jurisdiction of Hendrick's Reef on November 7, 1812, Tompkins to Armstrong, November 7, 1812, in Hastings, *Tompkins Papers*, 3:182–83.
55. Williams to Tompkins, December n.d. 1807, in Hastings, *Tompkins Papers*, 2:29–30.
56. Tompkins to Williams, July 25, 1807, in Hastings, *Tompkins Papers*, 2:5–8; Tompkins to Dearborn, May 16, 1808, in Hastings, *Tompkins Papers*, 2:85–86; Tompkins to Senate, November 4, 1808, *Journal of the Senate, 1808*, 1457. Eustis to Cheves, December 10, 1811, ASP:MA, 1:87–91.
58. Some sources refer to the Southwest Battery as the West Battery.
59. Cochrane to Cockburn, July 1, 1814, and Cochrane to Melville, July 17, 1814, in Dudley and Crawford, *Naval War of 1812*, 3:129 and 3:132–35.
60. *Annals of Congress: Debates and Proceedings in the Congress of the United States, 1789-1824*, 1st Session, 12th Congress, 373–77. The War Hawks were those congressmen who pressured their colleagues and President Madison into declaring war against Britain. A short biography of Porter is found in Kohler, "Peter Porter of Black Rock," in DeCroix, *War of 1812*, 3:42–47.
61. Tompkins to Cook, December 12, 1811, in Hastings, *Tompkins Papers*, 2:371–73.
62. Tompkins to Paulding, December 30, 1811, in Hastings, *Tompkins Papers*, 2:390–92; Tompkins to Macomb, January 4, 1812, in Hastings, *Tompkins Papers*, 2:400–401.

Chapter 2

1. Donald Hickey sums up Republican optimism, Hickey, *War of 1812*, 26–28.
2. Every worthy study of operations notes the vulnerability of the British supply line. See Charles P. Stacey, "Another look at the Battle of Lake Erie."
3. Porter's speech in the House of Representatives as published in the *National Intelligencer*, February 25, 1812. However, by April, Porter realized that preparations for war were proceeding too slowly. He wrote to Madison that declaring war at that time would be "an act of madness." See Stagg, "Between Black Rock and a Hard Place," for Porter's strategic analysis and shifting views. See also Madison to Wirt, September 30, 1813, in Hunt, *Writings of James Madison*, 8:261–65, for the president's thought process in initiating the war in 1812.
4. Tompkins's address to the Legislature, January 28, 1812, in Hastings, *Tompkins Papers*, 2:446; Stagg, *Mr. Madison's War*, 232–40.
5. Tompkins's address to the Legislature, January 28, 1812, in Hastings, *Tompkins Papers*, 2:445.
6. Jefferson to Duane, August 4, 1812, Thomas Jefferson Papers, LOC. "Jack the painters" referred to James Aiken, a Scot who sympathized with the American colonists and burned the rope yard at the naval base at Portsmouth in 1776.
7. See Kert, *Privateering*, 149–56. An extract of the law is found in Dudley and Crawford, *Naval War of 1812*, 1:166–70.

292 NOTES TO CHAPTER 2

8. See Barbuto, "1812: The United States Builds an Army."
9. Tompkins to Miller, January 19, 1812, in Hastings, *Tompkins Papers*, 2:437–38.
10. See Stagg, *Mr. Madison's War*, and Skelton, "High Army Leadership," 253–74.
11. Cortlandt, P. Van Cortlandt Jr., E. Sage, et al. to Madison, on or about January 1, 1812, James Madison Papers, Series 1, Reel 14, LOC. Myers's recollections provide valuable insight on politics and military operations. For the regimental nickname, see Yetwin, *Mordecai Myers*, 121–22.
12. Yetwin, *Mordecai Myers*, 82. For an analysis of the officer corps, see Stagg, "United States Officers in the War of 1812."
13. Smyth to Schuyler, April 22, 1812, RG 94, Adjutant General Letters Sent, NARA. An example of a recruiting district commander's instructions to a recruiting officer is found in Chrystie to Caldwell, May 12, 1812, Moffat Library of Washingtonville, Caldwell Correspondence, Washingtonville, N.Y.
14. Bloomfield left valuable observations of his service in the Revolution. See Lender, Mark E. and James Kirby Martin, *Citizen Soldier*.
15. Smyth to Gansevoort, April 10, 1812, and Smyth to Armistead, April 9, 1812, RG 94, Adjutant General Letters Sent, NARA.
16. Smyth to Gansevoort, March 17, 1812, RG 94, Adjutant General Letters Sent, NARA.
17. Smyth to Boerstler and Smyth to Parker, June 15, 1812, RG 94, Adjutant General Letters Sent, NARA.
18. Mann, *Medical Sketches*, vi–vii, 12. For an overview of medical operations, see Gillett, *Army Medical Department*.
19. Eustis to Tompkins, March 24, 1812, Record Series A0802-78, vol. 21, NYSA/OSC; Brant, *James Madison Commander in Chief*, 44.
20. Britain waged war against revolutionary France starting in 1793 with a short break of about a year in 1802–3.
21. An overview of Britain's organization and financing for war and the evolution of strategy and diplomacy is found in Grodzinski, "American 'Independence is not threatened'" found in Hickey and Clark, *The Routledge Handbook of the War of 1812*.
22. Tompkins to Eustis, March 31, 1812, in Hastings, *Tompkins Papers*, 2:520–21; General Order dated April 2, 1812, in Hastings, *Tompkins Papers*, 1:315–17; Hall, "Militia Service," 27–28. A fine study of the naval base on Lake Ontario is Gibson's "Militia, Mud, and Misery."
23. Brown to Widrig, April 24, 1812, Record Series A0802-78, vol. 21, NYSA/OSC.
24. "An Act Authorizing the President of the United States to accept and organize certain Volunteer Military Corps," dated February 6, 1812. This law was amended in July to allow the president to directly commission officers. See Johnson, "The U.S. Voluntary Corps."
25. Eustis to Tompkins, April 15, 1812, in Irwin, *Daniel D. Tompkins*, 143.
26. Record Series A0802-78, vol. 21, General Order dated 21 April 1812, NYSA/OSC; Hastings, *Tompkins Papers*, 1:318–21.
27. Tompkins to Eustis, June 26, 1812, in Hastings, *Tompkins Papers*, 1:649–51.
28. Tompkins to State Legislature, February 27, 1813, in Hastings, *Tompkins Papers*, 3:277; Reed, "Decius Wadsworth," 530. The Albany arsenal was later named the Gibbonsville Supply Depot and Arsenal and is now the Watervliet Arsenal.

29. Tompkins to Porter, April 18, 1812, in Hastings, *Tompkins Papers*, 2:553–58. Porter departed Washington in mid-April and did not participate in the congressional debates relative to the declaration of war.
30. Tompkins to Armstrong, January 29, 1814, in Hastings, *Tompkins Papers*, 3:444–48.
31. Tompkins to Brent, July 14, 1813, in Hastings, *Tompkins Papers*, 3:346–49; Noon to Porter, May 20, 1812, Porter Papers, roll 2, item A-28, BHM.
32. Tompkins to Van Vechten, February 4, 1812, in Hastings, *Tompkins Papers*, 2:459–67; Tompkins to Paulding, March 21, 1812, in Hastings, *Tompkins Papers*, 2:517–18.
33. Tompkins's report to the Legislature dated November 11, 1812, in Hastings, *Tompkins Papers*, 3:184.
34. General Order dated June 18, 1812, in Hastings, *Tompkins Papers*, 1:336–42.
35. A visitor to Plattsburgh in August 1814 noted that the "dirty" town was "overrun with grog shops and taverns." See Dulles, "Extracts," 283.
36. Jenkins, *Lives of the Governors*, 182.
37. General Order dated July 13, 1812, in Hastings, *Tompkins Papers*, 1:370; Tompkins to Van Rensselaer, July 13, 1812, in Hastings, *Tompkins Papers*, 3:27–28.
38. Tompkins to John Smith, February 22, 1812, in Hastings, *Tompkins Papers*, 2:491; Tompkins to Van Rensselaer, July 13, 1812, in Hastings, *Tompkins Papers*, 1:370.
39. For the fight on State Street in Albany, see Barbagallo, "Fellow Citizens, Read a Horrid Tale . . ."
40. Tompkins to Brown, August 7, 1812, in Hastings, *Tompkins Papers*, 3:56–57.
41. Lovett to Alexander, August 5, 1812, in Bonney, *Legacy of Historical Gleanings*, 203.
42. Tompkins to Bellinger, May 14, 1812, in Hastings, *Tompkins Papers*, 2:608–9; Hough, *History of Jefferson County*, 461. The details of posting militiamen in Ogdensburg is found in Austin, *St. Lawrence County*, 39–45.
43. Tompkins to Swift, April 29, 1812, in Hastings, *Tompkins Papers*, 2:569–70; Swift to Tompkins, June 24, 1812, in Emerson, "An Industrious and Worthy Woman," 8–9.
44. Tompkins to Eustis, April 30, 1812, in Hastings, *Tompkins Papers*, 2:574–78.
45. Smyth to Gansevoort, May 19, 1812, RG 94, Adjutant General Letters Sent, NARA.
46. Tompkins to Porter, June 20, 1812, in Hastings, *Tompkins Papers*, 2:631–33; Tompkins to Porter, May 12, 1812, in Hastings, *Tompkins Papers*, 2:598–600.
47. Tompkins to Anderson, June 13, 1812, in Hastings, *Tompkins Papers*, 2:623–24.
48. Snyder, *Red & White*, 30. A cultural, social, and operational look at the Iroquois written from a Six Nation's perspective is Hill, *War Clubs Wampum Belts*.
49. Granger to the Iroquois Council, September 1808, in Snyder, *Red & White*, 38.
50. Tompkins to Morton, May 9, 1812, in Hastings, *Tompkins Papers*, 2:589.
51. Guernsey, *New York City and Vicinity*, 1:84.
52. General Order dated June 20, 1812, in Hastings, *Tompkins Papers*, 1:343–44; Gero, *Excelsior's Citizen Soldiers*, 74.
53. Tompkins to Porter, June 20, 1812, in Hastings, *Tompkins Papers*, 2:633–34; Stagg, *Mr. Madison's War*, 239–41.
54. Unlike the Royal Navy, the title "commodore" was an honorific in the U.S. Navy, not an official rank. A commodore commanded a squadron of warships. Thus, it would have been appropriate for Rodgers, as well as Chauncey, Perry, and Macdonough, to be addressed as commodore.
55. Strum, "New York Federalists and Opposition," 170; Hickey, *War of 1812*, 39–40; Stagg, *Mr. Madison's War*, 232.

56. For the workings of the Washington Benevolent Society in the 1812 draft of militia, see Dorsey, "Delinquency of George Holcomb."

57. Ellis, *Ruinous and Unhappy War*, 72.

58. Obadiah German, "Unprepared for War with England," 12th Congress, 1st Session, *Annals of America*, 4:319–24.

59. Heidler and Heidler, *Encyclopedia of the War of 1812*, app. 1, "Twelfth Congress votes on Declaration of War," 573. William Paulding Jr. served as the state adjutant general in 1809–1810 and again in 1811–1813, alternating with Solomon Van Rensselaer. He was mayor of New York City, serving three terms between 1825 and 1829.

60. Lampi, "Federalist Party Resurgence," 263; "DeDiemer's Intelligence Report," National Library and Archives of Canada, Ottawa, Canada, RG 8, C.676, 194–97.

61. Clinton's speech is found in *Niles' Weekly Register*, July 18, 1812; See Strum, "Federalists and Opposition" and "The Politics of the New York Antiwar Campaign," for a description of the antiwar cause.

62. Lampi, "Federalist Party Resurgence," 268. The election was conducted in December because the regular April election did not include the reapportioned seats and was subsequently revoked.

63. Tompkins had difficulty providing receipts acceptable to state officials and was never paid back to his satisfaction. Tompkins to Mclean, June 22 and 24, 1812, in Hastings, *Tompkins Papers*, 2:634 and 638.

64. Tompkins to Eustis, June 27, 1812, and Tompkins to Dearborn, June 28, 1812, in Hastings, *Tompkins Papers*, 1:652–58.

65. Tompkins to Clinton, June 24, 1812, in Hastings, *Tompkins Papers*, 2:639–41.

66. Tompkins to Bloomfield, June 27, 1812, in Hastings, *Tompkins Papers*, 1:651–52.

67. Paulding to Mooers and Pettit, June 23 and 26, 1812, in Hastings, *Tompkins Papers*, 1:349–57.

68. Brown to Tompkins, quoted in Hough, *History of Jefferson County*, 461–62.

69. Paulding to Hall, Wadsworth, and Porter, June 23, 1812, in Hastings, *Tompkins Papers*, 1:352–54; Wadsworth to Tompkins, June 28, 1812, in Babcock, *The War of 1812 on the Niagara Frontier*, 32–33.

70. Tompkins to Bullis, July 13, 1812, in Hastings, *Tompkins Papers*, 3:30–32.

71. "DeDiemer's Intelligence Report," National Library and Archives of Canada, Ottawa, Canada, RG 8, C.676, 194–97. The realm of military and naval intelligence has been inadequately treated.

Chapter 3

1. Kutolowski, "Commissioners and Canvasses," 8–11.

2. Turner, *Pioneer History*, 584. See also Densmore's *Red Jacket*.

3. Wadsworth to Tompkins, June 28, 1812, Cruikshank, DHNF, 3:77; Paulding to Hall, July 2, 1812, and Tompkins to Baldwin, August 8, 1812, in Hastings, *Tompkins Papers*, 1:366–67 and 3:68–70.

4. Galloway, "Firing the First Shot," 23–24.

5. Trace, "'Salt Boats Are A-Comin,'" in DeCroix, *War of 1812*, 1:24–29.

6. Petition dated July 30, 1812, Record Series A0802–78, vol. 21, NYSA/OSC.

7. Multiple council records, in Snyder, *Red & White*, 39–47.

8. There are three accounts of the Grand River council. See Snyder, *Red & White*, 47–51.

9. General Order, July 13, 1812, and Tompkins to Van Rensselaer, August 14, 1812, in Hastings, *Tompkins Papers*, 1:370 and 3:78–80.

10. Dearborn to Eustis, August 7, 1812; Dearborn to Mullany, August 8, 1812; Dearborn to Snyder, August 13, 1812, all found in Dearborn, *Defence*, 4–6. See also Johnson, *History of Erie County*, chap. 23.

11. Tompkins to Hall, July 8, 1812, and Tompkins to Macomb, July 12, 1812, in Hastings, *Tompkins Papers*, 3:21–27. The finest study of the Battle of Queenston Heights is Malcomson, *Brilliant Affair*.

12. Tompkins to Hamilton, January 16, 1812, in Hastings, *Tompkins Papers*, 2:428–29; Tompkins to Wadsworth, July 6, 1812, in Hastings, *Tompkins Papers*, 3:12–13; and Tompkins to Porter, July 8, and September 9, 1812, in Hastings, *Tompkins Papers*, 3:19–21 and 3:105–8.

13. Van Rensselaer to Tompkins, August 11, 1812, in Bonney, *Legacy of Historical Gleanings*, 203–5. A study of the preparation and battle is found in Barbuto, *Staff Ride Handbook*, chap. 3. See also Crissman, "Solomon Van Rensselaer."

14. Tompkins to Legislature, March 30, 1813, in Hastings, *Tompkins Papers*, 3:290–91; General Orders dated August 13 and 27, 1812, in Hastings, *Tompkins Papers*, 1:380 and 1:389–90. See Taylor, "Who Murdered William Cooper?"

15. Tompkins to Dearborn and Tompkins to Lewis, August 26, 1812, Tompkins to Hagner, October 9, 1816, in Hastings, *Tompkins Papers*, 3:91–95 and 3:669.

16. For a full treatment of Prevost, see Grodzinski, *Defender of Canada*.

17. The village of Newark was generally referred to by the *locals* as Niagara. Morgan Lewis to spouse Gertrude, September 1, 1812, Delafield, *Morgan Lewis*, 75; Anonymous undated letter held in the Historic Cherry Hill Manuscript Collection, Albany, N.Y.

18. Tompkins to Van Rensselaer, September 9, 1812, in Hastings, *Tompkins Papers*, 3:94–124. Tompkins wrote a flurry of orders between September 9 and 12 conveying a sense of urgency to his militia commanders. The battalion of Irish Greens was drawn very heavily from the state's First Rifle Regiment that garrisoned Staten Island.

19. Van Rensselaer to Tompkins, September 17, 1812, in Bonney, *Legacy of Historical Gleanings*, 236.

20. Van Rensselaer to Dearborn, September 17, 1812, in Bonney, *Legacy of Historical Gleanings*, 233–34. Apparently the writers used birch bark because paper was not available in camp.

21. Tompkins to Porter, September 9, 1812, in Hastings, *Tompkins Papers*, 3:105–8.

22. Dearborn's General Order, Greenbush, September 13, 1812, ASP:MA, 1:490; Smyth to Van Rensselaer, September 29, 1812, Van Rensselaer, *Affair of Queenstown*, 67–68; Van Rensselaer to Smyth, October 5 and 6, 1812, in Bonney, *Legacy of Historical Gleanings*, 242–43.

23. Van Rensselaer to Harriot, October 10, 1812, in Bonney, *Legacy of Historical Gleanings*, 247; Solomon Van Rensselaer's undated letter to the editors of the *Columbian*, Historic Cherry Hill, Albany, N.Y.

24. From a certificate drawn up by Mead November 2, 1821, NYSA/OSC Record Series A0802–78, vol. 22. See also Mead's statement in the *Albany Argus*, March 30, 1813.

25. Inspector's Reports on the Twelfth and Fourteenth Infantry, October 5, 1812, ASP: MA 1:491–92. The two regiments were recruited in Virginia and Maryland.

26. Elliott to Hamilton, October 9, 1812, and Jones to Chauncey, July 14, 1813, in Dudley and Crawford, *Naval War of 1812*, 1:328–31 and 2:500–501. Dr. Cyrenius Chapin, although a Federalist, was an active militia leader. See Kohler, "Colonel Cyrenius Chapin"; Warren, "Two Dramatic Incidents"; Clark, *Military History of Wayne County*, 247–50.

27. Chauncey to Hamilton, October 22, 1812, in Dudley and Crawford, *Naval War of 1812*, 1:339–40.

28. *Buffalo Gazette*, October 27, 1812; Van Rensselaer to Dearborn, October 8, 1812, Cruikshank, DHNF, 4:41.

29. Van Rensselaer to Dearborn, October 8, 1812, in Bonney, *Legacy of Historical Gleanings*, 244–46.

30. Gray to Van Rensselaer, August 31, 1812, Goodyear Collection, BHM. After the battle, Lt. Col. Thompson Mead of the Seventeenth Regiment of Detached Militia claimed that there were an additional eighty boats within ten miles of Lewiston. See *Albany Argus*, March 30, 1813.

31. Van Rensselaer to Smyth, October 10, 1812, Van Rensselaer, *Affair of Queenstown*, 71; Smyth to Van Rensselaer and Hall to Smyth, October 12, 1812, ASP:MA 1:492; Mead, *Albany Argus*, March 30, 1813.

32. Wool's narrative of the Battle of Queenston Heights, Wool Papers, New York State Library, Albany, N.Y.

33. Mead, *Albany Argus*, March 30, 1813.

34. Malcomson's appendices in *Brilliant Affair* are a wealth of information on units and individuals. Van Rensselaer to Dearborn, October 14, 1812, in Bonney, *Legacy of Historical Gleanings*, 256–58. Judge Jedediah Peck was a veteran of the Revolution and served eleven years in the state legislature. He is considered the father of the New York state common school system. He was sixty-four years old at the Battle of Queenston Heights.

35. Willson to Stewart, November 9, 1812, Willson, "Rifleman of Queenston," 374.

36. Shepard, *Autobiography*, 45.

37. *Buffalo Gazette*, October 27, 1812; Gillett, *Army Medical Department*, 161; Van Rensselaer to Dearborn, October 14, 1812, in Bonney, *Legacy of Historical Gleanings*, 256–58.

38. Howe, "Recollections," 382.

39. Lewis to spouse Gertrude, October 22, 1812, Delafield, *Morgan Lewis*, 78; Van Rensselaer to Tompkins, October 23, 1812, *Buffalo Gazette*, December 22, 1812; Bonney, *Legacy of Historical Gleanings*, 275.

40. Smyth to Dearborn, October 24 and November 9, 1812, in Severance, "Alexander Smyth," 221–25; Lovett to Alexander, November 4, 1812 and Livingston to Smyth, November 4, 1812, Cruikshank, DHNF, 2:180–81. Fort Schlosser was an unfortified supply point south of Niagara Falls and Manchester.

41. *Buffalo Gazette*, October 27, 1812.

42. *Buffalo Gazette*, October 27 and November 3, 1812; Tompkins to Van Rensselaer, October 6, 1810, and Tompkins to Smith, February 22, 1812, in Hastings, *Tompkins Papers*, 1:556–57 and 2:491; Wool to Macomb, April 6, 1813, Wool Papers, New York State Library, Albany, N.Y.; Washington Benevolent Society to Van Rensselaer, in Bonney, *Legacy of Historical Gleanings*, 281–83.

43. Address to the Legislature, November 3, 1812, in Hastings, *Tompkins Papers*, 3:179–81.

44. Smyth to Eustis, October 20, 1812, and Eustis to Smyth, November 4, 1812, ASP:MA 1:493.

45. Severance, "Alexander Smyth," 226–27; "Answer of the Men of New York, Inhabiting the Western District," and Livingston to Tompkins, November 14, 1812, Cruikshank, DHNF, 2:194–95 and 213.

46. Parker to Smyth, October 22; Dearborn to Smyth, October 21; and Smyth to Dearborn October 24, 1812, ASP:MA 1:493; Smyth to Dearborn, October 30, 1812, Cruikshank, DHNF, 2:172.

47. Parker to Smyth, October 30, 1812, ASP:MA 1:495. The New York Greens arrived the same day that Parker penned this letter.

48. Smyth to Eustis, undated; Merchant to Smyth, November 23, and Winder to Smyth, November 7, 1812, ASP:MA 1:497, 500 and 509.

49. McFeely to Smyth, November 25, 1812; Scott to the Secretary of War, January 30, 1812, ASP: MA 1:346; Fredriksen, "Chronicle of Valor," 250–52. The story of this American heroine is told by Catherine Emerson in "Worthy Woman."

50. Campbell to Smyth, November 27, 1812, ASP:MA 1:500–501; *Buffalo Gazette*, November 17, 1812.

51. Governor Simon Snyder of the Commonwealth of Pennsylvania, in the General Order dated August 25, 1812, in "Simon Snyder's Mobilization Order to Pennsylvania Militia, August 1812," *Journal of the War of 1812* 11, no. 4 (2009): 25. Sapio notes the particular difficulties in mobilizing Pennsylvania's militia in *Pennsylvania and the War of 1812*, 184–86, in which he cites the "unbelievable lack of coordination between state and national officials."

52. Tannehill to Smyth, November 22, 1812, and undated roster, ASP:MA 1:498–99.

53. Smyth to council of the Six Nations, November 22, 1812; Smyth's proclamation addressed to his "Companions in Arms," November 17, 1812, Cruikshank, DHNF, 2:215–17.

54. Angus to Hamilton, December 1, 1812, in Dudley and Crawford, *Naval War of 1812*, 1:355–59; Smyth's statement found in Severance, "Alexander Smyth," 235–40; King to Smyth, November 28, 1812, and Bisshop to Sheaffe, December 1, 1812, and Winder to Smyth, December 7, 1812, all Cruikshank, DHNF 2:245–46; 253–56; and 2:260–63.

55. General Order dated November 27, 1812, ASP:MA 1:500.

56. Dearborn to Smyth, October 21, 1812, ASP:MA 1:493–44; Smyth to Dearborn, December 8, 1812, in Cruikshank, DHNF, 2:287–91.

57. Severance, "Alexander Smyth," 240–41. Chapin to Van Rensselaer, December 13, 1812, Cruikshank, DHNF, 2:301.

58. Tompkins to Fleming, dated January 2, 1813, in Hastings, *Tompkins Papers*, 3:218–19; Dearborn to Madison, December 13, 1812, James Madison Papers, Series 1, reel 14, LOC.

59. Morning Reports for infantry and artillery regiments dated December 1, 1812, ASP:MA 1:504–6; McFeely to Smyth, December 1, 1812, ASP:MA 1:507; Winder to Smyth, December 2, 1812, ASP:MA 1:507; Cummings to Magraw, December 11, 1812, BHM; Tannehill to Smyth, December 7, 1812, ASP:MA 1:507.

60. The documentary evidence of Smyth's period in command is found in "On the Manner in Which the War has been Conducted," February 8, 1814, ASP:MA 1:490–513.
61. Yetwin, *Mordecai Myers*, 91.
62. Chauncey to Hamilton, January 8, 1813, in Dudley and Crawford, *Naval War of 1812*, 2:407–10.
63. The main camp was Flint Hill, located in what is now Delaware Park and Forest Lawn Cemetery in Buffalo.
64. Drs. Daniel Chapin and Cyrenius Chapin, unrelated, were professional rivals and both contributed notably to their communities. One source addressing the deaths at Flint Hill is "Public Ceremonies," in *Report of the Buffalo Park Commissioners*, 95–128.

Chapter 4

1. For a detailed design study of Woolsey's brig, see Gibson, *Oneida*.
2. Malcomson, *Lords of the Lake*, 17–22.
3. Malcomson, *Lords of the Lake*, 29–34.
4. The story of the 32-pounder is found in Hough, *Jefferson County*, 464.
5. Steppler's "A Duty Troublesome Beyond Measure" remains the best scholarly study of British wartime logistics. A summary of Steppler's work is found in "Logistics on the Canadian Frontier."
6. Brown to Tompkins, August 4 and 10, 1812, Hough, *Jefferson County*, 465–66.
7. General Order dated August 13, 1812, and Tompkins to Woolsey, September 9, 1812, in Hastings, *Tompkins Papers*, 1:377–79 and 3:101–2; *Buffalo Gazette*, October 13, 1812.
8. General Orders dated September 9 and 15, 1812, in Hastings, *Tompkins Papers*, 1:396–403.
9. Benjamin Forsyth led his riflemen with skill and daring in numerous engagements until his death near Odelltown. For a sketch of his service, see Lemmon, *Frustrated Patriots*, 65–67 and 97–107.
10. Brown to Tompkins, September 17, 1812, Hough, *Jefferson County*, 466–67.
11. Gibson, *Oneida*, 37–38. For an evaluation of Chauncey, see Brodine, "Cautious Commodore?"
12. Chauncey to Hamilton, October 8, 1812, in Dudley and Crawford, *Naval War of 1812*, 1:336–37.
13. Tompkins to Dearborn, October 8, and Tompkins to Dodge, October 10, and Tompkins to Brown, October 9, 1812, in Hastings, *Tompkins Papers*, 3:156–69. See Darby Noon's contract with Samuel Hooker to build barracks, June 6, 1812, Sackets Harbor Battlefield Library, Sackets Harbor, N.Y.
14. Chauncey to Hamilton, October 21 and 22, and November 6, 13, and 17, 1812, in Dudley and Crawford, *Naval War of 1812*, 1:338–49.
15. Third Artillery Regiment Orderly Book, New York State Library, Albany, N.Y., Manuscript Collection, entry for 14 November 1812. Lieutenant John Biddle was a member of the wealthy and influential Biddle family of Philadelphia.
16. Chauncey to Hamilton, November 22, 1812, in Dudley and Crawford, *Naval War of 1812*, 1:352; Barbuto, *Long Range Guns*, 47–51.
17. Tompkins to Parish, October 9, 1812, in Hastings, *Tompkins Papers*, 3:163–64. See also Hitsman, "David Parish" and Austin, *St. Lawrence County*, chap. 2, "David

Parish and His Money Tree." Although born in Hamburg, Parish was raised in an English-speaking household. Austin makes the case that Parish dealt with authorities in both the U.S. and Canada to ensure the preservation and prosperity of his land and financial holdings.

18. Tompkins to Dodge, October 10, 1812, in Hastings, *Tompkins Papers*, 3:166–67.

19. Forsyth was promoted to major on January 20 and brevetted to lieutenant colonel on February 6 for distinguished service. Tompkins to Brown, February 25, 1813, in Hastings, *Tompkins Papers*, 1:440–41; Forsyth to Macomb, February 22, 1813, ASP:MA 1:441; General Order, Kingston, February 23, 1813, and General Order, Montreal, February 25, 1813, in Wood, *Select British Documents*, 2:17–20. See also Graves, "War on the Ice," and Austin, *St. Lawrence County*, chap. 4, "The Lion Scratches Back."

20. As an example, Commodore Isaac Chauncey had Samuel Stacy of Ogdensburg arrested at Sackett's Harbor for espionage. Stacy was a civilian and could not be tried by court-martial. Charges against civilians were addressed in civil court. See Chauncey to Jones, July 4, 1813, in Dudley and Crawford, *Naval War of 1812*, 2:521; Benedict to Lewis, July 10, 1813, RG 45, M222, Roll 7, NARA; and Jones to Chauncey, July 19, 1813, RG 45, T829, Roll 453, Private Letters, item 30, NARA. As further evidence of collaboration, see Austin, *St. Lawrence County*, chap. 1, "The Emperor Ford."

21. Tompkins to Young, January 6, 1813, in Hastings, *Tompkins Papers*, 3:223.

22. Gibson, "Militia, Mud and Misery," 250–53.

23. Chauncey to Dearborn, November 30, and Chauncey to Hamilton, December 1, 1812, in Dudley and Crawford, *Naval War of 1812*, 1:361–64.

24. Angus to Hamilton, December 27, 1812, in Dudley and Crawford, *Naval War of 1812*, 1:327–28; Chauncey to Pettigrew, January 9, 1813, in Dudley and Crawford, *Naval War of 1812*, 2:411.

25. Tompkins report to the Legislature, November 11, 1812, in Hastings, *Tompkins Papers*, 3:185.

26. Tompkins to Armstrong, February 6, 1813, and Tompkins to Legislature, March 31, 1813, in Hastings, *Tompkins Papers*, 3:241–43 and 3:291–96.

Chapter 5

1. Lewis to Madison, August 21, 1812, James Madison Papers, series 1 reel 14, LOC.

2. Tompkins to Galusha and Tompkins to Clark, June 30, 1812, in Hastings, *Tompkins Papers*, 2:648–52; Muller, "Traitorous and Diabolical Traffic," 79.

3. Tompkins to Livingston, August 7, 1812, in Hastings, *Tompkins Papers*, 3:67–68; Livingston to Tompkins, August 12, 1812, in Irwin, *Daniel D. Tompkins*, 152–53.

4. Yetwin, *Mordecai Myers*, 86–87.

5. Yetwin, *Mordecai Myers*, 122.

6. Tompkins to Mooers, September 14, 1812, in Hastings, *Tompkins Papers*, 3:125–26.

7. Tompkins to Bloomfield, September 18 and 22, 1812, in Hastings, *Tompkins Papers*, 3:134–41.

8. Dearborn to Madison, September 30, 1812, James Madison Papers, series 1 reel 14, LOC.

9. Macdonough to Hamilton, October 14 and 26, 1812, and Macdonough to Jones, January 22, 1813, in Dudley and Crawford, *Naval War of 1812*, 1:325–27 and 2:424–25. See also Skaggs, *Thomas Macdonough*.

10. "Treaty for Release of Prisoners," Cruikshank, DHNF, 2:195–97.
11. Tompkins to the St. Regis Nation, November 7, 1812, in Hastings, *Tompkins Papers*, 3:181–82.
12. Dearborn to Smyth, October 28, 1812, Cruikshank, DHNF, 2:168; Dearborn to Eustis, November 8 and 24, 1812, Secretary of War, Letters Received, RG 107, NARA; Erney, "Dearborn," 297–99.
13. Dearborn to Eustis, November 24, 1812, Secretary of War, Letters Received, RG 107, NARA.
14. Malcomson, *Historical Dictionary*, 276–77.
15. Orderly Book of Captain John Straight's Company of Detached Militia, Feinberg Library, SUNY Plattsburgh.
16. Graves, "Hard School of War," 4.
17. Horsman, *Frontier Doctor*, 28–29. Beaumont was born in Connecticut but moved to Champlain, New York at the age of 21. After the war he established a practice in Plattsburgh and later continued his career as an army surgeon.
18. Mann, *Medical Sketches*, 19–24 and 45.
19. Tompkins to Hathaway and Ross, December 9, 1812, in Hastings, *Tompkins Papers*, 3:211–12.

Chapter 6

1. Three General Orders dated June 27, 1812, in Hastings, *Tompkins Papers*, 1:345–48.
2. Record Series A0802-78, vol. 23, NYSA/OSC; Mohl, *Poverty*, 85.
3. The use of the navy is ably presented in Kastor, "Maritime War Only."
4. Guernsey, *New York City*, 1:8.
5. Arthur, *How Britain Won the War*, 66; Tompkins to Legislature, November 3, 1812, in Hastings, *Tompkins Papers*, 3:180.
6. Statement by Tompkins found in "Spirit and Manner in Which the War is Waged by the Enemy," ASP:MA, 1:345–65.
7. Galpin, "Grain Trade," 29–39. In 1811, 60 percent of American grain exports went to Portugal and Spain. About 20 percent of the ships arriving in the port of Lisbon had come directly from New York City. For an analysis of the impact of U.S. grain trade on Wellington's campaign, see Watson, "The United States and the Peninsular War."
8. Jaffe, *New York at War*, 132–33. Prevost's policy was issued on July 11, 1812, *Niles' Weekly Register*, August 1, 1812. The *Ontario Repository* of August 11, 1812, shows Prevost's edict pertaining to Lower Canada, issued on July 10 and offering some Americans release from the requirement to bear arms against their fellow Americans.
9. Woodworth suspended the paper on September 6, 1814, but published a large 'wrap up' issue following the termination of the conflict. *The War* is available from the Lilly Library at the University of Indiana and Brock University, Canada. Woodworth is best known for his poem, "The Old Oaken Bucket."
10. Armstrong to Madison, August 3, 1812, James Madison Papers, series 1, reel 14, LOC; Tompkins to Armstrong, July 28, 1812, Adjutant General Letters Received, RG 94, NARA; Fredriksen, *Officers*, 33–35.
11. Hull to Hamilton, October 15, 1812, in Dudley and Crawford, *Naval War of 1812*, 1:532–33.

12. Jefferson to Duane, August 4, 1812, Thomas Jefferson Papers, LOC; Kert, *Privateering*, Introduction.

13. For the financial aspects of privateering, see Leiner's "Privateers and Profit."

14. Guernsey, *New York City*, 1:123; Kert, *Privateering*, 153.

15. There were no privateers on Lake Ontario; the probability of meeting a British warship was too high. Gibson, "Pirates and Robbers," 3. *The War*, August 8, 1812.

16. "Spirit and Manner in Which the War Is Waged by the Enemy," ASP:MA, 1:345–65.

17. Guernsey, *New York City*, 1:119; Hastings, *Tompkins Papers*, 1:99 and 1:425–35.

18. Steenshorne, "Evacuation Day," 13.

19. Tompkins to Eustis, September 9, 1812, in Hastings, *Tompkins Papers*, 3:103–5.

20. Tompkins to Legislature, March 31, 1813, in Hastings, *Tompkins Papers*, 3:291–96.

21. Tompkins to Brent, January 11, 1813, and Tompkins to Dobbin, March 13, 1813, in Hastings, *Tompkins Papers*, 3:226–30 and 3:310–11.

22. Benedict to McIntyre, Comptroller, June 22, 1818, and Statement of John McMahan, December 11, 1822, Record Series A0802-78, vol. 23, NYSA/OSC.

23. Report on the petition of James McMahan, March 27, 1822, Record Series A0979, Reports, NYSA/OSC.

24. Record Series A0802-78, vol. 10, NYSA/OSC.

25. Spencer to Dox, June 8, 1815, Record Series A0802-78, vol. 10, NYSA/OSC.

26. Dearborn to Madison, December 13, 1812, James Madison Papers, Series 1, reel 14, LOC.

Chapter 7

1. Jones to Chauncey, January 27, 1813, in Dudley and Crawford, *Naval War of 1812*, 2:419–20.

2. Brant, *James Madison, Commander in Chief*, 126–28; Gallatin to Madison, January 4 and 7, 1813, Rutland et al., *Papers of James Madison, Presidential Series*, 5:552 and 5:557–58.

3. Fulton to Madison, March 18, 1813, James Madison Papers, series 1, reel 15, LOC. Worth wrote a lengthy memoir covering the 1813 campaigns, Graves, *First Campaign*.

4. Gibson, "Profits vs. Patriotism"; Storm, "War on Business."

5. The best study of the 1813 gubernatorial election is Strum's "House Divided."

6. Jenkins, *Lives of the Governors*, 184–86.

7. Armstrong to the Cabinet, February 8, 1813, ASP:MA, 1:439. The finest book-length study of the battle for York is Malcomson's *Capital in Flames*.

8. Armstrong to Dearborn, February 10, 1813, Armstrong, *Notices*, 221–22; Dearborn to Armstrong, March 3 and March 9, 1813; ASP:MA, 1:441. Over twenty of Pike's soldiers were hospitalized for frozen feet following their trek from Lake Champlain to Sackett's Harbor, Gillett, *Army Medical Department*, 167.

9. Dearborn to Armstrong, March 16, 1813; Dearborn to Armstrong, undated, and Armstrong to Dearborn, March 29, 1813, ASP:MA, 1:442; Chauncey to Jones, March 18, and Jones to Chauncey, April 8, 1813, in Dudley and Crawford, *Naval War of 1812*, 2:430–34.

10. Tompkins to Hopkins, February 11, 1813, in Hastings, *Tompkins Papers*, 3:251.

11. Fredricksen, "Plow-Joggers," 17–18.

12. Chauncey to Jones, April 24, 1813, in Dudley and Crawford, *Naval War of 1812*, 2:448.

13. This peninsula is now the Toronto Islands.

14. Malcomson, *Capital in Flames*, 346–98; Malcomson, "New Yorkers at York."

15. Sheaffe's full report is found in Sheaffe to Prevost, May 5, 1813, in Dudley and Crawford, *Naval War of 1812*, 2:455–57.

16. For casualties see Malcomson's *Capital in Flames*, chap. 11 and appendix 8.

17. *Capital in Flames*, chap. 13; Chauncey to Jones and Dearborn to Armstrong, April 28, 1813, in Dudley and Crawford, *Naval War of 1812*, 2:449–52; Terms of Capitulation, April 28, 1813, in Wood, *Select British Documents*, 2:84–85; Sheaffe to Prevost, May 5, 1813, in Wood, *Select British Documents*, 2:89–94. Captured public property included artillery pieces, batteaux, anchors, and immense quantities of tools, rigging, nails, iron, ammunition, uniforms, flour, salt meat, and farm implements.

18. Horsman, *Frontier Doctor*, 37.

19. Fredriksen, "Plow-Joggers," 19. Many of the creeks draining into the western end of Lake Ontario were named by the number of miles from the mouth of the Niagara River, e.g., Four Mile Creek in New York and Forty Mile Creek in Upper Canada.

20. Dearborn to Armstrong, May 3 and May 13, 1813, ASP:MA, 1:444–45. Before he entered the U.S. Army, John Boyd spent nine years in India commanding native troops and amassing a small fortune.

21. Chauncey to Jones, May 15 and 28, 1813, in Dudley and Crawford, *Naval War of 1812*, 2:462–64.

22. William Beaumont to Samuel Beaumont, June 1, 1813, William and Samuel Beaumont Papers, U.S. Army Military History Institute, Carlisle Barracks, Pa.

23. Scott to Gardner, Gardner Papers, New York State Library, Albany, N.Y.

24. Dearborn to Armstrong, May 27, 1813, ASP:MA, 1:444–45.

25. Scott to Gardner, June 4, 1813, Gardner Papers, New York State Library, Albany, N.Y.

26. Yetwin, *Mordecai Myers*, 101.

27. Vincent to Prevost, May 28, 1813, in Wood, *Select British Documents*, 2:103–7.

28. Chauncey to Jones, May 29, 1813, in Dudley and Crawford, *Naval War of 1812*, 2:480.

Chapter 8

1. Tompkins to Clark, February 11, 1813, in Hastings, *Tompkins Papers*, 3:252–53.

2. Chauncey to Jones, February 5, 1813, in Dudley and Crawford, *Naval War of 1812*, 2:425; Tompkins to Brown, February 11, 1813, and Tompkins to Dearborn, February 12, 1813, in Hastings, *Tompkins Papers*, 3:253–56.

3. Tompkins to Armstrong, May 13, 1813, ASP:MA, 1:444; General Order dated October 2, 1812, in Hastings, *Tompkins Papers*, 1:403–4; Gero, *Excelsior's Citizen Soldiers*,116–17; Gillett, *Army Medical Department*, 167. The navy and marines had their own hospital on Navy Point that was burned during the raid.

4. Macomb to Dearborn, February 28, 1813, Third Artillery Regiment Orderly Book, Manuscript Collection, New York State Library, Albany, N.Y.

5. February 25, 1813, Third Artillery Regiment Orderly Book, Manuscript Collection, New York State Library, Albany, N.Y.

6. Malcolmson, *Lords of the Lake*, chap. 5.
7. Yeo to Admiralty, May 26, 1813, in Dudley and Crawford, *Naval War of 1812*, 2:469–70. The lines of command in Canada were somewhat blurry. Prevost believed he commanded Yeo; however, Yeo understood that he should cooperate with Prevost but report to Admiral Sir John Borlase Warren, commander of the Royal Navy North America Station at Halifax, Nova Scotia.
8. Admiralty to Yeo, March 19, 1813, in Dudley and Crawford, *Naval War of 1812*, 2:435–36.
9. Isaac Chauncey to Wolcott Chauncey, May 20, 1813, in Dudley and Crawford, *Naval War of 1812*, 2:467. The book-length study of the battle is Wilder's *Sackett's Harbour*. For the new warship, see Gibson, "U.S. Frigate *General Pike*."
10. Officers could not directly command forces of their sister service. Operational command of a joint operation was given to the senior officer. A commodore outranked a colonel. Thus, Yeo would have operational command of the raiding force—army and navy. Prevost was unwilling to allow this arrangement, and by his presence on the ground, he retained overall direction of the battle and responsibility for it.
11. Brown to Armstrong, June 1, 1813, in Dudley and Crawford, *Naval War of 1812*, 2:473–77.
12. See Morris, *Sword of the Border*, chap. 3, for Brown's role.
13. Wilder provides a good review of the confusion leading to the command to burn the shipyard. See *Sackett's Harbour*, 99–105. Drury was cleared of responsibility in his court-martial.
14. Baynes to Prevost, May 30, 1813, and Prevost to Bathurst, June 1, 1813, Wood, *British Documents*, 2:123–34.
15. Brown to Armstrong, June 1, 1813, in Dudley and Crawford, *Naval War of 1812*, 2:473–77; Brown to Tompkins, June 1, 1813, quoted in Wilder, *Sackett's Harbour*, 121–22.
16. Tompkins to Brown, July 2, 1812, in Hastings, *Tompkins Papers*, 3:328–29.
17. Extract from "Memoir of Lieutenant David Wingfield, R.N.," in Dudley and Crawford, *Naval War of 1812*, 2:470–73.
18. This is John Morris's assessment in *Sword of the Border*, 48.
19. Chauncey to Jones, June 2, 1813, in Dudley and Crawford, *Naval War of 1812*, 2:477–78.

Chapter 9

1. Chauncey to Jones, June 11, 1813, in Dudley and Crawford, *Naval War of 1812*, 2:493–94. Malcomson estimates that at the end of May 1813, the American squadron had eighty-two guns, while British vessels had ninety, hardly a decisive difference, *Lords of the Lake*, 142.
2. Perhaps the best history of the failed pursuit of Vincent's force is Elliott's *Strange Fatality*.
3. Anon. "1813, The Battle of Stoney Creek," 58.
4. Fredriksen, "Memoirs of Captain Ephraim Shaler," 419; For the order of battle, see Elliott, *Strange Fatality*, Appendix E.
5. Yetwin, *Mordecai Myers*, 103; Harvey to Baynes, June 6, 1813, and Vincent to Prevost, June 6, 1813, in Wood, *Select British Documents*, 2:139–45.
6. Yeo to Admiralty, June 29, 1813, in Hanford, *Notes*, 5–6.

7. Fredriksen, "Plow-Joggers," 19.

8. Dearborn to Armstrong, June 6 and 8, and Lewis to Armstrong, June 14, 1813, ASP:MA, 1:446.

9. Lewis to Armstrong, June 14 and 20, 1813, ASP:MA, 1:446–49; Mann, *Medical Sketches*, 62–63 and 89.

10. *Montreal Gazette*, July 6, 1813. Laura Secord was married to Canadian militiaman James Secord, who had been badly wounded at the Battle of Queenston Heights. Somehow she learned of the American expedition to attack FitzGibbon's men and set off to warn him.

11. Terms of Capitulation, June 24, 1813, and Boerstler to Dearborn June 25, 1813, in Wood, *Select British Documents*, 2:160–62. For detailed narratives, see Cruikshank, *Beechwoods*; Armstrong, *Notices*; and Chapin, *Review*.

12. *Buffalo Gazette*, July 29, 1813; Kohler, "Colonel Cyrenius Chapin," 28–29.

13. Armstrong to Dearborn, July 6, 1813, ASP:MA, 1:449; Armstrong to Boyd, July 7, 1813, Mann, *Medical Sketches*, 204. Madison sent Dearborn a conciliatory note to offset Armstrong's heavy hand. See Madison to Dearborn, August 8, 1813, , in Hunt, *Writings of James Madison*, 8:256–57.

14. Armstrong to the Six Nations, April 9, 1813, in Snyder, *Red & White*, 58–59; Benn, *Iroquois*, 130–31.

15. Cornplanter, Black Snake, Johnston Silverheals, and Big John to Granger, 3 June 30, 1813, in Snyder, *Red & White*, 65.

16. Clark to Harvey, July 5, 1813, in Wood, *Select British Documents*, 2:174–75.

17. A good account of this skirmish is found in Benn, *Iroquois*, 124–27. See also Yetwin, *Mordecai Myers*, 104–5.

18. Porter to Armstrong, August 9, 1813, in Snyder, *Red & White*, 68–70.

19. Allen, "Bisshopp Papers," 22–29; Clark to Harvey, July 12, 1813, in Wood, *Select British Documents*, 2:176–79.

20. Aigin, "Affair of June 4, 1813." See also Dorsheimer, "Village of Buffalo,"192–93; Rutland, "Guardsman of Buffalo," 867–70; Porter to Armstrong, August 9, 1813, in Snyder, *Red & White*, 70. For another firsthand report, see James Sloan's Memoir, Manuscript Collection, Buffalo & Erie County Public Library, Buffalo, N.Y..

21. Tompkins to Hall, July 27, 1813, in Hastings, *Tompkins Papers*, 3:357–58.

22. Records of the Council held at Buffalo on July 25, 1813, in Snyder, *Red & White*, 65–67; Fredriksen, "Chronicle of Valor," 267; Benn, *Iroquois*,130.

23. Scott, *Memoirs*, 98; Benn, *Iroquois*, 138–40.

24. Yeo to Admiralty, June 29, 1813, in Dudley and Crawford, *Naval War of 1812*, 2:498; Woolsey to Chauncey, June 19, 1813, in Dudley and Crawford, *Naval War of 1812*, 2:495–96; Hanford, *Notes*, 5–6. Visitors to the Charlotte neighborhood in Rochester will find the shoreline much further north than that of 1812. Although it was built after the battle, the Charlotte–Genesee lighthouse marks the approximate shoreline in the early nineteenth century.

25. *The Ontario Messenger*, Canandaigua, June 29, 1813; Clark, *Wayne County*, 197–210; Burnet to Tompkins, June 26, 1813, in Hastings, *Tompkins Papers*, 3:351–52. The shoreline at Sodus Point was considerably different at the time of the raid than it is today. The peninsula traversed by Greig Street is the 1812 feature, not the more northerly peninsula tipped by Sodus Point Beach Park.

26. Jones to Chauncey, June 17; Strachan to Baynes, August 2; Chauncey to Jones, August 4,1813, in Dudley and Crawford, *Naval War of 1812*, 2:494–95 and 2:526–29; Scott to Boyd, August 3, 1813, ASP:MA, 1:450.

27. Chauncey to Jones, August 13, 1813, in Dudley and Crawford, *Naval War of 1812*, 2:537–41.

28. Yeo to Admiralty, July 16, 1813, in Dudley and Crawford, *Naval War of 1812*, 2:502–3.

29. Yeo to Prevost, August 11, and Chauncey to Jones, August 13, 1813, in Dudley and Crawford, *Naval War of 1812*, 2:535–41. James Fenimore Cooper served as a militia captain in 1814 in Otsego County.

30. Yeo to Warren and Chauncey to Jones, September 12, 1813, in Dudley and Crawford, *Naval War of 1812*, 2:579–81.

31. Chauncey to Jones, October 1, 1813, in Dudley and Crawford, *Naval War of 1812*, 2:586–88; Yeo to Warren, September 29, 1813, in Wood, *Select British Documents*, 2:208–9. The story of the Burlington Races is well told in Malcomson, *Lords of the Lake*, chap. 12.

32. Prevost to Bathurst, August 25, 1813, in Wood, *Select British Documents*, 2:185–86.

33. Mann, *Medical Sketches*, 66–68 and 73–74.

34. The standard biography is Jacobs, *Tarnished Warrior*. See also Linklater, *Artist in Treason*.

Chapter 10

1. Tompkins to Fleming, January 2, 1813, in Hastings, *Tompkins Papers*, 3:219.

2. Tompkins to State Assembly, March 15, 1813, in Hastings, *Tompkins Papers*, 3:282–90.

3. Clinton to Tompkins, January 23, 1813, in Hastings, *Tompkins Papers*, 3:259–60.

4. Swift, *Memoirs*, 109–10; Aimone, "West Point's Contribution," 39–41; Forman, "Military Academy."

5. Randall to father, March 23, 1813, Randall Papers, Maryland Historical Society, Baltimore.

6. Fredriksen, "Tempered Sword," 7.

7. Guernsey, *New York City*, 1:213; Fredriksen, *The United States Army in the War of 1812*; Records of the Third Military District, RG 98, NARA.

8. Stevens to Fenwick, September 9, 1813, Stevens Letter Book, Manuscript Collection, New-York Historical Society.

9. Stevens to Fenwick, November 8, 1813, Stevens Letter Book, Manuscript Collection, New-York Historical Society.

10. Tompkins to Richard Platt, July 17, 1813, and Tompkins to Fenwick, October 19, 1813, Hastings *Tompkins Papers*, 3:354–57 and 3:398–99.

11. Guernsey, *New York City* 1:228–34. Captain William Hawley resigned his militia commission in 1814, *Military Minutes*, 2:1465.

12. General Orders dated July 31 and September 1, 1813, in Hastings, *Tompkins Papers*, 1:445–61.

13. Guernsey, *New York City*, 1:204.

14. Guernsey, *New York City*, 1:208–10.

15. Melville to Warren, March 26, 1813, in Dudley and Crawford, *Naval War of 1812*, 2:78–79; Guernsey, *New York City*, 1:212.

16. Jones to Lewis, April 23, and Jones to Fish, May 15, 1813, and Lewis's rejoinder to Jones, May 23, 1813, in Dudley and Crawford, *Naval War of 1812*, 2:106–11.
17. Guernsey, *New York City*, 1:216.
18. The evolution of the blockade is described in Dudley, "1813: The Grip Tightens," in *Splintering the Wooden Wall*, 79–109.
19. Guernsey, *New York City*, 1:292.
20. On September 27, 1813, the number of larger idle merchant vessels was reported as 122, plus eighteen sloops and schooners, Guernsey, *New York City*, 1:383. See also Arthur, *How Britain Won the War*, 92–94, 101–2, 146.
21. Tompkins to Jones, June 18, 1813, in Hastings, *Tompkins Papers*, 3:330–32.
22. Guernsey, *New York City*, 2:4–6.
23. Leiner, "Privateers and Profit," 1246–47; Guernsey, *New York City*, 1:383–84.
24. Guernsey, *New York City*, 1:211 and 1:386; Kert, *Privateering*, 153.
25. Kert, *Privateering*, 107; Tanner, "Young Teazer."
26. Fulton to Jones, April 27, Lewis to Jones, June 20 and 28, 1813, in Dudley and Crawford, *Naval War of 1812*, 2:111–14; Gibson, "Oddities," 3–6.
27. Fulton to Decatur, August 5, and Decatur to Fulton, August 9, 1813, in Dudley and Crawford, *Naval War of 1812*, 2: 211–12.
28. Hardy to Warren, June 26, and Lewis to Jones, June 28, 1813, in Dudley and Crawford, *Naval War of 1812*, 2:161–62.
29. Guernsey, *New York City*, 1:359–80.

Chapter 11

1. See Graves, *Field of Glory*, for a comprehensive narrative of the campaign. Lewis arrived at Sackett's Harbor on July 2, Armstrong to Lewis, July 3 and 9, 1813, ASP:MA, 1:451.
2. Purdy to Wilkinson, undated, ASP:MA, 1:479.
3. Armstrong to Wilkinson, August 5, 1813, ASP:MA, 1:463.
4. Wilkinson to Armstrong, August 6, 1813, ASP:MA, 1:464.
5. Armstrong to Wilkinson, August 8 and 9, 1813, ASP:MA 1:464–65.
6. Tompkins to Hawkins, August 21, 1813, in Hastings, *Tompkins Papers*, 3:371–72.
7. Tompkins to Hopkins, September 16, 1813, in Hastings, *Tompkins Papers*, 3:384–88. In March 1813, Armstrong ordered the army to use William Duane's *A Hand Book for Infantry*. Tompkins wanted the militia to use the same tactical doctrine.
8. Armstrong to Harrison, September 22 and October 30, and Harrison to Armstrong, October 24, 1813, ASP:MA, 1:455–56.
9. Macdonough to Jones, May 1, 1813, in Dudley and Crawford, *Naval War of 1812*, 2:460.
10. Macdonough to Jones, June 4 and July 22, and Jones to Macdonough, June 17, 1813, in Dudley and Crawford, *Naval War of 1812*, 2:490–91 and 2:513–16; Taylor to Stovin, June 3, 1813, in Wood, *Select British Documents*, 2:221–23.
11. Instructions for Lieutenant Colonel Murray, July 27, 1813, and Macdonough to Jones, August 3, 1813, in Dudley and Crawford, *Naval War of 1812*, 2:517–19; Samuel Beaumont Jr. to father, August 8, 1813, Beaumont Papers, U.S. Army Military History Institute, Carlisle Barracks, Pa.; Murray to Sheaffe, August 3, 1813, in Wood, *Select British Documents*, 2:235–36.
12. Hampton to Armstrong, September 7, 1813, ASP:MA, 1:458.

13. Regarding the disparity of spelling between village, river, and battle: I defer to the national spellings. Thus, the village of Chateaugay and the Battle of Chateauguay. While the river originates in New York, the engagement took place across the border in Lower Canada.

14. Armstrong to Hampton, September 28, 1813, ASP:MA, 1:460.

15. Hampton to Armstrong, October 4, 1813, ASP:MA, 1:460.

16. Hampton to Armstrong, October 12, and Armstrong to Hampton, October 16, 1813, ASP:MA 1:460–61.

17. Hampton to Armstrong, November 1, 1813, ASP:MA, 1:461.

18. Purdy to Wilkinson, undated, ASP:MA, 1:479. The best analysis of Hampton's campaign is found in Graves, *Field of Glory*, chap. 5.

19. Hampton to Armstrong, November 1, 1813, ASP:MA, 1:461.

20. De Salaberry to De Watteville, October 26, 1813, and Prevost to Bathurst, October 30, 1813, in Wood, *Select British Documents*, 2:386–87 and 2:392–95; Graves, *Field of Glory*, 110–11 and appendices B and C.

21. Wilkinson to Hampton, November 6, and Hampton to Wilkinson, November 8, 1813, ASP:MA, 1:462.

22. Hampton to Armstrong, November 12, 1813, ASP:MA, 1:462–63; Mann, *Medical Sketches*, 116.

23. Fredriksen, "Tempered Sword," 13; Fredriksen, "General George Izard's Journal," 197.

Chapter 12

1. The British refer to this engagement as the Battle of Goose Creek. While the engagement is recorded in Hough, *Jefferson County*, 494–95, the most recent analysis is *The Pork Barrel Fort* by Lewis P. Beers Jr. See also Gibson, "Pirates and Robbers," 15–23; Malcomson, *Historical Dictionary*, 123–34; and *Buffalo Gazette*, August 10, 1813.

2. See Graves, *Field of Glory* for an analysis of the Chateauguay-Crysler's Farm campaign. Wilkinson to Armstrong, August 21 and 26, 1813, ASP:MA, 1:465. "To take the stud" was to be obstinate and uncooperative.

3. Wilkinson to Armstrong, August 26 and 30, 1813, ASP:MA, 1:465–66.

4. General Order dated September 4, 1813, in Hastings, *Tompkins Papers*, 1:462–66.

5. Powers to Ingersoll, Ingersoll Papers, box 2, folder 15, Historical Society of Pennsylvania, Philadelphia.

6. Wilkinson to Armstrong, September 11, 16, and 18, 1813, ASP:MA, 1:466–67.

7. Wilkinson to Armstrong, September 20, 1813, ASP:MA, 1:468–69.

8. Wilkinson to Armstrong, October 2 and October 2, 1813; Armstrong to Wilkinson October 9 and October 19, 1813, ASP:MA, 1:470–71.

9. Armstrong to Wilkinson August 8, and October 20, 1813, ASP:MA, 1:464 and 1:473.

10. Wilkinson to Armstrong, November 16, 1813, ASP:MA, 1:475.

11. Chauncey to Jones, October 30, 1813, in Dudley and Crawford, *Naval War of 1812*, 2:594–96; Hough, *Jefferson County*, 502–5.

12. Mulcaster to Yeo, November 2, 1813, in Dudley and Crawford, *Naval War of 1812*, 2:596–97.

13. Morrison to De Rottenburg, November 12, 1813, in Wood, *Select British Documents*, 2:441–44.

14. Fredriksen, "Reynold M. Kirby," 71; Gardner to Wood, November 20, 1813, Gardner Papers, New York State Library, Albany, N.Y.; Fredriksen, "Georgia Officer," 683.
15. Wilkinson to Hampton, November 12, and Wilkinson to Armstrong, November 16, 1813, ASP:MA, 1:463 and 475.
16. Orders issued by the Assistant Adjutant at French Mills, RG 98, item no. 46, NARA.
17. Armstrong to Wilkinson, 25 November 1813, ASP:MA, 1:480.
18. Gardner to mother, November 30, 1813, Gardner Papers, New York State Library, Albany, N.Y.
19. Miller to spouse, December 8, 1813, War of 1812 Collection, Clements Library, University of Michigan; Fredriksen, "Reynold M. Kirby," 75.
20. Mann, *Medical Sketches*, 117–20.
21. Fredriksen, "Chronicle of Valor," 270.

Chapter 13

1. General Orders dated August 25 and 28, 1813, in Hastings, *Tompkins Papers*, 1:452–57.
2. Tompkins to McClure, August 27, 1813, in Hastings, *Tompkins Papers*, 3:373–79.
3. Tompkins to Wilkinson, August 31, 1813, in Hastings, *Tompkins Papers*, 3:382–84.
4. Porter, Cyrenius Chapin, and Joseph M'Clure to Wilkinson, September 17, Wilkinson to Porter, September 18, and Armstrong to Wilkinson, September 22, 1813, ASP:MA, 1:467–69.
5. Graves, *Field of Glory*, 61; "McClure to the Public," January 1, 1814, Brannan, *Official Letters*, 290–92.
6. Council at Buffalo, September 8, 1813, in Snyder, *Red & White*, 59–60.
7. Scott to Wilkinson, October 11, 1813, ASP:MA, 1:482–83; Rochester to his father, October 15, 1813, Towle, "Militia Myth."
8. Chapin, *Review*, 25; Chauncey to Jones, November 21, 1813, in Dudley and Crawford, *Naval War of 1812*, 2:599–600.
9. Harrison to McClure, November 15, 1813, ASP:MA, 1:484; Colquhoun, "Joseph Willcocks"; Graves, "Canadian Volunteers."
10. Mann, *Medical Sketches*, 94–96.
11. Tompkins's Report to the Legislature, January 31, 1814, and Tompkins to McClure, November 26, 1813, in Hastings, *Tompkins Papers*, 3:448 and 3:400–401.
12. McClure to Armstrong, December 10, 1813, in Cruikshank, *Drummond's Winter Campaign*, 14.
13. Cruikshank, *Drummond's Winter Campaign*, 14–15; Chapin's public letter recorded in Ketchum, *History of Buffalo*, 405–6; McClure to Armstrong, December 10, 1813, ASP:MA, 1:486; "McClure to the Public," January 1, 1814, DHNF, 9:48–50; McClure, *Destruction of the American Towns*, 18. The story of the burning of the village of Newark and British retaliation is found in Graves, "Reaping the Whirlwind," DeCroix, *War of 1812*, 2:40–51.
14. "McClure to the Public," January 1, 1814.
15. Murray to Vincent, December 12 and 13, 1813, in Wood, *Select British Documents*, 2:481–83.
16. McClure to Armstrong, December 13, 1813, ASP:MA, 1:486; General Orders issued by McClure on December 12, 1813; Granger to McClure, December 11, 1813, in Snyder, *Red & White*, 72–73; Benn, *Iroquois*, 148–52.

17. Harvey to Murray, December 17, and Drummond to Prevost, December 18, 1813, in Wood, *Select British Documents*, 2:485–88. See also Cruikshank, *Drummond's Winter Campaign*.
18. McClure's address "To the Inhabitants of Niagara, Genesee and Chautauqua," December 18, 1813, Ketchum, *Buffalo*, 378–79.
19. Learned to Walbach, April 5, 1814, RG 94, Letters Received, NARA. Office of the Adjutant General, 1805–1821.
20. Murray to Gordon, December 19, 1813, and Driscoll, "Capture of Fort Niagara," DHNF, 9:11–13 and 18–20.
21. Driscoll, "Capture of Fort Niagara," Cruikshank, DHNF, 9:20.
22. *Geneva Gazette*, February 2, 1814.
23. Drummond to Prevost, December 20, 1813, in Dudley and Crawford, *Naval War of 1812*, 2:624–25.
24. McClure to Armstrong, December 22 and 25, 1813, ASP:MA, 1:487.
25. A view of the Tuscarora contribution to the fight at Lewiston is found in Hill, *War Clubs and Wampum Belts*, 42.
26. Drummond to Prevost, December 20 and 22, 1813, and Drummond's General Order, December 19, 1813, in Wood, *Select British Documents*, 2:492–505.
27. Howe, "Recollections," 386.
28. Turner, *Pioneer History*, 593; Scrantom to father, December 26, 1813, in Hanford, *Notes*, 10.
29. Tompkins to McClure, December 24, 1813, and Tompkins to Hall, December 25, 1813, in Hastings, *Tompkins Papers*, 3:402–4.
30. McClure to Armstrong, December 25, 1813, ASP:MA, 1:487; Hall to Tompkins, December 26 and 29, 1813, Hall, "Militia Service," 30–35.
31. Harvey to Riall, December 29, 1813, in Wood, *Select British Documents*, 2:509–11. The three craft were the *Little Belt* and *Chipaway*, captured at the Battle of Lake Erie, and *Trippe*, Elliott to Jones, January 5, 1814, in Dudley and Crawford, *Naval War of 1812*, 3:373–74. A detailed narrative of the destruction of Buffalo is found in Johnson, *Erie County*, chap. 25.
32. Hall to Tompkins, December 31, 1813.
33. Drummond to Prevost, December 30, 1813, in Wood, *Select British Documents*, 2:511–12; Turner, *Pioneer History*, 597–607; Dorsheimer, "Village of Buffalo," 194–99; *Buffalo Gazette*, February 1, 1814; Howe, "Recollections," 389; Skinner, "Story of the St. John House"; Report on "Property Lost or Destroyed," the House Committee on Claims, March 16, 1832, *New American State Papers: Military Affairs*, 5:266–95.
34. Return of the Killed and Wounded of the Militia of the State of New York on the Niagara frontier to repel the Invasion of the Enemy on 30 December 1813, BHM.
35. Brayman, "Pioneer Patriot," 364.
36. McMahan to Pell, January 11, 1820, Record Series A0802–78, vol. 21, NYSA/OSC.
37. Tompkins to Armstrong, December 24, 1813, in Hastings, *Tompkins Papers*, 3:405–7.
38. Armstrong to Tompkins, December 26, 1813, Cruikshank, DHNF, 9:54.
39. Tompkins to Hall and Tompkins to Madison, January 3, 1814, in Hastings, *Tompkins Papers*, 3:410–13. Fragmentary records of the state militia who responded to Tompkins's orders are found in Record Series A0802–78, vol. 22, NYSA/OSC. A narrative of events after the battle is found in Hall, "Militia Service," 37–59.

40. Cass to Armstrong, January 12, 1814, ASP:MA, 1:487–88.
41. Governor's Annual Report to the Legislature, January 25, 1814, in Hastings, *Tompkins Papers*, 3:426–32.
42. Prevost's Proclamation, January 12, 1814, Cruikshank, DHNF, 9:112–16.
43. Guernsey, *New York City*, 2:12–17; Turner, *Pioneer History*, 603–4. The estimate of 12,000 refugees is probably overstated. The 1810 census records the population of Niagara County at 6,032. Some number of these departed for safety when the declaration of war arrived in June 1812. Of course, there were births and new settlers arriving between the census and December 1813.
44. *Laws of the State of New-York passed at the Thirty-Seventh Session of the Legislature*, "An Act for the Relief of Late Sufferers of the Western Frontier of the State," February 18, 1814, Chap. 16: 20, Record Series A0802–78, vol. 21, NYSA/OSC.
45. Record Series A0802–78, vol. 21, and Record Series A0979, Reports, Act of April 15, 1815, NYSA/OSC.
46. Hall, "Militia Service," 55–59.

Chapter 14

1. Madison to Armstrong, May 20, 1814, James Madison Papers, reel 27, LOC.
2. "An act making further provision for filling the ranks of the regular army, encouraging enlistments, and authorizing the re-enlistments, for longer periods, of men whose terms of service are about to expire." The mythology of the war asserting that these British reinforcements came principally from Wellington's forces is refuted by Graves. See "The Redcoats are Coming!"
3. "Bounties and Premiums for Recruits" and "General Return of Recruits," ASP:MA, 1:511–13.
4. Tompkins to Armstrong, January 2, 9 and 16, 1814, in Dudley and Crawford, *Naval War of 1812*, 3:372–73 and in Hastings, *Tompkins Papers*, 3:416–20.
5. Cochrane to Cockburn, July 1, Cochrane to Bathurst, July 14, and Cochrane to Admiralty, July 17, 1814, in Crawford, *Naval War*, 3:129–35.
6. Jones to Chauncey, January 15, 1814, in Dudley and Crawford, *Naval War of 1812*, 3:386–87.
7. Izard to Wilkinson, December 6, 1813, ASP:MA, 1:481.
8. *Niles' Weekly Register*, March 12, 1814; British Intelligence Report, February 7, 1814, National Library and Archives of Canada, Ontario, Canada, RG 8, C.682, 116; Ashdown, "Invasion Flotilla," np; Fredriksen, "Chronicle of Valor," 272.
9. Mann, *Medical Sketches*, 126–27; Fredriksen, "Chronicle of Valor," 272–73.
10. Mann, *Medical Sketches*, 144.
11. Williams to Vincent, March 31, 1814, in Wood, *Select British Documents*, 3:14–17; Fredriksen, "Chronicle of Valor," 275–77; Gosling, "Lacolle Mill."
12. Fredriksen, "Tempered Sword," 14–15; Izard to Madison, May 24, 1814, Manuscript Division, New York Public Library, New York; Macomb to Izard, May 23, 1814, M221, Secretary of War Letters Received, Registered Series, roll 62; Fredriksen, "Georgia Officer," 689.
13. Macdonough to Jones, December 28, 1813 and February 7, March 7, and April 11, 1814, Jones to Macdonough, January 28 and February 22, 1814, and Tompkins to Jones, March 10, 1814, in Dudley and Crawford, *Naval War of 1812*, 2:606, 2:393–99, and 3:428.

14. Tompkins to De Ridder and Petit, April 18, and Tompkins to Armstrong, May 7, 1814, in Hastings, *Tompkins Papers*, 3:466–67 and 3:471–72. De Ridder commanded the 16th Brigade and Pettit the 17th Brigade of common militia. Pettit had served as a presidential elector in 1808.

15. Macdonough to Jones and Pring to Williams, May 14, 1814, in Dudley and Crawford, *Naval War of 1812*, 3:480–83. See also Everest, *Champlain Valley*, 149–51.

16. Izard to Armstrong, June 24, 1814 and July 3, 1814, Izard, *Correspondence*, 40–47. The 24 June letter is incorrectly dated as Forsyth was killed on June 28. Izard and the British returned civilian hostages in early July.

17. "Governor's Annual Report to the Legislature," in Hastings, *Tompkins Papers*, 3:428.

18. "Reply of the Federalist Assembly," in Hastings, *Tompkins Papers* 3:433–35.

19. Jenkins, *Lives of the Governors*, 186.

20. "Governor's Report on the Invasion of the Niagara Frontier to the Legislature," January 31, 1814, in Hastings, *Tompkins Papers*, 3:448–52.

21. Strum, "Federalists and Opposition," 178–79. Strum sees evasion of militia service as primarily an anti-war response. Beyond a protest of the war, a citizen might refuse to answer a call up because of the obvious disruption to life and possibility of loss of life or limb. The cost to the evader would be a minor cash penalty and perhaps a loss of prestige within the community.

22. "Governor's Annual Report to the Legislature," in Hastings, *Tompkins Papers*, 3:429–30.

23. "Governor's Report on the Invasion of the Niagara Frontier to the Legislature," January 31, 1814, in Hastings, *Tompkins Papers*, 3:451–52.

24. Tompkins to Legislature, dated March 13, 1813 and "Reply of the Federalist Assembly," in Hastings, *Tompkins Papers* 3:278–81 and 3:435.

25. Tompkins to Armstrong, March 30, 1814, in Hastings, *Tompkins Papers*, 3:460.

26. Harvey Strum's masterful analysis of the 1814 election is found in "Saving Mr. Tompkins' War."

27. Yeo to Warren, March 5, 1814, in Dudley and Crawford, *Naval War of 1812*, 3:403–4.

28. Chauncey to Jones, March 30, and Drummond to Prevost, April 27 and 28, and May 3, 1814, in Dudley and Crawford, *Naval War of 1812*, 3:411–12; 3:447–48, and 3:464.

29. Tompkins to Chauncey, April 17, 1814, in Hastings, *Tompkins Papers* 3:464–65; Tompkins to Gaines, April 17, 1814, in Hastings, *Tompkins Papers* 3:465–66.

30. Mitchell to Brown, May 8, 1814, in Dudley and Crawford, *Naval War of 1812*, 3:474–76.

31. Drummond to Prevost, May 7, 1814 and Yeo to Croker, May 9, 1814, in Wood, *Select British Documents*, 3:52–57 and 3:61–66.

32. Woolsey to Chauncey, May 7, and Mitchell to Brown, May 8, 1814, in Dudley and Crawford, *Naval War of 1812*, 3:472–76.

33. *History of Oswego County*, 67.

34. Porter to Tompkins, May 17, 1814, in Hanford, *Notes*, 12–15; *Ontario Repository*, May 24, 1814.

35. Clark, *Wayne County*, 211–20.

36. Mitchell to Ellis, May 9 and Appling to Ellis, May 25, 1814, Record Series A0802–78, vol. 22, NYSA/OSC.

37. There are a number of accounts of the engagement at Sandy Creek. See Chester, *Big Sandy*, and Malcomson, *Lords of the Lake*, 278–83.
38. Appling to Gaines, May 30, Popham to Yeo, June 1 and Woolsey to Chauncey, June 1, 1814, in Dudley and Crawford, *Naval War of 1812*, 3:508–13; Drummond to Prevost, June 2, 1814, in Wood, *Select British Documents*, 3:73–75.
39. Hough, *Jefferson County*, 512; Hibbard, "Recollection," 31.
40. Chambers to Armstrong, April 17, 1813, M221 Secretary of War Letters Received, Registered Series; Owen to Yeo, July 17, 1814, in Dudley and Crawford, *Naval War of 1812*, 3:536–37; Gibson, "Oddities," 16–22.
41. Third Military District Records, NARA RG 98; Fredriksen, *United States Army*. Pennsylvania Governor Simon Snyder and his political allies in Congress engineered Fotterall's failure to win Senate approval. See Edward Coles to Madison, May 22, 1813, *PJM:PS*, 6:331–32. Although a regimental commander, Talmadge was never promoted to colonel.
42. Guernsey, *New York City*, 2:33–40.
43. Guernsey, *New York City*, 2:42–44.
44. Graves, "Hard School of War," 7.

Chapter 15

1. See Barbuto, *Niagara 1814* for an analysis of the 1814 campaign on the Niagara River.
2. General Order dated March 13, 1814, in Hastings, *Tompkins Papers*, 1:478–79.
3. Scott, *Memoirs*, 116.
4. Barbuto, *Niagara 1814*, chap. 6; Graves, "Handsome Little Army," *War along the Niagara*; McGurty, "Lambs Prepared for Slaughter," DeCroix, *War of 1812*, 3:14–21.
5. Mann, *Medical Sketches*, 160.
6. Inspector General Report of Intelligence, May 4, 1814, BHM.
7. Parish to Porter, June 7, 1814, Manuscript Collection, Buffalo & Erie County Public Library, Buffalo, N.Y.
8. Scott to Brown, May 23, 1814, Brown Collection, University of Michigan, Clements Library, Ann Arbor, Mich.
9. Graves, "Handsome Little Army," found in *War along the Niagara*, 49.
10. Ghent was then situated in the French Republic. In 1815, the city was a part of a new creation, the United Kingdom of the Netherlands. Today, Ghent is a Belgian city.
11. Notes on Cabinet Meeting, June 7, 1814, in Dudley and Crawford, *Naval War of 1812*, 3:497–98.
12. ASP:MA, 1:535 and 1:550.
13. Armstrong to Brown, June 10, 1814, Dudley and Crawford, *Naval War of 1812*, 3:499–501.
14. Brown to Chauncey, June 21 and Chauncey to Brown, June 25, 1814, in Dudley and Crawford, *Naval War of 1812*, 3:526–27.
15. See Porter's Statement, May 25, 1840, BHM.
16. This battle is known to Americans as the Battle of Chippewa. That was the spelling used by American veterans of the battle. Because the battle occurred in Upper Canada, I use the Canadian name for the river and battle.
17. Porter's Statement, May 25, 1840, BHM. See also Graves, *Red Coats & Grey Jackets*.

18. For a thumbnail biography of Eleazar Wood, see Aimone, "West Point's Contribution," 42–43.
19. Porter's Statement, May 25, 1840, BHM.
20. There is no documentation of Riall's quote other than Scott's autobiography, *Memoirs*, 1:128–29.
21. Brown to Armstrong, July 6, Drummond to Prevost, July 9, and Riall to Drummond, July 6, 1814, in Wood, *Select British Documents*, 3:110–20.
22. Adams, *History*, 2:45.
23. Porter's Statement, May 25, 1840, BHM.
24. Ibid.
25. Porter to Tompkins, July 29, 1814, Cruikshank, DHNF1814, 101–3. See also Hill, *War Clubs and Wampum Belts*, 57–58.
26. Warren, "Two Dramatic Incidents," Smith, *Buffalo*, 71; Efner, "Memoir," 50. Efner recalled an attempt to persuade the natives not to murder the alleged spy.
27. Brown to Chauncey, July 13, 1814 and Hamilton to Chauncey, August 31, 1812, in Dudley and Crawford, *Naval War of 1812*, 3:550–51 and 1:297–301.
28. Howe, "Recollections," 392.
29. Swift's Obituary in the *Ontario Messenger*, republished in *The War*, August 2, 1814.
30. Brown to Armstrong, August 7, 1814, in Dudley and Crawford, *Naval War of 1812*, 3:577–81. A full treatment of the Battle of Lundy's Lane is Graves, *Where Right and Glory Lead!*
31. Scott, *Memoirs*, 140.
32. Graves, *Soldiers of 1814*, 35.
33. Towson was brevetted to major for his role in capturing the *Caledonia* and to lieutenant colonel for gallant conduct at Chippawa.
34. Graves, *Soldiers of 1814*, 37.
35. Scott, *Memoirs*, 141.
36. Jesup to the *National Intelligencer*, September 25, 1852, reprinted in "Who Captured General Riall?" *Historical Magazine*, July 1870, 54–55.
37. *Memoranda of Occurrences*.
38. Brown to Armstrong, August 7, 1814; "Brown's Memoranda," Library of Congress. David B. Douglass presented his memoirs as a series of lectures. See Douglass, "Reminiscences."
39. Drummond to Prevost, July 27, 1814, in Wood, *Select British Documents*, 3:144–51.
40. Lord, "War on the Canadian Frontier," 209.
41. Leavenworth's Statement, BHM; Scott, *Memoirs*, 143.
42. Jesup, *Memoirs*; *Memoranda of Occurrences*; Drummond to Prevost, July 27, 1814, in Wood, *Select British Documents*, 3:144–51.
43. Brown to Armstrong, August 7, 1814, in Dudley and Crawford, *Naval War of 1812*, 3:577–81.
44. Howe, "Recollections," 395–96.
45. Porter to Tompkins, July 29, 1814, Cruikshank, DHNF1814, 1:101–3.
46. Casualty figures are found in Graves, *Where Right and Glory Lead!*, chap. 12 and appendix A.
47. Brown to Armstrong, August 7, 1814, in Dudley and Crawford, *Naval War of 1812*, 3:577–81.

48. *Buffalo Gazette*, July 28, 1814.
49. Jones to Chauncey, July 20 and 24 and August 3, Jones to Decatur, July 28, Chauncey to Brown, August 10, and Chauncey to Jones, August 10, 1814, in Dudley and Crawford, *Naval War of 1812*, 3:551–57 and 3:584–87.

Chapter 16

1. Douglass, "Reminiscences," 128; Drummond to Prevost, in Wood, *Select British Documents*, 3:166. Douglass was born in New Jersey but entered the army from New York. He was a longtime professor at West Point and a consultant on the building of the Erie Canal. He died while serving as a professor at Hobart College, then known as Geneva College.
2. Expanded narratives of the siege of Fort Erie are found in Graves, *And All Their Glory Past*; Barbuto, *Niagara 1814*; and Barbuto, "The 1814 Siege of Fort Erie."
3. Dorsheimer, "Village of Buffalo," 203–4. See also Fredriksen, "Memoirs of Johnathan Kearsley," 9–11, for a description of this key engagement.
4. Drummond to Prevost, August 4, 1814, and Morgan to Brown, August 5, 1814, Cruikshank, DHNF1814, 116–18 and 121–24; Tucker to Conran, August 4, 1814, in Wood, *Select British Documents*, 3:177–78.
5. Brown to Tompkins, August 1, 1814, Cruikshank, DHNF1814, 103–4; Brown to Armstrong, August 5, 1814, *Brown's Letter Book*, BHM; Tompkins to Yates, Tompkins to Brown, August 13, 1814, and Brown to Tompkins, September 20, 1814, in Hastings, *Tompkins Papers*, 3:495–98 and 3:562.
6. Mann, *Medical Sketches*, 162.
7. Brown to Armstrong, August 5, 1814, *Memoranda of Occurrences*.
8. Dobbs to Yeo, August 8, 1814, and Conkling to Kennedy, August 16, 1814, in Dudley and Crawford, *Naval War of 1812*, 3:588–91.
9. Fredriksen, "Kearsley," 11–12.
10. Douglass, "Reminiscences," 130.
11. Right Division Order, August 14, 1814, Cruikshank, DHNF1814, 136–39.
12. Douglass, "Reminiscences," 132.
13. Douglass, "Reminiscences," 134.
14. Graves, *Soldiers of 1814*, 39.
15. Howe, "Recollections," 398–99.
16. Drummond to Prevost, August 15 and 16, 1814, in Wood, *Select British Documents*, 3:178–82 and 3:189–94; Gaines's report, Cruickshank, DHNF1814, 150.
17. Horner, "Surgical Sketches," 772.
18. Madison to Armstrong, July 27; August 12, 1814; and August 13, 1814, James Madison Papers, reel 27, LOC. As evidence of delays and mischance in communication, on August 7, 1814, Izard complained to Armstrong that he had just then received Armstrong's letter of July 30 and still had not received Armstrong's July 27 letter or any correspondence from the secretary of war between July 2 and 30. RG 94, War Department Letters (M221), roll 62, NARA.
19. Armstrong to Izard, August 2, 10, and 12, 1814, and Izard to Armstrong, August 11, 1814, Izard, *Official Correspondence*, 61–74; Armstrong to Brown, August 16, 1814, in Brown's Orderly Book, LOC.
20. Howe, "Recollections," 400; Barbuto, *Niagara 1814*, 267.

21. Sinclair to Jones, September 7, 1814, in Dudley and Crawford, *Naval War of 1812*, 3:600–601.
22. Brown to Tompkins, August 21, 1814, in Brown's Orderly Book, LOC.
23. Efner, "The Adventures and Enterprises of Elijah D. Efner," 41 and 50–51.
24. Turner, *Pioneer History*, 607–11.
25. Brown to Secretary of War, September 29, 1814, Cruickshank, DHNF1814, 211.
26. A short biography of Gibson is found in Aimone, "West Point's Contribution," 44–45. See also Efner, "The Adventures and Enterprises of Elijah D. Efner," 53.
27. Porter's report to Brown, September 23, 1814, Cruickshank, DHNF1814, 208–11.
28. Graves, *Soldiers of 1814*, 57.
29. Brown to Monroe, September 18, 1814, *Memoranda of Occurrences*; Brown to Tompkins, September 20, 1814, Cruickshank, DHNF1814, 207.
30. Drummond to Prevost, September 19, 1814, in Wood, *Select British Documents*, 3:195–99.
31. Mann, *Medical Sketches*, 163; Record Series A0802–78, vol. 22, NYSA/OSC.
32. Response of the Assembly to Governor Tompkins, October 9, 1814, in Hastings, *Tompkins Papers*, 3:549–51.
33. Tompkins to Fisk, October 3, 1814, in Hastings, *Tompkins Papers*, 3:560–63.
34. Tompkins to Davis and Swift, December 24, 1814, in Hastings, *Tompkins Papers*, 3:631–32.
35. Brown to Izard, September 10, 1814, Izard, *Official Correspondence*, 86.
36. Chauncey to Jones, September 24 and October 12, 1814, in Dudley and Crawford, *Naval War of 1812*, 3:620–22; Hough, *Jefferson County*, 516.
37. Fredriksen, "Tempered Sword," 8–10; Monroe to Izard, September 27, and Izard to Monroe, October 7, 1814, Izard, *Official Correspondence*, 95–99.
38. Barbuto, *Niagara 1814*, 292–96; Fredriksen, "Tempered Sword," 10–11.
39. Izard to Monroe, October 16, 1814, Izard, *Official Correspondence*, 100–104.
40. The Battle of Cook's Mill is found in Barbuto, *Niagara 1814*, 296–301.
41. Drummond to Prevost, October 20, and Myers to Drummond, October 19, 1814, in Wood, *Select British Documents*, 3:221–26.
42. Izard anticipated instructions from Monroe to reinforce Sackett's Harbor. Monroe to Izard, October 24, 1814, in Dudley and Crawford, *Naval War of 1812*, 3:623–24; Henderson to unknown recipient, September 18, 1844, Lilly Library at the University of Indiana, War of 1812 Collection; Stacy, *Memoir*, 263.
43. Gillett, *Army Medical Department*, 175.
44. Porter, "Jacob Porter Norton," 54.

Chapter 17

1. Henry Clay, February 22, 1810, *Annals of Congress*, 11th Congress, 2nd Session, 580.
2. Guernsey, *New York City*, 2:98–108.
3. Madison to Armstrong, July 2, 1814, in Hunt, *Writings of James Madison*, 8:281–82; ASP:MA, 1:550.
4. General Orders dated July 20 and August 4, 1814, in Hastings, *Tompkins Papers*, 1:490–500.
5. Madison to Armstrong, August 2, 1814, James Madison Papers, reel 27, LOC.
6. Record Series A0802–78, vol. 22, NYSA/OSC.

7. General Order dated August 29, 1814, in Hastings, *Tompkins Papers*, 1:504-7.

8. Churchill, *Life of Sylvester Churchill*, 117.

9. Bathurst to Prevost, June 3, 1814, National Archives of the United Kingdom, Colonial Office Records, Kew, England.

10. See Schroeder, *Battle of Lake Champlain*, Chapter 3, for the evolution of Prevost's decision to move on Lake Champlain.

11. Prevost to Bathurst, August 5, 1814, in Wood, *Select British Documents*, 3:345-46.

12. Armstrong to Izard, July 27, and Izard to Armstrong, August 11, 1814, Izard, *Official Correspondence*, 64-67.

13. Tompkins to Mooers, September 2, and Tompkins to Prior and Davis, September 9, 1814, in Hastings, *Tompkins Papers*, 3:515-16 and 3:520. Armstrong to Izard, August 10, 1814, Izard, *Official Correspondence*, 67.

14. Guernsey, *New York City*, 1:211.

15. Mann, *Medical Sketches*, 145 and 152-53.

16. *Albany Argus*, October 4, 1814. For the British perspective, see Robinson, "Expedition to Plattsburgh."

17. "Rifles Promised to a Corps of Juvenile Volunteers," ASP:MA, 1:361-63.

18. Wool to Simms, January 8, 1850, *Historical Magazine*, vol. 2, October 1873. See also "Major Wool's Account of the Battle of Plattsburgh," *North Country Notes*, September 1961, n.p.

19. Wool to Roberts, January 6, 1859, published in "The Battle of Beekmantown in 1814," *North Country Notes*, September 1965, n.p.; Mann, *Medical Sketches*, 145-46. For the composition of British forces, see Graves, "Finest Army Ever."

20. John Rochester to his father, Nathaniel Rochester, September 9, 1814, found in Nelson, "Plattsburg," 31.

21. Macdonough to Jones, September 13, 1814, in Dudley and Crawford, *Naval War of 1812*, 3:614-15; Pring to Yeo, September 12, 1814, in Wood, *Select British Documents*, 3:368-73. For the naval battle, see Schroeder, *Battle of Lake Champlain*.

22. Stevens to his brother, December 5, 1814, *Proceedings of the Vermont Historical Society*, March 1938, 16-19.

23. Everest, *Recollections*, 26.

24. Prevost to Bathurst, September 11, 1814, in Wood, *Select British Documents*, 3:350-53.

25. Baynes to Robinson, September 11, 1814, quoted in ibid.

26. Macdonough to Jones, September 11 and 13, 1814, in Clark, *Pensioners*, 56-57, and prisoner list, 69-70.

27. Macomb to Monroe, September 12, 1814, in Dudley and Crawford, *Naval War of 1812*, 3:609; Macomb to Monroe, September 15, 1814, in Wood, *Select British Documents*, 3: 353-60.

28. Mann, *Medical Sketches*, 147.

29. Speech by Augustus Wright, October 8, 1814, Hastings *Tompkins Papers*, 1:104.

30. Tompkins to Monroe, September 29, 1814, in Hastings, *Tompkins Papers*, 3:555.

31. Lossing, *Pictorial Field-Book*, 878. Alexander Saranac Macomb graduated from West Point in 1835 and served in the First Dragoon Regiment. He also served as aide-de-camp to his father when General Macomb was commanding general of the army.

32. Lewis, "Citizen Soldier."

33. Madison to Tompkins, September 28, 1814, in Hunt, *Writings of James Madison*, 8:312–13; Irwin, *Daniel D. Tompkins*, 181. Tompkins was also concerned that he could not support his family in a home in Washington. Tompkins to Betts, February 12, 1816, in Hastings, *Tompkins Papers*, 3:655.

34. Tompkins to Generals Haile, Hurd, and Dodge, August 16, 1814, in Hastings, *Tompkins Papers*, 3:503.

35. Arthur, *How Britain Won the War*, 178.

36. Tompkins commissioned Irving by brevet; there is no record that this commission was awarded by the Council of Appointment. Irving's time in military service appears in Irving, *Life and Letters*, 232–47.

37. Solomon Van Rensselaer to Harriet Van Rensselaer, November 14, 1814, in Bonney, *Legacy of Historical Gleanings*, 320–21.

38. Guernsey, *New York City*, 2:135–38.

39. "Report of the Special Committee of Defence," July 14, 1814, Guernsey, *New York City*, 2:151–54.

40. "Report of the Special Committee of Defence," July 14, 1814, and "Report Made to Common Council," July 26, 1814, Guernsey, *New York City*, 2:153–54 and 2:166–68.

41. Guernsey, *New York City*, 2:188–89; Hastings, *Tompkins Papers*, 3:495.

42. DeWitt Clinton's address to the citizens of New York, Guernsey, *New York City*, 2:177–80.

43. Speech by Marinus Willett, Guernsey, *New York City*, 2:196–99. See also General Joseph Swift's Report on Fortifications, December 31, 1814, Guernsey, *New York City*, 2:535–40.

44. For the *New York Herald*, see Gero, *Excelsior's Soldiers*, 89. See also Wilson, *United Irishmen*, 85, and Clark, *Seventh Regiment*, 72–74.

45. Guernsey, *New York City*, 2:234–40.

46. Tompkins to Platt, August 3 and August 4, 1814, in Hastings, *Tompkins Papers*, 3:482–83; Tompkins to Lewis, August 24 and September 5, 1814, and Annual Report to the Legislature, September 30, 1814, in Hastings, *Tompkins Papers*, 3:507–11; 3:518 and 3:542.

47. General Order dated August 27, 1814, Guernsey, *New York City*, 2:241–43. Tompkins to Heermance and Haight, August 28, 1814, in Hastings, *Tompkins Papers*, 3:511–12.

48. General Order dated August 29, 1814, Guernsey, *New York City*, 2:245.

49. General Order dated August 29, 1814, Guernsey, *New York City*, 2:246.

50. General Order dated August 29, 1814, Guernsey, *New York City*, 2:248–51.

51. Rules and Regulations to be Observed in the Camp Daily, issued by the Third Military District, August 29, 1814, Guernsey, *New York City*, 2:258–62.

52. Clinton's Address to the opening of the Court of Sessions, September 5, 1814, Guernsey, *New York City*, 2:283–87.

53. *Letter to Archibald M'Intyre*, 19.

54. Tompkins to the Legislature, September 27, 1814, in Hastings, *Tompkins Papers*, 3:535–39.

55. Hastings, *Tompkins Papers*, 1:75; Hastings, *Military Minutes*, 1437–39. On October 24, 1814, the legislature passed thirteen acts on the state's defenses. See *Laws of the State of New York*, 38th Session, Chaps. 16 through 28, 15–31.

318 NOTES TO CHAPTER 17

56. Tompkins to Lewis, September 15, 1814, and Annual Report to the Legislature, September 30, 1814, in Hastings, *Tompkins Papers*, 3:528–29 and 3:543–44.
57. General Orders dated October 3, 5, and 7, 1814, and Tompkins to Irving, September 28, 1814, and Tompkins to King, October 12, 1814, in Hastings, *Tompkins Papers*, 1:514–16, 3:551–52, and 3:567–68.
58. Committee of Defence to William Irving, October 1, 1812, James Madison Papers, Series 1, reel 16, LOC. Irving was a U.S. Representative from New York City and brother of Washington Irving.
59. Monroe to Tompkins, October 14, 1815, in Hastings, *Tompkins Papers*, 1:699.
60. Washington Irving to William Irving, October 14, 1814, found in Irving, *Life and Letters*, 240.
61. Tompkins to Monroe, September 29, 1814, in Hastings, *Tompkins Papers*, 3:555.
62. Tompkins to Monroe, October 29, 1814, in Hastings, *Tompkins Papers*, 3:578–79.
63. Tompkins to the Legislature, October 17, 1814, in Hastings, *Tompkins Papers*, 3:570–73.
64. Monroe to Senate Committee on Military Affairs, October 17, 1814, ASP:MA, 514.
65. Gero, "New York's Black Regiments," 36; Gero, *Excelsior's Soldiers*, 89–91; *Laws of the State of New York*, 38th Session, Chap. 18:22.
66. Irving, *Life and Letters*, 243.
67. Clinton to Tompkins, January 24, 1814, in Hastings, *Tompkins Papers*, 3:436–37; Swift to Clinton, September 24, 1814, *Tompkins Papers*, 3:477–78; Fortification Commission report, September 23, 1814, in Hastings, *Tompkins Papers*, 3:532–35.
68. Jones to Madison, October 26, 1814, in Dudley and Crawford, *Naval War of 1812*, 3:631–36.
69. Hutcheon, *Fulton*, chap. 5; Tompkins to Steddiford, July 14, 1814, in Hastings, *Tompkins Papers*, 1:488–89.
70. Kert, *Privateering*, 138–40 and 153; Tompkins to Reid, April 24, 1815, in Hastings, *Tompkins Papers*, 3:643–44.
71. Monroe to Giles, October 17, 1814, ASP:MA, 514–17; Madison to Jefferson, October 10, 1814, in Hunt, *Writings of James Madison*, 8:313–16.
72. *The Columbian*, November 15, 1814; Final Report of the Common Council Committee of Defence During the War 1812–15, Guernsey, *New York City*, 2:544–51.
73. Tompkins to the Legislature, September 27, 1814, and Senate to Tompkins, October 4, 1814, and Assembly to Tompkins, October 9, 1814, in Hastings, *Tompkins Papers*, 3:539, 3:548 and 3:550.
74. Third Military District Order dated November 21, 1814, and Tompkins to Monroe, September 29, 1814, and November 6, 1814, in Hastings, *Tompkins Papers*, 3:555 and 3:595.
75. Irwin, *Daniel D. Tompkins*, 194–95; Tompkins to Monroe, December 12, 1814, in Hastings, *Tompkins Papers*, 3:613–16; General Order dated November 17, 1814, Hastings *Tompkins Papers*, 2:719–20.
76. Solomon Van Rensselaer to Harriet Van Rensselaer, November 30, 1814, in Bonney, *Legacy of Historical Gleanings*, 321–22; General Order dated November 26, 1814, in Hastings, *Tompkins Papers*, 1:727–29.
77. Madison to Nicholas, November 26, 1814, in Hunt, *Writings of James Madison*, 8:319; Monroe to Tompkins, November 26, 1814, RG 94, M7, NARA; Monroe to Jesup, November 26, 1814, RG 94, M7; Monroe to Izard, November 26, 1814, RG

94, M7; and Monroe to Madison, January 10, 1815. See also Brant, *James Madison, Commander in Chief*, 359–61; and Buel, *America on the Brink*, 212–31.
78. Ellis, *Ruinous and Unhappy War*, 242–44.
79. Tompkins to Monroe, December 24, 1814, in Hastings, *Tompkins Papers*, 3:629–30.

Chapter 18

1. Cochrane to Bathurst, July 14, 1814, in Dudley and Crawford, *Naval War of 1812*, 3:131. See also Grodzinski, "American 'Independence is not Threatened,'" Hickey and Clark, *Routledge Handbook*, 23–29; and Mills, "Wellington and the Peace Negotiations," 26–32. J. C. A. Stagg offered that the three American victories were "ultimately adequate for its diplomatic needs." See Stagg, "The Politics of Ending the War," 99. Another analysis of competing strategies is Lambert, "Sideshow?"
2. Hastings, *Military Minutes*, 2:1535–37.
3. Cooper, *Some Old Letters*, 54; Porter's Statement, May 25, 1840, BHM. Reactions to the news of the peace treaty are found in the February 13, 1815, issues of the New York City dailies, the *Columbian* and the *Commercial Advertiser*.
4. *Albany Register*, February 14, 1815.
5. Common Council Resolutions, February 20, 1815, Guernsey, *New York City*, 2:468–70.
6. *Albany Argus*, February 24, 1815; *Albany Register*, March 3, 1815.
7. State General Order dated February 22, 1815, and Military District General Order dated February 20, 1815, Guernsey, *New York City*, 2:479–82; *Albany Register*, January 10, 1815.
8. Mohl, *Poverty*, 20 and 113–14; Hastings, *Tompkins Papers*, 1:105.
9. Dallas to Tompkins, April 10, 1815, in Hastings, *Tompkins Papers*, 1:764.
10. Report of the Committee of Claims, March 27, 1818, *New American State Papers: Military Affairs*, 5:222–24. A large number of witness statements, including several by Canadian officers, are included in the Report of the Committee of Claims, March 16, 1832, *New American State Papers: Military Affairs*, 5:266–95.
11. Record Series A0802-78 vol. 21, NYSA/OSC.
12. Monroe to the Six Nations, March 11, 1815; Parrish to Granger, April 10, 1815; Red Jacket at Council at Buffalo, November 27, 1815; Granger to Graham, January 20, 1817, in Snyder, *Red & White*, 80–86.
13. Zabecki, "Medals, Decorations, and Military Honors," in Tucker, *Encyclopedia*, 963–68.
14. Calhoun to the House of Representatives, "List of Brevet Officers," December 23, 1817. Award narratives are derived from Heitman, *Historical Register*.
15. Cullum, *Register of Graduates*, 51.
16. Calhoun to Barbour, March 13, 1822, ASP:MA, 2:360–61; Barbuto, *Niagara 1814*, 323–24.
17. Stagg, "Enlisted Men in the United States Army," Table IV. Vermont provided 445 recruits per 10,000 of its white male population of military age. New York provided 427 recruits per 10,000. Stagg estimated that 21.1 percent of the regular army was recruited in New York. Pennsylvania came in second, with 13.6 percent of the army.
18. Calhoun to Taylor, "Number of Militia Called into Service in the Years 1812, 1813, 1814," January 16, 1821, ASP:MA, 2:279–82; Butler to Polk, December 12, 1836

ASP:MA, 5:927–62. There is a distinction between the words "term of service" and "period of service." "Term of service" is the amount of time that a recruit agreed to in his enlistment contract, regardless of how long he actually served. For example, a recruit might enlist for a "term of service" of eighteen months. Interim Secretary of War B. F. Butler used "period of service" to be a length of time a militiaman actually served when called into service. A militiaman called into service on two separate occasions would have served two "periods of service." This is not how Secretary of War John C. Calhoun used "period of service" in his 1821 report to Congress. Calhoun used "period of service" to refer to the number of militiamen from a state who served for some time in a specific year. For example, 14,888 New York militiamen were called up and served for some length of time during the 1812 "period of service." The length of service could vary from a few days to several months.

19. According to J. C. A. Stagg, Virginia's leaders, despairing of protection by the federal government, called out large numbers of militiamen to serve along the coast. See Stagg, "The American Homefront, 1812–1815," 160.

20. Butler to Polk, December 12, 1836, ASP:MA, 5:935–36; Drinkard to Buchanan, February 23, 1858, *New American State Papers: Military Affairs*, 5:337–38.

21. Final Report of the Common Council Committee of Defence During War 1812–15, November 6, 1815, found in Guernsey, *New York City*, 2:544–51.

22. Tompkins to the Legislature, February 2, 1816, in Hastings, *Tompkins Papers* 1:645–52.

23. Tompkins to the Legislature, February 2, 1816.

24. Tompkins to the Legislature, February 24, 1817, in Hastings, *Tompkins Papers* 3:657–58.

25. Tompkins to Thompson, September 2, 1817, in Irwin, *Daniel D. Tompkins*, 223.

26. Tompkins recorded the acerbic correspondence between him and Archibald M'Intyre in a lengthy document he published as *A Letter to Archibald M'Intyre*.

27. Irwin, *Daniel D. Tompkins*, 254–60 and 264–78.

28. Guernsey, *New York City*, 2:414–26; and Hastings, *Tompkins Papers*, 1:108–12.

29. *Albany Register*, March 3, 1815.

30. Meacham, *American Lion*, 83–84.

31. Van Rensselaer, *Narrative*, iv.

32. Brown's postwar career is told in Morris, *Sword of the Border*, chaps. 9 through 15.

33. For a fuller treatment of the Scott-Gaines controversy, see Peskin, *Scott*, 75–81.

34. Delafield, *Morgan Lewis*, 121.

35. *The Albany Argus*, March 5, 1815; McMaster, *Steuben County*, 97–98.

36. Monroe to Tompkins, February 4, 1815, Secretary of War Confidential Letters Sent (M7); Bell, *Secretaries of War*, 42.

37. Porter's Statement, May 25, 1814, BHM.

38. Worth's biography is Edward Wallace's *General William Jenkins Worth*.

39. Aimone, "West Point's Contribution," 39–41. This railroad line is now the Harlem line of the Metro-North Railroad.

40. Emerson, "An Industrious and Worthy Woman."

41. War of 1812 Pension Records, War Department.

42. Donald Hickey estimates that as many as 20,000 American servicemen, privateers, and civilians died as a direct cause of the war. Hickey, *187 Things*, 136.

43. Lampi, "Federalist Party Resurgence," 276–77.

44. Stagg, "Enlisted Men in the United States Army," 626–29.

45. Stagg, "Enlisted Men in the United States Army," 627–28; Horsman, "Dartmoor," 14.

46. Emerson, "An Industrious and Worthy Woman."

47. *Laws of the State of New York, passed at the Forty-second, Forty-third, and Forty-fourth Sessions of the Legislature*, Forty-second session, chap. 117, "An Act to Authorize the payment of claims for services rendered and supplies furnished the Militia and Volunteers," 139.

48. *Albany Register*, February 17, 1815.

49. *Laws of the State of New York, passed at the Thirty-ninth, Fortieth, and Forty-first Sessions of the Legislature*, Forty-first session, chap. 222, "An Act to organize the militia," 210–33; *Laws of the State of New York, passed at the Forty-second, Forty-third, and Forty-fourth Sessions of the Legislature*, Forty-second session, chap. 248, "An Act Making an Appropriation to defray certain Expenses," 316–17.

50. *Laws of the State of New York, passed at the Forty-second, Forty-third, and Forty-fourth Sessions of the Legislature*, Forty-second session, chap. 219, "An Act to Amend an Act entitled 'an act to organize the militia,'" 282–88.

51. *Laws of the State of New York, passed at the Forty-second, Forty-third, and Forty-fourth Sessions of the Legislature*, Forty-third session, chap. 247, "An Act to exempt the persons therein mentioned from the performance of military duty," 252.

52. Blatchford, *Statutes of the State of New-York*, 147 and 712–25; Skeen, *Citizen Soldiers*, chap. 10; Mahon, *History of Militia and National Guard*, chap. 6.

Bibliography

Archival Sources

"American Election Returns 1787–1825." http://elections.lib.tufts.edu.

Brock University, St. Catharines, Ontario
   Archives and Special Collections

Buffalo & Erie County Public Library, Buffalo, New York
   Manuscript Collection

Buffalo History Museum Manuscript Collection, Buffalo, New York
   Goodyear Collection
   Peter B. Porter Papers
   War of 1812 Collection

Delaware County Historical Association, Delhi, New York
   Sherwood Collection

East Hampton Library, East Hampton, New York
   Manuscript Collection

Feinberg Library, SUNY Plattsburgh, Plattsburgh, New York
   Manuscript Collection

Fenimore Art Museum, Cooperstown, New York

Founders Online. https://founders.archives.gov.

Historic Cherry Hill, Albany, New York
   Manuscript Collection

Historical Society of Pennsylvania, Philadelphia, Pennsylvania

Internet Archive. https://founders.archives.gov.Library of Congress, Washington, D.C.
   Thomas Jefferson Papers, microfilm
   James Madison Papers, microfilm
   James Monroe Papers, microfilm

Lilly Library at the University of Indiana, Bloomington, Indiana
   War of 1812 Manuscripts

Little Falls Public Library, Little Falls, New York
   Muster Rolls

Maryland Historical Society, Baltimore, Maryland

Moffat Library of Washingtonville, Washingtonville, New York
    Caldwell Correspondence
National Archives and Records Administration, Washington, D.C.
    Records Group 45, Naval Records Collection of the Office of Naval Records and
        Library, 1794–1927
    Records Group 94, Records of the Adjutant General Office, 1780–1917
    Records Group 98, Records of the United States Army Commands, 1784–1821
    Records Group 107, Records of the Office of the Secretary of War, 1791–1947
        U.S. Department of War, Letters Sent by the Secretary of War Relating to Mili-
            tary Affairs, 1800–1889 (M6)
        U.S. Department of War, Confidential and Unofficial Letters Sent by the Secre-
            tary of War, 1814–1847 (M7)
        U.S. Department of War, Letters Received by the Secretary of War, Registered
            Series, 1801–1870 (M221)
        U.S. Department of War, Letters Received by the Secretary of War, Unregistered
            Series (M222)
National Archives of the United Kingdom, Kew, England
    War Office 28, General Orders Canada
National Library and Archives of Canada, Ottawa, Ontario
    Admiralty Records
    British Military Records, Records Group 8, C Series
    F. W. Robinson Journals
New-York Historical Society, New York, New York
    Ebenezer Stevens Letter Book
New York Public Library Archives and Manuscripts, New York, New York
    John Armstrong Letters
    Henry Dearborn Letters and Documents
    James Monroe Papers, 1772–1836
    Joseph G. Swift Correspondence
    Stephen Van Rensselaer Correspondence
New York State Archives, New York State Office of State Comptroller, Albany, New York
    Record Series A0269, General Account Ledgers, 1775–1918, Volumes 25–26
    Record Series A0802–78, Volumes 6, 10, and 21–23
    Record Series A0862, Comptroller's Office Daybooks, Day Book No. 9
    Record Series A0979, Reports to Legislature, 1789–1843
    Record Series A1263, Ledger of the State Treasurer, 1812–1816
New York State Library, Albany, New York
    Gardner Papers
    U.S. Army Third Artillery Regiment Orderly Book
    William Jenkins Worth Papers
    John Ellis Wool Papers
Sackets Harbor Battlefield Library, Sackets Harbor, New York
University of Michigan, Clements Library, Ann Arbor, Michigan
    Thomas Brisbane Papers
    Brown Collection
U.S. Army Military History Institute, Carlisle Barracks, Pennsylvania

Primary Sources

Aigin, James. "The Affair of June 4, 1813." In *Publications of the Buffalo Historical Society* 9: 371–72, edited by Frank H. Severance. Buffalo: Buffalo Historical Society, 1906.

Allen, Robert S., ed. "The Bisshopp Papers during the War of 1812." *Journal of the Society for Army Historical Research* 61 (Spring 1983): 22–29.

American State Papers: Military Affairs. 7 vols. Washington, D.C.: Gales and Seaton, 1832–1861. https://memory.loc.gov/ammem/amlaw/lwsp.html.

The Annals of America. 18 vols. Chicago: Encyclopedia Britannica, Inc., 1968.

Annals of Congress: Debates and Proceedings in the Congress of the United States, 1789–1824. 42 vols. Washington, D.C.: n.p., 1834–1856.

Archer, Mary Roach, ed. "Journal of Major Isaac Roach." *Pennsylvania Magazine of History and Biography* 17, no. 2 (1893): 129–58 and 281–315.

Armstrong, John. *Notices of the War of 1812.* New York: Wiley & Putnam, 1840.

Benn, Carl, ed. *Native Memoirs from the War of 1812: Blackhawk and William Apess.* Baltimore: Johns Hopkins University Press, 2014.

Bidwell, Mrs. Benjamin. "In the Midst of Alarms: Experiences of Buffalo Families under the fire of the enemy in the War of 1812." In *Publications of the Buffalo Historical Society,* 9: 357–59, edited by Frank H. Severance. Buffalo, N.Y.: Buffalo Historical Society, 1906.

Blatchford, Samuel. *Statutes of the State of New-York, of a public and general character passed from 1829 to 1851, both inclusive; with Notes and References to Judicial Decisions, and the Constitution of 1846.* Auburn, N.Y.: Derby and Miller, 1852.

Bonney, Catherine V. R., *A Legacy of Historical Gleanings.* Albany, N.Y.: J. Munsell, 1875.

Brannan, John. *Official Letters of the Military and Naval Officers of the United States during the War with Great Britain in the Years 1812, 13, 14, & 15.* Washington, D.C.: Way & Gideon, 1823.

Brayman, Daniel. "A Pioneer Patriot: Narrative of a Notable Defender of the Niagara Frontier in the Strenuous Old Days." In *Publications of the Buffalo Historical Society* 9: 361–67, edited by Frank H. Severance. Buffalo, N.Y.: Buffalo Historical Society, 1906.

Burt, Helen, ed. "Reminiscence of Benjamin Burt during the War of 1812." In *Twenty-Seventh Publication of the Oswego County Historical Society,* 95–96. Oswego, N.Y.: Oswego County Historical Society, 1964–65.

Chapin, Cyrenius. *Chapin's Review of Armstrong's Notices of the War of 1812.* Black Rock, N.Y.: D. P. Adams, 1836.

Clark, Byron N. *A List of Pensioners of the War of 1812.* Burlington, N.Y.: Research Publication Company, 1904.

Cooper, James Fenimore, ed. *Ned Myers: Or a Life before the Mast.* London: Richard Bentley, 1843.

Cooper, Margaret Adelia. *Some Old Letters & Bits of History.* New York: privately printed, 1901.

Cruikshank, Ernest, ed. *Documentary History of the Campaigns upon the Niagara Frontier in 1812–1814.* 9 vols. Welland, Ontario: Tribune Press, 1896–1908.

———, ed. *Documentary History of the Campaign on the Niagara Frontier in 1814.* Welland, Ontario: Lundy's Lane Historical Society, 1896.

Cullum, George W. *Register of the Officers and Graduates of the U.S. Military Academy at West Point, N.Y., from March 16, 1802, to January 4, 1850.* New York: J. F. Trow, 1850.

Dearborn, Henry. *Defence of Gen. Henry Dearborn against the Attack of Gen. William Hull.* Boston, Mass.: Edgar W. Davies, 1824.

Douglass, David B. "Reminiscences of the Campaign of 1814 on the Niagara Frontier." *Historical Magazine* 1–4 (July–October 1873).

Driscoll, Henry. "The Capture of Fort Niagara." In *The Documentary History of the Campaigns upon the Niagara Frontier in 1812-14.* 9:18–20, edited by Ernest Cruikshank. Welland, Ontario: The Lundy's Lane Historical Society. Welland, Ontario: Tribune Press, 1896–1908.

Duane, William. *A Hand Book for Infantry.* 5th ed. Philadelphia: Published by the author, 1813.

Dudley, William S., and Michael J. Crawford, eds. *The Naval War of 1812: A Documentary History.* 3 vols. Washington, D.C., 1985–2002.

Dulles, Charles W., ed. "Extracts from the Diary of Joseph Heatly Dulles." *Pennsylvania Magazine of History and Biography* 35 (1911): 276–89.

Efner, Elijah D. "The Adventures and Enterprises of Elijah D. Efner." In *Publications of the Buffalo Historical Society,* 4: 34–54, edited by Frank H. Severance. Buffalo, N.Y.: Buffalo Historical Society, 1896.

Everest, Allan S. ed. *Recollections of Clinton County and the Battle of Plattsburgh, 1800–1840,* Plattsburgh, N.Y.: Clinton County Historical Association, 1964.

Frederiksen, John C., ed. "Chronicle of Valor: The Journal of a Pennsylvania Officer in the War of 1812." *Western Pennsylvania Historical Magazine* 67 (July 1984): 243–84.

———. "A Georgia Officer in the War of 1812: The Letters of Colonel William Clay Cumming." *The Georgia Historical Quarterly* 71, no. 4. (Winter 1987): 668–91.

———. "Memoirs of Captain Ephraim Shaler: A Connecticut Yankee in the War of 1812." *New England Quarterly* 57 (September 1984): 411–20.

———. "The Memoirs of Johnathan Kearsley: A Michigan Hero from the War of 1812." *Indiana Military History Journal* 10 (May 1985): 4–16.

———. "'Plow-Joggers for Generals': The Experiences of a New York Ensign in the War of 1812." *Indiana Military History Journal* 11, no. 3 (October 1986): 16–27.

———. "Reynold M. Kirby and His Race to Join the Regiment: A Connecticut Officer in the War of 1812." *Connecticut History* 32 (November 1991): 51–82.

———. "The War of 1812 in Northern New York: General George Izard's Journal of the Chateaugay Campaign." *New York History* 76 (April 1995): 173–200.

———. "The War of 1812 in Northern New York: The Observations of Captain Rufus McIntire." *New York History* 68, no. 3 (July 1987): 297–324.

Galloway, Archer. "Firing the First Shot: As Told by the Man Who Fired It." In *Publications of the Buffalo Historical Society* 5: 21–25. Buffalo, N.Y.: Buffalo Historical Society, 1902.

Graves, Donald E., ed. *First Campaign of an A.D.C.: The War of 1812 Memoir of Lieutenant William Jenkins Worth, United States Army.* Youngstown, N.Y.: Old Fort Niagara Association, 2012.

———. *Soldiers of 1814: American Enlisted Men's Memoirs of the Niagara Campaign.* Lewiston, N.Y.: Old Fort Niagara Association, 1995.

Hall, Amos. "Militia Service of 1813-1814." In *Publications of the Buffalo Historical Society* 5: 27–62. Buffalo, N.Y.: Buffalo Historical Society, 1902.

Harrison, Jonas. "Extracts from the Correspondence of Jonas Harrison." In *Publications of the Buffalo Historical Society* 5: 99–109. Buffalo: Buffalo Historical Society, 1902.

Hastings, Hugh, ed. *Military Minutes of the Council of Appointment of the State of New York, 1783–1821.* 3 vols. Albany, N.Y.: James B. Lyon, 1901.
———. *Public Papers of Daniel D. Tompkins, Governor of New York, 1807–1817.* 3 vols. New York: Wynkoop Hallenbeck Crawford Co., 1898.
Heitman, Francis B. *Historical Register and Dictionary of the United States Army.* Washington, D.C.: Government Printing Office, 1903.
Hibbard, N. W. "A Participant's Recollection of the Battle of Sandy Creek." In *Transactions of the Jefferson County Historical Society,* No. 3, 29–31. Watertown, N.Y.: Jefferson County Historical Society, 1895.
Hodge, William. "A Buffalo Boy of 1813." In *Publications of the Buffalo Historical Society,* 9: 349–56. Buffalo, N.Y.: Buffalo Historical Society, 1906.
Horner, William E. "Surgical Sketches: A Military Hospital at Buffalo, New York, in the Year 1814," *The Medical Examiner and Record of Medical Science* 16 (December 1852): 753–74.
Howe, Eber D. "Recollections of a Pioneer Printer." In *Publications of the Buffalo Historical Society,* 9: 377–406. Buffalo, N.Y.: Buffalo Historical Society, 1906.
Hunt, Gaillard, ed. *The Writings of James Madison: Comprising his public and private papers and his private correspondence, including numerous letters and documents now for the first time printed.* 9 vols. New York: G. P. Putnam's Sons, 1900–1910.
Irving, Pierre M. *The Life and Letters of Washington Irving.* 3 vols. New York: G. P. Putnam and Son, 1869.
Irwin, Ray W., and Edna L. Jacobsen, eds. *A Columbia College Student in the Eighteenth Century: Essays by Daniel D. Tompkins.* New York: Columbia University Press, 1940.
Izard, George. *Official Correspondence with the Department of War: Relative to the Military Operations of the American Army under the command of Major General Izard, of the Northern Frontier of the United States, in the Years 1814 and 1815.* Philadelphia, Pa.: Thomas Dobson, 1816.
The Journal of the Senate of the State of New York, 1808. Albany, N.Y., 1808.
Laws of the State of New York, passed at the Forty-second, Forty-third, and Forty-fourth Sessions of the Legislature. Albany, N.Y.: William Gould and Company, 1821.
Laws of the State of New York, passed at the Thirty-fifth Session of the Legislature. Albany, N.Y.: S. Southwick, 1812.
Laws of the State of New York, passed at the Thirty-ninth, Fortieth, and Forty-first Sessions of the Legislature. Albany, N.Y.: Websters and Skinners, 1818.
Laws of the State of New York, passed at the Thirty-sixth, Thirty-seventh, and Thirty-eighth Sessions of the Legislature. Albany, N.Y.: Websters and Skinners, 1815.
Leavenworth, Henry. Undated statement on the battle of Bridgewater [Lundy's Lane]. Manuscript Collection, Buffalo History Museum, Buffalo, N.Y.
Lender, Mark E., and James Kirby Martin, eds. *Citizen Soldier: The Revolutionary War Journal of Joseph Bloomfield.* Newark, N.J.: New Jersey Historical Society, 1982.
McClure, George. *Causes of the Destruction of the American Towns on the Niagara Frontier, and Failure of the Campaign of the Fall of 1813.* Bath, N.Y.: Benjamin Snead, 1817.
Mann, James. *Medical Sketches of the Campaigns of 1812, 13, 14.* Dedham, Mass.: H. Mann and Co., 1816.
Memoranda of Occurrences Connected with the Campaign of Niagara. Manuscript Collection, Buffalo History Museum, Buffalo, N.Y.

Nelson, Gladys G., ed. "The Battle of Plattsburg." *University of Rochester Library Bulletin*. 3, no. 2. (Winter 1948): 30–34.

New American State Papers: Military Affairs. 19 vols. Wilmington, Del.: Scholarly Resources, 1979.

New American State Papers: Naval Affairs. 10 vols. Wilmington, Del.: Scholarly Resources, 1981.

Penny, Joshua. *The Life and Adventures of Joshua Penny, a Native of Southold, Long Island, Suffolk County, New York.* New York: Joshua Penny, 1815 (Printed by Alden Spooner).

Porter, Daniel R., ed. "Jacob Porter Norton, a Yankee on the Niagara Frontier in 1814." *Niagara Frontier* 12 (Summer 1965): 51–57.

Rutland, Robert A., William T. Hutchinson, William M. E. Rachal, and John C. A. Stagg, eds. *The Papers of James Madison, Presidential Series.* 7 vols. Charlottesville: University Press of Virginia, 1986.

Salisbury, Hezekiah. "A Guardsman of Buffalo." In *Publications of the Buffalo Historical Society,* 9: 867–70. Buffalo, N.Y.: Buffalo Historical Society, 1906.

Scott, Winfield. *Memoirs of Lieut.-General Scott.* 2 vols. New York: Sheldon & Company, 1864.

Shepard, Elihu H. *The Autobiography of Elihu H. Shepard.* St. Louis, Mo.: George Knapp, 1869.

Shriver, Phillip R., ed. "Brocken Locks and Rusty Barrels: A New York Militia Company on the Eve of the War of 1812," *New York History* 67, no. 3. (July 1986): 353–57.

Sidway, Mrs. Jonathan [Parnell Sidway]. "Recollections of the Burning of Buffalo." In *Publications of the Buffalo Historical Society,* 9: 311–36. Buffalo, N.Y.: Buffalo Historical Society, 1906.

Skinner, Martha St. John. "Story of the St. John House." In *Publications of the Buffalo Historical Society,* 9: 337–48. Buffalo, N.Y.: Buffalo Historical Society, 1906.

Sloan, James. *James Sloan Memoir.* Manuscript Collection, Buffalo Historical Museum. Buffalo, N.Y.

Spalding, Lyman A. *Recollections of the war of 1812 and Early Life in Western New York.* Lockport, N.Y.: Niagara County Historical Society, 1949.

Stacy, Nathaniel. *Memoirs of the Life of Nathaniel Stacy.* Columbus, Pa.: Abner Vedder, 1850.

Swift, Joseph G. *The Memoirs of Gen. Joseph Gardner Swift, LL.D., USA.* Worcester, Mass.: F. S. Blanchard & Co., 1890.

———. *Report on the Defence of the City of New-York, Accompanied with Maps, Views, and Topographical Plans.* New York: New-York Historical Society, 1814.

Third Artillery Regiment Orderly Book. New York State Library Manuscript Collection: Albany, N.Y.

Tompkins, Daniel D. *A Letter to Archibald M'Intyre, Esq., Comptroller of the State of New-York.* N.p.: n.p., 1819.

Towle, Edward L., ed. "The Militia Myth: Letters from Lt. William B. Rochester on the Niagara Frontier, 1813." *University of Rochester Library Bulletin* 19, no. 3. (Spring 1964).

Van Rensselaer, Solomon. *A Narrative of the Affair of Queenston in the War of 1812.* New York: Leavitt, Lord and Co., 1836.

Von Steuben, Friedrich Wilhelm. *Regulations for the Order and Discipline of the Troops of the United States.* Boston, Mass.: Henry Ranlet, 1794.

Warren, Asa. "Two Dramatic Incidents." In *Publications of the Buffalo Historical Society*, 9: 373–76. Buffalo, N.Y.: Buffalo Historical Society, 1906.

Willson, Jared. "A Rifleman of Queenston." In *Publications of the Buffalo Historical Society*, 9:373–76. Buffalo, N.Y.: Buffalo Historical Society, 1906.

Winder, William H. *Statements by Colonel William H. Winder of Occurrences on the Niagara Frontier, 1812*. Washington, D.C.: Printed by Duff Green, 1829.

Wingfield, David. "Memoir of Lieutenant David Wingfield." In William S. Dudley and Michael Crawford, eds. *The Naval War of 1812: A Documentary History*. 3 vols. Washington, D.C., 1985–2002, 2:470–73.

Wood, William, ed. *Select British Documents of the Canadian War of 1812*. 4 vols. Toronto: Champlain Society, 1920–28.

Wool, John E. "The Battle of Beekmantown in 1814." *North Country Notes* (September 1965).

———. "Major Wool's Account of the Battle of Plattsburgh." *North Country Notes* (September 1961).

Yetwin, Neil B., ed. *The Life & War Remembrances of Captain Mordecai Myers, 13th United States Infantry, 1812–1815*. Youngstown, N.Y.: Old Fort Niagara Association, 2013.

Newspapers

Albany Argus (Albany, New York)
Albany Gazette (Albany, New York)
Albany Register (Albany, New York)
Buffalo Gazette (Buffalo, New York)
The Columbian (New York City)
Commercial Advertiser (New York City)
Geneva Gazette (Geneva, New York)
Montreal Gazette (Montreal, Lower Canada)
The National Advocate (New York City)
National Intelligencer (Washington, D.C.)
New-York Evening Post (New York City)
New-York Spectator (New York City)
Niles' Weekly Register (Baltimore)
Ontario Messenger (Canandaigua, New York)
Ontario Repository and Western Advertiser (Canandaigua, New York)
Plattsburgh Republican (Plattsburgh, New York)
The War (New York City)

Secondary Sources

Adams, Henry. *History of the United States during the Administrations of Jefferson and Madison*. 9 vols. New York: Charles Scribner's Sons, 1931.

Aimone, Alan. "West Point's Contribution to the War of 1812." *The Journal of America's Military Past* 25, no. 2. (Fall 1998): 37–48.

Arthur, Brian. *How Britain Won the War of 1812: The Royal Navy Blockades of the United States, 1812–1815*. Woodbridge, U.K.: Boydell Press, 2011.

Ashdown, Dana W. "Wilkinson's Invasion Flotilla of 1813: A paper examining the American flotilla of Major-General James Wilkinson, and its potential survival in the Salmon River at Fort Covington, New York." *The War of 1812 Magazine*, no. 23

(February 2015). https://napoleon-series.org/military-info/Warof1812/2015/Issue23 /Wilkinson'sInvasionFlotilla.pdf.

Austin, John M. *St. Lawrence County in the War of 1812: Folly and Mischief.* Charleston, S.C.: The History Press, 2013.

Babcock, Louis L. *The Siege of Fort Erie: An Episode of the War of 1812.* Buffalo, N.Y.: The Peter Paul Book Company, 1899.

———. *The War of 1812 on the Niagara Frontier.* Buffalo, N.Y.: Buffalo Historical Society, 1927.

Barbagallo, Tricia A. "Fellow Citizens, Read a Horrid Tale . . ." *New York Archives* 7, no. 1 (Summer 2007): 20–23.

Barbuto, Richard V. "Daniel D. Tompkins, War Governor." *The War of 1812 Magazine* no. 25 (May 2016). http://napoleon-series.org/military/Warof1812/2016/Issue25 /Tompkins.pdf

———. "1812: The United States Builds an Army." *Journal of the War of 1812* 15, no. 1. (Summer 2012): 71–77.

———. "The 1814 Siege of Fort Erie." *The Journal of America's Military Past* 39, no. 3. (Fall 2014): 13–28.

———. *Long Range Guns and Close Quarter Combat: The Third United States Artillery Regiment in the War of 1812.* Youngstown, N.Y.: Old Fort Niagara Association, 2010.

———. *Niagara 1814: America Invades Canada.* Lawrence: University Press of Kansas, 2000.

———. *Staff Ride Handbook for the Niagara Campaigns, 1812–1814, War of 1812.* Youngstown, N.Y.: Old Fort Niagara Association, 2016.

Beers, Lewis P. Jr. *The Pork Barrel Fort: A Documented Account of the Battle of Cranberry/Goose Creek, July 21, 1813.* N.p.: published by the author, 2019.

Bell, William Gardner. *Commanding Generals and Chiefs of Staff, 1775–2005.* Washington, D.C.: Center of Military History, 2005.

———. *Secretaries of War and Secretaries of the Army.* Washington, D.C.: Center of Military History, 2005.

Benn, Carl. *The Iroquois in the War of 1812.* Toronto: University of Toronto Press, 1998.

Benn, Carl, and R. Arthur Bowler, eds. *War along the Niagara: Essays on the War of 1812 and Its Legacy.* Youngstown, N.Y.: Old Fort Niagara Association, 1991.

Bixby, George. *Peter Sailly: A Pioneer of the Champlain Valley.* New York State Library History Bulletin 12 (1919). Albany: University of the State of New York, 1919.

Black, Jeremy. "The North American Theater of the Napoleonic Wars, or, As It Is Sometimes Called, The War of 1812." *The Journal of Military History* 76, no. 4 (October 2012): 1053–66.

———. "The Problems of a Great Power: Britain and the War of 1812." *The RUSI Journal* 157, no. 4 (August 2012): 80–84.

———. *The War of 1812 in the Age of Napoleon.* Norman: University of Oklahoma Press, 2009.

Brant, Irving. *James Madison, Commander in Chief, 1812–1836.* Vol. 6, James Madison Book Series. Indianapolis: Bobbs-Merrill, 1961.

Brodine, Charles E. Jr. "The Cautious Commodore?" *U.S. Naval Institute Naval History* (October 2013): 30–35.

Brooke, John L. *Columbia Rising: Civil Life on the Upper Hudson from the Revolution to the Age of Jackson.* Chapel Hill: University of North Carolina Press, 2010.

Brown, Leon N. "Commodore Melancthon Taylor Woolsey, Lake Ontario Hero of the War of 1812." In *Fifth Publication of the Oswego County Historical Society*, 141–52. Oswego, N.Y.: Oswego Historical Society, 1941.

Buel, Richard Jr. *America on the Brink: How the Political Struggle over the War of 1812 Almost Destroyed the Young Republic.* New York: Palgrave Macmillan, 2005.

The Centenary of the Battle of Plattsburgh. Albany: The University of the State of New York: 1914.

Chartrand, Rene. *Forts of the War of 1812.* New York: Osprey Publishing, 2012.

———. "New York City Artillery Regiments ca. 1806–1815." *Military Collector and Historian* 64, no. 2 (Summer 2012): 133–34.

———. "Volunteer Units of Newburgh, New York, ca. 1790s—1815." *Military Collector and Historian* 63, no. 2. (Summer 2011): 142.

Chester, Gregory. *Battle of Big Sandy: War of 1812.* Watertown, N.Y.: Published by the author, 2007.

Churchill, Franklin Hunter. *Sketch of the Life of Brig. Gen. Sylvester Churchill, Inspector General U.S. Army.* New York: Willis McDonald & Co., 1888.

Clark, Emmons. *History of the Seventh Regiment of New York, 1806–1889.* New York: Seventh Regiment, 1890.

Clark, Lewis H. *Military History of Wayne County, N.Y.* Sodus, N.Y.: Lewis H. Clark, Hulett & Gaylord, 1883.

Cole, Stephanie. *Buffalo's 300.* Buffalo, N.Y.: Buffalo Aurora Comics, 2012.

Coles, Harry L. *The War of 1812.* Chicago: University of Chicago Press, 1965.

Colquhoun, A. H. U. "The Career of Joseph Willcocks." *The Canadian Historical Review* 7 (December 1926): 287–93.

Coombs, Howard G. "The Search for Certainty: Sackets Harbor—May 28/29, 1813." (Master's thesis, Queens University, 2003).

Crissman, Erin E. "Solomon Van Rensselaer: 'A Man of [no] Business Whatsoever'" (Master's thesis, SUNY Oneonta, 2004).

Cruikshank, Ernest. "The Contest for the Command of Lake Ontario in 1814." In *Ontario Historical Society Papers and Records* 21: 99–159. Toronto: Ontario Historical Society, 1924.

———. *Drummond's Winter Campaign.* 2nd ed. Welland, Ontario: Lundy's Lane Historical Society, n.d.

———. *The Fight in the Beechwoods,* 2nd ed. Welland, Ontario: Lundy's Lane Historical Society, 1895.

DeCroix, Douglas W., ed. *The War of 1812: A Three-Volume Commemoration of the Bicentennial, 2012–14.* Cheektowaga, N.Y.: Western New York Heritage Press, 2012–14.

Delafield, Julia. *Biographies of Francis Lewis and Morgan Lewis.* 2 vols. New York: Anson D. F. Randolph & Company, 1877.

Densmore, Christopher. *Red Jacket: Iroquois Diplomat and Orator.* Syracuse: Syracuse University Press, 1999.

Dorsey, Jennifer H. "The Delinquency of George Holcomb: Civil Disobedience in the Upper Hudson River Valley, 1812." *Hudson River Valley Review* 34, no. 1. (Autumn 2017): 2–17.

Dorsheimer, William. "The Village of Buffalo during the War of 1812." In *Publications of the Buffalo Historical Society* 1: 185–209. Buffalo, N.Y.: Bigelow Brothers, 1879.

Doty, Lockwood L. *A History of Livingston County, New York.* Geneseo, N.Y.: Edward E. Doty, 1876.

Dudley, Wade G. *Splintering the Wooden Wall: The British Blockade of the United States, 1812–1815.* Annapolis: Naval Institute Press, 2003.

Dunnigan, Brian Leigh. *A History and Guide to Old Fort Niagara.* Youngstown, N.Y.: Old Fort Niagara Association, 2007.

Egli, Bruce. "United States Volunteers in the War of 1812—The Legislative History." Unpublished paper, July 9, 2014.

"1813, The Battle of Stoney Creek." *Grimsby Historical Society Proceedings,* no. 1, (1950): 56–59.

Elliott, James E. *Strange Fatality: The Battle of Stoney Creek, 1813.* Toronto: Robin Brass Studio, 2009.

Ellis, James H. *A Ruinous and Unhappy War: New England and the War of 1812.* New York: Algora Publishing, 2009.

Emerson, Catherine. "An Industrious and Worthy Woman: The Chronicle of Betsy/ Mary Doyle and Her Husband Andrew." *Fortress Niagara* 13, no. 2. (December 2011): 3–15.

Emerson, George D. "The Episode of the Adams and Caledonia." In *Publications of the Buffalo Historical Society* 8: 405–8. Buffalo, N.Y.: Buffalo Historical Society Publications, 1905.

Erney, Richard A. "The Public Life of Henry Dearborn." Ph.D. dissertation, Columbia University, 1957.

Everest, Allan S. *The War of 1812 in the Champlain Valley.* Syracuse: Syracuse University Press, 1981.

———, ed. *Recollections of Clinton County and the Battle of Plattsburgh, 1800–1840.* Plattsburgh, N.Y.: Clinton County Historical Association, 1964.

Fitz-Enz, David G. *The Final Invasion: Plattsburgh, the War of 1812's Most Decisive Battle.* New York: Cooper Square Press, 2001.

Forman, Sidney. "Why the United States Military Academy was Established in 1802." *Military Affairs* 29, no. 1 (Spring 1965): 16–28.

Fredriksen, John C. *Officers of the War of 1812.* Lewiston, N.Y.: Edwin Mellon Press, 1989.

———. "A Tempered Sword, Untested: The Military Career of General George Izard." *The Journal of America's Military Past* 25, no. 2 (Fall 1998): 5–18; 25, no. 2 (Winter 1999): 5–16.

———. *The United States Army in the War of 1812.* Jefferson, N.C.: McFarland & Company, 2009.

Fredriksen, John C., comp. *War of 1812 Eyewitness Accounts: An Annotated Bibliography.* Westport, Conn.: Greenwood Press, 1997.

———. *The War of 1812 U.S. War Department Correspondence, 1812–1815.* Jefferson, N.C.: McFarland & Company, 2016.

Galpin, W. Freeman. "The American Grain Trade to the Spanish Peninsula, 1810–1814." *The American Historical Review* 28, no. 1 (October 1922): 24–44.

"George McClure." *Journal of the War of 1812* 12, no. 3 (Fall 2009): 6.

Gero, Anthony F. "Capt. John Richardson's Corps of Indian Riflemen, New York State Militia, 1812–1815: A Uniform Study." *Military Collector and Historian* 60, no. 2 (Summer 2008): 151–53.

———. *Excelsior's Citizen Soldiers: The Uniforms and Equipage of the New York State Militia, 1787–1847.* Auburn, N.Y.: Jacobs Press, 2016.

———. "Some Notes on New York's Black Regiments." *Military Collector and Historian* 31, no. 1 (Spring 1979): 36.

Gibson, Gary M. "Militia, Mud, and Misery: Sackets Harbor during the War of 1812." *New York History* (Summer/Fall 2013): 241–66.

———. "Oddities and Experiments: A Design and Operational History." Unpublished manuscript, 2013.

———. "Pirates and Robbers: American Privateers on the St. Lawrence River." *The War of 1812 Magazine* no. 26 (November 2016). http://napoleon-series.org/military/Warof1812/2016/Issue26/PiratesandRobbers.pdf.

———. "Profits vs. Patriotism in 1813." Sackets Harbor Battlefield Alliance, 2015. http://sacketsharborbattlefield.org/profit.htm.

———. "Target! Sackets Harbor during the War of 1812." Unpublished Manuscript, 2017.

———. "The U.S. Brig *Oneida*: A Design & Operational History." *The War of 1812 Magazine*, no. 19 (December 2012). http://napoleon-series.org/military/Warof1812/2012/Issue19/Oneida.pdf.

———. "The U.S. Frigate *General Pike*: A Design & Operational History." *The War of 1812 Magazine*, no. 23 (February 2015). http://napoleon-series.org/military/Warof1812/2015/Issue23/USFrigateGeneralPike.pdf.

Gillett, Mary C. *The Army Medical Department, 1775–1818.* Washington, D.C.: U.S. Army Medical Department Office of Medical History, 1981.

Gilpin, Alec R. *The War of 1812 in the Old Northwest.* East Lansing: Michigan State University Press, 1958.

Gosling, D. C. L. "The Battle at Lacolle Mill." *Journal of the Society for Army Historical Research* 47 (1969): 169–74.

Graves, Donald E. *And All Their Glory Past: Fort Erie, Plattsburgh and the Final Battles in the North.* Toronto: Robin Brass Studio, 2013.

———. "The Canadian Volunteers, 1813–1815." *Military Collector and Historian* 31 no. 3 (Fall 1979): 113–17.

———. "'Dry Books of Tactics': U.S. Infantry Manuals of the War of 1812 and After." *Military Collector and Historian* 38, no. 2 (Summer 1986): 50–61; 38, no. 3 (Winter 1986): 173–77.

———. *Field of Glory: The Battle of Crysler's Farm, 1813.* Toronto: Robin Brass Studio, 1999.

———. "The Finest Army Ever to Campaign on American Soil?" *The War of 1812 Magazine* no. 24 (November 2015). http: //www.napoleon-series.org/military/Warof1812/2015/Issue24/FinestArmy.pdf.

———. "The Hard School of War: A Collective Biography of the General Officers of the United States Army in the War of 1812." *The War of 1812 Magazine* no. 2 (February 2006); no. 3 (June 2006); no. 4 (September 2006).

———. *Red Coats and Grey Jackets: The Battle of Chippawa, 5 July 1814.* Toronto: Dundurn Press, 1994.

———. "The Redcoats are Coming!: British Troop Movements to North America in 1814." *Journal of the War of 1812* 6, no. 3 (Summer 2001): 12–18.

————. "War on the Ice: The British Attack on Ogdensburg, 21 February 1813." *The War of 1812 Magazine*, no. 16 (September 2011). http://www.napoleon-series.org/military /Warof1812/2011/Issue16/c_WaronIce.html.

————. *Where Right and Glory Lead!: The Battle of Lundy's Lane, 1814.* Toronto: Robin Brass Studio, 1997.

Griswold, William A. "A Reasoned Approach to the Defense of New York Harbor for the War of 1812." *Journal of America's Military Past* 30, no. 1 (Winter 2004): 26–42.

Grodzinski, John R. "American 'Independence is not threatened.'" In *The Routledge Handbook of the War of 1812*, edited by Donald R. Hickey and Connie D. Clark. New York: Routledge, 2016.

————. *Defender of Canada: Sir George Prevost and the War of 1812.* Norman: University of Oklahoma Press, 2013.

Guernsey, R. S. *New York City and Vicinity during the War of 1812–15.* 2 vols. New York: Charles L. Woodward. 1889.

Hammack, James W. Jr. *Kentucky and the Second American Revolution: The War of 1812.* Lexington: University Press of Kentucky, 1976.

Hanford, Franklin. *Notes on the Visits of American and British Naval Vessels to the Genesee River, 1809–1814.* Rochester, N.Y.: The Genesee Press, 1911.

Hatfield, Mark O. *Vice Presidents of the United States, 1789–1993.* Washington, D.C.: U.S. Government Printing Office, 1997.

Heidler, David S., and Jeanne T. Heidler, eds. *Encyclopedia of the War of 1812.* Santa Barbara, Calif.: ABC-CLIO, 1997.

Heitman, Francis B. *Historical Register and Dictionary of the United States Army.* 2 vols. Washington, D.C.: Government Printing Office, 1903.

Herkalo, Keith A. *September Eleventh 1814: The Battle of Plattsburgh.* Plattsburgh, N.Y.: The Battle of Plattsburgh Association, 2007.

Hickey, Donald R. "Federalist Defense Policy in the Age of Jefferson, 1801–1812." *Journal of Military History* 45, no. 2 (April, 1981): 63–70.

————. *187 Things You Should Know About the War of 1812.* Baltimore, Md.: Maryland Historical Society, 2012.

————. *The War of 1812: A Forgotten Conflict.* Urbana: University of Illinois Press, 1989.

Hickey, Donald R., and Connie D. Clark, eds. *The Routledge Handbook of the War of 1812.* New York, N.Y.: Routledge, 2016.

Hill, Richard W. Sr. *War Clubs and Wampum Belts: Hodinöhsö: ni Experiences of the War of 1812.* Brantford, Ontario: Woodland Cultural Centre, 2012.

History of Cayuga County New York. Auburn, N.Y.: Cayuga County Historical Society, 1908.

History of Oswego County, New York. Philadelphia: L. H. Everts & Co., 1877.

Hitsman, J. Mackey. "Alarum on Lake Ontario, Winter 1812–1813." *Military Affairs* 23, no. 3 (Fall 1959): 129–38.

————. "David Parish and the War of 1812." *Military Affairs* 26, no. 4 (Winter 1962–63): 171–77.

————. *The Incredible War of 1812: A Military History.* Toronto: Robin Brass Studio, 1999.

Holden, James Austin, ed. *The Centenary of the Battle of Plattsburg: 1814 September 11, 1914, At Plattsburg, N.Y., September 6 to 11, 1914.* Albany: University of the State of New York, 1914.

Horsman, Reginald. *Frontier Doctor: William Beaumont, America's First Great Medical Scientist*. Columbia: University of Missouri Press, 1996.

———. "The Paradox of Dartmoor Prison." *American Heritage* 26, no. 2 (February 1975): 13–17 and 85.

Hough, Franklin B. *History of Jefferson County*. Albany, N.Y.: Joel Munsell, 1854.

Hutcheon, Wallace S. Jr. *Robert Fulton: Pioneer of Undersea Warfare*. Annapolis, Md.: Naval Institute Press, 1981.

Irwin, Ray W. *Daniel D. Tompkins: Governor of New York and Vice President of the United States*. New York, N.Y.: The New-York Historical Society, 1968.

Jacobs, James R. *Tarnished Warrior: Major-General James Wilkinson*. New York: Macmillan, 1938.

Jaffe, Steven H. *New York at War: Four Centuries of Combat, Fear, and Intrigue in Gotham*. New York, N.Y.: Basic Books, 2012.

Jenkins, John S. *History of Political Parties in the State of New-York*. Auburn, N.Y.: Alden & Markham, 1846.

———. *Lives of the Governors of the State of New York*. Auburn, N.Y.: Derby and Miller, 1851.

Johnson, Crisfield. *History of Erie County, New York*. Buffalo, N.Y.: Matthews & Warren, 1876.

Johnson, Eric. "The U.S. Voluntary Corps." *Journal of the War of 1812* 9, no. 1 (Spring 2005): 15–19.

Johnson, Timothy D. "Lundy's Lane: Winfield Scott's Blunder to Glory." *Military History Quarterly* 8, no. 1 (Autumn 1995): 78–87.

Kastor, Peter J. "Toward 'The Maritime War Only": The Question of Naval Mobilization, 1811–1812." *Journal of Military History* 61, no. 3 (July 1997): 455–80.

Kerby, Robert L. "The Militia System and the State Militias in the War of 1812." *Indiana Magazine of History* 73 (June 1977): 102–24.

Kert, Faye M. *Privateering: Patriots & Profits in the War of 1812*. Baltimore: Johns Hopkins University Press, 2015.

Ketchum, William. *Authentic and Comprehensive History of Buffalo*. Buffalo, N.Y.: Rockwell, Baker, and Hill, 1865.

Kirkpatrick, David. *The War of 1812 in the West: From Fort Detroit to New Orleans*. Yardley, Pa.: Westholme Publishing, 2019.

Kohler, C. Douglas. "Colonel Cyrenius Chapin: The Brave Soldier, The Good Citizen, The Honest Man." *Western New York Heritage* 12, no. 4 (Winter 2010): 28–34.

Kutolowski, John F., and Kathleen Smith Kutolowski. "Commissioners and Canvasses: The Militia and Politics in Western New York, 1800–1845." *New York History* 63, no. 4 (January 1982): 5–38.

Lambert, Andrew. "Sideshow? British Grand Strategy and the War of 1812." *British Commission for Military History Newsletter* (Spring 2012): 17–47.

Lampi, Philip J. "The Federalist Party Resurgence, 1808–1816." *Journal of the Early Republic* 33, no. 2 (Summer 2013): 255–81.

Lear, Paul A. "An Objective of Lesser Proportions: The May 5–6, 1814, Battle of Oswego." Unpublished manuscript.

Leiner, Frederick C. "Privateers and Profit in the War of 1812." *Journal of Military History* 77, no. 4 (October 2013): 1225–50.

Lemmon, Sarah M. *Frustrated Patriots: North Carolina and the War of 1812*. Chapel Hill: University of North Carolina Press, 1973.

Lewis, Dennis M. "Citizen Soldier: The Militia in the Champlain Valley." *North Country Notes*, no. 187 (1983): 2–4.

Linklater, Andro. *An Artist in Treason: The Extraordinary Double Life of General James Wilkinson*. New York: Walker Publishing Company, 2009.

Lord, Norman C., ed. "The War on the Canadian Frontier, 1812–14: Letters Written by Sergt. James Commins, 8th Foot." *Journal of the Society for Historical Research*. 18 (1939): 199–211.

Lossing, Benson L. *The Pictorial Fieldbook of the War of 1812*. New York, N.Y.: Harper and Brothers, 1868.

Mahon, John K. *History of the Militia and the National Guard*. New York: Macmillan Publishing Company, 1983.

———. *The War of 1812*. Gainesville: University Presses of Florida, 1972.

Malcomson, Robert. *Capital in Flames: The American Attack on York, 1813*. Montreal: Robin Brass Studio, 2008.

———. *Historical Dictionary of the War of 1812*. Lanham, Md.: The Scarecrow Press, Inc., 2006.

———. *Lords of the Lake: The Naval War on Lake Ontario, 1812–1814*. Annapolis: Naval Institute Press, 1998.

———. "New Yorkers at York." *New York Archives* 8, no. 4 (Spring 2009): 28–31.

———. *A Very Brilliant Affair: The Battle of Queenston Heights, 1812*. Annapolis: Naval Institute Press, 2003.

———. "'When our country calls': The New York State Militia in the War of 1812." Unpublished paper, November 15–16, 2007, New York State Library, Albany, N.Y.

McClure, George. *Causes of the Destruction of the American Towns on the Niagara Frontier and the Failure of the Campaign of the Fall of 1813*. Bath, N.Y.: Benjamin Snead, 1817.

McMaster, Guy H. *History of the Settlement of Steuben County, N.Y.* Bath, N.Y.: R. S. Underhill & Co., 1853.

Meacham, Jon. *American Lion: Andrew Jackson in the White House*. New York, N.Y.: Random House, 2008.

Mills, Dudley. "The Duke of Wellington and the Peace Negotiations at Ghent in 1814." *The Canadian Historical Review* 2 (March 1921): 19–32.

Mohl, Raymond A. *Poverty in New York, 1783–1825*. New York: Oxford University Press, 1971.

Morris, John D. *Sword of the Border: Major General Jacob Jennings Brown, 1775–1828*. Kent: Kent State University Press, 2000.

Muller, H. N., III. "A 'Traitorous and Diabolical Traffic:' The Commerce of the Champlain-Richelieu Corridor During the War of 1812." *Vermont History* 44, no. 2 (Spring 1976): 78–96.

Parker, Arthur C. "The Senecas in the War of 1812." *New York State Historical Association Proceedings* 15 (1916): 78–90.

Parmeter, Irving. "The Battle of Sandy Creek." *United States Naval Institute Proceedings* 84, no. 1 (January 1958): 136–37.

Peskin, Allan. *Winfield Scott and the Profession of Arms*. Kent: Kent State University Press, 2003.

"Public Ceremonies in Connection with the Dedication of the Monument." *Twenty-seventh Annual Report of the Buffalo Park Commissioners* (January 1897): 95–128.

Reed, C. Wingate. "Decius Wadsworth: First Chief of Ordnance, U.S. Army, 1812–1821." *Army Ordnance* 24 (May–June 1943): 527–30 and (July–August 1943): 113–16.

Robinson, C. W. "The Expedition to Plattsburgh, Upon Lake Champlain, Canada, 1814." *Journal of the Royal United Services Institution* 61, no. 443 (August 1916): 499–522.

St-Denis, Guy. "In Search of the Fisherman's Path: Rethinking the American Assault on Queenston Heights." *Canadian Military History* 27, no. 1 (May 2018), Article 16. http://scholars.wlu.ca/cmh/vo127/iss1/16.

Sapio, Victor A. *Pennsylvania and the War of 1812.* Lexington: University Press of Kentucky, 1970.

Schecter, Barnet. *The Battle for New York: The City at the Heart of the American Revolution.* New York, N.Y.: Walker & Company, 2002.

Schroeder, John H. *The Battle of Lake Champlain: A "Brilliant and Extraordinary Victory."* Norman: University of Oklahoma Press, 2015.

Scott, Winfield. *Memoirs of Lieutenant General Scott, LLD.* New York, N.Y.: Sheldon & Co., 1864.

Severance, Frank H., ed. "The Case of Alexander Smyth." In *Publications of the Buffalo Historical Society*, vol. 18, 215–55. Buffalo, N.Y.: Buffalo Historical Society Publications, 1914.

Sims, Doris M. *The Battle of Sodus Point: War of 1812.* Lyons, N.Y.: Wayne County Historical Society, 1985.

Skaggs, David Curtis. "More Important than Perry's Victory." *Naval History Magazine* 27, no. 5 (October 2013): 20–28.

———. *Thomas Macdonough: Master of Command in the Early U.S. Navy.* Annapolis: Naval Institute Press, 2003.

Skeen, C. Edward. *John Armstrong, Jr., 1758–1843: A Biography.* Syracuse: Syracuse University Press, 1981.

Skelton, William B. "High Army Leadership in the Era of the War of 1812: The Making and Remaking of the Officer Corps." *William and Mary Quarterly* 51, no. 2 (April 1994): 253–74.

Slosek, Anthony M., and Helen Moore Breitbeck, eds. *Oswego and the War of 1812.* Oswego, N.Y.: Heritage Foundation of Oswego, 1989.

Snyder, Charles M., ed. *Red & White on the New York Frontier: A Struggle for Survival.* Harrison, N.Y.: Harbor Hill Books, 1978.

Spafford, Horatio Gates. *A Gazetteer of the State of New York.* Albany, N.Y.: H. C. Southwick, 1813.

Stacey, Charles P. "Another Look at the Battle of Lake Erie." *The Canadian Historical Review* 39, no. 1 (March 1958): 41–51.

Stagg, J. C. A. "The American Homefront, 1812–1815." In *The Routledge Handbook*, edited by Donald R. Hickey and Connie D. Clark, 152–63.

———. "Between Black Rock and a Hard Place: Peter B. Porter's Plan for an American Invasion of Canada in 1812." *Journal of the Early Republic* 19, no. 3 (Autumn 1999): 385–422.

———. "Enlisted Men in the United States Army, 1812–1815: A Preliminary Survey." *The William and Mary Quarterly* 43, no. 4 (October 1986): 615–45.

——. "Freedom and Subordination: Disciplinary Problems in the U.S. Army during the War of 1812." *Journal of Military History* 78, no. 2 (April 2014): 537–74.

——. "James Madison and the Coercion of Great Britain: Canada, the West Indies, and the War of 1812." *William and Mary Quarterly* 38, no. 1 (January 1981): 3–34.

——. *Mr. Madison's War: Politics, Diplomacy, and Warfare in the Early American Republic, 1783–1830.* Princeton: Princeton University Press, 1983.

——. "The Politics of Ending the War of 1812." In *War along the Niagara: Essays on the War of 1812 and Its Legacy,* edited by Carl Benn and R. Arthur Bowler. Youngstown, N.Y.: Old Fort Niagara Association, 1991.

——. "United States Army Officers in the War of 1812: A Statistical and Behavioral Portrait." *Journal of Military History* 76, no. 4 (October 2012): 1001–34.

——. *The War of 1812: Conflict for a Continent.* Cambridge, England: Cambridge University Press, 2012.

Stanley, George F. G. *The War of 1812: Land Operations.* Toronto, Ontario: Macmillan of Canada, 1983.

Steenshorne, Jennifer E. "Evacuation Day." *New York Archives* 10, no. 2 (Fall 2010): 10–13.

Steppler, Glenn A. "A Duty Troublesome Beyond Measure." (Master's thesis, McGill University, 1974).

——. "Logistics on the Canadian Frontier 1812–1814." *Military Collector and Historian* 31, no. 1 (Spring 1979): 8–10.

Storm, Geoffrey. "The War on Business." *New York Archives* 13, no. 3 (Winter 2014): 20–23.

Strum, Harvey J. "A House Divided: The New York Gubernatorial Election of 1813." *Journal of the War of 1812* 13, no. 2 (Summer 2010): 17–23; no. 3 (Fall 2010): 4–9; no. 4 (Winter 2010–2011): 10–16.

——. *New York and the War of 1812.* (Ph.D. dissertation. Syracuse University, 1978).

——. "New York Federalists and Opposition to the War of 1812." *World Affairs* 142, (Winter 1980): 169–87.

——. "The Politics of the New York Antiwar Campaign, 1812–1815." *Peace and Change* 8 (September 1982): 7–18.

——. "Saving Mr. Tompkins' War: From Reluctant Warriors to War Hawks in the 1814 Election." *The War of 1812 Magazine,* no. 28 (April 2018). http: //napoleon-series .org/military/Warof1812/2018/Issue28/SavingMrTompkinsWar.pdf.

Tanner, Dwight. "Young Teazer—The Making of a Myth." *Nova Scotia Historical Quarterly* 6 (1976): 405–12.

Taylor, Alan. *The Civil War of 1812.* New York: Alfred A. Knopf, 2010.

——. "Who Murdered William Cooper?" *New York History* 72, no. 3 (July 1991): 261–83.

Thatcher, Joseph M. "A Fleet in the Wilderness: Shipbuilding at Sackets Harbor." In *War along the Niagara: Essays on the War of 1812 and Its Legacy,* edited by Carl Benn and R. Arthur Bowler. Youngstown, N.Y.: Old Fort Niagara Association, 1991.

Thomson, John Lewis. *Historical Sketches of the Late War between the United States and Great Britain.* Philadelphia: Thomas Desilver, 1816.

Tiro, Karim M. "The Widow's Son." *New York Archives* 9, no. 3 (Winter 2010): 20–23.

Trace, Jacqueline. "Salt Boats are A-Comin': The War of 1812 Touches Down in Chautauqua County." In *The War of 1812: A Three-Volume Commemoration of the*

Bicentennial, 2012–14, edited by Douglas W. DeCroix. 1:24–29. Cheektowaga, N.Y.: Western New York Heritage Press, 2012–14.

Tucker, Spencer, ed. *The Encyclopedia of the War of 1812.* 3 vols. Santa Barbara: ABC-CLIO, 2012.

Turner, Orsamus. *Pioneer History of the Holland Purchase of Western New York.* Buffalo, N.Y.: Jewett, Thomas & Co., 1850.

Tuttle, William H. *Madison County, New York Soldiers in the War of 1812.* Mt. Airy, Maryland: Pie Creek Publications, 1994.

Wade, Arthur. *Artillerists and Engineers: The Beginnings of American Seacoast Fortifications, 1794–1815.* McLean, Virginia: CDSG Press, 2011.

Wallace, Edward. *General William Jenkins Worth: Monterrey's Forgotten Hero.* Dallas: Southern Methodist University Press, 1953.

Watson, G. E. "The United States and the Peninsular War, 1808–1812." *The Historical Journal.* 19., no. 4. (December 1976): 859–76.

Watson, Samuel. "Trusting to 'the Chapter of Accidents': Contingency, Necessity, and Self-Restraint in Jeffersonian National Security Policy." *Journal of American History.* 76., no. 4. (October 1812): 973–1000.

Whitehorne, Joseph. *While Washington Burned: The Battle for Fort Erie 1814.* Baltimore: Nautical & Aviation Publishing Company of America, 1992.

Wilder, Patrick A. *The Battle of Sackett's Harbour: 1813.* Baltimore: The Nautical & Aviation Publishing Company of America, 1994.

Williams, Ames W. "The Old Fortifications of New York Harbor." *Military Collector and Historian.* 22., no. 2. (Summer 1970): 37–45.

Williams, Samuel, and Gideon Miner Davison. *Sketches of the War, Between the United States and the British Isles.* 2 vols. Rutland, Vt.: Fay and Davison, 1815.

Wilson, David A. *United Irishmen, United States: Immigrant Radicals in the Early Republic.* Ithaca: Cornell University Press, 1998.

Wood, Gordon S. *Empire of Liberty: A History of the Early Republic, 1789–1815.* New York: Oxford University Press, 2009.

Young, Andrew W. *History of Chautauqua County, New York from its First Settlement to the Present Time.* Buffalo: Matthews & Warren, 1875.

Zabecki, David T. "Medals, Decorations, and Military Honors," in *The Encyclopedia of the War of 1812*, edited by Spencer Tucker. 3 vols. Santa Barbara, Calif.: ABC-CLIO, 2012.

INDEX

Niagara River, 3, 26, 44–45, 47–49, 57–58,
  60, 64, 66–67, 77, 79, 83, 90, 93, 121–22,
  138, 158, 168, 176, 183, 205, 207–8, 210–11,
  222, 224, 234–35, 264–65, 275, 284
Nicholas, Wilson Cary, 257
Nolan, Maurice, 180
Non-Intercourse Act, 15
Noon, Darby, 43, 47
North Battery (Red Fort), 25–26
North River Steam Boat (*Clermont*), 50
Norton, Jacob Porter, 235
Norton, John, 61, 71, 134, 140, 212

Odelltown, Lower Canada, 161, 194, 196
O'Flyng, Patrick, 265, 267
Ogdensburg, N.Y., 47, 55, 63, 80, 82–83,
  86–87, 107–8, 157, 164–65; British raid in
  1813, 87, 114
Oneida County, 19, 117, 233, 279
Oneida Tribe, 202, 208
Onondaga, N.Y., 20, 185
Onondaga County, 19
Onondaga Tribe, 208
Ontario County, 19, 48, 58, 275
Ontario Messenger (Canandaigua), 215
Orange County, 21, 150
Orders in Council, 64
Orne, Azor, 208
Oswego, N.Y., 15, 38–39, 46–47, 49, 64, 80,
  82–83, 85, 89, 101, 141, 167; Battle of,
  199–201
Oswego Falls, 8, 199–201
Otter Creek, 195–96

Parish, David, 87
Parker, Thomas, 75, 160
Parrish, Jasper, 8, 13, 208
Paulding, William, 22, 52, 98
Pearson, Thomas, 211
Peck, Jedediah, 71
Pennington, William S., 250–51, 253
Perry, Oliver Hazard, 69, 89, 101, 116, 120,
  122, 132, 143, 155–56, 159, 204
Pettigrew, John, 89
Pettit, Micajah, 54, 93, 196
Pike, Zebulon, 93, 95–96, 114, 116–19, 127
Plattsburgh, N.Y., 15, 20, 44, 47, 54, 83, 91, 93,
  96–97, 103, 130, 148, 159–61, 164–65, 172,
  193–95, 240; Battle of, 3, 193, 229, 232, 238
Plattsburgh Bay, 241, 244, 246–47; Battle of,
  241–44, 247, 257, 261, 263, 265–66, 280
Plenderleath, Charles, 134, 136

Pomeroy, Lemuel, 20
Popham, Stephen, 202
Porter, David, 100, 255
Porter, Moses, 78
Porter, Peter B., 26, 32–33, 35, 42–43, 50, 52,
  55–56, 62, 66–67, 69, 73, 77, 139–40, 168,
  175–76, 192, 201, 207–8, 210–14, 217–20,
  223, 228–33, 235–36, 262, 265, 275–76
Power, Manley, 192
Powers, Thomas, 167
Prescott, Upper Canada, 86–87, 170, 227, 240
Prevost, Sir George, 64, 86, 101, 126–30,
  137–38, 144, 181–82, 185–86, 192–93, 199,
  222, 227, 230, 239, 242–46, 261, 268
Presque Isle, Pa., 88–89, 116, 120, 122
Pring, Daniel, 126, 196
privateering, 34, 80, 104–5, 153–54, 166, 255
privateers, 2, 4, 32–34, 80, 98, 100–101,
  104–5, 151, 153–54, 166, 195, 255, 281
Provincial Marine, 46–47, 63, 68, 80, 82,
  84–85, 126
Pultneyville, N.Y., 141, 201, 214
Purdy, Robert, 158, 162–65

Quebec, Lower Canada, 2, 32–33, 46, 64, 72,
  82, 101, 122, 135, 137, 142, 184, 186, 239
Queenston, Upper Canada, 69, 71, 120–21,
  136, 214–15, 272
Queenston Heights, 69, 74, 162, 214–15;
  Battle of, 3, 57, 61, 71, 75, 79, 88–90, 104,
  106, 115, 156, 204, 236, 248, 261, 284

Red Jacket (Seneca), 57, 63, 140, 208, 211, 214,
  276, 282
Reid, Samuel C., 255
Republican Party, 8, 10, 16, 31, 45, 115, 133,
  261, 280
Rhode Island, 22, 51, 143, 151
Riall, Phineas, 179, 181–84, 210–13, 215, 217,
  264
Richard (American sloop), 6
Richardson, John, 228
Richelieu River, 8, 16, 80, 126, 142, 160–61,
  194, 196
Riddle, David, 229
Ripley, Eleazar, 206, 210–11, 217–19, 222–24,
  229–31, 273
Robertson, James, 245
Robinson, Frederick, 192, 244–45
Rochester, John C., 243
Rochester, William B., 176
Rodgers, John, 50, 100, 203

CPSIA information can be obtained
at www.ICGtesting.com
Printed in the USA
LVHW031237110822
725707LV00001B/46